The Right to
Private Property

The Right to Private Property

Jeremy Waldron

CLARENDON PRESS · OXFORD

Oxford University Press, Walton Street, Oxford OX2 6DP
Oxford New York Toronto
Delhi Bombay Calcutta Madras Karachi
Petaling Jaya Singapore Hong Kong Tokyo
Nairobi Dar es Salaam Cape Town
Melbourne Auckland
and associated companies in
Berlin Ibadan

Oxford is a trade mark of Oxford University Press

Published in the United States
by Oxford University Press, New York

First published 1988
First issued in paperback 1990

British Library Cataloguing in Publication Data
Waldron, Jeremy
The right to private property.
1. Private property
I. Title
330'.17
ISBN 0–19–823937–8

Library of Congress Cataloging in Publication Data
Waldron, Jeremy.
The right to private property/Jeremy Waldron.
Bibliography: p.   Includes index.
1. Right of property. I. Title.
JC605.W36 1988   323.4'6—dc19   88–4841
ISBN 0–19–823937–8

Printed in Great Britain by
Biddles Ltd,
Guildford and King's Lynn

For the memory of
Francis Herbert Waldron
Clerk in Holy Orders
1913–1986

ACKNOWLEDGEMENTS

This project is the culmination of eight years' work, six of them studying (part-time) for a doctoral degree at Oxford. From 1978 to 1980, it was funded by the British Council under the Commonwealth Scholarship plan. I am grateful to them for their support, and also to University College, Oxford, Lincoln College, Oxford, the University of Edinburgh, and the University of California at Berkeley, for the assistance and facilities they provided in the years that followed.

Many people have heard, read, and commented on portions of the text in earlier drafts. Chapters have been read in seminars as far afield as Stirling and Dunedin. For comments, criticisms, and encouragement, I am particularly grateful to the following: Ruth Adler, Malcolm Anderson, Patrick Atiyah, Stanley Benn, Gerry Cohen, Robert Cooter, Penelope Dubroff, Antony Duff, Bob Durrant, John Finnis, Sean Gallagher, Robert Goodin, Leslie Green, James Griffin, Richard Gunn, Vinit Haksar, Bob Hargrave, Herbert Hart, Don Herzog, Ted Honderich, Desmond King, Martin Krygier, Nicola Lacey, David Lieberman, Neil MacCormick, Chris McCrudden, Richard Milin, David Miller, Alan Musgrave, Philippe Nonet, Denise Reaume, Andrew Reeve, John Robertson, Mike Rosen, Kim Scheppele, Philip Selznick, Jeremy Shearmur, Henry Shue, Hillel Steiner, Susan Sterett, Christine Swanton, Neil Tennant, Jack Tweedie, and Howard Williams. I am grateful also to Peggy White, Anne Jenkins, and Mona Bennett for typing several of the chapters. Angela Blackburn has been a helpful and supportive editor at Oxford University Press. I wish to express my thanks to the editors of the *Philosophical Quarterly, Political Studies, The Locke Newsletter, Oxford Journal of Legal Studies*, and the *Journal of the History of Philosophy* for permission to use some material first published in their journals.

Special mention should be reserved for five special people. Gwen Taylor first interested me in the theory of property and, indeed, in political philosophy. Alan Ryan was temporary supervisor of my project in 1979 and has been continually encouraging ever since; his own work, *Property and Political Theory*, does elegantly and persuasively what I can do only clumsily and unconvincingly. The support, friendship, advice, and intellectual stimulation of Joseph Raz have been invaluable over the years. And I owe more than I can say to Helen Waldron for all she has given.

The greatest debt I have run up in this project is to my doctoral supervisor, Ronald Dworkin. He read all of this in several drafts, and the penetrating comments and criticisms he offered were indispensable for its progress. This book is not as good as it could be, but without Dworkin's encouragement and advice from start to finish, it would have been considerably worse.

Re-reading these pages in proof, I am acutely embarrassed by my use of 'he' where I mean 'he or she' and my use of 'man' where I mean 'person'. Everything that is said applies to men *and* women, unless the context clearly indicates otherwise.

J. W.

Berkeley, May 1988

CONTENTS

Le premier qui ayant enclos un terrain s'avisa de dire, ceci est à moi, et trouva des gens assez simples pour le croire, fut le vrai fondateur de la société civile.

Jean-Jacques Rousseau, Discours sur l'inégalité
(Seconde partie)

Eh bien! n'est-il pas vrai que si la liberté de l'homme est sainte, elle est sainte au même titre dans tous les individus; que si elle a besoin d'une propriété pour agir au dehors, c'est-à-dire pour vivre, cette appropriation d'une matière est d'une égale nécessité pour tous? Et de tout cela ne doit-on pas conclure que toutes les fois qu'il nait une personne douée de liberté, il faut que les autres se serrent?

Pierre-Joseph Proudhon, Qu'est-ce que la Propriété?
(Premier Mémoire, II. 2)

PART I

THE FRAMEWORK

I

Introduction

1. CONCLUSIONS

This is a long book, and it may help readers if I state at the beginning what its main conclusions are.

The book addresses the issue of the justification of private property. It asks whether individuals have a *right* to private property, or (which I think is the same thing) whether there are any good right-based arguments for private property. A right-based argument is an argument showing that an individual interest considered in itself is sufficiently important from a moral point of view to justify holding people to be under a duty to promote it. So my question can be rephrased as follows. What individual interests are served by the existence of private property as opposed to some other sort of property regime (such as communism)? Are any of these interests so important from a moral point of view that they justify holding governments to be under a duty to promote, uphold, and protect property-owning? Or is it rather the case that, taken one by one, the interests which individuals have in the matter do not have this level of importance, and that these interests should be dealt with in the aggregate, in the form of utilitarian arguments about property institutions, rather than treated as the basis of rights?

Those are the questions. What are my answers? I examine two lines of right-based argument: one associated with John Locke and Robert Nozick, the other associated with G. W. F. Hegel. Both lines of argument hold that individuals have an interest in owning things which is important enough to command respect and to constrain political action. On the Hegelian approach, this is a basic human interest which everyone has: owning property contributes immensely to the ethical development of the individual person. On the Lockean approach, the interest which commands respect is one which people have only on account of what they happen to have done or what has happened to them. A man who has mixed his labour with a piece of land, or acquired it legitimately from someone else, has an interest in ownership which the government must respect; but a man who has done neither of these things, but would simply *rather like* to own something, has no such constraining interest. The Lockean right to property, in other words, is a special right, whereas the Hegelian one is a general right.

Examining these arguments, I found the details of the Locke/Nozick approach unconvincing. Locke's argument about mixing one's labour is incoherent, and Nozick offers no detailed argument at all for a Labour (or a First Occupancy) Theory of acquisition. Locke does provide a good argument for a general right of a rather different sort: a general right to subsistence which imposes welfarist constraints on whatever property system there may be. But no such general right is recognized in Nozick's theory. I maintain that this is a fatal flaw: no theory of the kind that Nozick intimates could possibly be made acceptable in the absence of a background general right to subsistence.

There are fewer difficulties with the Hegelian approach, though it has to be said that the link between private property and the ethical development of the person is rather obscure and, in any case, never established as an absolutely necessary connection. However, the Hegelians have probed important relations between the existence of private property and things like individual self-assertion, mutual recognition, the stability of the will, and the establishment of a proper sense of prudence and responsibility. Though the arguments are tentative and difficult, they do establish a connection between respect for property and respect for persons—a connection which in most libertarian writings of the Nozickian sort is never established except at the level of rhetoric.

The interesting thing about the Hegelian approach is its distributive implication. If the argument works, it establishes, not only that private property is morally legitimate, but also that, in Hegel's words, 'everyone must have property'. We cannot argue, on the one hand, that property-owning is necessary for ethical development, and then, on the other hand, affect unconcern about the moral and material plight of those who have nothing. Just as a right-based argument for free speech establishes a duty to see to it that everyone can speak freely, so a general-right-based argument for private property establishes a duty to see to it that everyone becomes a property-owner. It is in effect an argument against inequality and in favour of what has been called 'a property-owning democracy'.

Now it may be thought that this leads to a contradiction. If everyone must have property, then we will have to limit the rights of owners to deal and trade with their holdings as they please, for nothing is more certain than that untrammelled liberty in this regard will lead quickly to inequality. It may be thought that to limit owners' rights in this way is to undermine the very idea of private property, which is the freedom of a person to do as he pleases with the goods that are under his control. I claim, however, that this argument proceeds too quickly. For one thing, private property is a concept of which there are many conceptions: legal systems recognize all sorts of constraints on the rights of owners, and the crucial question is not whether there should be constraints, but whether the particular constraints we need defeat the original aims of our right-based argument. If they do, then there is a problem; but they may not. For another thing, property rights are going to have to be constrained by a general background right to subsistence anyway; this is what I argue in the context of Lockean theory, and it applies here as well. So it is possible that the restrictions which are necessary to ensure property for all can ride in on the back of the general right to welfare, which has to be conceded on any account. Finally, though the thrust of the argument is broadly egalitarian, the right to property is unlikely to establish a case for absolute equality. More likely, it will call for everyone to have an amount of property sufficient for him to take seriously his responsibility for its use and management. So, though the right to property has these consequences, it leaves considerable leeway for variations in social policy and economic distribution.

The important conclusion, then, is this. Under serious scrutiny, there is no right-based argument to be found which provides an adequate justification for a society in which some people have lots of property and many have next to none. The slogan that property is a human right can be deployed only disingenuously to legitimize the massive inequality that we find in modern capitalist countries.

2. UTILITARIAN ARGUMENTS FOR PRIVATE PROPERTY

The arguments I shall explore in this book are not the only (nor even necessarily the most influential) ones put forward in favour of private property. I shall not, for example, have room to say anything about the view that a capitalist economy is conducive to political liberty, nor will I be able to give utilitarian or economic efficiency arguments anything like the attention they deserve. However, because rights are often defined by contrast with utilitarian arguments, it may be worth starting with a brief sketch of the latter.

Many of the most familiar arguments in favour of private property and against socialism are utilitarian arguments. They purport to show that the total or average happiness of society will be greater, or that the general welfare (under some other utilitarian conception) will be better served, if material resources and in particular the main material means of production are owned and controlled by private individuals and firms rather than by the state or the community as a whole.

Early examples of such arguments are found in Book Two of Aristotle's *Politics*. 'What is the proper system of property for citizens who are to live under an ideal constitution?' Aristotle asks, 'Is it a system of communism or one of private property?'[1] He points out some difficulties in systems of common ownership, in particular common ownership of land. If those who own also work the land, then quarrels are likely to break out continually about the proportion between work and recompense: 'Those who do more work and get less recompense will be bound to raise complaints against those who get a large recompense and do little work.'[2] Such social disharmony will be avoided, Aristotle suggests, if each person is the exclusive owner of the plot that he works upon. To this he adds the suggestion that the net product of privately owned land is likely to be greater than that of commonly owned land: 'When everyone has his own separate sphere of interest, there will not be the same ground for quarrels; and the amount of interest will increase, because each man will feel he is applying himself to what is his own.'[3] The latter suggestion is discussed in more detail earlier in Book Two:

What is common to the greatest number gets the least amount of care. Men pay most attention to what is their own: they care less for what is common; or, at any rate, they care for it only to the extent to which each is individually concerned. Even when there is no other cause for inattention, men are more prone to neglect their duty when they think another is

[1] Aristotle, *Politics*, 1262^b (trans. Barker, p. 48).
[2] Ibid. 1263^a (p. 49).
[3] Ibid.

attending to it: this is exactly what happens in domestic service, where many attendants are sometimes of less assistance than a few.[4]

But although he makes out these arguments for private ownership, Aristotle is in favour of the communal *use* of resources. The property of each should be made 'to serve the use of all, in the spirit of the proverb which says "Friends' goods are goods in common" '.[5] (In this regard, his position is not so distant from Plato's. Plato believes that in an ideal state land will be owned privately by farmers; the farmers will provide produce to the Guardians as a class and it will be consumed by them in common.)[6] But Aristotle does not think this should be one of the rules of property. Virtue not legal compulsion should lead men to share their wealth.[7] Certainly, he thinks it the function of the legislator 'to ensure that men shall be good men, to consider what practices will make them so, and what is the end or aim of the best life'.[8] But this function is fulfilled, not by the direct legislative prescription of morally good acts, but by the constitution of a society in which moral virtue is nurtured and encouraged.[9] (Here Aristotle differs from Plato, who calls explicitly for legislation to govern the Guardians' common mode of consumption.)[10] This combination, then, of private ownership and communal virtue is more conducive to prosperity and social harmony, on Aristotle's account, than any other arrangement for the ownership and use of material resources.

Aristotle's second argument—that individuals are likely to care more for what is their own—has been taken up by some modern defenders of private property.

According to Harold Demsetz, the 'primary function of property rights is that of guiding incentives to achieve a greater internaliz- ation of externalities'.[11] If land, for instance, is held in common, it is likely each user will not feel the full impact, in terms of the

---

[4] Ibid. 1261^b (p. 44).

[5] Ibid. 1263^a (p. 49; cf. Barker's useful Note J on p. 55).

[6] Plato, *Republic*, 416D–417B (trans. Lee, pp. 184–5).

[7] Aristotle, *Politics*, 1263^a (pp. 49–50).

[8] Ibid. 1333^a (p. 317). (In this passage, I have preferred the translation by Sinclair, p. 286.)

[9] Ibid. 1263^a (p. 50): 'the function proper to a legislator is to make men so disposed that they will treat property in this way'. See also the more general discussion in Aristotle, *Nicomachean Ethics*, 1103^a–1104^b (trans. Ross, pp. 28–31) and 1179^a–1181^b (pp. 269–76).

[10] Plato, *Republic*, 417B (p. 185).

[11] Demsetz, 'Toward a Theory of Property Rights', p. 348.

benefits but particularly the costs of his use. When, for example, many individuals hunt in the same territory, no one has any incentive to increase or maintain the stock of game, since the benefits of *his* doing so will redound to others as well as himself whether the others are also conservationists or not. Unless the benefits exceed the costs of his action by a huge amount, he is unlikely to find conservation personally advantageous. (This rests, of course, on controversial assumptions about human motivation: Demsetz is working within a tradition which regards such assumptions as axiomatic.) The result is that over intensive hunting is likely to occur. The cost of each hunter's activity in terms of the depleted game stock will be felt not only by him but by his fellow hunters and by the generations of hunters who follow. Thus when individual hunting decisions are made, the full benefits but only some of the costs of a decision to hunt will be taken into account, and, in the aggregate, a level of hunting may be maintained which is in fact against the long-term interests of all.[12] The more this happens (i.e. the greater the level of costs not taken into account in individual decision-making about hunting), the more defensible a scheme of private property rights over game and territory will begin to seem in utilitarian terms, and (on Demsetz's view) the more likely it is that such a scheme of property will emerge.[13] A communal form of ownership 'fails to concentrate the costs associated with any person's exercise of his common right on that person'.[14] A scheme of private ownership, on the other hand,

will internalize many of the external costs associated with communal ownership, for now an owner, by virtue of his power to exclude others, can generally count on realizing the rewards associated with husbanding the game and increasing the fertility of his land. This concentration of benefits and costs on owners creates incentives to utilize resources more efficiently.[15]

Of course, owners-in-common, perceiving the tendency of their over-exploitation of resources, could get together and agree to limit their use. But Demsetz suggests that the transaction costs involved in securing such an agreement together with the costs (and the assurance problem) involved in its policing might be prohibitive. An advantage of private property rights is that they reduce

---

[12] Demsetz, 'Towards a Theory of Property Rights', pp. 351–3.
[13] Ibid. 350 and 352.
[14] Ibid. 354.
[15] Ibid. 356.

transaction costs, at least in resolving subsequent problems of externalities.[16]

Another utilitarian argument for private property concerns the role of markets in promoting productive efficiency and social prosperity. It is now accepted that a centralized command economy, in which all productive decisions were taken on the basis of the central allocation of scarce resources, would lead, in the conditions of modern industry, to radically inefficient and perhaps catastrophic results.[17]

The *locus classicus* of this argument is in the work of Ludwig von Mises. Socialist planners, von Mises points out, face two problems: first, the problem of what to produce and, secondly, the problem of how to produce it.[18] It is conceivable that socialist planners might solve the first problem, particularly if they adhered to some 'objective' theory of human and social 'need' which was not dependent on the interplay of the subjective preferences of actual consumers.[19] But the second problem, he claims, will be intractable as a problem of planning. How will a planner know where a given quantity of (say) coal or iron ore is best applied, or to what purposes certain machine parts should be devoted? The use of what are called 'production goods' is not related directly to the need for specified consumption goods, since each of the former could go through any one of a series of stages in contributing to the production of the latter.

Von Mises' suggestion is that the only way through this decisional morass is via a system of prices, fixed by the interaction of a plurality of entrepreneurs, each risking the capital commodities under his control in production or exchange, and adjusting his

---

[16] Ibid. (This last point, though, raises the question of the transaction costs involved in the actual shift from common to property rights. As James Buchanan notes, Demsetz does not indicate why the latter costs should be substantially lower than those associated with an agreement among owners-in-common to limit the exercise of their common rights. (See Buchanan, *Limits of Liberty*, pp. 22-3.) We cannot go into this matter in any great detail here, except to note Buchanan's own suggestion that a 'natural' distribution of private *control* of resources might emerge without agreement from a Hobbesian process of interaction, and that, given Hobbes's arguments about security and Demsetz's arguments about efficiency, everyone would have an incentive to ratify as a structure of private *rights* that 'natural' distribution of private *control*. (Buchanan, *Limits of Liberty*, pp. 23 ff.)

[17] For socialist recognition of this point, see e.g. Nove, *Economics of Feasible Socialism*, and Anderson, *On the Tracks of Historical Materialism*.

[18] Von Mises, 'Economic Calculation', pp. 77 ff.

[19] Ibid. 77-8.

activity to his perception of the similarly adjusted activity of others: in other words, a system of market prices. A market economy has powerful tendencies in the direction of efficient resource allocation. But a centrally planned economy will have no grip on these processes at all—nowhere to start and no idea of which direction to go.[20]

Von Mises' argument has evoked two sorts of response. Some say that in principle a set of market prices might be arrived at by calculation or by trial and error. Mathematically, it is said, all the equations exist for the solution of the pricing problem; the only issue is the practical one of solving them. But there are reasons for scepticism about this 'hypothetical market' approach. First, it depends on the availability to the socialist planners of perfect knowledge about the economy and on a high degree of stability and predictability in the circumstances of the society they are administering. But that hypothesis misses the point of von Mises' approach. As Murray Rothbard points out, 'the Mises demonstration of the impossibility of economic calculation under socialism and of the superiority of private markets in the means of production applied only to the real world of uncertainty, continuing change, and scattered knowledge'.[21] Secondly, the abstract possibility of this 'hypothetical market' solution relies on the concept of Walrasian general equilibrium, which von Mises—in common with his socialist opponents (in other contexts)—regards as inapplicable in the real world. The von Mises defence of the market does not derive from any expectation of equilibrium but from a recognition of powerful *equilibrating tendencies* in the interactive decision-making of capitalist entrepreneurs adjusting to one another's activity on a self-interested basis under conditions of risk and uncertainty. These tendencies prevail, but only to a certain extent, in the face of disequilibrating forces such as unexpected change and the inconsistency of human plans. Von Mises' point is just that in a socialist economy there is no real tendency at all to oppose the forces of disequilibrium.

The other main response to von Mises' argument has been the suggestion that socialist economies might operate, not with calculation based on 'hypothetical markets', but with the reintroduction of actual markets for certain goods. (To a certain extent

---

[20] See also Von Mises, *Socialism*.
[21] Rothbard, 'Von Mises and Economic Calculation', p. 68.

anyway, socialist planners in the Eastern bloc have been able to rely on the prices established by capitalist markets outside their bloc; almost all intra-bloc trade appears to be conducted with reference to prices fixed in this way.)[22] Thus it is suggested that feasible socialism must allow a place for quasi-entrepreneurial market competition between producers and firms, and that this can be done without abandoning state or common ownership of productive resources. To answer this point, the defender of von Mises' line has to rely on something like the earlier argument from self-interest. Unless individual 'entrepreneurs' in a market socialist economy are motivated by something like considerations of personal profit in their investment and allocative decisions and generally in the use of the resources under their control, they will not respond efficiently to the market situation. But then it seems that socialism can compete in efficiency with a private property economy only to the extent that it reintroduces the idea of private property by the back door.[23]

Partly this will resolve itself into a controversy about the definitions of socialism and private property.[24] Do we still have a socialist system, when individual managers have effective control of capital resources in a competitive environment? A market socialist may say 'Yes', stressing the fact that the managers' decisions are still subject to social control in a number of respects. But private owners in capitalist societies are subject to various forms of social control too; planning restrictions, pollution controls, minimum wage laws, and the like mean that they cannot dispose of their property exactly as they please. These problems of definition will be confronted in Chapter 2. For the time being we should note that it may well be that the sort of economy envisaged by market socialists is poised perhaps too finely on the dividing line between private and collective property to be decisive in an argument about the superiority of one form of property to the other.

Anyway, in brief and sketchy form, these are the main utilitarian arguments about the justifiability of private property. In what

[22] Ibid. 72.

[23] There is an immense literature on the possibility of 'market socialism'. See e.g. the exchange between Sirc and Nuti in Kolakowski and Hampshire (eds.), *The Socialist Idea*, Chs. 14–15.

[24] See e.g. the exchange between Lessnoff and Miller: Lessnoff, 'Capitalism, Socialism and Democracy'; Miller, 'Jerusalem Not Yet Built'; Lessnoff, 'Not Talking About Jerusalem'.

follows, however, I am going to concentrate on certain *non-utilitarian* arguments in favour of private property.

3. NON-UTILITARIAN THEORIES

The idea of a non-utilitarian argument is apt to seem at first bewildering to a layman, a politician, or an economist. What, they will ask, could possibly count in favour of or against an institution like private property except its effects on the welfare of everyone in the society, assessed in a roughly aggregative way?

But the situation is quite different in moral and political philosophy. Philosophers have never been more aware than they are today of the grave ethical defects (as well as the technical difficulties) of utilitarian argument.[25] Two points in particular may be mentioned. First, utilitarianism is criticized for the fact that it takes human interests and desires as given: in utilitarian theory, the satisfaction of any preference and the fulfilment of any interest is taken to have a positive value in itself no matter what it is a preference for or an interest in. So when one section of the population takes pleasure in persecuting another, that satisfaction may conceivably be taken as decisive in justifying on utilitarian grounds a decision not to extend social protection to the persecuted group.[26] Secondly, quite apart from the question of the quality of desires and interests, there is the more general problem of distribution. A utilitarian concerned to maximize the sum of happiness or satisfaction in a society cares little about the distribution of that sum: the slightly greater happiness of many, over the long term, is capable of outweighing, in a utilitarian calculation, the intense suffering and abject deprivation of a few. This leaves no room in social decision-making for considerations of justice and equality, except perhaps as subordinate maxims.[27] But ethical thinking about social and political issues has always been informed by a conviction that justice and equality are independent

[25] See e.g. Hart, 'Between Utility and Rights', p. 77. Also Sen and Williams (eds.), *Utilitarianism and Beyond*, esp. 'Introduction'.

[26] Cf. Rawls, *A Theory of Justice*, pp. 30 ff.

[27] For the idea of equality as a subordinate maxim in a utilitarian system, see Bentham, *Theory of Legislation*, p. 103; for a similar though less rigorous treatment of justice, see Mill, *Utilitarianism*, Ch. 5; also Sidgewick, *Methods of Ethics*, Bk. III, Ch. 5.

values, co-ordinate with if not superior to considerations of aggregate utility.[28]

Can the theories known as rule- or indirect utilitarianism provide adequate utilitarian solutions to these problems?[29] I have my doubts. Either they cease to be utilitarian, and take on a commitment to rules and moral institutions for their own sake; or, if they remain utilitarian, they produce at best rules and institutions which, in their foundations and justification, continue to evince a commitment to the very aspects of utilitarian theory that have been found objectionable. Their sophistication gives us a reason perhaps to believe that utilitarians can have *a* theory of justice and rights; but it does not give us any confidence that the principles of that theory will have anything in common with the principles underlying our fundamental 'intuitive' misgivings about utilitarianism.[30] It therefore does nothing to allay the widespread suspicion that the difficulties in utilitarian theory are very deep-set, reflecting a failure of that theory to take seriously the moral significance of certain fundamental individual interests in security, autonomy, and independence.[31]

The decline of confidence in utilitarian argument has been accompanied by a growth in moral and political theories of a non-utilitarian kind. Explicitly or implicitly, the dominant idea in recent non-utilitarian thought has been that of *rights*: the idea that people have certain key interests (in specific freedoms or in specific aspects of their material well-being) which they are not to be required to sacrifice, and which therefore may not be overridden, for the sake of the collective welfare or other goals of their society.

For example, many liberal philosophers argue that each person has a right to life, and a right to at least the minimum amount of negative liberty necessary for his development as an autonomous moral agent. Some argue also that each person has a right to certain conditions of positive liberty, such as the material conditions which

---

[28] See e.g. Ross, *The Right and the Good*, Ch. 2, and Rawls, *A Theory of Justice*, pp. 26 ff.

[29] See e.g. the survey of the problems with this approach in Lyons, *Forms and Limits*, esp. Chs. 4–5 and in his 'Utility and Rights'. But for continued confidence in the viability of a 'two-level' utilitarianism, see Hare, *Moral Thinking*.

[30] Cf. Dworkin, 'Right to Pornography?', p. 193; also Waldron (ed.), *Theories of Rights*, 'Introduction', pp. 18–19.

[31] Cf. Rawls, *A Theory of Justice*, pp. 22–33 and 175–92; Nozick, *Anarchy, State, and Utopia*, pp. 30–4 and 48–51; Williams, 'Critique of Utilitarianism', pp. 108 ff. (See also the discussion in Ch. 3, below.)

make his negative freedom worth exercising and the spiritual conditions (like education and the support of secure human relationships) which make its exercise humanly fulfilling.[32] These, it is said, are morally crucial interests for each person, and they are not to be sacrificed merely for the sake of the greatest happiness or prosperity of society in general. As this sort of argument becomes more common, it is interesting to see whether the individual interest in having private property can plausibly be regarded in the same sort of way.

Often accounts of human rights have not gone beyond a list of these crucial interests and the bare assertion that they are to be accorded special respect. Since the mid- 1970s, however, moral and political philosophy has seen a growing interest in systematic theories of rights. Philosophers have become interested in the foundations of the idea that certain individual interests are worthy of special respect, and there have been several impressive attempts to work out systematically the sort of theory that is needed to connect the surface rhetoric of rights-assertions, so common in political life, with the deep values and assumptions about morality and human nature that we find in moral philosophy.[33]

In this book, I shall not be looking in any detail at modern theories of rights. There are three exceptions: I shall draw on some aspects of Ronald Dworkin's theory in my definition of 'right-based argument' in Chapter 3 and criticize others; I shall make extensive reference to Robert Nozick's account of historical entitlement in my discussion of what I want to call special-right-based arguments for private property in Chapter 7; and, again in that chapter, I shall make use of certain aspects of John Rawls's theory of justice and his conception of political philosophy.

No modern philosopher of rights has produced a fully developed discussion of property on the scale of the historical theories we will be examining—the theories of Locke and Hegel. On Rawls's view, the question of the private or collective ownership of the means of production is a question of practical political judgement not a matter for a theory of justice.[34] (At first sight, this seems to conflict

---

[32] For 'positive' liberty, see Berlin, *Four Essays*, Ch. 2, and Taylor, 'What's Wrong with Negative Liberty?' For an approach along these lines based on liberty, see Plant, *Equality, Markets, and the State*.

[33] Cf. Waldron (ed.), *Theories of Rights*, 'Introduction', pp. 2–5.

[34] Rawls, *A Theory of Justice*, pp. 258 and 271–4. (But see Schweicart, 'Should Rawls be a Socialist?')

with his view that the right to own property is one of the basic liberties protected by the first principle of justice. However, he does not explore this tension and there is no space to go into it here.)[35] Dworkin makes no more than a passing reference to private property in his work, indicating simply that his favoured form of argument for rights—the argument concerned with the corruption of the egalitarian character of utilitarian calculations by the inclusion of external preferences—does not require social decision-making to be constrained by any right to private property (or for that matter, freedom of contract).[36] Nozick's discussion is the fullest of the philosophers I have mentioned. But on his own account he does not offer a full theory of private property, only a sketch of what the form of such a theory might be.[37] Aspects of that form will be discussed in Chapter 7; but he has not put sufficient flesh on the bones to warrant a more substantial discussion.

Instead, my aim is to take hold of some of the analytical apparatus used in the modern discussion of rights, and see if it can be brought usefully to bear on one or two much older arguments for property. In a way, this exercise is bound to be anachronistic, and the hermeneutical problems it raises will be discussed in Chapter 5. But everyone involved in the modern debate about property and justice is aware of how much reference back there is to works of philosophers who have trodden these paths before.[38] There is an obvious debt to Locke in Nozick's work, and in much other libertarian writing.[39] And, particularly among conservative defenders of property (in the English tradition of conservatism) there is an evident debt to Hegel.[40] Both those who trace their lineage back to the *Second Treatise* and those who paddle in the murky waters of the *Philosophy of Right* are apt to talk about a right to (or a right of) property as one of the fundamental elements in a theory of respect for persons. My suspicion is that talk of 'a right to property' means something different in each case: it is not just a different theory or a different justification, but a different conception of what it is that has to be justified. My aim, then, in

---

[35] Rawls, *A Theory of Justice*, p. 61. See also Hart, 'Rawls on Liberty', pp. 227 ff.
[36] Dworkin, *Taking Rights Seriously*, pp. 277–8. But see also Dworkin, 'Liberalism', pp. 129 ff. and 'Equality of Resources', pp. 283–5.
[37] Nozick, *Anarchy, State, and Utopia*, pp. xii, 9, and 202–3.
[38] See Ryan, *Property and Political Theory*, 'Introduction'.
[39] See, e.g., Nozick, *Anarchy, State, and Utopia*, pp. 9–12 and 174 ff.
[40] e.g. Scruton, *Meaning of Conservatism*, pp. 94–118.

this work is to use certain concepts drawn from the modern analytical discussion of rights (particularly H. L. A. Hart's categories of *special* right and *general* right)[41] to elucidate that difference.

4. THE RIGHT TO PRIVATE PROPERTY

In 1789, the French National Assembly published a *Declaration of the Rights of Man and the Citizen*, in which it was asserted: 'The end in view of every political association is the preservation of the natural and imprescriptible rights of man. These rights are liberty, property, security, and resistance to oppression.'[42] To this, the derisive response of the English utilitarian Jeremy Bentham is as well known as the rhetoric of the *Declaration* itself: 'Natural rights is simple nonsense: natural and imprescriptible rights, rhetorical nonsense,—nonsense upon stilts.'[43] Less well known, however, are Bentham's criticisms of the particular rights which the Assembly had declared to be fundamental. Here are his remarks on the right of property:

Man—that is, every man . . . has a right to property, to proprietary rights, a right which cannot be taken away from him by the laws. To proprietary rights. Good: but in relation to what subject? For as to proprietary rights— without a subject . . . in relation to which they can be exercised—they will hardly be of much value, they will hardly be worth taking care of with so much solemnity. . . . As there is no such subject specified with relation to each man, or to any man (indeed how could there be?) the necessary inference . . . is, that every man has a right to everything. Unfortunately, in most matters of property, what is every man's right is no man's right; so that the effect of this part of the oracle . . . would be, not to establish property, but to extinguish it—and this is one of the rights declared to be imprescriptible![44]

Now, of course this response is excessive and Bentham's 'interpretation' fastidious and pedantic. But as so often his hyperbole puts us

---

    [41] Hart, 'Are There Any Natural Rights?', pp. 83–8. See Ch. 4, below.
    [42] *Declaration of the Rights of Man and the Citizen*, Art. 2. (See Waldron, *Nonsense Upon Stilts*, p. 26).
    [43] Bentham, 'Anarchical Fallacies', p. 53.
    [44] Ibid. 57–8. Bentham also inveighed against the alleged natural right to property with some of his strongest anti-rights invective in 'Supply Without Burthern', pp. 70–76.

on the alert to a serious and important confusion. The statement that property is one of the rights of man is an ancient and familiar one; but it is ambiguous, concealing perhaps a variety of quite different claims. These claims may be divided initially into four broad categories.

(i) Immunities Against Expropriation

The statement may intend to make reference to existing rights of ownership or to rights of ownership which, at any rate, exist independently of the statement itself. If someone is already the owner of some good, then he is said to have the right not to have that ownership undermined or taken away from him, even if public policy demands that property arrangements should be altered to that effect. This seems, in fact, to be roughly what the National Assembly intended, for in their later expansion of the right of property they wrote: 'Since property is an inviolable and sacred right, no individual may be deprived of it unless some public necessity, legally certified as such, clearly requires it; and subject always to a just and previously determined compensation.'[45]

Property is protected, then, to the extent that peremptory expropriation without compensation is banned. But there is no implication from this that everyone is entitled to have or obtain property or that people who are not owners have a right to be put in that position. If somebody does not have and has never had any ownership rights over anything, he has no ground for complaint under this provision; indeed it does not concern him. It is only the rights of proprietors that are in question here: the *Declaration* adds an immunity against expropriation to existing rights of property and insists that henceforth no property rights will exist without the conjunction of this immunity. For the purposes of the *Declaration*, then, it is assumed that there are methods for determining who has property rights—methods which fall outside this provision itself. Property may be acquired by commerce, distribution by the state, the lottery of natural acquisition, or however; but the right of property, on this interpretation, assumes that that question has been settled independently.

Into this category fall some of John Locke's political arguments

[45] *Declaration of the Rights of Man and the Citizen*, Art. 17. (See Waldron, *Nonsense Upon Stilts*, p. 28.)

about the right to property. Locke argues that this right, along with
the rights to life and liberty, is the basis of all political morality. It
follows that property must not be taken, even for the sake of the
general good, without the owners' consent in civil society:

> For the preservation of Property being the end of Government, and that for
> which men enter into Society, it necessarily supposes and requires that the
> People should have Property, without which they must be suppos'd to lose
> that by entring into Society, which was the end for which they entered into
> it, too gross an absurdity for any Man to own.[46]

Thus, *given* a distribution of property (which Locke believes can be
determined independently of political organization, and which we
will discuss in Chapter 6), individual property-holders are said to
have a right, against their government, that their holdings should be
respected.[47]

Into this category, too, fall many of the clauses protecting
property in the constitutions of the nations of the world. Perhaps
the most famous is the Fifth Amendment to the Constitution of the
United States of America: 'No person . . . shall be deprived of life,
liberty, or property, without due process of law; nor shall private
property be taken for public use without just compensation.'[48] And
there are scores of similar provisions in constitutions and bills of
rights all around the world.[49]

I shall not on the whole be concerned with claims of this first
kind. The reason is simple. The right to property, understood in this
way, does not provide any sort of argument for the existence of
private property. It assumes and builds on independent arguments
about the basis and distribution of property: it adds a particular
immunity to what is otherwise a pre-existing bundle of property
rights. Since we are concerned with right-based arguments *for*

---

[46] Locke, *Two Treatises*, II, sect. 138; of course, Locke equivocates on what is to
count as owners' consent—see sects. 140–2.

[47] For the idea that property was distributed independently of civil society, see
Locke, *Two Treatises*, II, Ch. 5. As James Tully has rightly seen, a claim in this First
Category is perfectly compatible with the view that the distribution of property is
conventional. Tully is mistaken, however, in attributing this view to Locke. (See
Tully, *A Discourse on Property*, p. 98 *et passim*. See also the discussion in Ch. 6,
below, and in Waldron, 'Locke, Tully and the Regulation of Property'.)

[48] See Finer, (ed.), *Five Constitutions*, p. 106.

[49] e.g. *Constitution of Panama* (1946–56), Art. 45: 'Private property acquired in
accordance with the law by natural and juridical persons is guaranteed and may not
be disregarded or impaired by subsequent laws.' (See Peaslee, *Constitutions of
Nations*, Vol. IV.)

private property (as against socialism or some other system), we should look behind this sort of claim to the substance of those independent arguments.

(ii) Natural Property Rights

When it is said that the right to property is one of the *natural* rights of man, sometimes what is meant is that property rights are themselves natural rights. The idea of natural rights is far from clear, as Bentham never tired of pointing out; but what might be meant is something along the following lines. As a matter of fact, individuals left to their own devices will gain control of natural resources in a variety of ways. Some of those ways (for example, being the first to labour on something) create relationships between the individual holder and the resources he controls which are, from a moral (or perhaps religious) point of view, so important as to impose duties on others to refrain from interfering with or undermining that control (either in general or in certain specified ways). These duties, then, correspond to natural rights to some sort of exclusive control of the resources, in other words natural rights of property. They are natural, not in the sense that the individuals concerned are born with them (in one of the ways that, say, rights to life and liberty are said to be natural), but rather in the sense that the force of these rights obtains and can be recognized as valid by moral and rational people quite apart from any provisions of positive law. And they are perhaps also natural in the sense that the sort of relationship out of which these rights and duties are generated has important roots in the nature of human beings.[50]

This sort of claim forms the independent moral background to Locke's political views about the right to property, which we examined under heading (i). Locke believes that citizens have a right to an immunity against expropriation; but he also believes that the property rights which have a claim to be protected in this way are natural rights, established along the lines that I have outlined in the previous paragraph. This latter part of his view constitutes Locke's argument for the existence of private property. Private property, he maintains, is morally required by the respect commanded by certain relations established between individuals and resources in a state of nature. In Chapter 6, I shall devote a lot

[50] See D'Entrèves, *Natural Law*, Chs. 2–3.

of attention to the detail of the arguments with which Locke attempts to support this view; and in Chapter 7, I shall look at a more recent version of the same kind of approach, put forward by Robert Nozick.

For the time being, the interesting and important thing to note about the Lockean approach is what we might call the contingency of the individual rights it establishes. Natural rights to property are, on Locke's view, rooted in certain relations that some individuals happen to establish between themselves and certain things—in particular the relation of labouring on virgin resources.[51] Though Locke believes it is in some sense natural for individuals to establish such relations, he does not believe that every individual will, or even that every individual must, establish a relation of this kind between himself and some significant resource. Some will and some will not. Those who do so, acquire natural property rights, but those who do not, acquire none (or at any rate none of the rights with which we are at present concerned).[52] The situation of the latter is therefore analogous to that of a person to whom no promises happen to have been made. A person to whom no promises have been made has no promissory rights (whatever other rights he has), and that is entirely compatible with the view that making and receiving promises is a natural human activity, and also with the view that the promising relation generates rights and duties that can be recognized as morally binding independently of any considerations of positive law. Natural property rights, then, on this interpretation are universal human rights at most only in the formal sense that anyone *might* have them; no one is ruled out of the domain of these rights a priori. (This sort of universal claim is considered in type (iii), below.) They are not universal rights in the way that the natural right to life and liberty is usually taken to be.

(iii) Eligibility to Hold Property

That rather modest claim may sometimes be all that is meant by the statement that property is one of the rights of man. At its weakest, the claim is simply the claim not to be ruled out of the class of

---

[51] Locke, *Two Treatises*, II, sects. 27 ff.

[52] Locke did believe that everyone had certain common property rights—e.g. the right to a minimum subsistence—see *Two Treatises*, I, sect. 42; see also Ch. 6, sect. 2, below.

people who *may* own property. This appears to be the gist of the provision on property in the Universal Declaration of Human Rights: 'Everyone has the right to own property alone as well as in the association of others.'[53] The right is one which everyone is supposed to have unconditionally and *ab initio*. It is a right not to be excluded from the class of potential property-owners in the way that, say, slaves or women have been excluded in the past. Such a right, of course, does not guarantee that anyone (let alone everyone) will actually get to *be* an owner; it does not feed the baby and it will not pay the rent. But it is something. (Rawls's liberty to hold personal property, to which we have already referred, probably also fits into this category.)[54]

Occasionally, the meaning of a claim like this has been stretched to prohibit the wholesale socialization of property in a society. If, for example, all resources are taken into public ownership and private ownership is prohibited, say, on socialist grounds, then in a sense everyone has been excluded from the class of potential property-owners. A requirement that no one be excluded from potential ownership, therefore, can be read as meaning that private property should not be ruled out altogether for a society. We find an idea along these lines in the Constitution of the Republic of Eire:

The state acknowledges that man, in virtue of his rational being, has the natural right, antecedent to positive law, to the private ownership of external goods. The state accordingly guarantees to pass no law attempting to abolish the right of private ownership, or the general right to transfer, bequeath, and inherit property.[55]

On a superficial reading, this looks like a claim of type (ii). Certainly it makes reference to the 'naturalness' of property-owning. But it need not involve any claim about the existence or otherwise of natural property rights, that is, property rights established independently of legal provisions. All it maintains is that there is something about human nature (the nature we all share) which makes it wrong to exclude any (or all) of us from the class of potential proprietors. Similarly, it looks as though it

---

[53] *Universal Declaration of Human Rights*, Art. 17. (See Keith (ed.), *Essays on Human Rights*, p. 197.) See also *Constitution of India* (1949–63), Art. 19 (1): 'All citizens shall have the right ... to acquire, hold, and dispose of property.' (See Peaslee, *Constitutions of Nations*, Vol. II.).

[54] Rawls, *A Theory of Justice*, p. 61.

[55] *Constitution of the Republic of Eire*, Art. 43 (1) and (2); see the discussion in Exshaw, 'Right of Private Ownership'.

extends protection to existing property rights along the lines of the provisions of type (i)—and an interpretation along these lines has occasionally been urged in the Irish courts.[56] But in theory, at least, it is possible to expropriate some existing property-owners *without* attacking the idea of private property itself or the idea that everyone is a potential proprietor. (A programme of redistribution, based on the view that the existing rich did not morally deserve their wealth would have exactly that effect.)

I think claims of this third kind (and the arguments that might be used to support them) are interesting and important. But perhaps rather arbitrarily, I shall spend most of my time looking only at those interpretations of the idea of a right to property from which it would follow that the person who has the right actually must have property if his right is to be respected. Claims of type (ii) and, as I shall argue, type (iv) have this consequence. But claims of type (iii) do not: an individual's right here is satisfied so long as there are institutions of private property in his society from which he is not as a matter of law a priori excluded. I shall examine this claim in Chapter 11.

(iv) The General Right to have Private Property

It is sometimes said that the ownership of private property has a great moralizing effect on the individual owner. It promotes virtues like responsibility, prudence, and self-reliance; it gives him a place to stand in the world, a place where he can be confident that his freedom will be recognized and respected; and it affords him control of at least a minimum of those natural resources access to which is a necessary condition of his agency. (Often indeed it is said that private ownership has such moralizing effects that only those who own property are fit to be citizens in a republic.)

We find an early version of this kind of argument in Aristotle's *Politics*, alongside the utilitarian arguments we have already mentioned. Like many of the ancients, Aristotle treats the moral issues of monogamy and private property as on a par. Both, he suggests, promote individual virtue, and in both cases important forms of moral goodness are liable to be destroyed by the socialization of the relations in question:

---

[56] *Pigs Marketing Board* v. *Donnelly (Dublin) Ltd.* [1939] IR 413; *Buckley and others (Sinn Fein)* v. *Attorney-General* [1950] IR 67.

The first of these [forms of goodness] is temperance in the matter of sexual relations (it is an act of moral value to refrain from loving the wife of another in the strength of temperance): the second is liberality in the use of property. In a state which is excessively unified no man can show himself liberal, or do a liberal act; for the function of liberality consists in the proper use which is made of private property.[57]

We may not find this argument particularly convincing: other modes of liberality (and sexual restraint!) may be available even in a communist state. But it provides the prototype of a category of argument that becomes very important in the ideology of private property in the nineteenth century and which remains influential in conservative ideology today. In later chapters we shall be looking in general at this sort of argument, and in particular at Hegel's formulation of a view linking ownership with the necessary conditions for the ethical development of individual freedom in the *Philosophy of Right*.

The connection between private property and moral virtue is not always seen as a matter of individual right. (Often this approach may be seen as a duty-based rather than as a right-based argument for private property.) But increasingly philosophers are prepared to argue that individuals have a right to the conditions necessary for the full development of their autonomy, their ethical personality, and their capacity for responsible agency. Mere negative freedom is not enough: we must look, at least in the abstract, at the quality of choice which it is open to individuals to exercise, otherwise we risk attracting the accusation that we do not after all take the issue of human freedom seriously.[58] Since this position is increasingly common, and since it has been argued that private property is a necessary element in the ethical development of individual choice, it seems appropriate to consider claims of this sort as a fourth category of interpretations of the statement that property is one of the rights of man.

Predictably, this sort of view is found more in philosophical monographs than in political constitutions. I know of no provision of any constitution in the world which asserts a universal right to property on this sort of basis. Such claim would certainly be a very radical one, for it would entail, not merely that private property should exist in the society, but also that everyone should be a

---

[57] Aristotle, *Politics* 1263[b] (trans. Barker p. 50).
[58] See Plant, *Equality, Markets, and the State*, Chs. 3–4.

proprietor. If someone were propertyless, then his claim to
autonomy and the development of his free agency would not have
been satisfied; it would have been undermined and violated just as
much as if he had been excluded from the scope of religious or
political toleration extended by the state. On this account, then, the
mere legal opportunity to own property is not enough. Property
only does the work for which, it is argued, it ought to exist if
individuals actually have it. An equal concern, then, for the ethical
development and autonomy of all dictates an equal concern that
each individual should have property.

5. AIMS

My main concern in the pages that follow is to outline and compare
arguments of type (ii)—arguments about natural property rights—
with arguments of type (iv)—arguments asserting a general right to
have private property. The former establish contingent and only
formally universal natural rights to property; the latter establish
rights that are concerned substantially with the interests and
development of everyone. The point of this comparison is, first and
foremost, to understand the arguments themselves and to see how
compelling a case they make for private property; in particular I
shall be concerned with the arguments of John Locke (and to a
lesser extent Robert Nozick) in (ii) and G. W. F. Hegel in (iv). But
secondly, I also want to drive home this point that the idea of *a
right to property* is not straightforward, and that in its ambiguity it
conceals at least four ideas, two of which are radically different
from one another. If that shakes the confidence of those who invoke
the idea of a right to property glibly in defence of existing capitalist
relations without considering what talk of *rights* in this context
might imply, then at least one of my aims will have been fulfilled.

The substance of these arguments will be set out in the second
part of the book, and in Chapter 5 I shall say more by way of
introduction to the theories that I am going to examine.

Chapters 2 to 4, however, are concerned with more abstract
issues. It was D. G. Ritchie who remarked in his book *Natural
Rights* that 'the confusions which permeate the theory of natural
rights come out most conspicuously of all in the case of the right to

private property'.[59] The same, I believe, can be said about the confusions surrounding the concept of private property itself. I hope in these early chapters to cast some light on both these areas.

In what I have been saying about the right to private property, I have assumed that private property is a clearly identifiable social institution (so that we can tell whether a society has it or not, and therefore whether and to what extent the alleged right is satisfied), and that it is quite different from other forms of property regime such as socialism. But this claim is very controversial. Many jurists deny that we have any useful or coherent notion of ownership, and they insist that there is no distinction in principle (only at most a difference of degree) between a private property economy and a socialist one. In both systems, they say, individuals have rights which can be called property rights, and the only interesting question is how these rights are to be packaged and bundled together. My first task is to criticize this view and to argue the case for a reasonably clear and distinctive concept of private property.

Secondly, as I have already intimated, I want to make some general comments about rights and about Ronald Dworkin's distinction between right-based, duty-based, and goal-based political arguments.[60] I shall make out a case for a very broad notion of right-based argument: an argument counts as right-based just in case it takes the moral importance of some individual interest as a reason for assigning duties or imposing moral requirements.

Then, in Chapter 4, I want to draw a distinction between two types of right (and accordingly between two types of right-based argument). This is based on H. L. A. Hart's distinction between *special* rights, i.e. rights arising out of particular events and transactions, and *general* rights, i.e. rights which the right-bearer is conceived to have independently of the contingent events and transactions in which he has been involved. This distinction, I hope, will provide a formal basis for the substantial comparisons I want to make in the second half of the book.

[59] Ritchie, *Natural Rights*, p. 263. I am indebted to Pennock, 'Thoughts on the Right to Private Property', p. 172, for this reference.
[60] Dworkin, *Taking Rights Seriously*, Ch. 6.

2

What is Private Property?

Although private property has found its way again to the forefront of attention in jurisprudence and political philosophy,[1] serious discussion is hampered by the lack of a generally accepted account of what private property is and how it is to be contrasted with alternative systems of property rules. As R. H. Tawney pointed out:

It is idle . . . to present a case for or against private property without specifying the particular forms of property to which reference is made, and the journalist who says that 'private property is the foundation of civilization' agrees with Proudhon, who said it was theft, in this respect at least that, without further definition, the words of both are meaningless.[2]

Many writers have argued that it is, in fact, impossible to define private property—that the concept itself defies definition. If those arguments can be sustained, then a work like this is misconceived. If private property is indefinable, it cannot serve as a useful concept in political and economic thought: nor can it be a point of interesting debate in political philosophy. Instead of talking about property systems, we should focus perhaps on the detailed rights that particular people have to do certain things with certain objects, rights which vary considerably from case to case, from object to object, and from legal system to legal system. But, if these sceptical arguments hold, we should abandon the enterprise of arguing about private property as such—of saying that it is, or is not, conducive to liberty, prosperity, or rights—because the term does not pick out any determinate institution for consideration.

Why has private property been thought indefinable? Consider the

---

[1] See, for example, Nozick, *Anarchy, State, and Utopia*; Becker, *Property Rights*; Macpherson (ed.), *Property: Mainstream and Critical Positions*; Tully, *A Discourse on Property*; Pennock and Chapman (eds.), *NOMOS XXII: Property*; Ryan, *Property and Political Theory*. This chapter is a condensation of a longer piece—see Waldron, 'What is Private Property?'.

[2] Tawney, 'Property and Creative Work', p. 136.

relation between a person (call her Susan) and an object (say, a motor car) generally taken to be her private property. The layman thinks of this as a two-place relation of ownership between a person and a thing: Susan owns that Porsche. But the lawyer tells us that legal relations cannot exist between people and Porsches, because Porsches cannot have rights or duties or be bound by or recognize rules.[3] The legal relation involved must be a relation between persons—between Susan and her neighbours, say, or Susan and the police, or Susan and everyone else. But when we ask what this relation is, we find that the answer is not at all simple. With regard to Susan's Porsche, there are all sorts of legal relations between Susan and other people. Susan has a legal liberty to use it in certain ways; for example, she owes no duty to anyone to refrain from putting her houseplants in it. But that is true only of some of the ways that the car could (physically) be used. She is not at liberty to drive it on the footpath or to drive it anywhere at a speed faster than 70 m.p.h. Indeed, she is not at liberty to drive it at all without a licence from the authorities. As well as her liberties, Susan also has certain rights. She has what Hohfeld called a 'claim-right' against everyone else (her neighbours, her friends, the local car thief, everyone in the community) that they should not use her Porsche without her permission. But Susan also owes certain duties to other people in relation to the vehicle. She must keep it in good order and see that it does not become a nuisance to her neighbours. She is liable to pay damages if it rolls into her neighbour's fence. These rights, liberties, and duties are the basic stuff of ownership. But legal relations can be changed, and, if Susan owns the Porsche, then *she* is in a position to change them. She has the power to sell it or give it to somebody else, in which case all the legal relations change: Susan takes on the duties (and limited rights) of a non-owner of the Porsche and someone else takes on the rights, liberties, duties, and powers of ownership. Or perhaps Susan lends or hires the car; that involves a temporary and less extensive change in legal relations. She can bequeath the car in her will so that someone else will take over her property rights when she dies. These are her powers to change her legal situation and that of others. She may also, in certain circumstances, have her own legal position altered in relation to the Porsche: for instance, she is liable to have the car

---

[3] See American Law Institute, *Restatement of Law of Property*, Vol. I, p. 11. See also Noyes, *Institution of Property*, p. 290.

seized in execution of a judgement summons for debt. All these legal relations are involved in what we might think of as a clear case, indeed a paradigm, of ownership. Private property, then, is not only not a simple relation between a person and a thing, it is not a simple relationship at all. It involves a complex bundle of relations, which differ considerably in their character and effect.[4]

If that were all, there would be no problem of definition: private property would be a bundle of rights, but if it remained constant for all or most of the cases that we want to describe as private property, the bundle as a whole could be defined in terms of its contents. But, of course, it does not remain constant, and that is where the difficulties begin.

Each of the legal relations involved in Susan's ownership of the Porsche is not only distinct, but in principle separable, from each of the others. It is possible, for example, that someone has a liberty to use an automobile without having any of the other rights or powers which Susan has. Because they are distinct and separable, the component relations may be taken apart and reconstituted in different combinations, so that we may get smaller bundles of the rights that were involved originally in this large bundle we called ownership. But when an original bundle is taken apart like this and the component rights redistributed among other bundles, we are still inclined, in our ordinary use of these concepts, to say that one particular person—the holder of one of the newly constituted bundles—is the *owner* of the resource. If Susan leases the car to her friend Blair so that he has exclusive use of the Porsche in return for a cash payment, we may still say that Susan is really the car's owner even though she does not have many of the rights, liberties, and powers outlined in the previous paragraph. We say the same about landlords, mortgagors, and people who have conceded various encumbrances, like rights of way, over their real estate: they are still the owners of the pieces of land in question. But the legal position of a landlord is different from that of a mortgagor, different again from that of someone who has yielded a right of way, and different too from that of a person who has not redistributed any of the rights in his original bundle: depending on the particular transactions that have taken place, each has a different bundle of rights. If lay usage still dignifies them all with the title 'owner' of the land

---

[4] This analysis is obviously indebted to Honoré's paper, 'Ownership'. I shall refer to Honoré's discussion of the way in which ownership is to be defined in sect. 6, below.

in question, we are likely to doubt whether the concept of ownership, and the concept of private property that goes with it, are doing very much work at all. The lawyer, certainly, who is concerned with the day-to-day affairs of all these people, will not be interested in finding out which of them really counts as an owner. His only concern is with the detailed contents of the various different bundles of legal relations.[5]

As if that were not enough, there are other indeterminacies in the concept of ownership. In America, an owner can leave his goods in his will to more or less anyone he pleases. But an owner's liberty in this respect is not so great in England; it is even more heavily curtailed by statute law in, say, New Zealand; and in France the operation of the doctrine of *legitima portio* casts a different complexion on wills, bequest, and inheritance altogether.[6] What does this show? Does it show that the French have a different concept of ownership from the Americans and the English, so that it is a linguistic error to translate '*propriété*' as 'ownership'? Or does it show that the power of transmissibility by will is not part of the definition of ownership, but only contingently connected with it? If we take the former alternative, we are left with the analytically untidy situation in which we have as many ambiguities in the term 'ownership' as there are distinct legal systems (and indeed distinct momentary legal systems—for each may change in this respect over time). But if we take the latter option, we run the risk of leaving the concept of ownership without any essential content at all. It will become rather like *substance* in Locke's epistemology: a mere substratum, a hook on which to hang various combinations of legal relations.

In fact, I think many legal scholars now do take this latter option. In their view, the term 'ownership' serves only as an indication that some legal relations, some rights, liberties, powers, etc., are in question. On their view, the term does not convey any determinate idea of what these legal relations are. In every case, we have to push the words 'ownership' and 'private property' aside and look to the detail of the real legal relations involved in the given situation.[7]

For completeness, I should mention a third source of indeterminacy.

---

[5] For a particularly strong statement of this view, see Grey, 'Disintegration of Property', pp. 69–85.

[6] See Tyler, *Family Provision*; Maurice, *Family Provision Practice*; and, for the doctrine of *legitima portio*, Guest, 'Family Provision and *Legitima Portio*'.

[7] Cf. Grey, 'Disintegration of Property', p. 70; also Ackerman, *Private Property and the Constitution*, pp. 26 ff.

The objects of property—the things which in lay usage are capable of being owned—differ so radically in legal theory, that it seems unlikely that the same concept of ownership could be applied to them all, even within a single legal system. In England, the ownership of a Porsche is quite a different thing from the ownership of a piece of agricultural land. There are different liberties, duties, and liabilities in the two cases. Private property in these comparatively concrete objects is a different matter again from the ownership of intangible things like ideas, copyrights, corporate stock, reputations, and so on. Once again the common word 'ownership'—'X owns the car', 'Y owns the land', 'Z owns the copyright'—may be unhelpful and misleading, for it cannot convey any common content for these quite different bundles of legal relations. There is also a similar, though perhaps less spectacular, variation in ownership with different types of *owner*: the ownership of a given resource by a natural person may be a different matter from its ownership by a corporation and different again from its being the property of the Crown. Variations in 'subject' as well as variations in 'object' can make a difference to the nature of the relation.[8]

2. CONCEPTUAL DEFINITION

We owe to H. L. A. Hart the point that in jurisprudence, as in all philosophy, it is a mistake to think that particulars can be classified under general terms only on the basis of their possession of specified common features.[9] But when jurists express doubts about the usefulness of general terms such as 'private property' or 'ownership', it is usually this sort of definition that they have in mind. They imply that if we are unable to specify necessary and jointly sufficient conditions which an insitution must satisfy in order to be regarded as a system of private property, or which a legal relation must satisfy in order to be regarded as a relation of ownership, then those terms are to be regarded as ambiguous or confused and certainly as analytically unhelpful.[10]

If Hart's point is accepted, however, this scepticism begins to

---

[8] Cf. Friedmann, *Law in a Changing Society*, pp. 96 ff.
[9] Hart, 'Definition and Theory', pp. 21–47.
[10] These points are put forcefully by Grey, 'Disintegration of Property', pp. 76–81.

seem a little premature. Conceptual definition is a complicated business and the idea that it always involves the precise specification of necessary and sufficient conditions must be regarded as naive and outdated. A term which cannot be given a watertight definition in analytic jurisprudence may nevertheless be useful and important for social and political theory; we must not assume in advance that the imprecision or indeterminacy which frustrates the legal technician is fatal to the concept in every context in which it is deployed. In the rest of this chapter, I want to consider whether any of the more interesting recent accounts of the nature and meaning of political concepts—such as Wittgenstein's idea of family resemblance, the idea of persuasive definitions, the distinction between concept and conception, or the idea of 'essential contestability'—casts any light on the question of the definition of private property. Briefly, what I want to say (the main argument is in section 6) is that private property is a *concept* of which many different *conceptions* are possible, and that in each society the detailed incidents of ownership amount to a particular concrete conception of this abstract concept.

That will be the core of my argument in this chapter. In the other sections, I shall try to relate this approach to some of the other difficulties we have noticed: difficulties about different types of property object, split ownership, alternative property systems, corporations, and so on. However, before doing any of that, I want to start by distinguishing the concept of private property (of which, as I have said, there are many different conceptions) from the much more general concept of a property system.

3. THE CONCEPT OF A PROPERTY SYSTEM

The concept of property is the concept of a system of rules governing access to and control of material resources. Something is to be regarded as a material resource if it is a material object capable of satisfying some human need or want. In all times and places with which we are familiar, material resources are scarce relative to the human demands that are made on them. (Some, of course, are scarcer than others.) Scarcity, as philosophers from Hume to Rawls have pointed out, is a presupposition of all sensible talk about property. If this assumption were ever to fail (as Marx believed it some day would) then the traditional problem of the nature and justification of rival types of property system would probably disappear.[11] But so long as it obtains, individuals (either on their own or in groups) are going to disagree about who is to make which use of what. These disagreements are often serious because, in many cases, being able to make use of a resource that one wants is connected directly or indirectly with one's survival. A problem, then, which I shall call the problem of *allocation*, arises in any society which regards the avoidance of serious conflict as a matter of any importance. This is the problem of determining peacefully and reasonably predictably who is to have access to which resources for what purposes and when. The systems of social rules which I call property rules are ways of solving that problem.

The concept of property does not cover all rules governing the use of material resources, only those concerned with their allocation. Otherwise the concept would include almost all general rules of behaviour. (Since almost all human conduct involves the use of material resources, almost all rules about conduct can be related to resources in some way.) For example, most societies have rules limiting the use of weapons: they are not to be used to wound or kill people. Some jurists have suggested (in relation to private property systems) that rules prohibiting harmful use should be included among the standard incidents of ownership.[12] (In our discussion of Susan and her Porsche, we suggested that speed restrictions might also be treated in this way.) Nothing much hangs on this, but I suspect a better approach is to treat prohibitions on harmful behaviour as general constraints on action, setting limits to what may be done in a given society. Then we can locate rules about property within those limits, as rules determining which (generally permissible) actions may be performed with which resources. As Nozick puts it, the rules of property determine for each object at any time which individuals are entitled to realize which of the constrained set of options socially available with respect to that object at that time.[13] So, for example, the rule that

[11] The classic discussion is Hume, *Treatise*, Bk. III, Pt. II, sect. 2. See also Hart, *Concept of Law*, pp. 192 ff., and Rawls, *A Theory of Justice*, pp. 126 ff. For the Marxist position on scarcity, see e.g. Marx and Engels, *German Ideology*, p. 56; and Marx, *Critique of the Gotha Programme*, pp. 17–18. See also Macpherson, *Democratic Theory*, pp. 19 ff.

[12] See e.g. Honoré, 'Ownership' p. 123.

[13] Nozick, *Anarchy, State, and Utopia*, p. 171.

knives are not to be used murderously nor cars driven at a certain speed are not to be seen as property rules. They are part of the general background constraints on action which place limits on what anyone can do with any object whether it is his property—or something he has some sort of entitlement to use—or not.[14] Once we have settled what the background rules of action are, we can then turn to the property rules. If a particular action, say, riding bicycles, is permitted by law, it does not follow that the law permits me to ride any bicycle I please. The specific function of property rules is to determine, once we have established that bicycles may be ridden, who is entitled to ride which bicycle and when.

4. MATERIAL OBJECTS

I have defined property in terms of *material* resources, that is, resources like minerals, forests, water, land, as well as manufactured objects of all sorts.[15] But sometimes we talk about objects of property which are not corporeal: intellectual property in ideas and inventions, reputations, stocks and shares, choses in action, even positions of employment. As we saw, this proliferation of different kinds of property object is one of the main reasons why jurists have despaired of giving a precise definition of ownership. I think there are good reasons for discussing property in material resources first before grappling with the complexities of incorporeal property.

[14] Cf. Salmond, *Jurisprudence*, p. 251 n.

[15] It is tempting to follow John Austin and draw a sharp line between *persons* and *things*—persons being humans and things 'such permanent external objects as are not persons'—and then insist that property is a matter of rules governing access to and control of things by persons. (See Austin, *Lectures on Jurisprudence*, Vol. I, Lect. xiii, pp. 357–8.) This has what appears to be the moral advantage of ruling out slavery as a form of property a priori. But, as Austin himself notes, that analysis does nothing to rule out the possibility that a slave, though not a chattel, might occupy in a certain legal system 'a position analogous to a thing' in virtue of the law of personal status (ibid. Lect. xv, p. 385). A more common-sense approach is to recognize that humans *are* material resources (in the sense we defined): they can be used to lift loads or drive mills, as footstools, and even as food. Slavery is wrong, no doubt; but the objection to systems which treat humans as one another's chattels ought to be ethical rather than conceptual. Moreover, Austin's approach has the disadvantage of driving a conceptual wedge between the idea of property in oneself and property in external objects: indeed the former locution must be, for him, impermissible. But some philosophers (notably Locke, *Two Treatises*, II, sect. 27) have wanted to use that idea as the basis of their argument for private property. Maybe there are problems with such arguments. But we should not define our concepts in such a way as to make them impossible in advance.

First, we should recall that the question of how material resources are to be controlled and their use allocated is one that arises in every society. All human life involves the use of material resources and some of the most profound disagreements among human beings and human civilizations concern the basic principles on which this is to be organized. The allocation of material resources, we may say, is a primal and universal concern of human societies (though if Marx's optimism is justified, it may not concern us for ever). The question of rights in relation to *in*corporeal objects cannot be regarded as primal and universal in the same way. In some societies, we may speculate, the question does not arise at all either because incorporeals do not figure in their ontology or, if they do, because human relations with them are not conceived in terms of access and control. That is a point about incorporeals in general. Turning to the incorporeal objects we are interested in, it is clear that questions about patents, reputations, positions of employment, etc. are far from being universal questions that confront every society. On the contrary, one suspects that these questions arise for us only because other and more elementary questions (including questions about the allocation of material objects) have been settled in certain complex ways.[16]

Once these prior questions have been answered, it is often illuminating to characterize the solutions in terms which bring out analogies with the way in which questions about property have been answered. For example, once it is clear that individuals have rights not to be defamed, it may be helpful to describe that situation by drawing a parallel between the idea of owning a material object and the idea of having exclusive rights in a thing called one's 'reputation'. Such talk may take on a life of its own so that it becomes difficult to discuss the law of defamation except by using this analogy with property. I certainly do not wish to suggest that such talk about incorporeal property should be abandoned or 'reduced' to more complicated talk about other legal relations. But it is important to see that there is a reason for concentrating first and foremost on property rules about material resources, for that gives us the raw material on which the analogies are based.[17]

[16] For a discussion of the variety of incorporeal objects recognized in primitive societies, see Lowie, 'Incorporeal Property'.

[17] Thus I reject the approach of Honoré, 'Social Justice', p. 62, who claims that 'no rational distinction can be drawn' between property rights in material goods and property rights in incorporeal things. I believe that our understanding of the latter is increased immeasurably by having a grip *first* on an understanding of the former.

A more extreme materialist view was taken by Bentham, who insisted that all talk of incorporeal property is 'fictitious', 'figurative', 'improper', and 'loose and indefinite':

In almost every case in which the law does anything for a man's benefit or advantage, men are apt to speak of it, on some occasion or other, as conferring on him a sort of property. . . . The expedient then has been to create, as it were, on every occasion, an ideal being and to assign to a man this ideal being for the object of his property: and these are the sort of objects to which men of science . . . came . . . to give the name of 'incorporeal'.[18]

(Austin took a similar view.)[19] However, Bentham and Austin may be wrong in thinking that this talk causes confusion in the law: there are topics, like copyright and patents, which are probably most lucidly discussed in these terms. The only point I wish to make is that the analysis of concepts and arguments about incorporeal property must be postponed until we have clear concepts of property and private property for material objects.

Is it possible to postpone discussion of incorporeals in this way? Maybe even our ordinary property talk involves incorporeals more often than we think. For example, it is often said that the English law of real property is not concerned with land as a material resource but only with estates in land. Since there can be several different estates in a single piece of land, each with a different owner, it is impossible to identify an estate with anything corporeal. The law of real property therefore concerns incorporeal objects (estates) not corporeal things like rocks and soil.[20]

This argument is plausible only if we have already identified property with private property. If we insist that the function of a property rule is to assign particular objects exclusively to particular individuals, then we *will* have to say that the objects of English real property law were estates not pieces of land. But that is not my view. The concept of property is the concept of rules governing access to and control of material resources, and such a system of rules may assign to several people rights in the same resource. In its origins the English system of real property was not a private property system at all but a highly structured system of collective

---

[18] Bentham, *Introduction to Principles of Morals and Legislation*, p. 211.

[19] Austin, *Lectures on Jurisprudence*, Vol. I, Lect. xlvi, pp. 775 ff.

[20] See, e.g. Lawson, *Law of Property*, p. 16; Cheshire, *Modern Law of Real Property*, p. 32.

property.[21] Talk of incorporeal estates attaching to particular individuals was a way of characterizing that system (just as talk of 'reputations' as property objects was a way of characterizing the complexities of the law of defamation). Today, however, some of these incorporeal estates (notably fee simple) are so far-reaching that they are tantamount to private ownership of land. We should say then that the forms of a feudal system of collective property have been adapted by English law to express the modern reality of private property in pieces of land.[22]

What about the corporeality of land itself? A piece of land is not usually taken to be identical with the soil and rock etc. at a given location.[23] If anything, the land is identified with the location—a region of three-dimensional space rather than the sort of material object that one might locate *in* space.[24] The suggestion might be made therefore that land itself is an incorporeal thing. There are two ways of responding to this. We might accept the argument but insist that spatial regions can still be regarded as material resources. Although they differ ontologically from cars and rocks they also seem to be in quite a different category from the complexes of rights that constitute familiar incorporeals—patents, reputations, etc. It is philosophically naive to think that the fact that we have to regard regions as property objects adds anything to the case for regarding, say, choses in action in that way. The second response is more subtle. We may concede that land, as conceived in law, is too abstract to be described as a material resource. But we may still insist that the primary objects of real property are the actual material resources like arable soil and solid surfaces which are located in the regions in question. Until recently, these resources have been effectively immovable and so there has been no reason to distinguish 'land as material' from 'land as site'.[25] But developments like modern earth-moving and high-rise building necessitate a more complex and sophisticated packaging of rights over these resources. Thus the concept of land as site has now had to be

[21] See Philbrick, 'Changing Conceptions of Property', pp. 707–8; see also Noyes, *Institution of Property*, pp. 232 ff.

[22] See Megarry and Wade, *Law of Real Property*, pp. 14–15; also Kahn Freund, 'Introduction' to Renner, *Institutions of Private Law*, p. 42.

[23] But the Californian Civil Code defines land as 'the solid material of the earth': see Paton, *Textbook of Jurisprudence*, pp. 508–9. See also Salmond, *Jurisprudence*, pp. 416–7.

[24] This is the view of Kocourek, *Jural Relations*, p. 336.

[25] This distinction is from Noyes, *Institution of Property*, p. 438.

detached from its association with immovable resources and employed on its own as an abstract idea for characterizing these more complicated packages of rights. Still, in the last analysis, the system of property in land is a set of rules *about* material resources and nothing more.

Both worries about land can be seen as stemming from a desire to preserve a link between the concept of property and that of 'economic reality'. Real estate is about interests and fees, or about desirable sites, but not about soil and rocks. And similar suggestions have been made more generally in the literature: in the modern commercial world wealth no longer consists in the possession and control of material objects, but is a matter of less tangible considerations—stocks, shares, funds, and options— complicated economic relations which cannot be reduced to the ownership of things.[26]

Once again, this worry seems to be based on the identification of property with private property. If we ask, 'What things do modern men *own* which are definitive of their wealth?', we will certainly have to conjure up incorporeal things to correspond to the complex legal relations that in fact define their economic position. But if we say instead that property is a matter of rules about access to and control of material resources, but not necessarily about private ownership, then we may still say that a man's wealth is constituted for the most part by his property relations. He may not be the owner of very many resources; but the shares he holds, the funds he has claims on, and the options and goodwill he has acquired, together define his position so far as access to and control of material resources is concerned. This view, I think, reflects the complexity of modern economic life much more faithfully than the rival view which purports to treat shares, options, goodwill as though they were objects simply and straightforwardly on a par with minerals, land, and factories.

5. THE CONCEPT OF PRIVATE PROPERTY

I now want to say what distinguishes a system of *private* property from other types of property system. Some jurists give the impression that by making out a case for the establishment of some

---

[26] Ibid. See also Friedmann, *Law in a Changing Society*, p. 96.

system of settled rules about material objects, they have thereby refuted socialism.[27] This is a mistake. A socialist system, as much as a system of private property, is a system of rules governing access to and control of material objects. A case for private property must relate to what is distinctive about this type of system, and not merely to the concept of property rules, something to which socialists and capitalists have a common commitment. Marx, for example, regarded it as obvious that all forms of society require some system of property: 'That there can be no such thing as production, nor, consequently, society, where property does not exist in any form, is a tautology. . . . But it becomes ridiculous when from that one jumps at once to a definite form, e.g. private property.'[28]

The definition of private property I shall give is abstract. But it has the advantage of separating the question of what sort of system private property is from any particular theory of how private property is to be defended.

(i) Private Property

In a system of private property, the rules governing access to and control of material resources are organized around the idea that resources are on the whole separate objects each assigned and therefore belonging to some particular individual.

This claim requires clarification. We need to know what it is for a system of property rules to be organized around an idea, and what exactly, in the case of private property, this organizing idea of *belonging* involves. Let me say something about the latter issue first.

The organizing idea of a private property system is that, in principle, each resource belongs to some individual. At its simplest and most abstract, the idea can be elucidated in the following way. Imagine that the material resources available for use in a society have been divided into discrete parcels (call each parcel an object), and that each object has the name of an individual member of the society attached to it. (There are many ways in which this division of resources and the allocation of names to objects could be made. I

---

[27] e.g. Benn and Peters, *Social Principles and the Democratic State*, p. 155.
[28] Marx, *Grundrisse*, p. 349.

make no assumptions about the way in which these processes take place. Both are matters for a theory of distributive justice.)[29]

A private property system is one in which such a correlation is used as a basis for solving what we earlier called the problem of allocation. Each society faces the problem of determining which, among the many competing claims on the resources available for use in that society, are to be satisfied, when, by whom, and under what conditions. In a private property system, a rule is laid down that, in the case of each object, the individual person whose name is attached to that object is to determine how the object shall be used and by whom. His decision is to be upheld by the society as final. When something like the idea of a name/object correlation is used in this way as a basis for solving the problem of allocation, we may describe each such correlation as expressing the idea of *ownership* or *belonging*. 'Ownership', then, on my stipulation, is a term peculiar to systems of private property. The owner of a resource is simply the individual whose determination as to the use of the resource is taken as final in a system of this kind.

Clearly, this idea of ownership is a possible way of solving the problem of allocation. But everything would depend on whether people accepted it and were prepared to abide by its fundamental rule. Partly this would be a matter of the acceptability of the name/object correlation. People would not be happy with an arbitrary correlation or one which did not assign their name to any object worth using. That is a matter for the theory of justice. But there might also be controversies about the very idea of ownership. People might ask, 'Why should *one* individual be put in a specially privileged position with regard to a given resource? Why not insist that, for all resources (or at least all the most important resources), the claims of every citizen are to be treated on an equal basis? Or why not insist that resource use is to be determined in each instance by reference to collective aims of the society?' These questions constitute the ancient problem of the justification of private property. The definition of private property that I have given enables us to see, in the abstract, just what is at stake when these questions are asked. It enables us to see what is distinctive and controversial about private property.

I should now say something about the organizing ideas of those types of property system that are usually opposed to private

[29] See Dworkin, 'Equality of Resources', esp. pp. 285–7.

property in such debates. The two most common alternatives are *common property* and *collective property*.

(ii) Collective Property

In a system of collective property, the problem of allocation is solved by a social rule that the use of material resources in particular cases is to be determined by reference to the collective interests of society as a whole. If there is any question about how or by whom resources like land, industrial plant, housing, and so on are to be used, those questions are to be resolved by favouring the use which is most conducive to the collective social interest. (We are familiar with this in the way that the control of major productive resources is organized in socialist countries.)

This leaves open two important questions. First, what is the collective interest? Is it defined in an aggregative welfarist way, or a statist way, or in some other holistic way, or what? Secondly, given some conception of collective interest, what procedures are to be used to apply that conception to particular cases? Are we to have a central economic planning committee, or the delegation of collective responsibility on trust to expert managers, or some sort of national democratic structure of decision-making, or local decision-making with certain national reservations, or what? A conception of collective property is not completely specified until these questions have been answered. But the general idea is clear enough: in principle, material resources are answerable to the needs and purposes of society as a whole, whatever they are and however they are determined, rather than to the needs and purposes of particular individuals considered on their own. No individual has such an intimate association with any object that he can make decisions about its use without reference to the interests of the collective.[30]

Collective property is sometimes presented as though it were a special case of private property, with the state as the equivalent of a private owner. This may be true at the level of the legal rules, particularly when we are talking about elements of collective property in, say, a predominantly capitalist society: those few industries that are controlled by the state are controlled by it as nominal owner. But at a deeper level of theoretical analysis, it is

---

[30] Macpherson describes substantially the same idea under the heading of 'state property', in 'Meaning of Property', pp. 5–6.

clear that 'ownership' by the state or its agencies is in quite a different category from ownership by a private firm or individual. It is the effect of a decision by a sovereign authority, which determines the rules of property, to retain control of a resource itself, and not to allow a resource to be controlled exclusively by any private organization.

(iii) Common Property

The idea of common property is superficially similar to that of collective property in that no individual stands in a specially privileged situation with regard to any resource. But it is different inasmuch as the interests of the collective have no special status either. In a system of common property, rules governing access to and control of material resources are organized on the basis that each resource is in principle available for the use of every member alike. In principle, the needs and wants of every person are considered, and when allocative decisions are made they are made on a basis that is in some sense fair to all.

Our familiarity with this idea does not stem from our knowledge of any society in which it is the dominant form of property, for there is no such society. It stems rather from our familiarity with the way in which the allocation of certain resources is handled in almost all societies: parks and national reserves are the best example. Many philosophers have used the idea of common property to characterize the initial situation of men in relation to resources in the so-called 'State of Nature'.[31]

In the case of finite resources, or resources which cannot be used simultaneously by everyone who wants to use them, the operation of a system of common property requires procedures for determining a fair allocation of use to individual wants. This is the task of a theory of justice, once a system of common property has been adopted.[32] The fact that the implementation of such a principle is likely to involve in practice a state apparatus for determining authoritatively whose claim to use a given resource should justly prevail at a given time may lead to a blurring of the distinction

[31] For the tradition in Natural Law theory which considers the possibility of common property without a state apparatus, see the discussion in Tully, *A Discourse on Property*, pp. 68 ff. See also Tuck, *Natural Rights Theories*, pp. 60–1.

[32] See Panichas, 'Prolegomenon', p. 340. See also Cohen, 'Capitalism, Freedom and the Proletariat', pp. 16–17.

between common property systems and (statist) collective property systems. But in principle the ideas may be distinguished and each is different from the idea of private property.

In all three cases—private, common, and collective property— what I have outlined is rather simplistic compared with the complicated property rules of most actual societies. It may be thought unrealistically simple in two ways. First, the terms in which I have described the different types of system are very abstract. For example, in real private property systems, nothing like a deliberate name/object correlation ever actually takes place. Secondly, as we all know, there are no examples of pure systems of any of these three types. All systems combine the characteristics of private, common, and collective property to some degree. I want to consider both points.

(iv) The 'Organizing Idea' of a Property System

First, the point about the abstractness of my characterization. In relation to private property systems my claim is not that people ever actually get together to divide resources into parcels or objects and to allocate names to objects in the way I described. The point is rather that the idea of ownership, which is crucial to the operation of these systems, is *something like* the idea of such a correlation. An idea of this sort—an idea whose gist is expressible in terms of this image—serves as an essential point of reference by which the operation of these systems of very detailed and complicated rules is to be understood.

What is it for a system to have such a point of reference, and why is such an 'organizing idea' necessary? It is possible that a property system might exist without any organizing idea at all. There might be nothing but a set of rules governing the allocation of resources without any sense of a point or organizing idea behind these rules. Or, if the rules are thought to have a point, it may be understood in terms of general goals like utility and prosperity rather than any abstract property idea. However, if a society of this sort were at all complex, then citizens would have great difficulty following the rules. Everyone would need to become a legal expert to determine at any point what he could or could not do in relation to the resources that he came across. He would have to acquire a detailed knowledge of the rules for each resource and of his rights, powers, liberties, and duties in relation to it. There would be no other way of ensuring, in ordinary life, that one abided by the rules except to find out what they were and learn them by heart.

On the whole, our society is not like that. It is possible for the layman to go about his business most of the time without this detailed knowledge. As Bruce Ackerman points out, every day the layman has to make countless decisions as to whether one thing or another may be used by him for some purpose that he has in mind. In making these decisions it is rare for him to find it necessary to obtain professional legal advice. 'Indeed, most of the time Layman negotiates his way through the complex web of property relationships that structures his social universe without even perceiving a need for expert guidance.'[33] He can do this because he knows in an informal and non-technical way which things are 'his' and which are not. If something is 'his' then (roughly) he determines what use is to be made of it; if not, somebody else does. Of course this is rough and ready knowledge by the standards of legal science. But it is there and it is socially very important: in the case of the overwhelming majority of citizens, it provides the main basis on which they learn to apply the property rules of their society.

The organizing idea of a given property system may also be important for its legitimation. The problem of allocation, as we have seen, is both difficult and dangerous. Disputes about property are likely to be among the most deadly disputes that can arise. If violence is not to erupt continually, they must be settled on terms whose legitimacy is widely acknowledged. But the complexity and detail of economic life is such that there is no question of securing a consensus for the justification of each particular property rule (e.g., 'Cheryl to have a right of way across Blackacre', 'The factory foreman to have responsibility for the maintenance of that type of machine', and so on). Justification and legitimation necessarily proceed on a fairly broad front; and the organizing idea of a property system (the basis on which its rules are learned and understood for application in everyday life) provides a natural point of contact between legitimizing considerations and the grasp which ordinary citizens have on the rules.

---

[33] Ackerman, *Private Property and the Constitution*, p. 116 and also the discussion at pp. 97 ff. For the claim that some ability of the sort Ackerman describes is essential to the operation of a market economy, see Buchanan, *Limits of Liberty*, p. 18.

(v) Ideal Types

But all this talk about the organizing idea of a private property system makes sense only on the assumption that we can say whether a given system, in real life, *is* a system of private, common, or collective property. Is this a warranted assumption? This raises the second of the issues I said we had to consider.

As categories of social, economic, or political science, these ideas of a private property system, a collective property system, and a common property system are clearly 'ideal typic' categories. To quote Max Weber out of context, 'none of these ideal types . . . is usually to be found in historical cases in "pure" form'.[34] In Britain, for example, some industries (like British Leyland) are held as collective property, while others (like Times Newspapers) are privately owned. In the Soviet Union, the most recent constitution makes explicit provision for the private ownership of houses and small holdings, even while it insists that the land and basic means of production are the property of the state.[35] Both these systems, with their respective mixes of private property rules and collective property rules, also have certain common property rules, controlling resources like Hyde and Gorky Parks, respectively. This means that our ideal types of property system are somewhat difficult to apply in the real world. We can identify four sources of difficulty here.

(1) As we have seen, the ideas of common, collective, and private property represent focal points for political disagreement and debate in each society. To put it crudely: socialists argue for a system of collective property, radicals for something like common property, and capitalists and their liberal ideologues for private property. In practice these arguments seldom result in outright victory for one side or the other. More likely there will be a measure of compromise, with access to and control of some resources being private, others common, and others organized on a collective basis. That has certainly been our experience in the West. The mix will often reflect the relative political strength of the competing factions; for example, the recent spate of 'privatization' in Britain is an indication of the declining political power of socialism.

---

[34] Weber, *Economy and Society*, p. 216 (referring to his three ideal types of legitimate domination). For Weber's discussion of the notion of ideal types, see ibid. 9 ff.

[35] *Constitution of the Union of the Soviet Socialist Republics*, Art. 13; see Finer (ed.), *Five Constitutions*, p. 151.

(2) Sometimes debate about the problem of allocation is conducted in a way that makes direct reference to social goals (like prosperity or stability) without the mediation of any organizing idea like private or collective property at all. We have seen that this can hardly happen across the board, but it may happen occasionally and haphazardly. These debates, then, may yield 'pragmatic' solutions to particular allocation problems which fit only loosely with the general approach to property rules in the society concerned.

(3) No society, whatever its ideological predilections, can avoid the fact that some resources are more amenable to some types of property rule than others. In the case of sunlight and air, for example, it seems hard to envisage anything like private property. Common property seems the 'obvious' solution: people simply make use of them as they want to. For other resources, like clothes, toothbrushes, and food for the table, it is hard to see how they could be regulated except on a private property basis. Finally, there are resources like highways and artillery pieces, over which most societies have found it necessary to exercise collective control. These are certainly not hard-and-fast a priori truths: the circumstances of human life may change; and, even if they remain the same, someone could be committed so fanatically to a particular property idea that he sought to apply it across the board to all resources.[36] But for practical purposes, they represent outer parameters within which different systems of property may be established.[37]

(4) As we shall see in section 8, systems of private property have the peculiarity that they permit individual owners to split up their rights, thereby producing new property arrangements which, considered in isolation, may imitate the arrangments of other non-private property systems. (By this means, for example, joint ownership and common ownership can come to be categories of a private property system.)

Even in the face of these complications, it is still possible to say,

---

[36] See the discussion in Salmond, *Jurisprudence*, p. 252.

[37] Of course, there are disputes about these parameters. Many of the arguments in favour of socialist collective property, for example, boil down eventually to the claim that the nature of human production (in advanced societies, at least) is such that the means of production are intrinsically apt for collective property relations and peculiarly inapt for private ownership. They even suggest that the prevalence of corporate ownership in private property systems indicates the truth of this claim (see n. 67, below). Needless to say defenders of private property deny this.

of most societies, whether their property system is one of common, collective, or private property. Partly this is a matter of the society's self-understanding. In Britain despite considerable nationalization, people feel that property rules are still organized primarily around the idea of private ownership. In the Soviet Union, by contrast, despite some leeway for private property, the official ideology and self-understanding of the society points firmly towards state or collective property as the dominant property idea. This is expressed in the Soviet Constitution where it is said that state property is 'the principal form of socialist property'.[38]

Of course, all this may be controversial in a given society; perhaps it is possible for a society to deceive itself in this regard. As an objective constraint, we may want to look at the way in which 'the commanding heights' of the economy—that is, the resources deemed most important in the life of the society (or those resources in relation to which the problem of allocation is in the long run most acute, or those resources that occupy strategic positions in relation to the economy as a whole)—are controlled. The dominance of the Marxist paradigm in social theory has generally meant that property rules in relation to the main material means of production are taken as the crucial index.

The existence of these disagreements need not worry us here. An argument for or against private property may be sustained even where it is unclear whether the society in which that debate is taking place has a private property system or not. Further, even if the practical upshot of such an argument can never be the establishment of a system which is indisputably private or collective, still such arguments are not without practical significance. The effect of a politically successful argument will be to push the property system a certain distance in one direction or the other. The inevitability, then, of what has become known as 'the mixed economy' does not deprive us of our subject-matter. As long as the balance of the mixture remains a matter of contention, there is room for argument about the respective merits of private, common, and collective property systems as rival bases for social and economic reform.

---

[38] *Soviet Constitution*, Art. 11; see Finer (ed.), *Five Constitutions*, p. 151.

6. THE CONCEPT AND CONCEPTIONS OF OWNERSHIP

I return now to the problem of *defining* private ownership. Ownership, as we have seen, expresses the abstract idea of an object being correlated with the name of some individual, in relation to a rule which says that society will uphold that individual's decision as final when there is any dispute about how the object should be used. The owner of an object is the person who has been put in that privileged position.

How is this very abstract idea related, in a particular system, to the detailed legal rules conferring particular rights, powers, liberties, on particular individuals? Until we have given some account of this, we will not be able to say how the idea of ownership performs the functions outlined in the preceding section. For example, does the idea operate as some sort of informal or shorthand summary of the rules? If so, we should be able to indicate how it works by stating in a definition what the legal rights of owners are characteristically taken to be. Or perhaps the idea of ownership has the same relationship to the detailed legal rules of property as the moralistic idea of infidelity has to the detailed matrimonial law of adultery: it determines the spirit, rather than abbreviates the content, of the legal rules. Or maybe there is some other relationship.[39] That is the question I will consider in this section.

As we saw in section 1, most jurists agree that it is impossible to capture the relation between the idea of ownership and the detailed rules of a private property system in a precise legal definition of the analytical type. We cannot say that a person *owns* a resource if and only if he has certain specified rights, powers, liberties, and duties. How should we respond to this?

One possibility is that we conclude the term is simply ambiguous— rather like 'right' before Hohfeld went to work on it— covering a variety of quite distinct legal phenomena from usage to usage.[40] If we take this approach, we should probably abandon 'ownership' altogether (as Hohfeld suggested we should abandon 'right'), replacing it in every context by a less ambiguous statement

---

[39] For an account of different views of the relation between the legal term 'ownership' and ordinary language, see Ackerman, *Private Property and the Constitution*, pp. 10 ff.

[40] See Hohfeld, *Fundamental Legal Conceptions*, pp. 36 ff.

of the legal relations to which we want to refer. This suggestion is reinforced by the view (in fact still controversial in the literature)[41] that, in modern legal practice, it is seldom necessary in the course of pleading to set up a claim to the ownership of a disputed good. Litigation, in common law at least, revolves around the idea of *a better title to possess*, and in general around some of the particular rights which we might take to be connected with ownership, rather than ownership itself.

However, before being panicked into abandoning the concept, we ought to consider other possible relations between the 'intuitive' idea of ownership and the detailed property rules.

One possible approach is described (but not ultimately accepted) by Honoré: 'If ownership is provisionally defined as *the greatest interest in a thing which a mature system of law recognizes*, then it follows that, since all mature systems admit the existence of "interests" in "things", all mature systems have, in a sense, a concept of ownership.'[42] A similar suggestion is made by Austin:

[T]hough the possible *modes* of property are infinite, and though the indefinite power of user is always restricted more or less, there is in every system of law, some one mode of property in which the restrictions to the power of user are fewer [the power of indefinite user more extensive] than in others. . . . And to this mode of property, the term dominion, property, or ownership is pre-eminently and emphatically applied.[43]

The trouble with these suggestions is that they lead us to identify 'owners' in even the most collectivist systems. Even with regard to a harvester on a Soviet farm, there may be someone who has more rights in respect of it than anyone else. Thus the link between ownership and private property is in danger of being severed.

Moreover, this approach is perhaps too pessimistic about the prospects for a more substantial definition. Although there are the variations that we noticed in section 1,

There is indeed a substantial similarity in the position of one who 'owns' an umbrella in England, France, Russia, China and any other modern country one may care to mention. Everywhere the 'owner' can, in the simple

---

[41] See Hargreaves, 'Terminology and Title'; Holdsworth, 'Terminology and Title—A Reply'; Turner, 'Reflections on Ownership in English Law'; Kiralfy, 'Problem of Law of Property in Goods'; Hargreaves, 'Modern Real Property'. See also Dias, *Jurisprudence*, pp. 396 ff.

[42] Honoré, 'Ownership', p. 108.

[43] Austin, *Lectures on Jurisprudence*, Vol. II, p. 824.

uncomplicated case . . . use it, stop others using it, lend it, sell it, or leave it by will. Nowhere may he use it to poke his neighbour in the ribs or knock over his vase. Ownership, *dominium*, *propriété*, *Eigentum* and similar words stand not merely for the greatest interest in particular systems but for a type of interest with common features transcending particular systems.[44]

Honoré has done valuable work, setting out a list of what these common features are: he calls them 'the standard incidents' of 'the full liberal concept of ownership' in ordinary 'uncomplicated' cases.[45] I shall only list them here, very briefly, for (with one exception) I have no wish to improve on the details of his account. In standard cases, Honoré suggests that an owner of an object X will have: (1) a right to the possession of X; (2) a right to use X; (3) a right to manage X (that is, determine the basis on which X is used by others if it is so used); (4) a right to the income that can be derived from permitting others to use X; (5) a right to the capital value of X; (6) a right to security against the expropriation of X; (7) a power to transmit X by sale, or gift, or bequest to another; (8) the lack of any term on the possession of any of these rights etc.; (9) a duty to refrain from using X in a way that harms others; (10) a liability that certain judgements against him may be executed on X; and (11) some sort of expectation that, when rights that other people have in X come to the end of their term or lapse for any reason, those rights will, as it were, return 'naturally' to him. My only quarrel is with Honoré's feature (9)—the prohibition on harmful use. As I have already indicated (in section 3 above), these prohibitions are better regarded as general background constraints on action than as specific rules of property (let alone as specific incidents of *private* property).

It would be a mistake to think that Honoré intends this list of standard incidents to be taken as necessary or jointly sufficient conditions of ownership. It is intended more as an elucidation of certain rather common features of ownership along the lines of a Wittgensteinian 'family resemblance' analysis.[46] The idea of family resemblance enables us to accommodate a certain amount of variation here and there, without abandoning our faith in some

[44] Honoré, 'Ownership', p. 108.
[45] Ibid. 112–28. See also Snare, 'Concept of Property', p. 205, and Becker, *Property Rights*, pp. 18 ff. , for other approaches along these lines.
[46] For the idea of 'family resemblance', see Wittgenstein, *Philosophical Investigations*, pp. 32 ff.

constancy in the way the term is used. Thus, for example, the fact that, in particular regimes, incident (7)— the power of transmission—is limited or incident (6)—the immunity against expropriation—is not guaranteed need not deter us from describing persons in that regime as 'owners' or the regime itself as a system of private property. It need not deter us from that any more than the fact that a particular member of the Churchill family lacks the Churchillian Roman nose deters us from attributing 'the Churchill face' to him. We do not have to insist on a strictly analytical definition in order to understand these concepts: providing we can see what Wittgenstein called the 'complicated network of similarities overlapping and criss-crossing . . . sometimes overall similarities, sometimes similarities of detail', we can account for the usefulness of the concept in social life.[47]

But there is an important aspect of the variability that this approach fails to capture. It concerns the role of critical argument. Because the content of ownership varies from society to society, it becomes possible for people to argue that the idea of ownership prevalent in their society is better or worse than the idea prevalent elsewhere. Such suggestions, which on the surface seem purely conceptual arguments, can easily become vehicles for advancing practical proposals for changes in property rules.

Suppose, for example, that, in society A, intestate goods are taken over and redistributed by the state, whereas in society B they are transmitted by rules of inheritance to the owners' relatives and dependents. A citizen of society A who is in favour of the latter arrangement may argue: 'We don't *really* have a system of ownership in our society; a *real* system of ownership (like that in society B) is one which recognizes not only the power of bequest but also the right of inheritance.' To this suggestion, a defender of the arrangements in society A (call him John Stuart Mill) may reply:

Nothing is implied in [private] property but the right of each to his (or her) own faculties, to what he can produce by them, and to whatever he can get for them in a fair market; together with his right to give this to any other person if he chooses, and the right of that other to receive and enjoy it. It follows, therefore, that although the right of bequest, or gift after death, forms part of the idea of private property, the right of inheritance, as distinguished from bequest, does not.[48]

What sort of disagreement is this? At one level Mill and his

[47] Ibid. 32e.
[48] Mill, *Principles of Political Economy*, Bk. II, Ch. 3, sect. 3, p. 221.

opponent are simply disagreeing about what rules of property to have. We give individuals a certain package of rights over resources; should we give their relatives the same rights over those resources after the individuals have died? If the question is stated blandly like that, it can be resolved in the way that all social questions about the detailed assignment of rights are resolved—by direct appeal to the goals of the community such as liberty, prosperity, stability, or whatever.

But what if Mill insists that, whatever the answer to *that* question may be, his point about the true meaning of ownership and private property still remains? 'That the property of persons who have made no disposition of it during their lifetime, should pass first to their children, and failing them, to their nearest relations, may be a proper arrangement or not, but it is no consequence of any principle of private property.'[49] Is this anything more than an empty verbal quibble?

A cynic may suggest that Mill's tactic is one of 'persuasive definition': he is attempting to give 'a new conceptual meaning to a familiar word without substantively changing its emotive meaning . . . with the conscious or unconscious purpose of changing, by this means, the direction of people's interests'.[50] But that would presuppose that the term once had a settled descriptive meaning which is now being altered. This seems false in the case of 'ownership': the difficulties relating to its definition have always existed.

A more fruitful approach draws on the use that political philosophers have made recently of W. B. Gallie's idea of 'essentially contested concepts': 'concepts whose proper use inevitably involves endless disputes about their proper uses on the part of their users'.[51] There are many difficulties with Gallie's claims about essential contestability, not least the essentialism implied in his terminology and in his claim that what holds a conceptual contest together and gives it its point is a reference back to the achievement of some 'exemplar' made in common by all the contesting parties.[52]

[49] Ibid.
[50] See Stevenson, 'Persuasive Definitions', p. 331.
[51] Gallie, 'Essentially Contested Concepts'. For the initial reception of Gallie's idea, see esp. Connolly, *Terms of Political Discourse*, Ch. 1; Lukes, *Power*, p. 9 *et passim*; and Gray, 'Contestability of Social and Political Concepts'.
[52] See e.g. MacDonald, 'Is "Power" Essentially Contested?'; Lukes, 'Reply to MacDonald'; Clarke, 'Eccentrically Contested Concepts'; Connolly, *Terms of Political Discourse* (2nd edn.), Ch. 6; Gray, 'Political Power, Social Theory, and Essential Contestability', pp. 94 ff.

I think it is possible to avoid buying into these controversies, if we are content simply to distinguish between a *concept* and various *conceptions* of that concept. Dworkin, for example, in his work distinguishes between the abstract concept of *fairness* and various more concrete conceptions of it which attempt to characterize what fairness is and involves at a practical level. Rawls, likewise, distinguishes between the abstract concept of *justice* and various competing conceptions of it, of which he takes his own construction to be one.[53] In the same way, we may want to characterize the relation between the idea of ownership and the detailed rules of particular systems of private property in terms of the relation between concept and conception.[54] The concept of ownership is the very abstract idea described in section 5: a correlation between individual names and particular objects, such that the decision of the named individual object about what should be done with an object is taken as socially conclusive. The rules of real or postulated legal systems assigning rights, liberties, powers, immunities, and liabilities to people in regard to particular resources amount to conceptions of that abstract concept. To the extent that two or more conceptions are opposed to one another (as they were in the John Stuart Mill argument about inheritance that we considered a moment ago) to that extent, the conceptions can be regarded as contestant uses of the concept in Gallie's sense.

We can also see now why ownership *appears* practically dispensable from the point of view of the technical lawyer. Since he is concerned (most of the time) with the law as it is in the society in which he and his clients live, and not with the law as it might be or as it is anywhere else, he never has occasion to raise his attention above the level of the particular conception of ownership constituted by the property rules of the legal system he is dealing with. For his purposes, that conception can be described exhaustively in terms which make no reference to ownership, nor even to the fact that it is a conception of ownership. The detailed rights, powers, liberties, and so on which his particular client has, or does not have,

[53] For the distinction between concept and conception, see Rawls, *A Theory of Justice*, pp. 5–11 (competing conceptions of justice); Dworkin, *Taking Right Seriously*, pp. 103, 134–6 (competing conceptions of fairness and cruelty), and 226 (competing conceptions of equality); and Gray, 'On Liberty, Liberalism and Essential Contestability' (competing conceptions of liberty).

[54] I am grateful to Ronald Dworkin for suggesting this approach to me. For somewhat similar aproaches to property, see Ackerman, *Private Property and the Constitution*, pp. 97–8, and Snare, 'Concept of Property', p. 201.

are all that he need concern himself with. Others, however, who are concerned with questions about the justification of those rules may need to raise their attention to a somewhat higher level of abstraction.

I think the concept–conception contrast also applies to the other property ideas we have been considering: common property and collective property. Each can be characterized in terms of a very abstract idea; and each may be realized in particular societies in various concrete forms. If we compare a particular conception of (say) collective property with a particular conception of private property—the Soviet Union and the United Kingdom, for example— we may be sceptical about whether there are any differences in principle between them. But if we see each property system as a concrete conception of a particular concept—as we must, in my opinion, if we are concerned with justification— then the important theoretical differences will be apparent.

7. OWNERSHIP AND MARKETS

Is an argument for private property necessarily an argument for a free market economy? Does the ownership of a resource necessarily entail a power of alienation over it?[55]

In theory, the answer is 'No'. An economic system might allocate resources to individuals on the basis that it is for each individual to say how and on what terms the resource allocated to him is to be used, without anyone having the power to transfer that right of decision to anyone else.[56] There might be a rule that whenever a question of transfer arises, it should be decided by the society as a whole, perhaps on the same sort of basis as the original allocation was determined. So we could say about exchange and alienation what we have already said (in section 6) about inheritance and bequest. Particular rules about the transmission of deceased estates—and indeed the whole idea of an individual having a power over his deceased estate—may characterize particular conceptions of private ownership, but the association of all this with the concept of private ownership will be contingent and necessarily controversial. Similarly, while the inclusion of powers of alienation and

---

[55] For an affirmative answer, see Lindsay, 'Principle of Private Property', p. 99.

[56] This possibility is discussed in relation to land in Caldwell, 'Rights of Ownership or Rights of Use?', p. 764. See also Salmond, *Jurisprudence*, p. 415 n.

free exchange along with exclusive use is perhaps characteristic of the modern Western conception of ownership, there may be competing conceptions of ownership that do not have these characteristics.

But although we could take that approach, it would be wrong not to recognize that the link between ownership and alienation is somewhat tighter than the connection which ownership has with inheritance and bequest. Its tightness is indicated by what we have said already about the problem of allocation. The problem of allocation arises because members of a society disagree on how scarce material resources are to be used. In a private property system society must decide to whom to allocate particular resources. However this distributive issue is resolved, it will seldom be satisfactory in the circumstances of the modern world for it to be resolved rigidly once and for all. Circumstances change: whatever principle was used for determining the initial distribution of resources, that same principle might dictate a different distribution if it were applied again later. For example, if the ownership of a given resource were vested initially in the person who most deserved it, or in the person who could exploit it most efficiently, there would be no guarantee that at the end of a year, say, that person would still be the one who deserved it most or who could make the best use of it. Or if the initial distribution were based on equality, that equality might subsequently be upset by the birth or arrival of new individuals or by the uneven consumption or depreciation of the distributed resources.[57] Now we could as a society redistribute resources authoritatively from time to time to preserve the application of the principle to which we had initially committed ourselves.[58] But redistribution of that sort has its costs, as many of its critics have pointed out: it disappoints expectations, it undermines security and stability, and it leaves people without the ability to undertake long-term planning of resource use except to the extent that they can prophesy changes in social circumstances and how the society will respond to them.[59] If these costs are thought too high, we may stick with the given distribution even

[57] See Dworkin, 'Equality of Resources', pp. 308–11, and Proudhon, *What is Property?*, p. 78.

[58] Cf. the famous 'Wilt Chamberlain' argument in Nozick, *Anarchy, State, and Utopia*, pp. 160–4.

[59] The classic argument to this effect is found in Bentham, 'Principles of the Civil Code'. There is a convenient excerpt in Macpherson (ed.), *Property: Mainstream and Critical Positions*.

though it now lacks the justification which was the reason for setting it up in the first place. But there is a third possibility. Instead of redistributing resources authoritatively from the centre, we could leave individual owners free to redistribute the resources they owned whenever it pleased them to do so. This would avoid the costs of insecurity, for a person would know a resource of his would never be redistributed until he was ready to redistribute it. Of course, the operation of this system might make matters worse: since it could not be controlled from the centre, it might take the distribution even further away from the original pattern. But it need not have that effect. Particularly if the original distributive principle made reference to the will and preferences of the distributees (as in Lockean principles of acquisition, or distributions on the basis of a principle of efficiency), allowing owners to transfer resources among themselves as they pleased might well promote the application of the original principle in changing circumstances rather than further undermine it.[60]

8. SPLIT OWNERSHIP

We have used the concept–conception distinction to analyse the differences between ownership in different societies. But it cannot be used to characterize the differences between the rights of owners that arise out of the 'fragmentation' or 'splitting' of ownership within a given society. The rights of a landlord are different from those of a mortgagor and different again from those of an owner-occupier who has no debts secured on his property. We still tend to describe them all as owners; but we can hardly say that there are three different *conceptions* of ownership in play here. Another explanation is necessary.

In this connection, two points seem to be important. First, it seems necessary to settle the meaning of ownership in the fullest sense before we consider the splitting up and recombination of property rights. If our conception of full ownership varies from society to society, then the account we give of the splitting and recombination of property rights will vary accordingly. Thus, for

---

[60] A suggestion along these lines in relation to the principle of efficiency is developed in Calabresi and Melamed, 'Property Rules, Liability Rules and Inalienability', p. 1092.

example, the rights of a landlord in England are different from those of a landlord in America, not just because the law of landlord and tenant is different but also because of the underlying differences in the respective conceptions of full ownership in the different societies. (For example, a landlord in America has more testamentary freedom than his counterpart in England.)

Secondly, we should note that once we start talking about cases of split ownership, we are introducing a dynamic element into what has up till now been a rather static analysis. The idea that an owner-occupier, a landlord, and a mortgagor, can all be described as private owners despite the differences in the particular rights they have, is paradoxical only if we take what might be called a 'time-slice' view of property systems, that is, only if we think we can tell who is and who is not an owner by concentrating on the rights, powers, and duties distributed around a society at a particular moment in time. But to approach matters with this expectation is already to beg the question against the concept of private ownership. The idea of ownership, I have maintained, is the idea of solving the problem of allocation by assigning each resource to an individual whose decision about how the resource is to be used is final. Thus in order to see whether a society has a system of ownership, and what its conception of ownership is, we must examine not just the way that resources are being used at this minute but how it was determined that *that* use, rather than some other possible pattern of use, came about. We have to examine something of the history of the uses and rights to use in the society. A static time-slice view, will not do justice to the essentially dynamic character of the private property systems.[61]

Thus, for example, when we describe a landlord as an owner, despite his having no right to live in 'his' house, we do so because we want to say something about the history—or about the likely future—of the property rights involved. Perhaps it is politically important to indicate that a given distribution of rights arose out of a private rather than a collective decision. Or we may want to draw attention to the fact that it was *this* person rather than any other whose decision led to this distribution of rights. We may also want to indicate, for reasons of planning and predictability, that certain rights will revert back to a certain person, or to his successors in

---

[61] For a more general critique of 'time-slice' approaches to property and distributive justice, see Nozick, *Anarchy, State, and Utopia*, pp. 153–60.

title, after some period of time.[62] Whatever the reason, it will have to do primarily with a dynamic rather than a static analysis of the society we are considering. It will be because we want to convey information about what has happened in the past or what may be expected to happen in the future. Once this is understood, the special position of landlord-owners, mortgagor-owners, and so on becomes clear. They do not fall directly under the conception of ownership in their society, but they stand in a dynamic relationship to that conception which is evident and important, and which may explain and justify the use of the word 'owner' to describe them.

9. CORPORATE OWNERSHIP

I shall be brief on the subject of corporate ownership. A society in which the main means of production are held by large corporations and managed by executives and boards responsible to a large and dispersed body of shareholders differs so markedly from a society dominated by individual private ownership that it is tempting to describe corporate property as a distinct type of property regime.[63]

However, I am inclined to view corporate property rather as a mutation of private property than as a distinct form of property in its own right. We have seen that one of the distinctive features of private property systems is that owners often have the power to split up and recombine the rights over resources originally allocated to them. Sometimes this leads to mortgages, sometimes to complicated leasehold arrangements, sometimes to trusts—and

---

[62] Hence the insistence in modern law of property on a mortgagor's equity of redemption. This sort of point is reflected in those theories which attempt to define ownership in terms of a 'residuary' interest: e.g. Pollock, *Jurisprudence and Legal Essays*, p. 98; Dias, *Jurisprudence*, pp. 395–6; Noyes, *Institution of Property*, pp. 298–9. For doubts about that approach, see Honoré, 'Ownership', pp. 127–8. However, if there is no realistic expectation that the rights will revert back to the original owner, we may find it difficult to resist describing the person who has acquired those rights as the real owner of the goods. An interesting example concerns modern developments in the law of consumer credit and hire purchase: though in strict theory the purchaser is not the owner of the goods he is paying for, the law has come increasingly to regard him as the 'real' owner of the goods and to give him certain security and protection on the basis of that. The uncertainty in cases like these reflects exactly the different 'dynamic' pressures that I have been describing. (I am grateful to Patrick Atiyah for drawing these examples to my attention.)

[63] This suggestion is mooted, for example, in Schumpeter, *Capitalism, Socialism and Democracy*, pp. 139–42.

sometimes, I want to say, it leads to corporate property. Individual owners have the power, acting with others, to constitute a corporate person and to transfer their holdings to it. Once that has been done, those holdings will be used, controlled, and managed on a basis that is different from the paradigm of private ownership, where an individual's determination is taken as socially decisive. A wedge is driven, for example, between what Honoré calls the right to manage and the right to the capital. (The split, however, is not total because of the the the control that shareholders have over a board of directors, at least in theory, in the last resort.)[64]

We may still, however, want to class the resulting arrangement as private property, for two reasons. We may do it, first, to draw attention to the fact that the arrangement was brought about as a result of private initiatives and for the purposes of the particular private individuals (and their successors in the arrangement) who were involved. To emphasize this, we may even say that, in the last analysis, the shareholders are the '*real* owners' of the company's assets. (Of course, they do not have all the rights of ownership on, say, Honoré's list, but then neither does a landlord or a mortgagor.)[65] Secondly, we may want to draw attention to the fact that the corporation, as a legal entity, may act as a private owner, using and allocating the resources that 'it' owns as 'it' sees fit rather than on the basis of the common or the collective interest. If we take this line, we may be inclined to say that the corporation is the '*real* owner' of 'its' assets.[66]

I have said that corporate property can be a form of private property. But it can also be a form of collective property too. Sometimes corporations are constituted not by private initiatives but by the state, and sometimes private corporations are taken over by the state (or 'nationalized') and made to serve public purposes rather than 'their own' purposes or those of their shareholders. In these cases, we should say that corporate property is a form of collective property inasmuch as it is constituted collectively and resources are controlled, ultimately, by collective rather than private purposes. The corporate form, then, has a protean amenability to property systems of different sorts. (Marx regarded

[64] The best discussion remains Berle and Means, *Modern Corporation and Private Property*.

[65] For difficulties with this approach, see ibid., Bk. II, and Bk. IV, Ch. 1.

[66] For a useful discussion, see Chaudhuri, 'Toward a Democratic Theory of Property and the Modern Corporation'.

this as evidence for his view that the inevitability of the transformation of capitalist into communist societies was a matter of the internal logic of the institutions involved.)[67] For this reason, then, I do not regard it as a distinct type of property system. Confronted with a society in which resources are controlled and managed by corporations, there are further questions to ask, and one of the most crucial of these will be: is the property system of this corporate economy predominantly private or collective? An answer to that question may not always be easy (as we saw in section 6). But in answering it, we will have to look as always to the basis on which access to and control of material resources is organized and the extent to which that determines the constitution and the operation of the corporate entities.

10. SUMMARY

There are several difficulties with the concept of private property, and they can be made to seem daunting or overwhelming if they are simply lumped together in the way that many jurists present them. I have tried to show that if we deal with them one at a time and in a certain order, using the full range of techniques of analysis, definition, and understanding that are available in modern philosophy, we can reach a reasonably clear understanding of what it is that people are disagreeing about when in a dispute about the justifiability of private property. To sum up, the main moves I have made have been the following.

(1) I have insisted that we should deal with the question of property rights in relation to material resources first, and come back to the issue of rights in relation to intangible objects at the end of our analysis when we are in a position to see more clearly the complex structures of analogy that are involved. (The latter task has not been attempted here.)

(2) I drew a distinction between the concept of property and the concept of private property. The latter (like the rival ideas of collective and common property) indicates a particular sort of way in which a property system might be organized.

---

[67] See especially Karl Marx, *Capital*, Vol. III, pp. 437 ff. There is a useful discussion of this idea in Avineri, *Social and Political Thought of Karl Marx*, pp. 174–84.

(3) Next, I drew a distinction between the concept of private property and particular conceptions of that concept. The latter may be defined as the particular bundles of rights, liberties, powers, duties, etc. associated with full ownership in particular legal systems. Though they differ from one another in their details (and those differences may sometimes be far-reaching), they have in common that they are conceptions of the same concept so that for the purposes of lay understanding and perhaps also for legitimation the component elements in the bundle can be regarded as being held together by a single organizing idea—the idea that it is for a certain specified person (rather than for anyone else or for society as a whole) to determine how a specified resource is to be used. This distinction, I suggested, provides our best way through the morass of difficulties generated by the diversity of rights associated with private ownership in different legal systems.

(4) Finally, I distinguished between a static conception of private ownership and a dynamic understanding of that conception. An approach which relates a conception of private ownership to a given distribution of rights in terms of its history, or in terms of its likely future, is helpful for understanding the point of continuing to describe landlords, mortgagors, and others who have alienated some of their ownership rights as being nevertheless still the private owners of the resources in question.

Together, these four moves are helpful for sorting out the various difficulties involved in the legal definition of private property. For the purposes of political philosophy, however, the second is the most important. When philosophers argue about the justifiability of private property, they are not interested (at least in the first instance) in the detail of the property rules of any society in particular—the property rules of nineteenth-century England, for example, or twentieth-century Singapore—though what they say will have consequences for the evaluation of those detailed rules. Rather they are talking in the first instance about a certain *type* of institution: a type described by the abstract idea outlined in section 5. We are asking whether there are good right-based reasons for preferring property systems of this type rather than property systems of any of the other types that I outlined.

Because the question is being posed in this abstract way, we must not expect an answer to determine a complete blueprint for a property system. Only so much can be done at the philosophical level, and philosophers do their discipline no service by insisting, for example, that traditional arguments such as Locke's, for example, should be rejected because they are not conclusive on the details of property arrangements.[68] A philosophical argument can determine only, as it were, the general shape of a blueprint for the good society. Even if we find that there are good moral grounds for preferring private property to collective property, we still face the question of what conception of private property to adopt. In other words, we still face the question of what detailed rights, powers, liberties, immunities, and so on should be accorded to owners at the level of concrete legal rules. Occasionally, the philosophical argument may indicate a particular answer to that question. For example, Hegel's very general argument for private property in the *Philosophy of Right* claims that it is crucial that an owner should have a complete power of alienation over the goods that he owns. But in other cases, the argument may not indicate any answer either way. Does Locke's Labour Theory of property generate any case for an unlimited power of testamentary bequest?[69] Does Aristotle's argument in the *Politics* provide any basis for evaluating English common law requirements about the procedures for the conveyance of land? That the answer in both cases is clearly negative does not mean that these arguments are not worth considering. I hope that by isolating and identifying the abstract concept of private ownership, and by distinguishing it from its particular conceptions, I have managed to show why.

[68] For the approach criticized here see e.g. Becker, *Property Rights*, p. 22 *et passim*.

[69] Locke, *Two Treatises*, I, sect. 86 ff. For a discussion see Waldron, 'Locke's Account of Inheritance'.

3

Right-Based Arguments

Private property, as we have seen, is a possible solution to the problem of allocation. To argue for private property is to indicate reasons for adopting a solution of this type rather than any of the others (such as common property or collective property) that may be suggested. The arguments in which I am particularly interested I shall call '*right-based arguments*'. In this chapter, I want to provide a framework which distinguishes right-based arguments from other arguments such as utilitarian ones.

As the term implies, a right-based argument is an argument which involves an appeal to *rights*: one defends a social arrangement by showing how it respects or promotes respect for the rights that people have, such as their right not to be attacked or their right to freedom of speech. Unfortunately, we cannot simply define a right-based argument as an argument that appeals to rights. There are two reasons.

First, we must leave room for the possibility that an argument may be right-based even though the term 'a right' is not used in its formulation. There is a common view that the concept of *a right* was unknown to the ancient philosophers, and the evidence for this view is supposed to be that the Greeks had no word that is translated by our term 'a right'. Now, even if this is true about Greek vocabulary, it does not follow that in Greek political philosophy there is no sentence, paragraph, or chapter that presents an argument sufficiently close in spirit to modern arguments appealing to rights to justify being regarded as a right-based argument. Whether any Greek arguments are of this sort is a matter of interpretation; it is a matter of our understanding of the substance of what they wrote not of the particular terms in which they expressed themselves.

Secondly, disputes about whether certain arguments are right-based or not must not be confused with disputes about what rights people actually have. Those who appeal to rights in political argument do not agree about what rights it is appropriate to appeal to. Some believe people have a right to a certain minimum standard of living, and they argue for the welfare state on the basis of an appeal to this sort of right. Others deny such rights exist and they say this sort of talk debases the currency of rights.[1] In their view, the only rights we have are rights to the familiar 'negative' freedoms of classical liberal theory: the right to free speech, free trade, and free association, etc. It is tempting, then, for the old-fashioned liberal to say that his opponents' arguments are not really right-based, since the considerations they appeal to cannot be regarded as having the force or importance that he thinks rights have. The trouble is that, if this approach is taken by every philosopher interested in rights, we will end up with as many definitions of 'right-based argument' as there are distinct theories of rights; in those circumstances, it would be difficult to see what useful classificatory work the concept was doing in political philosophy.

The better option, it seems to me, is to define 'right-based argument' in a way that is, as far as possible, neutral as between competing theories of the rights people have.[2] Such a definition would have to distinguish right-based from other arguments more in terms of their formal character than their content. It would offer an account of what it was to appeal to rights which would capture what competing theorists of rights have in common and what distinguishes them from other political theorists (such as utilitarians). Thus, for example, this type of definition would enable us to say that a given argument was right-based even though we wanted to deny the rights that it purported to rely on, or even though we denied the existence of rights altogether and doubted whether this form of argument had any force in political theory.

The last point has some importance in the present context. I do not accept all the premises of the arguments for property that I will be referring to—Hegel's and Nozick's, for example—and certainly they would not accept each other's. But I think that their arguments have important structural features in common that distinguish them from, say, the utilitarian arguments I sketched earlier. In providing a neutral definition of 'right-based argument' I hope to capture this common character as clearly as I can.

---

[1] See e.g. Cranston, 'Human Rights: Real and Supposed'. For the contrary view, see the reply to Cranston in Raphael, 'Human Rights: Old and New', and more recently, Golding, 'Primacy of Welfare Rights'.

[2] Dworkin, *Taking Rights Seriously*, pp. 90–1.

2. DWORKIN'S CATEGORIES

The terminology I am using was developed by Ronald Dworkin. In *Taking Rights Seriously*, Dworkin proposed a 'tentative initial classification of political theories' into right-based, duty-based, and goal-based theories.[3]

The idea is that, in any but the most intuitionistic moral or political theory, it is possible to distinguish between judgements or propositions that are more or less *basic* in the sense that less basic judgements are derivable from or justified by more basic ones (perhaps with the help of premisses concerning matters of fact). If we analyse moral and political theories in this way, we expect eventually to reach a basis beyond which it is impossible to go: this will be a small set of moral judgements underpinning and justifying the whole theory, from which the rest of the theory can in some sense be derived. Utilitarians pride themselves on the fact that their moral theory is organized explicitly in this way, and part of Dworkin's enterprise is to see whether such a structure can be discerned in non-utilitarian theories as well.

Nearer the surface of a theory, as it were, and among its subordinate and derivative principles, we would expect to find judgements of all sorts. For example, in the derivative levels of utilitarian theory, there are judgements that people have certain rights (for example, secure rights of property), judgements indicating the desirability of the pursuit of certain subordinate goals (such as an equal distribution of resources), and rules laying down certain strict duties and obligations (such as the obligation to fulfil contracts one has made). We expect that this will be true of most moral and political theories. But Dworkin's enterprise is based on a hunch that in their basis, in their fundamentals, most theories 'will give pride of place to just one of these concepts': it will take some overriding goal, or some set of fundamental rights, or some set of transcendent duties as fundamental, and show other goals, rights, and duties as subordinate and derivative.[4] A theory, Dworkin says, may take some goal, like improving the general welfare as fundamental, in which case it is to be described as a goal-based theory; or it might take some right, like the natural right to liberty, as fundamental, in which case it is right-based; or it might regard

---

[3] Dworkin, *Taking Rights Seriously*, pp. 90–6 and 169–76. See Mackie, 'Can There Be A Right-Based Moral Theory?', for an attempt to apply the classification to moral theories as well.

[4] Dworkin, *Taking Rights Seriously*, p. 171.

some duty, like the duty to obey God's will set out in the Ten Commandments, as fundamental, in which case we will call it duty-based. He acknowledges, however, that some theories may be pluralistic even in their foundations: 'theories' such as those that John Rawls describes as intuitionistic need not give pride of place to any one of the concepts right, goal, and duty.[5] He should also perhaps have acknowledged that the classification may not be exhaustive. There may be certain types of theory—for example, Aristotle's theory of virtue—which defy classification in these terms, and others—such as theories of moral desert—which are irresolvably ambiguous in this regard. Since my aim here is only to reach an understanding of what it is for an argument to be based on rights, as opposed to some other moral idea, nothing I say should be taken to restrict the categories of moral argument that there might be.

Dworkin gave no formal definition of what it was for a theory to be *based* on a particular moral concept. John Mackie, however, has indicated three senses in which a theory might be said to be 'X-based': (1) the theory takes 'X' as its only undefined term, and defines other moral terms in relation to 'X'; (2) the theory forms a system in which some statements about Xs are taken as basic and the other statements in the theory are derived from them, (perhaps with the help of non-moral, purely factual premisses); or (3) the theory is a system of the sort described in (2) not only formally but also in its purpose, so that the basic statements about Xs can be seen as capturing what gives point to the whole moral theory.[6] Mackie favoured the third of these approaches, and I shall follow him in that. But there is this reservation: an X-based theory need not actually be held by its proponents as an axiomatically organized system; the discovery that the theory is X-based may be the first step towards its axiomatization rather than the other way round.

How does Dworkin distinguish *rights* from *goals* and *duties*? Various gestures towards the definition of these categories are made in *Taking Rights Seriously*. Rights and goals are said to be species of the genus 'political aim':

A political theory takes a certain state of affairs as a political aim if, for that

---

[5] Ibid. 171–2. For the idea of an 'intuitionist' theory, see Rawls, *A Theory of Justice*, pp. 34–40.

[6] Mackie, 'Can There Be a Right-Based Moral Theory?', p. 358.

theory, it counts in favor of any political decision that the decision is likely to advance, or to protect, that state of affairs, and counts against the decision that it will retard or endanger it. A political right is an individuated political aim. An individual has a right to some opportunity or resource or liberty if it counts in favor of a political decision that the decision is likely to advance or protect the state of affairs in which he enjoys the right, even when no other political aim is served and some political aim is disserved thereby, and counts against that decision that it will retard or endanger that state of affairs, even when some other political aim is thereby served. A goal is a nonindividuated political aim, that is, a state of affairs whose specification does not in this way call for any particular opportunity or resource or liberty for particular individuals.[7]

Of course, a goal such as economic efficiency may call for some particular distribution of individual burdens and benefits given particular facts: 'Economic efficiency as a goal will suggest that a particular industry be subsidized in some circumstances, but taxed punitively in others.'[8] But such an assignment of burden or benefit is not itself pursued as a political aim—political action does not 'track' it, as it were, or follow it wherever it may lead—and its achievement does not itself count in favour of any political decision. In cases like these, 'distributional principles are subordinate to some conception of aggregate collective good, so that offering less of some benefit to one man can be justified simply by showing that this will lead to a greater benefit overall.'[9] If, however, it is the case that our goals are best promoted by pursuing and tracking a particular assignment of benefits and burdens as (though it were) an aim in its own right, then it may make sense to talk about the derivation of rights from goals. This, as Dworkin notes, is a familiar two-level utilitarian idea: 'that treating the right . . . as a complete justification in particular cases, without reference to the more basic goal, will in fact advance the goal in the long run'.[10] When rights are derived from goals in this way (and vice versa) we get the sort of theoretical articulation we noticed earlier: a theory then counts as right-*based* (or goal-*based*) if in the final analysis justification, direct or indirect, comes to an end with some statement of individuated (or non-individuated) political aims.

Later, it will become clear that there are aspects of Dworkin's

[7] Dworkin, *Taking Rights Seriously*, p. 91.
[8] Ibid.
[9] Ibid.
[10] Ibid. 170–1.

approach to rights that I do not accept. Broadly, however, the contrast between individuated and non-individuated political aims is the sort of thing I want to capture in my definition of the categories of 'right-based' and 'goal-based' arguments for private property. Two things, though, need further elaboration before anything like Dworkin's definitions can be accepted. We need to say more clearly what makes an aim an individuated aim: we need to give some gloss to the dative idea of securing an opportunity, resource, or liberty *for* an individual. And we need to be clearer about the sense in which the achievement of some state of affairs '*counts in favour*' of a political decision. Briefly, the difficulty here is that we want utilitarian arguments to turn out as goal-based arguments: but, in a loose sense, it does count in favour of a political decision, so far as a utilitarian is concerned, that it gives satisfaction to some individual, and counts against it that it gives some individual pain. That seems to make utilitarian arguments right-based on the definition we are considering. So (to be brazen about it) I think we need to tighten up our characterization of 'counting in favour' in order to be able to exclude utilitarian arguments from the right-based category. (In 'Justice and Rights', Dworkin intersperses the term 'justify' with 'count in favour of';[11] in my view, the former idea moves us more in the direction we want.) These difficulties are better handled, I think, by the Interest Theory of Rights, developed by Neil MacCormick and Joseph Raz, which I shall outline in sections 4 and 5.

We have said nothing about Dworkin's account of the contrast between rights and duties. This contrast highlights the first difficulty, because as Dworkin acknowledges, rights and duties can both be described as individuated political aims. He says that right-based and duty-based theories place the individual, as opposed to society and its goals, at the centre of the stage, but that they cast him in different lights. To talk about an individual's rights, Dworkin says, is to concern oneself with his independence of action, whereas to talk about his duties is to concern oneself with the conformity of his actions to some code of rules.[12] By themselves neither of these descriptions will do. The account of rights seems too narrow to capture even the details of Dworkin's own theory let alone the proliferation of rights-theories in the modern world. It

---

[11] Ibid. 169–71.
[12] Ibid. 172.

captures perhaps the nature of those rights which protect individual liberties, but as Dworkin himself points out in other contexts, such rights are neither exhaustive nor in their general character definitive of all the rights there are.[13] The account of duties in terms of conformity to a code of rules begs the question of the basis of the code: it suggests that a duty-based theory is one which has at its basis a set of rules for which no further justification can be given. That is perhaps characteristic of certain intuitionistic theories of duty. But it is by no means evident that these are all the duty-based theories there are. The example of Kant's theory of the categorical imperative indicates that there may be theories whose fundamental spirit is captured by the idea of duty but which do not consist merely in a set of intuited rules. Much more, then, needs to be said about this distinction.

3. RIGHTS, DUTIES AND UTILITY AS BASES OF MORAL CONCERN

Before attempting a definition of *right-based argument*, I want to offer one or two general comments—again drawing on Dworkin's work—about the sort of contrasts I have in mind.

(i) The Distinction Between Rights and Duties

Someone might propose an objection to any distinction between right-based and duty-based theories along the following lines. When we try to understand what a right is, our tendency is to analyse it in terms of duties. Often, indeed, a statement like

(1)   X has a right (against Y) to do A

is regarded as logically equivalent to, indeed as a mere notational variation on, something like

(2)   Y has a duty (owed to X) not to do B

where Y's not B-ing is in some sense a condition of X's being free or able to do A. Certainly the most useful analysis of rights-talk that we have (Hohfeld's analysis of privileges, claim-rights, powers, and immunities) analyses rights-statements of all sorts in terms of what he appears to regard as the more primitive notion of a duty.[14]

---

[13] Dworkin, *Taking Rights Seriously*, pp. 266 ff. and 366–8.
[14] Hohfeld, *Fundamental Legal Conceptions*.

But if a statement or set of statements of form (1) lies at the basis of a theory, generating all its derivative and surface propositions and giving the whole theory its point, it seems odd to insist that the theory must be regarded as *right*-based rather than *duty*-based, since its foundations could as well be represented by statements of form (2). That is the objection.[15] How are we to answer it?

The start of an answer is to say that we should have doubts anyway about the thesis that rights-statements and duty-statements are logically equivalent. Often we want to talk about rights in advance of specifying who is to have the 'corresponding' duty. We may want to say, for example, that a child in Lebanon has a right to grow up in a peaceful community without having much idea about who exactly has a responsibility (to him) in this regard or how far the duty extends.[16] Even if we are sure that a particular person has a duty to him, we may still hesitate to regard that as *equivalent* to the right since this would foreclose the possibility of discovering other people with other duties to him also in this regard. And if Neil MacCormick is correct, this may be true not only of such vague moral rights but also of some of the strict legal rights conferred by legislation. MacCormick cites a case where legislation assigns a right to a class of individuals in respect of some property, where not only is the right assigned in advance of a determination of who is to have the 'corresponding' duty, but having the right (or rather being among the class of persons who have the right) is also held to be a *reason* for subsequently being assigned the duty in question.[17] In fact Dworkin appears to accept a position along these lines:

Your duty to respect my privacy, for example, may be justified by my right to privacy. I do not mean merely that rights and duties may be correlated as opposite sides of the same coin. That *may* be so when, for example, a right and the corresponding duty are justified as serving a more fundamental goal. . . . In many cases, however, corresponding rights and duties are not correlative, but one is derivative from the other and it makes a difference which is derivative from which.[18]

Thus the possibility that rights and duties may stand in generational or justificatory relationships to each other, rather than relationships

[15] This objection to Dworkin's distinction is put forward in MacCormick, *Legal Right and Social Democracy*, pp. 142–3.
[16] See e.g. McCloskey, 'Rights', p. 116, and 'Rights—Some Conceptual Issues', p. 103.
[17] MacCormick, 'Rights in Legislation', pp. 200–3.
[18] Dworkin, *Taking Rights Seriously*, p. 171.

of logical equivalence, provides an opening for the distinction between right-based and duty-based theories.

To explore the distinction further let us take a concrete example. According to Dworkin, 'there is a difference between the idea that you have a duty not to lie to me because I have a right not to be lied to, and the idea that I have a right that you not lie to me because you have a duty not to tell lies'.[19] What sense can we make of this claim? In both cases, we are dealing with a requirement on an *agent* not to tell lies to another person. Let us call the second person—the person who would be a victim of deception were a lie to be told— the *patient* of the requirement. If Dworkin is correct, there are (at least) two possible ways of justifying this requirement—or rather, there are (at least) two distinct types of justification that might be offered: one focusing primary attention on the patient and his rights, generating the duty not to lie out of that, and one focusing primary attention on the agent and his duties, and generating the patient's right not to be lied to out of that.

Here is an example of the first sort of justification. People have an interest in planning their lives, structuring them into what they take to be meaningful wholes in accordance with their conception of what makes life worth living. Each time he faces a choice an individual has an interest in being able to use his conception of the good life as a basis for guiding that choice. But he can do so only if he has accurate information about the situation he faces and the nature of the options before him. Without accurate information— or worse, working confidently with mistaken information—he may believe that a certain option facing him has a significance for his life plan that it does not have, or that some other option is unimportant when in fact it is very important for his purposes. Apart from his own senses, common sense, reason, and accumulated experience, the main source of such information is what other people pass on to him. If other people pass on mistaken information, to that extent they undermine the process of the formation, implementation, and review of a life plan. Because we take this interest in planning and structuring one's life to be an important one, we are prepared to hold others to be under a duty to pass on accurate information if they pass on any information at all. Certainly to pass on information that one knows is incorrect is to act as though the patient's planning of his life were unimportant, when in fact it is

[19] Dworkin, *Taking Rights Seriously*, p. 171.

important. In this line of argument, then, the duty not to lie is derived from the importance we are prepared to attach to the interest in not being in the position of relying on inaccurate information when addressing choices. This is one possible account of the requirement not to deceive, based on a concern for the individuals who stand to benefit from others' compliance with the requirement.

A duty-based account will be somewhat different. I guess the most familiar argument against lying and other forms of deception (e.g. false promising) which focuses primary moral concern on the agent (the potential liar) as opposed to the patient (the potential victim of deception) is the argument put forward by Kant in the *Groundwork*.[20] According to Kant, the wrongness of lying is a matter of the inevitable heteronomy of the will of the lying man. The argument goes something like this.

An autonomous will is one whose content is determined by the mere possibility of its being a law unto itself, rather than by any inclination or desire; a heteronomous will is determined in its content by something other than 'the fitness of its maxims for its own making of universal law'.[21] It does not matter particularly whether the heteronomous will is determined by the pursuit of self-interest or (sympathetically) by the interest of some other. Kant insists that 'I ask myself only, "Can you also will that your maxim should become universal law?" Where you cannot it is to be rejected, and that not because of a prospective loss to you, *or even to others* . . .'[22] Now a liar is a man who deceives others whenever this would gain a marginal advantage for himself. The maxim of the will of such a man cannot be represented as the prescription by the will to itself of a universal law. 'I will lie or (to use Kant's example) I will break my promise whenever I conceive it to be marginally in my interest to do so' cannot possibly be universalized. Its universalization involves a contradiction, for it destroys the hypothesis of the existence of language or a practice of promising which it nevertheless presupposes. Such practices depend on general acceptance of the principle that non-deception and fidelity take priority over perceived personal advantage at least at the margin. (In the case of promising that is part of the whole point of

---

[20] Kant, *The Moral Law* (Paton's translation of the *Groundwork*), pp. 70–1 and 89–90 (IV, 402–3 and 422 in the Prussian Academy edn.).

[21] Ibid. 108 (IV, 441).

[22] Ibid. 71 (IV, 403); my emphasis.

the practice.) Therefore the will of the liar must be determined not by the mere form of law but by something other than (and incompatible with) reverence for the pure form of law. Therefore the will of the liar is heteronomous.

Why is that an argument against lying? What is wrong with having a heteronomous will? Kant's concern is not about what will happen to the rest of us if heteronomous wills are let loose in the world. His concern is rather for the will itself, and, more broadly, for the integrity and self-sufficiency of an agent endowed with reason. The concern seems partly teleological in character. We have a capacity for reason and we should exercise it to the full. Early in the *Groundwork*, Kant insists that every organ and faculty of a natural being has some end or function. To find out what its function is we should find out what end its use would be 'most appropriate' or 'best fitted' for. He then argues (I will not go into the details) that our faculty for reason is not best suited for promoting happiness or for promoting any particular contingent end: for that, instinct would be at least as serviceable. So, he concludes, reason's true function must be what it can do on its own—apart from being at the service of the other inclinations—namely to prescribe laws to the will as an end in itself.[23] As beings endowed with a rational faculty, we are, by our very nature, subject to a certain discipline: 'We stand under a discipline of reason, and in all our maxims we must not forget our subjection to it, or withdraw anything from it.' Submission to such a discipline, he suggests, is the only way of life 'suitable to our position among rational beings as men'.[24]

Expounded in this way, the Kantian account can be taken as a paradigm of a duty-based argument. Of course, rights can be derived from the Kantian argument. From the Second Formulation of the Categorical Imperative, it is easy to derive the right not to be treated as a mere means. But the rationale of even this famous right is duty-based. It is an insult to your own rationality to treat the rationality of anyone (yourself or others) as a mere means. Treating it as an end is part of the discipline of reason that I referred to. The right is derivative from the deeper rational duty. At a more

[23] Kant, *The Moral Law*, pp. 62–4 (IV, 395–7). In the *Second Critique* Kant modifies this position a little, asserting that reason may serve our needs and our happiness as well as the end of its own self-sufficiency so long as the latter end is not lost sight of: see Kant, *Critique of Practical Reason*, trans. Beck, p. 63 (V, 61).

[24] Kant, *Critique of Practical Reason*, p. 85 (V, 83).

particular level, the same will be true of the right not to be deceived (and the right to have promises kept).

These two lines of argument for the requirement of non-deception appear to fit Dworkin's specifications: that there is a difference between the view that you have a duty not to lie to me because I have a right not to be lied to, and the idea that I have a right not to be lied to because you have a duty not to lie to me; and that this difference can be explained in terms of focusing moral concern on a human individual in two different sorts of ways.

(ii) The Distinction Between Rights and Utilitarian Considerations

What distinguishes utilitarian theories from theories of rights? Perhaps the difference lies in the greater individualism of the latter.

According to many philosophers, the 'arch-sin' of utilitarianism is its denial of moral individualism: what Rawls refers to as its failure to 'take seriously the distinction between persons'.[25] This criticism is based, of course, on the readiness of utilitarians to contemplate trading off the interests of one individual against those of others. The criticism is summed up by H. L. A. Hart: utilitarians treat 'the division between persons as of no more moral significance than the division between times which separates one individual's earlier pleasure from his later pleasure, as if individuals were mere parts of a single persisting entity'. Utilitarianism, he says, is not an individualistic doctrine, since it is interested in individuals only 'as the points at which fragments of what *is* important, i.e. the total aggregate of pleasure or happiness, are located'.[26] Theories of rights, by contrast, are supposed to be theories which respect the distinction between persons and which prohibit the sacrifice of individual interests for the greater good.

I believe this criticism is ill-founded and certainly unfair to the character of many utilitarian theories. Utilitarianism, it seems to me, is undeniably an individualistic theory. Surely it is impossible to understand the concepts *pleasure* or *satisfaction*—let alone *happiness* as it figures in Mill's *Utilitarianism*[27]—without reference to the notion of an individual. Satisfaction as a mere event, the

[25] See Rawls, *A Theory of Justice*, pp. 22–3 and 175–92; Nozick, *Anarchy, State, and Utopia*, pp. 30–4 and 48–51; Williams, 'Critique of Utilitarianism', pp. 108 ff.; Hart, *Essays in Jurisprudence*, pp. 17 and 204.

[26] Hart, *Essays in Jurisprudence*, p. 200.

[27] Mill, *Utilitarianism*, Ch. 2.

occurrence of which the utilitarian for some odd reason wants to maximize, makes no sense at all; what the utilitarian wants to maximize is individuals' being satisfied. (For instance, in Mill's case, the leading hedonistic value is happiness, conceived as a characteristic of a whole life; how this can be understood as anything other than an individualistic value is beyond me.) Well-being, happiness, and the satisfaction of preferences are not social or collective properties. It is not the society which is happy but the individuals who go to make it up. Nor on the other hand are well-being, happiness, and satisfaction transcendent states which exist independently of individuals or societies. (If somehow they were, it is difficult to see why anyone would think it important to maximize them.) The point is that utilitarianism has to be distinguished from genuinely collectivist theories which take certain states of affairs to be valuable which have no intrinsic connection with the state or condition of individuals; for example, a fascist theory may regard national glory as the goal to be promoted and be quite indifferent (except instrumentally) about how individuals fare in the course of its pursuit.

I have already noted that for a utilitarian, it counts in favour of a political decision that it gives pleasure to—or satisfies a preference or contributes to the happiness of—some individual, and counts against it that it gives him pain. Pleasure and pain do seem to be pursued as individuated political aims by utilitarians. But notoriously, a decision that gives one man pleasure may give others pain. Is there perhaps anything about the way utilitarians deal with conflicts of this sort that distinguishes them from theorists of rights?

I think there is, but the contrast I want to indicate has to be stated very carefully. It is not the case that theorists of rights must simply repudiate the sort of interpersonal trade-offs that utilitarians appear to embrace. For rights may also conflict in concrete situations. A's right to urgent medical care may conflict with Dr B's right to organize his career as he pleases. Or A's right to urgent medical care may conflict in an emergency with C's and D's rights to urgent medical care, where resources and services are scarce. One way out of these dilemmas is the approach favoured by Robert Nozick: adopt a theory of rights which excludes any rights that cannot be stated in negative terms (negative in the sense that they are nothing but rights that certain actions should not be performed), and then treat all remaining rights as side-constraints on agency, so that conflicts of the sort we are imagining do not arise.[28] But this approach cannot be taken as definitive of right-based theories—nor as an account of what distinguishes them from utilitarianism—for two reasons.

First, many theories of rights do recognize rights to positive assistance or to the use of scarce goods, and we do not want to rule these out by definition. Such rights can and do conflict in conditions of scarcity, and when they do there is no alternative to some sort of trade-off approach, to something like what Nozick disparagingly refers to as 'a utilitarianism of rights'.[29] A doctor in a medical emergency may well decide that the only way to deal with the competing rights of the injured is to operate some sort of triage system, or to abandon one patient after a short while in order to give equal attention to someone else. If he does that, we should not be forced to say that he has abandoned concern with rights and lapsed into utilitarianism. On the contrary, respect for the rights of all requires him to adopt some system which may have the result that not everyone receives all he has to offer in the way of urgent care.

Secondly, even among theories of negative rights, the Nozick approach is not the only nor even the most obvious one. We may decide, in a difficult situation ('punishment of the innocent' or 'Jim and the Indians'[30] cases are the ones that spring to mind), to violate some negative rights in order to prevent the violation of lots of similar rights by others. We may prefer doing that to the alternative, where the rights *we* might violate are respected but where the greater number of rights-violations we could prevent are permitted; and we may prefer it on right-based grounds. Certainly, our concern for the rights of individuals pulls us in both directions here; but if the numbers are much greater on one side, the concern is engaged more on that side than on the other. Once again, then,

---

[28] Nozick, *Anarchy, State, and Utopia*, pp. 28–35; Nozick, however, reserves the possibility of an exception 'in order to avoid catastrophic moral horror' (ibid. 30). For a slightly more extended discussion of this point, see Nozick, 'On the Randian Argument', p. 224. For other expressions of the 'side constraints' idea, see Anscombe, 'Modern Moral Philosophy', p. 40; Denyer, 'Chess and Life'; and Gewirth, 'Are There Any Absolute Rights?'.

[29] Nozick, *Anarchy, State, and Utopia*, p. 28.

[30] For the punishment of the innocent, see e.g. McCloskey, 'A Note on Utilitarian Punishment', and Nozick, *Anarchy, State, and Utopia*, pp. 28–9; For 'Jim and the Indians', see Williams, 'Critique of Utilitarianism', pp. 98–9.

we are heading in the direction of a 'utilitarianism of rights', except that the approach we take need not be aggregative. Even a concern for *equal* protection of rights may require us to violate some of the rights of a few in order to extend any protection at all to the others.

Nozick's approach, by contrast, insists that in this sort of case, our duty is simply not ourselves to violate any rights—whatever others are doing and whatever other rights could be protected as a result of our violations. I think that Thomas Nagel is right to notice that this is an approach which focuses its concern at least as much on the *agent* (the person whom the rights are supposed to constrain) as on the right-bearers. The Nozickian concern is that agency should not be exercised in certain ways with regard to individual rights, and not merely that certain things should not happen to individuals:

[R]ights of the kind that interest Nozick are not rights that certain things not *happen* to you . . . Rather they are rights not to be deliberately treated or used in certain ways, and not to be deliberately interfered with in certain activities. They give rise to claims not against the world at large, but only against someone who contemplates deliberately violating them. The *relation* between the possessor of the right and the actor, rather than just the intrinsic nature of the possessor and of his life, must enter into the analysis of the right and the explication of its basis.[31]

For example, the Nozickian right not to be assaulted is, as Nagel puts it, '*not* a right that everyone do what is required to ensure you are not assaulted'. It is a right that is correlated only with each person's duty that *he* should not assault you. In a footnote, Nozick wonders whether side constraints could be expressed in the notation of value, i.e. in a form which assigns value to certain states of affairs: any such representation would, he thinks, have to involve the assignment for each person of an infinite negative value to the state of affairs in which *he* attacks someone so that 'no amount of stopping others from violating rights can outweigh his violating someone's rights'.[32] The important thing is that the nature of the right, as Nagel puts it, 'cannot be explained simply by the fact that it is bad to be assaulted'.[33] For that fact does not explain why the prohibition on assault should function as a side constraint even on activities oriented towards the avoidance of many cases of people

[31] Nagel, 'Libertarianism Without Foundations', p. 198.
[32] Nozick, *Anarchy, State, and Utopia*, p. 29 n.
[33] Nagel, 'Libertarianism Without Foundations', p. 198.

being assaulted. Nozick's approach is in fact as much duty-based as right-based, for it is concerned primarily with what is wrong with assaulting people rather than with what is wrong with being assaulted.

My suggestion, then, is the paradoxical one that Nozick's theory of rights as side constraints is not straightforwardly a right-based theory. Rather it is dominated by a very strong component which is duty-based, in the terms we have discussed. (This suggestion is consistent with Nozick's invocation of Kantian foundations, and of course the appearance of paradox has a lot to do with Nozick's well-known failure ever to fully articulate the foundations of his theory.[34] In Nagel's own elaboration of the basis of side-constraints, by contrast, the duty-based aspect is quite evident.)[35] For these reasons, then, it would be quite wrong to take Nozick's approach as the feature which distinguishes right-based theories as such from utilitarianism. Theorists of rights can, do, and in my opinion must allow for the possibility of trade-offs between rights when they conflict—at least, when the conflict is between different individuals' rights of the same sort. To reiterate: such trade-offs need not evince a purely aggregative approach; the rights-theorist may believe in pursuing equal respect for rights rather than the maximization of such respect. But he cannot think that each right is absolutely inviolable, because the respect that a given right commands will often draw him in the direction of infringing another.

If a simplistic contrast between theories which permit trade-offs and theories which do not is inadequate, is there anything else about the utilitarian attitude to trade-offs that will serve our purposes? I think there is, and three points about utilitarianism will help indirectly to indicate what I mean.

First, utilitarians seek to maximize the promotion of pleasure or the satisfaction of preferences no matter what the pleasure is taken in or no matter what the content of the preferences. Preferences and satisfactions are intersubstitutable without regard to content: the only things that matter are quantitative features like duration, intensity, and fecundity (to use Bentham's terms).[36] This is the basis

[34] Waldron (ed.), *Theories of Rights*, 'Introduction', pp. 15–16 and n.
[35] Nagel, 'Limits of Objectivity', pp. 131 ff. Nagel's account has the virtue of setting out the way in which the controversies about acts and omissions and the Doctrine of Double Effect lock into this issue.
[36] Bentham, *Introduction to Principles of Morals and Legislation*, pp. 38–41.

of the utilitarian commitment to the commensurability of all values. The nature of an interest or the content of a preference gives it no special status in the utilitarian calculus except what can be established for it on quantitative grounds. Now precisely because interests are approached in this quantitative manner—because they are regarded for all practical purposes as commensurable and inter-substitutable—there is a sense in which the possibility of trade-offs is built into the very fabric of the utilitarian conception of value. Maybe each of the political aims of utilitarianism (each satisfaction) is an individuated aim in Dworkin's sense; but each is also conceived of in a way that makes it inherently apt for substitution for or by another item in the utilitarian calculus. Each aim is treated like a commodity: what Marx might call its 'use-value' (the qualitative features of its usefulness to particular human beings) is nothing; its 'exchange-value' (the ratio in which it exchanges with other political aims that are thought of in the same way) is everything. So while it is true, in the utilitarian calculus, that producing any individual satisfaction counts in favour of a decision, still the nature of what is thus taken into account— namely, the exchange value of each interest—points us immediately towards the possibility of trade-offs, and therefore highlights the fact that it is never on its own to be regarded as a conclusive political justification for anything.

Secondly, the principle of the quantitative commensurability of interests is itself a point of contrast between utilitarianism and theories of rights. A utilitarian believes that the value of all interests can be determined on a single metric. Even a man's life is worth, in the last resort, the same as a finite quantity of pleasure or a certain amount of comfort and enjoyment spread around the community. There is, then, in utilitarian theory a real prospect, not only that important interests such as the interest in survival will be traded off against other interests of the same kind, but that such interests may be traded off also against a greater mass of interests of substantially lesser importance. In my view, it is the prospect of this sort of trade-off—not the prospect of trade-offs as such—that the rights-theorist is opposed to. A theory of rights accords special importance to individual interests of certain types, and may express this importance in terms of the lexical priority of those interests over human interests generally.

Thirdly, in utilitarian calculations one never gets the sense which one gets in theories of rights and duties that, when one interest is traded off against another, any apology or explanation or making-good is owed to the unlucky interest. In theories of rights which allow for the possibility of conflict, there is usually a requirement that a prima facie right cannot be overridden in favour of others without some moral compunction and without a feeling that something extra is owed in the future if at all possible to the person whose right has had to be sacrificed. This requirement of making good may not be conclusive—and it is unlikely to be as strong as the original right itself—but it is there and it acts as a signal that the right continues to be taken seriously as a ground of moral constraint even when the direct constraints it purports to impose have had to be pushed to one side. In utilitarian theories, by contrast, one gets the sense that preferences by themselves generate no moral claim whatsoever until they have been fed into and processed by the utilitarian calculus. The utilitarian may regard each satisfaction as desirable and each pain as undesirable, but these values are not themselves the ground of any moral constraint. Moral constraints arise only out of the *aggregative interplay* of preferences.

So what I want to edge towards is a distinction between utilitarian and right-based theories which focuses on the fact that, though both are distinguished by their pursuit of *individuated* political aims, right-based theories take single individuated aims as the basis for generating genuine and full-blooded moral constraints whereas utilitarian theories do not. This is the essence of the so-called 'Interest Theory' of rights, which I shall outline in the sections that follow.

4. RIGHTS AND DUTIES: THE BENEFIT THEORY

The theory of rights that I want to use as the basis for my approach has been developed in recent work by Neil MacCormick and Joseph Raz. It is not a theory of what rights people have, but a theory of what it is to say or to argue that somebody has a right, and of what is distinctive (and controversial) about rights-talk. It can best be introduced by considering its relation to the somewhat better known 'Benefit Theory' of rights.

The Benefit Theory concerns the relation between rights and

rules, in particular rules which impose duties (or obligations—I do not think the asynonymy of these terms matters in this context). (It may be worth noting here that most theories recognize a sense of the term 'right' which is connected not with the existence of rules imposing duties but with the non-existence of such rules: sometimes 'I have a right to do X' means little more than 'There is no rule requiring me not to do X'. Following Hohfeld, these rights are sometimes referred to as *privileges*.[37] But we will not be concerned with them here. When privileges become important in political philosophy it is usually not on their own account, but because they are surrounded by other rights which *are* connected with duties— namely, duties on other people not to interfere with a person's performance of an action which he has no duty not to perform.[38] Since we are interested in right-based arguments which are understood to constrain or require certain political actions, we shall concern ourselves with those rights that are understood to be related to duties that political agents are under.)

At its simplest, the Benefit Theory holds that an individual can be said to have a right whenever he is the beneficiary of another's duty. If P stands to benefit from Q's duty to do (or to refrain from doing) X, then P has a right against Q—a right that may be characterized either as a right *that* Q should do X (or refrain from X-ing) or as a right *to* the benefit that he stands to gain in the matter.[39] Formulated in this way, however, the Benefit Theory is clearly too wide. On a utilitarian account, for example, all duties are conceived to promote a large number of individual benefits: a utilitarian account of promissory rights will draw attention not just to the benefit that promisees stand to gain if the duties are carried out but also to the (indirect) benefits that will be secured thereby to the whole of society. Since we do not want to say that when I make a promise almost everyone has a right that I should carry it out, we need a more restricted version of the Benefit Theory. If I perform my duty to repay the £100 I borrowed from you, all sorts of people stand to benefit: you, certainly, but also your aunt when you take her out to dinner to celebrate; someone bidding against me—

---

[37] Hohfeld, *Fundamental Legal Conceptions*. For a discussion, see Hart, 'Bentham on Legal Rights', pp. 175–6, and Waldron (ed.), *Theories of Rights*, 'Introduction', p. 6.

[38] Hart, 'Bentham on Legal Rights', p. 176.

[39] Lyons, 'Rights, Claimants and Beneficiaries', pp. 173–5. Lyons refers to this as the 'unqualified' Benefit Theory.

impoverished by the repayment—in an auction next week; the grocer down the road who gains marginally and indirectly from the contribution of this transaction to the climate of creditworthiness in the community; and so on. But these, we may say, are purely contingent benefits; they cannot be predicted in advance simply on the basis of a knowledge of the duty and of what would count as carrying it out. And that seems to be at least part of the reason why we would say that your aunt, the auction competitor, and the grocer do not have *rights* in the matter despite the benefit that is secured to them by the performance of my duty.[40]

A qualified Benefit Theory, then, might hold that an individual has a right when he is *intended* to benefit from another's performance of a duty, or—if, as I suspect, talk of intentionality is bewildering here— when the securing of a benefit to him is part of the point of holding another to be under the duty in question. A benefit giving rise to a right must be so intimately related to the duty that it becomes in a sense a test of the duty's performance—so that it is possible to say in advance that unless this benefit has been conferred, the duty has not properly been carried out. Conferring the benefit in question must lie at or near the immediate ground of the duty.

An important feature of this account is that it becomes impossible to tell whether a rule imposing a duty also confers a right without considering something like the rationale or the ground of the rule or duty in question. The fact that someone will benefit from the rule's operation is not sufficient unless that benefit is in some sense the *raison d'être* of the rule. An enquiry into which legal rules impose rights and which do not is partly an enquiry into legislative purpose. (It need not of course depend on ascertaining the precise intentions of those who formulated the rule; indeed sometimes that may be positively misleading, as in the cases when a legislator's intention in putting forward a certain rule about contracts was to benefit his brother-in-law's construction business. Looking to legislators' intentions is only one theory of legislative purpose. Another more plausible theory might be Dworkin's suggestion that we look at legal rules in the light of the best political theory we can construct which rationalizes the rules, principles, and precedents of that system as a whole.)[41]

---

[40] Ibid. 176. This is the 'qualified' Benefit Theory. See also Lyons, 'Correlativity of Rights and Duties'.

[41] Dworkin, *Taking Rights Seriously*, Ch. 4, and *Law's Empire, passim.*

The aspect of legislative purpose is emphasized strongly in Neil MacCormick's account of rights. In a critique of Hart's 'Choice Theory' (which we shall examine in section 6), MacCormick set out to examine the distinguishing characteristics of those legal rules which confer rights on individuals. His position is set out first in general terms: 'The essential feature of rules which confer rights is that they have as a specific aim the protection or advancement of individual interests or goods.'[42] Later he outlines three features which, he says, must be included in any characterization of rules which confer rights:

First, they concern 'goods' (or 'advantages', or 'benefit', or 'interests', or however we may express the point). Whatever x may be, the idea of anyone's having a right to x would be absurd unless it were presupposed that x is normally a good for human beings, at any rate for the people who qualify as having the 'right' in question. . . . *Secondly, they concern the enjoyment of goods by individuals separately*, not simply as members of a collectivity enjoying a diffuse common benefit in which all participate in indistinguishable and unassignable shares. . . . *Thirdly, benefits are secured to individuals in that the law provides normative protection for individuals in their enjoyment of them.*[43]

When a rule satisfies these conditions, MacCormick argues, we can say it confers rights on individuals, whether the language of rights has been used by the legislator or not.

In an earlier article discussing children's rights, MacCormick considered the rule that children ought to be cared for and nurtured. On any account of the purpose or point of this rule, children will benefit from its being obeyed. But on some accounts, MacCormick insists, that rule does not confer rights on children:

For example, along the lines of Swift's *Modest Proposal*, one could suggest as a reason why children ought to be cared for [and] nurtured . . . that that would be the best way of getting them to grow into plump and contented creatures fit to enhance the national diet. Or again, one could argue that a healthy society requires healthy and well-nurtured children who will grow up into contented and well-adjusted adults who will contribute to the GNP and not be a charge on the welfare facilities or the prison service.[44]

But these arguments do not present the benefit to the children as the *point* of the rule; they present it rather as 'a fit means to an ulterior

---

[42] MacCormick, 'Rights in Legislation', p. 192.
[43] Ibid. 204–5
[44] MacCormick, 'Children's Rights', p. 159.

end'.[45] MacCormick's position then is quite close to Dworkin's comments about political aims. It seems sensible to say that we take children to have a right when we actually aim at securing some benefit for them; the fact that we do secure some benefit for them in the course of aiming for something else is not sufficient (unless the best way to secure our ulterior purpose is to pursue the subordinate aim as though it were not subordinate to any further purpose, in which case we may talk about a derivative right).

The emphasis that MacCormick places on the purpose, the aim, or the concern of rules which confer rights has two very important consequences.

First, it permits some loosening of the very tight connection that the familiar Benefit Theory drew between rights and duties. On that theory, talk about rights was simply another way of talking about duties which conferred benefits: wherever there was a right, there was a beneficial duty; no duty—no right. But now that rights are associated not with duties *per se* but with the ground or point of duties, it may be possible to talk about a right to something in advance of the actual specification of a duty. A rule confers a right on an individual—we may say—if it indicates a ground on which duties to benefit that individual may be imposed, even if it does not itself impose any such duties.[46] This possibility, as we saw in section 3, helps to take care of the objection that since rights and duties are strictly correlative, there can be no distinction in principle between a right-based and a duty-based argument or theory.

Secondly, once we start talking about the point of rules rather than the rules themselves, it becomes easier to see how we can extend this analysis from the realm of legal rules and begin talking about moral rights. This point can best be illustrated in connection with Jeremy Bentham's comments on rights. In those moods when he was not disposed to dismiss talk of rights altogether, Bentham held that 'to assure to individuals the possession of a certain good, is to confer *a right* upon them'.[47] The only sort of assurance that Bentham was interested in here was the assurance provided by a *legal rule*; we have already referred to his denunciation of all talk of natural rights as 'nonsense upon stilts'.[48] He acknowledged that we

[45] Ibid.
[46] Ibid. 161 ff.
[47] Quoted in Lyons, 'Rights, Claimants and Beneficiaries', p. 175.
[48] Bentham, 'Anarchical Fallacies', p. 53.

might want to criticize existing legal rules and to suggest new legal rights:

> In proportion to the want of happiness resulting from the want of rights, a reason exists for wishing that there were such things as rights. But reasons for wishing there were such things as rights, are not rights;—a reason for wishing that a certain right were established is not that right—want is not supply—hunger is not bread.[49]

But now since we want to say that a rule establishes a right not simply by imposing a duty, but by laying down a certain ground for the imposition of duties, this point of Bentham's becomes less convincing. There is a sense in which, on MacCormick's analysis, a certain sort of (legal) reason or ground for imposing a duty counts as a (legal) right, so that a reason for imposing a right (in Bentham's sense of 'right') really is a right (in MacCormick's sense.) Likewise, without seriously distorting MacCormick's meaning, one could say that a certain sort of moral reason for holding someone to be under a duty counts as a moral right, and so— to paraphrase Bentham— that a certain sort of reason for wishing there were a right (in Bentham's sense) just *is* a right (in the sense that I want to pursue).

This approach has been taken further by Joseph Raz in his recent book, *The Morality of Freedom*. Rights, Raz insists, should be identified, 'by their role in practical reasoning':

> They indicate intermediate conclusions between statements of the right-holder's interests and another's duty. To say that a person has a right is to say that an interest of his is sufficient ground for holding another to be subject to a duty, i.e. a duty to take some action which will serve that interest, or a duty the very existence of which serves such an interest. One justifies a statement that a person has a right by pointing to an interest of his and to reasons why it is to be taken seriously. One uses the statement that a right exists to derive (often with the aid of other premises) conclusions about the duties of other people towards the right-holder.[50]

On Raz's account, the justificatory role of rights means that they cannot be regarded as strictly correlative to duties, and therefore that statements about rights are not strictly equivalent to statements about duties. The last point is crucial if rights are to be seen as justifications: one statement cannot justify another if the two are equivalent. Moreover, rights are open-ended with regard to the duties that they may ground:

---

[49] Bentham, 'Anarchical Fallacies', p. 53. See also Bentham, 'Supply Without Burthern', p. 75 n.   [50] Raz, 'Legal Rights', p. 5.

The existence of a right often leads to holding another to have a duty because of the existence of particular facts peculiar to the parties or general to the society in which they live. A change of circumstances may lead to the creation of new duties based on the old right. The right to political participation is not new, but only in modern states with their enormously complex bureaucracies does this right justify, as I think it does, a duty on the government to make public its plans and proposals before a decision is made . . . This dynamic aspect of rights, their ability to create new duties, is fundamental to any understanding of their nature and function in political thought.[51]

Of course, the 'dynamic aspect' could equally be captured by making the right correlative to a rather abstract duty and saying that changing circumstances etc. might lead to the derivation of different concrete duties from that.[52] But I think Raz's model leads to a clearer sense of the way in which statements of duty are justified. In the present context, it seems clearer to say that a right to private property might justify, in different circumstances, all sorts of duties and institutional requirements to secure the property of individuals against various forms of derogation, rather than that it is simply correlative to a very abstract and ill-defined duty to respect private property which is then broken down into particular concrete requirements in particular circumstances. But we could jump either way on this. The importance of Raz's analysis, on either account, is to emphasize the dynamic grounding relation (whether mediated by an abstract duty or not) that exists between talk of an individual's right and talk of the particular requirements that are brought to bear on other individuals.

Raz's phrase 'a reason for *holding another to be under a duty*' is an interesting one. Raz says that it is used 'advisedly to preserve the ambiguity between saying that rights are a reason for *judging* a person to have a duty, and saying that they are reasons for *imposing* duties upon him' (my emphasis).[53] Partly this is a matter of how we approach the vexed question of the existence of duties. In the legal sphere, duties are something we create: we impose them on people and they do not exist prior to their imposition. In morals, the matter is more controversial. Some philosophers might say, following Mackie, that our morality is something we invent rather

[51] Raz, 'Nature of Rights', pp. 199–200; the same point is made by MacCormick, 'Children's Rights', pp. 162–3.

[52] For the distinction between abstract and concrete rights and duties, see Dworkin, *Taking Rights Seriously*, pp. 93 ff.

[53] Raz, 'Nature of Rights', p. 200.

than something we discover;[54] in this case, it seems sensible to say that a right is a reason for inventing or imposing a duty rather than a reason for judging that one exists. But if we take a realist approach to ethics, the latter terminology might be more congenial.[55] It is a virtue of Raz's account that it leaves this open.

To say that there is *a* reason for holding someone to be under a duty is not to deny that there may be conflicting reasons for not holding this which we may want to say prevail in particular circumstances. We must be careful not to state this too weakly lest we run into the difficulties (discussed in the previous section) of distinguishing rights from utilitarian considerations. Raz's most lucid formulation is: ' "x has a right" is true if and only if . . . other things being equal, an aspect of x's well-being is a sufficient reason for holding some other person(s) to be under a duty.'[56] The reason must be weighty enough to be *normally sufficient* as a political justification. As Raz points out, 'where . . . conflicting considerations altogether outweigh the interests of the would-be right-holder, and no one could justifiably be held to be obligated on account of those interests, then there is no right'.[57] If, however, the right is outweighed by conflicting considerations only in certain cases, we may be willing to say either that the right exists (in something like a 'prima-facie' sense) but that it generates no duty in those particular cases, or that it generates duties but only prima-facie duties. If a right is characteristically outweighed in cases of a particular type, that may be, as Raz suggests, a reason for rethinking our specification of the right, or for denying that a certain concrete right (say the right to malign anyone you please) can be derived from an abstract right (like the right to free speech).[58]

Finally, we should note that, on Raz's account, duties are understood as a particular species of moral requirement: they are peremptory requirements in the sense that they express not merely reasons for acting but exclusionary reasons—reasons whose function it is to exclude action on the basis of the balance of

[54] Mackie, *Ethics*, Ch. 1.
[55] For a useful account of the options here, see Dworkin, *Taking Rights Seriously*, pp. 159–68.
[56] Raz, 'Nature of Rights', p. 195.
[57] Ibid. 211.
[58] Ibid. I use 'abstract' and 'concrete' here rather than Raz's terms to avoid confusion with my use of 'general right' later in Ch. 4.

reasons.[59] I shall not make much of this feature of Raz's analysis in the present work. It seems plausible as an account of the ordinary use of the language of rights: we say that many of the things I have a moral reason to do for others' benefit (like letting them read my magazines when I have finished with them) they do not have a right that I should do. But I suspect it is less important as a feature of right-based arguments in politics, so I shall largely overlook it in what follows.

5. THE INTEREST THEORY

Following Raz's approach, I shall say that an argument for private property is *right-based* just in case it takes some individual's interest (or the interests of some or all individuals severally) as a sufficient justification for holding others (usually governments) to be under a duty to create, secure, maintain, or respect an institution of private property.

There are two important features of this definition which I want to discuss before I go on to compare it in section 6 with a couple of rival accounts—the Choice Theory of rights (once espoused by Hart) and the theory of 'Rights as Trumps' espoused by Dworkin.

The first point concerns the role of the concept of *interests* in this definition. The concept of interests is vexed and controversial in the literature of political philosophy. On some accounts, interests are tied analytically to preferences, so that either an individual cannot be said to have an interest in something which he prefers to have nothing to do with, or (less rigidly) to say that an individual has an interest in some good or liberty or opportunity is to say that, at least, under conditions of adequate information and authentic consciousness he would prefer to have that good or liberty or opportunity. Other theorists offer a more objective account: an individual may have interests even though, under any plausible counterfactual conditions, he might prefer not to have these promoted. On the objective account, since a person's interests are determined essentially by his nature (what is good for entities of that sort, or what is in accordance with their end or *telos*) while his desires or preferences are not, there may be an irremovable

[59] See Raz, 'Right-Based Moralities', p. 184, and 'Promises and Obligations', pp. 221–6.

dissonance between a person's interests and his desires.[60] In my view, little is gained by pretending that there is a single right answer to the question 'What is the correct relation between the concept of interest and the concept of desire?'. Different answers will be appropriate for different tasks that the concept of interests is used to fulfil in political theory, and for different philosophical arguments in which it has a part to play. Individual interest (like harm, freedom, power, and, as we have seen, ownership) is a concept of which many different and perhaps competing conceptions are possible.

The point of my definition is to suggest a connection between rights, right-based arguments and the concept of interests, leaving open the question of the particular conception of interests that might be involved in the articulation of a particular theory of rights. At any rate, we should note that the Interest Theory of rights does not involve the claim that every individual interest provides the ground for a right (so that individuals could be conceived to have an abstract right to have all their interests promoted). It maintains only that to say that an individual has a right is to call attention to the importance of *some* interest of his as a basis for holding others to be under a duty (to promote that interest). Which interests are singled out in this way and why will be a matter of substantial argument for each theory of rights. So even if we were to set up what I have called an objective conception of interests in general, we would leave open the possibility that the only interests that are taken to matter *for the purposes of a particular theory of rights* (the only interests that ground duties in the way I have specified) are interests which in fact accord with the desires of the person who has them. I think it would be unwise to rule out this possibility a priori as a matter of conceptual analysis either of the concept of interests or of the concept of rights. (We will discuss this further when I look at the Choice Theory of Rights in the following section.)

The concept of interests that is in play in my definition, then, is simply the concept, as Raz puts it, of an aspect of an individual's well-being.[61] To cite a person's interest as part of a political justification is to focus one's concern specifically on him, on how

[60] There are excellent discusssions of the issues involved here in Barry, *Political Argument*, Ch. x; Lukes, *Power*, Chs. 6 and 8; Connolly, *Terms of Political Discourse*; Reeve and Ware, 'Interests in Political Theory'; and Swanton, 'Concept of Interests'.

[61] Raz, 'Nature of Rights', p. 195.

things go for him. That focus, as I say, may be determined by his preferences, his feelings, or by some more objective criterion of his health or good or welfare; the concept of an interest that I want to use leaves that open. It is no criticism of the idea of a right-based argument that it is defined in terms of a concept of which competing conceptions are possible and so, to this extent, that it is not, as it were, pinned down. For one thing, it is important to see how not only precise conceptions but also conceptual controversies fit together and lock into one another. For another, it is important to have a wide rather than restrictive idea of what counts as a right-based argument, for, as I have already suggested, we do not want to link that idea analytically with any particular theory about what rights people have. Of course, a definition will be vacuous if it uses concepts so indeterminate that it rules nothing out. But as we have already seen, certain arguments do not count as right-based despite the breadth and openness of the concept of interests used in the definition of that idea. Utilitarian arguments do not count as right-based because they do not usually regard individual interests taken one by one as political justifications for anything; the task of justification is only undertaken when the aggregate effect of a requirement on interests generally has been assessed. And duty-based arguments do not count as right-based because they do not take the interest of any person in a situation as a justification for imposing requirements on others; on the contrary, a duty-based argument takes the importance of some aspect of an individual's moral agency as a justification for imposing a requirement on him.

A related issue is this. Can an individual be said by a theorist to have a right to some good or opportunity or liberty which, in the circumstances, the theorist would have to agree it is not in his interest to have? At first glance, it looks as though the answer must be 'No', on the Interest Theory (as well as the Benefit Theory) of rights. But this, as Raz and MacCormick have conceded, would be counter-intuitive. 'A person may have property which is more trouble than it is worth'—as MacCormick puts it, 'some *heredi-tates* may be *damnosae*'—'It may be in a person's interest to be imprisoned, even while he has a right to freedom.'[62] And some theorists have suggested that criminals have a right to be punished at the same time as they want to say that punishment is, by definition, something which it is against one's interests to suffer.

[62] Ibid. 208; MacCormick, 'Rights in Legislation', p. 204.

(Actually, this last example can be dealt with easily. Usually when it is said that X has a right to be punished, what is meant is that he has a right to be punished rather than sent to a hospital for treatment; the background of this claim is usually some belief that it would be *less* against his interests to be punished than subjected to 'therapy', and therefore relatively speaking *in* his interests to be punished.) In other cases, however, the explanation may have more to do with the relation between *general* theories of human interests and accounts of the particular interests that particular people have in particular circumstances. Although right-based arguments focus on the interests of individuals considered one by one, these need not be interests which are peculiar to particular individuals; they may be interests which each individual is thought to have in common with every other. (This will always be so in the case of the so-called human rights.) Often, theories of rights will focus on interests which, on the whole, all individuals have, and they will give a general explanation of why this interest is so important for each individual who has it as to justify holding others to be under a duty to serve it. But, in the nature of things, the universalism of this approach cannot be watertight. The generalities in question are not rigidly nomological in the sense that a single counter-example is sufficient to refute them. Rather they will be sufficiently established if it can be shown that we should presume that every individual has this interest and that it has the importance in his case that we believe it has in most cases in the absence of peculiar considerations rebutting this presumption. To say, then, that an individual has a right to something which it is not in his interests to have, is simply to juxtapose the presumption with its rebuttal in a particular case. Again, depending on the shape of the particular theory of rights, there may be good (right-based) reasons for continuing to act as though the presumption were true even when we feel confident that, in a particular case, it has been rebutted. (Notice that this move in the direction of generality does not in any way blur the distinction between right-based and utilitarian arguments. To consider individual interests at a general rather than a particular level is not the same thing as considering 'the general interest' in the sense that utilitarians give to that phrase.)

The second point about my definition of right-based arguments concerns the emphasis on the interests of individuals taken one by one. As we saw, MacCormick insisted that rights 'concern the enjoyment of goods by individuals separately, not simply as members of a collectivity enjoying a diffuse common benefit in which all participate in indistinguishable and unassignable shares'.[63] Consider, for example, the good of *fraternity* in a human society. Many theorists believe that the government has a duty to foster this good. (Indeed, some non-liberal theorists believe that this duty lies at or near the foundations of political morality.)[64] Now it is certainly the case that all or most individuals have an interest in fraternity in their society, in the sense that they will be individually worse off—their lives impoverished or whatever—if their society is not fraternal. A right-based argument for the duty to foster fraternity, then, would regard these individual interests (severally) as crucial in justifying the imposition of this duty. But those who take fraternity to be an important political value are unlikely to agree that either its value or its importance can be explained on the basis of what it is worth to single individuals: what individuals like X or Y or Z get out of fraternity is not sufficient to explain why fraternity between or among X, Y, and Z is valuable. Rather they will say that an account of the value of fraternity should refer in the first instance to its being good for human communities, and only derivatively to its being good for individuals considered apart from their communities. It is arguable that individual persons are not the only human entities there are, and that, in this case, humanistic concern is more likely to be focused on a community considered as an entity in its own right than on the particular individuals who go to make it up.

The case of fraternity illustrates the point that there may be some values (or concerns or commitments) which, because of their communal character, cannot be captured in the language of rights. This is what we should expect. Though we do not want our account of what it is to say that someone has a right to commit us to any particular theory about what rights people have, we also do not want that account to present the language of rights as some sort of lingua franca in which *any* humanistic concern can be expressed. The idea of rights emerged with the growth of ethical and political individualism, and we should expect that rights will be associated at a fundamental level with specifically individualistic concerns.[65] If

[63] MacCormick, 'Rights in Legislation', p. 205.

[64] See Sandel, *Liberalism and Limits of Justice*; also Sandel (ed.), *Liberalism and its Critics*, 'Introduction'.

[65] Cf. Lukes, *Individualism*, Chs. 7–8.

we want to express a concern about human interests understood other than in an individualistic way—the interests of communities or ways of life, for example—we will find, I think, that other vocabularies of value are more apposite. (It should be stressed that the alternatives are not exhausted by the language of rights and the language of utility. As I argued in section 3, utilitarianism *is* an individualistic theory: what distinguishes it from an approach based on rights is its insistence on aggregating individual interests, its refusal to derive duties from the importance of individual interests taken one by one. The alternative I have in mind in this context is a style of evaluation concerned about the fate of communities and communal life as such which is not the same as a concern about all or any of the members of those communities considered either severally or in the aggregate.[66])

To the extent that values such as fraternity are taken seriously in political morality, to that extent it becomes implausible to argue that political morality as a whole is right-based. Certainly, it seems likely that any plausible theory will have *some* concerns which can only be expressed in the language of rights, and it is arguable that in any plausible theory some at least of these will be fundamentally right-based rather than derivative from utilitarian or communitarian evaluations. From a humanistic point of view, individuals are undoubtedly important in their own right even if they are not the only important human entities that there are.[67] But it is a matter of substantial moral controversy whether political morality is right-based in its entirety; many would want to argue that the right-based approach skews the balance too markedly in favour of individualistic concerns.[68] We cannot go very deeply into that controversy here. For the most part, I shall be talking about right-based *arguments* for private property and ignoring the larger question of whether any plausible arguments for property can be derived from fundamentally right-based *theories* of political morality. (This distinction, as we shall see, is particularly important in our characterization of Hegel's argument.)

Two issues in this controversy are worth further mention. As

[66] See e.g. Teitelman, 'The Limits of Individualism'; Taylor, 'Atomism'; and the articles in Sandel (ed.), *Liberalism and its Critics*, Pt. II.

[67] Cf. Raz, 'Right-Based Moralities'. I am indebted to Joseph Raz for many conversations about these matters.

[68] The *locus classicus* is, of course, Marx, 'On the Jewish Question'. See also Taylor, 'Atomism'.

indicated, I am inclined to accept the broad socialist point that theories of rights are concerned exclusively with individualistic values to the exclusion of other human concerns which cannot be expressed in individualistic terms. To say this, however, is not to accept the more specific point, for which many Marxists have argued, that the language of rights is a specifically *capitalist* language or that it is appropriate only for expressing the concerns of what C. B. Macpherson calls 'possessive individualism'.[69] There are other conceptions of the human individual than that of an insatiable utility seeker bent relentlessly on the pursuit of his own satisfactions, and there is therefore no reason why the partisan of rights should be stuck with the image of capitalist man. Only the the crudest historical materialism would be committed to the view that modern ethical individualism is wedded irrevocably to the particular economic framework of the society in which it was nurtured;[70] an ethical idea once conceived takes on a life (or lives) of its own, drawing sustenance not only from its immediate environment but from other sources, ancient and modern, which someone preoccupied exclusively with economic elements might not grasp. Since it is arguable that the Marxist theory itself expresses some non-derivative individualistic concerns (particularly concerns about individual freedom, self-development, and alien-ation)—concerns which *can* be expressed in the language of rights—its critique of liberal theories cannot be that individualistic concerns are in themselves intrinsically capitalist.[71]

The second issue is more analytic. Does it make sense to say that *groups* have rights?[72] Does it make sense, for example, to talk about a whole people having a right to self-determination, or a community having a right to the preservation of its culture? If the answer is 'Yes', do these provide counter-examples to the approach adopted in this chapter? I think these locutions do make sense, and that they can be accommodated within the interest theory as follows. When we talk of the rights of a group, we usually have in mind the relation between that group, as an entity, and either other similar entities or a wider entity of which it is a part. A people's

[69] See Macpherson, *Possessive Individualism, passim.* (For a critique, see Miller, 'The Macpherson Version'.) See also Pashukanis, *Law and Marxism.*
[70] Macpherson comes close to this in parts of *Possessive Individualism.* For a more considered view, see Dunn, *Politics of Socialism,* Ch. 2.
[71] See e.g. Brenkert, *Marx's Ethics of Freedom.*
[72] See e.g. Glazer, 'Individual Rights Against Group Rights'.

right to self-determination, for example, is usually understood to impose duties either upon other peoples or upon the international community at large. Formally, then, the right-bearing entities can be understood as individuals a concern for whose interests generates duties on other such individuals or on collectivities of such individuals. (The case is not markedly dissimilar from the way in which non-natural persons such as corporations are accorded rights in most legal systems: formally these entities operate as natural individuals do.)[73]

As far as I can see, there are only two serious worries about the idea of group rights. One concerns the difficulties we may have in defining and identifying the groups that are in question—particularly in cases where the identity of the group is exactly what is at stake in the substance of the alleged right. (The identity of natural individuals is seldom disputed in this sort of way.) The other worry concerns the suggestion that a group such as a people or a community may have rights *against the constituent members who make it up*. Though it is common in political rhetoric to talk about striking a balance between the rights of the individual and the rights of society, I agree with Dworkin that these ways of talking can easily become confused.[74] If individual rights are understood as 'trumps' over some collective aim, and if these 'trumps' are set up simply as a response to defects inherent in the conception of this collective aim (in the way, for example, that Dworkin's political rights are meant to compensate for the distortion of utilitarian calculations by the ineliminability of external preferences), then to set the problematic aim up as a group right, on a par with individual rights, would defeat the very *raison d'être* of the latter. But this second worry *only* arises if we adopt Dworkin's approach to rights. In the section that follows, I shall show that, despite the popularity of the 'trumps' image, that theory is quite distinct from the Interest Theory approach to rights.

Having said all that, in most of what follows we shall be concerned with the rights of natural human individuals (though reference should be made to the discussion of corporate property in section 9 of Chapter 2).

---

[73] Cf. Dworkin, *Taking Rights Seriously*, p. 91 n.
[74] Ibid. Ch. 7; though see my paper 'Can Communal Goods be Human Rights?'.

6. ALTERNATIVES: HART AND DWORKIN

The Interest Theory of rights that I shall be using has a lot in common with the approach to rights adopted in Hart's recent writings on the subject. It has in common with that approach a rejection of Hart's earlier view—the so-called Choice Theory—and of Dworkin's account of rights as trumps over social goals. In this section I shall first briefly contrast the Interest Theory with the Choice Theory, then outline Hart's current view, and finally note some contrasts between the latter view and Dworkin's approach to rights.

(i) The Choice Theory

In Hart's article, 'Are There Any Natural Rights?', the following theses about rights were put forward. (1) Since 'there may be codes of conduct quite properly termed moral codes . . . which do not employ the notion of a right', the notion of rights must make a distinctive contribution to a moral theory rather than being an idiom in which any moral claim can be expressed. (2) A person is said to have a moral right not by virtue of the fact that he stands to benefit from another's duty, but by virtue of the fact that he is morally in a position to claim the performance of a duty from another, or to waive it, and therefore to determine by his choice how the other ought to act. (3) 'It is . . . a very important feature of a moral right that the possessor of it is conceived as having a moral justification for limiting the freedom of another' so that rights express moral claims which it is deemed appropriate to enforce. (4) The justifications for limiting freedom which rights involve arise not only out of transactions like promises but also out of situations in which people who have conducted a joint enterprise to secure some benefit and who have submitted to rules restricting their liberty 'have a right to a similar submission from those who have benefited by their submission'. (This is Hart's so-called Principle of Fairness.) (5) The basis for rights may also be general in character—for example, Hart thinks that it follows from (3), perhaps together with (2), that 'if there are any moral rights at all, there is at least one natural right, the equal right of all men to be free'. Together these claims generated a conception of rights as essentially connected with 'a certain distribution of human freedom' in their nature, content and justification.[75]

In his recent collection of papers, Hart has chosen not to include this article, saying that the main argument 'seems to me to be mistaken and my errors not sufficiently illuminating to justify reprinting now'.[76]

But not all the positions outlined above have been rejected. As far as one can tell, Hart still maintains (1): though he has, as we shall see, modified his view of the distinctive contribution of a theory of rights, he believes that rights express a distinctive moral conception and that there are full moral theories, such as utilitarianism, which do not (and indeed cannot) take rights seriously. He also continues to maintain position (3): we are told that rights are regarded correctly by Mill as peremptorily enforceable moral claims: 'to have a right is to have a moral justification for demanding some liberty of action for oneself or some "service" . . . from others on the footing that even legal or social pressure is appropriate'.[77] He also says that thesis (4), the Principle of Fairness, is still worthy of discussion. Though that principle has come under powerful atack from Robert Nozick and others, Hart persists with it and regards it as an indispensable part of an adequate theory of political obligation.[78]

Thesis (2) has been perhaps the most controversial of the five. It formed the basis of the so-called Choice Theory of rights, usually contrasted with the Benefit and Interest Theories which we have already discussed. According to the Choice Theory, a right-holder is distinguished by the fact that, whether he stands to benefit by it or not, he has a certain moral 'sovereignty' over another's action: X has a right that Y should do A if and only if there is a justification for saying that X should have the power to determine what Y's duty is in regard to A-ing. Thus, for example, a promisee has a right, not because he stands to benefit if the promised act is performed, but because the circumstances of the promise justify our saying that he may insist on the promise being performed or release the promisor from his obligation, as he pleases. This theory has a number of controversial implications. It implies that it is a mistake to attribute

---

[75] Hart, 'Are There Any Natural Rights?', p. 80.

[76] Hart, *Essays in Jurisprudence*, p. 17.

[77] Hart, *Essays on Bentham*, p. 91.

[78] Hart, 'Are There Any Natural Rights?', pp. 85–6; Nozick, *Anarchy, State, and Utopia*, pp. 90–5; Hart, *Essays in Jurisprudence*, pp. 17 and 118–19.

rights to entities like foetuses or animals which are in principle incapable of exercising the choices which having rights essentially involves. (Hart regarded this as an advantage of his account.) It implies that one cannot have a right that one has a duty to exercise in a certain way. And in general it implies that rights cannot be regarded as inalienable—in the strong sense in which they provide protection for certain interests or freedoms which the individual in question is not thought to be morally competent to waive. A number of liberal philosophers (Locke and Mill, for example) have denied that people are morally competent to sell themselves into slavery: the freedom they might be tempted to exchange for contentment, security, or whatever is simply too precious to be traded in this way. But if Hart is correct, this position cannot be expressed in terms of a *right* to freedom or a *right* not to be enslaved. That seems to drive an unwelcome wedge between theories of rights, on the one hand, and contractarian theories like Locke's, on the other, which have derived almost all their normative implications from the idea that there are certain things that simply cannot be agreed to.[79]

In a later piece, Hart withdrew a little from this position. He acknowledged that the Choice Theory, though adequate for the purposes of 'the lawyer concerned with the working of the "ordinary" law', did not capture the way in which a constitutionalist or a political philosopher might want to talk about the rights that are or should be embodied, explicitly or implicitly, in a legal order. For their purposes, the 'focus of attention' is not usually the choice of the right-holder or his power of waiver, but those 'basic and fundamental individual needs' which generate particularly important moral demands. Talk of rights here is much better captured by the analyses of the Benefit or Interest Theories since it reflects the fact that 'certain freedoms and benefits are regarded as essential for the maintenance of the life, the security, the development, and the dignity of the individual'.[80] This represents a decisive abandonment of thesis (2), since that was supposed to be a thesis about rights in general, and about moral, indeed natural, rights in particular.

It would be a pity, however, if the controversy over the implications of the Choice Theory were regarded as closed as a

[79] See the discussion in Chapter 7, below, esp. n. 36.
[80] Hart, 'Bentham on Legal Rights', pp. 197.

result of this. Recently, Richard Tuck has shown how disputes about choice and alienability dominated the development of the early modern concept of a right—some theorists maintaining with Gerson and Molina that a man was *dominus* of his own life and liberty and indeed of all his rights (or *iura*), while others insisted with Vitoria and eventually Locke that liberty, though it was a right, was not exchangeable property and 'could not be traded for all the gold in the world'.[81] In the sixteenth and seventeenth centuries, these disputes about the analytic relation between *ius* and *dominium* were bound up with substantial political controversies about the justice of slavery and conventionalist defences of absolutism. Ultimately, they involved disagreements about the way in which the bearer of rights was to be seen: was he a free and independent agent with complete control over his own physical and spiritual destiny, or was he a creature whose rights were the reflection of his responsibilities and for whom the integrity of certain interests mattered more than the challenge of decision? Since our image of the right-bearer gives us at least the core of our image of the citizen, these are important questions. The answers that we give will flavour the whole of our political theory and indicate the substantial commitments we are taking on when we say that rights are fundamental to political morality. Since right-based approaches are increasingly common in modern thought, it is important that we should not lose sight of these questions as a result of an early capitulation to the Benefit Theory.

In the Choice Theory, a particular set of answers was associated analytically with the logic of rights. What it was to have a right told us that the right-bearer was to be conceived as an active, choosing agent. Perhaps that connection was in the end too tight, too analytical. We should remember, however, that the same issues may arise again— though in a looser way—in the context of a Benefit or Interest Theory. If we say (as Hart now appears to) that the function of a theory of rights is to pick out certain key elements of individual well-being as worthy of special protection, we are still left with the task of identifying those key interests and distinguishing them from other elements of preference and convenience which we might be prepared to see handled in, say, a utilitarian way. The criteria used to pick out the key interests or benefits regarded as the basis of rights may well reproduce all the substantial features of the

[81] For an excellent discussion, see Tuck, *Natural Rights Theories*, Chs. 1–3.

Choice Theory, identifying man's fundamental needs and ends in terms of what is necessary for his freedom, choice, and independence rather than, say, for his survival, sustenance, and welfare.

(ii) Hart on Rights and Interests

Hart's present position on theories of rights emerges most clearly in his discussion of the work of John Stuart Mill. In an assessment of Chapter V of Mill's *Utilitarianism*, Hart argues that the derivation of rights in the fullest sense from general utility (an enterprise common in modern philosophy and commonly attributed to Mill himself by those who undertake it) is hopeless, and he expresses doubt as to whether this was really what Mill intended. The gist of Mill's argument is that there are certain individual interests whose protection constitutes an 'extraordinarily important and impressive kind of utility', a utility which is 'vastly more important, and therefore more absolute and imperative' than—indeed 'not only different in degree but also in kind' from—the milder feeling attaching to the promotion of human pleasure or convenience. These utilities capture what Mill called 'the very groundwork of our existence' and 'the essentials of human well-being', and, as the ground of human rights, they demand respect, protection, and promotion in the case of every individual.[82] Hart argues that this approach represents a decisive repudiation of utilitarianism:

[T]he utilities which according to Mill are the stuff of those universal rights to which all individuals are entitled are forms of the individual good of those who have such rights. They are the essentials of individual human well-being and things no individual human being can do without. They are identified quite independently of general utility as if the criterion was to do exclusively with individual good, not general utility.[83]

To make this into a utilitarian doctrine, Mill would have to demonstrate a coincidence between the maximization of general utility and respect for these specific aspects of individual well-being. Hart shows that Mill never attempts anything like this. Whether he does or not, there is certainly no reason to expect such a coincidence. Even if we say that the important individual interests are to be given much greater weight than ordinary utilities in the

[82] Mill, *Utilitarianism*, Ch. 5; Hart, *Essays on Bentham*, pp. 90 ff.
[83] Hart, *Essays on Bentham*, p. 96; see also Hart, *Essays in Jurisprudence*, pp. 188 ff.

felicific calculus, still the sheer weight of numbers involved in calculations of the general interest make it unreasonable to expect that those interests will always come out on top in utilitarian calculations.[84] In demanding absolute respect nevertheless for certain specific aspects of individual well-being, Mill appears determined to put calculations of general utility on one side when they point in an opposite direction. As Hart puts it, 'claims to such rights are centrally claims to what is necessary, not merely to secure increases in totals of pleasure or happiness, but to what men, endowed with distinctively human capacities of thought, rational choice, and action, need if they are to be able to pursue their own individual ends as progressive beings.'[85] These are claims that individuals can make severally against one another, by-passing the aggregative calculations of general utility. A principle of rights, as Hart puts it, is 'a *distributive* and individualizing principle, according priority to specific basic interests of each individual subject'.[86]

Although in his recent papers Hart does not outline a theory of rights of his own, he lays great stress on the need for a theory of human nature that allows us to identify the 'essentials of human well-being'. Though utilitarianism cannot ground a theory of rights, still, theories of rights, he insists, must be more than a reaction to the excesses of aggregative utilitarianism: they must themselves offer and defend 'a specific conception of the human person and of what is needed for the exercise and development of distinctive human powers'.[87] It is for this reason, I believe, that Hart must now be supposed to reject the main argument of 'Are There Any Natural Rights?'—thesis (5), which argued transcendentally for the claim that 'if there are any moral rights at all, it follows that there is at least one natural right, the equal right of all men to be free'. The trouble with this argument is its abstraction from any plausible conception of human well-being. It proceeds on the purely analytic basis that rights provide justifications for coercion, which presupposes that coercion needs justifying, which indicates that coercion is prima facie wrong, which amounts in effect to a natural right to freedom. On Hart's present approach, an

[84] Hart, *Essays on Bentham*, pp. 96–7; see also Mill, *On Liberty*, pp. 103 ff. (Ch. 4, paragraphs 14 ff.) and Hart, *Essays on Jurisprudence*, p. 190.

[85] Hart, *Essays in Jurisprudence*, p. 189.

[86] Ibid. 182.

[87] Ibid. 17.

argument for rights must be more substantial, more full-blooded than this. Rights must be derived on the basis of a theory which accords importance to certain individual human interests rather than on the basis of the internal analytics of the language of rights itself.

(iii) Dworkin's Theory

It is for a similar reason, I think, that Hart repudiates Dworkin's approach to rights. On the issue of the derivation of rights from 'the essentials of human well-being', there is no question that Hart's approach and Dworkin's are fundamentally opposed. In a recent paper, Dworkin explicitly rejects the theory that 'whatever rights people have are at least in part timeless rights necessary to protect enduring and important interests fixed by human nature and fundamental to human development like interests in the choice of sexual partners and acts and choice of religious convictions'.[88] Instead Dworkin appears to make a virtue of what Hart regards as the main failing of modern theories of rights, by deriving a substantial theory of rights purely from his diagnosis of the shortcomings of utilitarianism. More generally, he favours a view which makes rights relative in each society to the background social values (general utility in our society, but perhaps national glory in another) which are normally accepted as decisive in that society. Briefly, in our society, rights are whatever individualistic constraints are necessary to make the application of the background value of general utility consistent with the fundamental but very abstract principle of equal concern and respect for persons.[89]

In 'Between Utility and Rights', Hart attacks Dworkin's specific deduction of rights against a utilitarian background (the argument based on the unfairness of including 'external preferences' in utilitarian calculations). I will not go into that here because I think his criticisms have been adequately answered.[90]

But the general issue remains: why does Dworkin believe that it is wrong to claim that the function of a theory of rights is to focus on specific individual interests and freedoms which are shown to be worthy of special protection by a substantial conception of human

[88] Dworkin, 'Rights as Trumps', p. 164.
[89] Dworkin, *Taking Rights Seriously*, pp. 232 ff. and 275 ff.; also 'Rights as Trumps', pp. 153–62; and 'Reply', pp. 281 ff.
[90] Dworkin, 'Rights as Trumps', pp. 159–64.

nature? Dworkin has never given any clear answer, but I suspect his worry concerns the *neutrality* of the conception of human nature which Hart's approach would involve.[91] Is it possible to pick and choose among human interests to distinguish those which constitute the essentials of well-being without committing oneself to a distinctive and controversial moral theory about what makes a life worth living? In the context of his discussions elsewhere, on the impossibility of establishing anything more than a 'minimum content' for theories of natural law, Hart has suggested that it is not.[92] If nevertheless he is, as I believe, correct about what modern declarations of human rights presuppose and about what theories of rights ought to articulate, then it is important to grasp the nettle of the neutrality issue and show how rights-theorists propose to reconcile the contestedness of their conceptions of human nature with the universal appeal that they want for the theories of rights they are building on these foundations.

7. RIGHTS AND SELFISHNESS

In his recent book on property, Alan Ryan notes that there has developed in the twentieth century 'a consensus that "it's his" invites the further question, "What good does its being his do for everyone else?" '[93] But it is a characteristic of right-based justifications of private property, as I have defined them, that they purport to bypass that question and ask instead, 'What good does its being his do for *him*—and why is that morally important?'. It might be thought, then, that right-based arguments are essentially selfish or egoistic arguments in contrast with the more altruistic concerns of utilitarianism. Many critics of rights see an almost definitional affinity between rights and egoism—it was Marx who wrote, 'None of the so-called rights of man goes beyond egoistic man, . . . an individual withdrawn into himself, into the confines of his private interest and private caprice, and separated from the community'[94]—and therefore a peculiar aptness in right-based

---

[91] For the idea of neutrality as expressive of the right to equal concern and respect, see Dworkin, 'Liberalism', p. 129. I am grateful to Leslie Green for suggesting this approach to me: see Green, 'Rights for Rights' Sake'.

[92] See e.g. Hart, *Concept of Law*, pp. 189 ff. , and *Essays in Jurisprudence*, p. 112.

[93] Ryan, *Property and Political Theory*, p. 177.

[94] Marx, 'On the Jewish Question', p. 147.

argumentation for private property. If you want to justify the institutional epitome of selfishness, they will say, what better set of moral considerations to turn to than those which themselves emphasize the demands that a man is entitled to make on his own account against his fellows?

Indeed, there is some superficial congruence even between the formulations we have adopted for our definitions of private ownership and right-based argument. A resource counts as being *owned* by an individual, we said in Chapter 2, if when disputes arise about how the resource is to be used that individual's say-so is taken as socially decisive without reference to the opinions or interests of others. And an individual, we have said, counts as having a right wherever the promotion or protection of some interest of his is regarded as sufficiently important in itself to warrant holding that others are under a duty to serve it in some way without further consideration of its impact on other interests or the social interest generally. In both cases there is concentration on a particular individual and a determination to see how far we can get in political morality by limiting ourselves to that to the exclusion of wider social considerations. Although it would be silly to maintain that institutions embodying individual rights are susceptible in the end only to right-based justifications—it is the achievement of modern utilitarianism to have put paid to that suggestion—still it may be thought that the easiest way to rationalize the dominance of individual will in the economic sphere is to adduce a mode of justificatory consideration which does not purport to go beyond the private interests of atomized individuals considered one at a time.

There is something in all this. Rights do represent what those who propound them regard as the ineliminable core of self-interest in political morality: our rights are, in a sense, those of our individual interests which it would be wrong or unreasonable to require us to sacrifice for the greater good of others.[95] Rights constitute for each agent the extent of the egoism he can proclaim against the community without moral embarrassment.

But two factors militate against any perception of this egoism as vicious. In the first place, it is essential to the language of rights that

[95] It does not follow that it is always wrong for the individual concerned to sacrifice these interests himself; that would be true, at most, only of inalienable rights. Nor does it follow that he is always morally justified in refusing to do so: see Waldron, 'Right to do Wrong' and 'Reply to Galston'. The present position is simply that it is always wrong to compel him to make the sacrifice.

the claims put forward therein are universalizable. In other areas of moral discourse, universalizability may be suspect; but claims of right are characteristically claims about the rights *of man*—the interests which require special moral protection in the case of all human individuals. (This universality is the source of both the main attraction and also, as we have seen, the main difficulties of right-based theories.) So the egoism proclaimed in a theory of rights is at least a universal egoism, and the claims made by each individual against the others are bound up necessarily with his recognition of the inescapability of similar claims made by each of the others against him. My rights are inseverable from those of my duties which are generated by the similar rights of others.[96] This, we will find, is important for an understanding of the notion that the right to property is one of the *general* rights of man

Secondly, it is assumed in all theories of rights—and indeed made into the explicit foundation of some of them—that there are certain interests which must be protected and promoted in the case of each human being before he becomes an agent capable of responding to the moral demands that may be made on him in the interests of others and in the service of other and higher ideals. Particularly when we look at general-right-based theories of property such as Hegel's, we shall see that the answer to the question 'What good does its being his do for him?' is often something like 'It contributes to his ethical development—it enables him to develop into a fully-fledged ethical agent'. If, as many of the critics of rights assert, social life and social responsibility are the most important part of what it is to be human, still it is open to a theorist of rights to maintain that there are certain individual interests—in education, in security, and in certain sorts of freedom—whose promotion is in all but exceptional cases a crucial prerequisite of the shouldering of that responsibility and of humanly fulfilling participation in communal relations with others. The egoism that permeates the language of rights, therefore, need not be conceived as standing on its own, but as locking into a wider moral theory that is far from exclusively egoistic in its foundations, aspirations and point.[97]

---

[96] This point, fundamental in the liberal tradition since Kant, is given great emphasis in Gewirth, *Reason and Morality*, esp. Ch. 3. (It is, by the way, quite separate from the further point that an individual with rights has a moral duty to exercise them responsibly.)

[97] See also Waldron (ed.), *Theories of Rights*, 'Introduction', pp. 19–20, and *Nonsense Upon Stilts*, pp. 190–209.

So to return to private property: right-based arguments in this area need not be seen exclusively as self-serving rationalizations of economic egoism. It is true that when we make out such an argument for someone's owning some resource, we are asking in the first instance, 'What's in it for him?' But that question does not get us anywhere near a right-based justification of his ownership until it is demonstrated that the sort of stake that he has in the matter is of sufficient moral importance in itself to warrant the imposition of duties on others.

4

Special Rights and General Rights

1. HART'S DISTINCTION

In his paper, 'Are There Any Natural Rights?', H. L. A. Hart drew a distinction between *special rights* and *general rights*. I am going to make use of a distinction along the lines of Hart's to elucidate the difference between two sorts of right-based argument for private property.[1]

Hart's distinction between special and general rights was related in the first instance to the idea of grounds for interference. The expression 'I have a right to. . .' is used, Hart argued, in two main types of situation:

(A) when the claimant has some special justification for interference with another's freedom which other persons do not have ("I have a right to be paid what you promised for my services'); (B) when the claimant is concerned to resist or object to some interference by another person as having no justification ('I have a right to say what I think').[2]

He continued:

When rights arise out of special transactions between individuals or out of some special relationship in which they stand to each other, both the persons who have the right and those who have the corresponding obligation are limited to the parties to the special transaction or relationship. I call such rights special rights to distinguish them from those moral rights which are thought of as rights against (i.e. as imposing obligations upon) everyone . . ..[3]

The latter rights Hart called 'general rights'. General rights, he said, differ from special rights in these respects:

(1) General rights do not arise out of any special relationship or transaction between men. (2) They are not rights which are peculiar to those who have

---

[1] Hart's distinction has also been used in discussions of property and justice by Nelson, 'Special Rights, General Rights, and Social Justice'.

[2] Hart, 'Are There Any Natural Rights?', p. 84.

[3] Ibid.

them but are rights which all men capable of choice have in the absence of those special conditions which give rise to special rights. (3) General rights have as correlatives obligations not to interfere to which everyone else is subject and not merely the parties to some special relationship or transaction . . .[4]

Let us look more closely at the distinguishing features of a special right. A first point is that it arises out of some special transaction or relationship, that is, a transaction or relationship which is, in some sense, peculiar to those who happen to have entered into it. A second point is that the parties involved in the right (the right-bearer and the person who bears or who is liable to bear[5] the corresponding obligation) are limited to those who were involved in the transaction or relationship. (In the terms of traditional jurisprudence, it is a right *in personam*.) Now these seem to be separate points and it is worth exploring the possibility that they might come apart. We need to introduce some terminology. Let us reserve the term 'special right' for rights satisfying the first of our points (and 'general right' for rights which do not satisfy it); and let us use the term 'rights *in personam*' for rights satisfying our second point (and 'rights *in rem*' for rights that do not satisfy it).

We may speculate now that there are not two but four distinct classes of right arising out of the combination of this pair of distinctions. The possibilities may be represented by diagram 1:

1. rights which are special and *in personam*	2. rights which are special and *in rem*
3. rights which are general and *in personam*	4. rights which are general and *in rem*

---

[4] Ibid. 88.
[5] Cf. ibid. pp. 80–2, for the 'Choice Theory' of rights.

Hart's paradigm of a promissory right is, of course, an example of (1). If A promises to pay B £5 for his services, then B has a right to be paid £5 and A has the corresponding obligation. Inasmuch as B's right arises out of the transaction between him and A, it is a special right. And since another person, C, for example, was not a party to that transaction, he has, so far as the example is concerned, neither a right like B's nor an obligation like A's; so the right to paid £5 in this case is *in personam*, a right of B against A only.[6]

Hart's paradigm of the right to say what one thinks is an example of (4). Most theories of rights which suppose a person to have this particular right suppose him to have it not on account of any special transaction or relationship in which he has been involved, but simply on account of what he is—a being such that it is a matter of moral importance that he should not be interfered with in this regard. Moreover, the right is a right *in rem* rather than *in personam*, for it carries a correlative duty for everyone not to interfere, not merely certain specified persons.

It is difficult to think of a right that could fill box (3) of the diagram: it would have to be a right which a person has, not because of any special transaction in which he has been involved, but which is nevertheless limited in an *in personam* sort of way. But in any case we can be confident that the two distinctions—special/general and *in personam/in rem*—come apart, because it is easy to think of a clear and uncontroversial case for box (2). On the view usually associated with John Locke and Robert Nozick, the right of an appropriator is a special right *in rem*, that is, a special right against the world. Consider the right of a Lockean farmer to the field he has enclosed and cultivated.[7] That right (to exclude others from the field, to control it for his own benefit, etc.) is a special right inasmuch as it is not a right he is supposed to have *ab initio* or as a matter of course: it arises out of a particular contingent event in which he was involved—namely, the event of his labouring on the field. Not everyone gets around to labouring on a field, and certainly only one person can be the *first* to labour on any particular field; so the right in question is, in Hart's terms, peculiar to him who has it. But the right so acquired is nevertheless a right against all the world, and thus a right *in rem*, because, on Locke's

---

[6] Hart, 'Are There Any Natural Rights?', p. 81. The dispute between 'Choice' and 'Benefit' Theories of rights is not relevant here. The idea of an *in personam* right can, I believe, be acommodated to both. For a discussion, see Ch. 3, sects. 4 and 6(i).

[7] Locke, *Two Treatises*, II, Ch. 5.

account, once the field has been laboured on, *anyone* who interferes with it without the labourer's consent will be in violation of his duty. Similarly, on Locke's account and particularly on Nozick's, rights arising out of the sale and purchase of fields and other appropriated resources are special rights *in rem*.[8] My right to my house arises out of the transaction I entered into with the vendors; apart from that transaction, I would have no rights at all to use or control that house. Nevertheless, the right is good against all the world: it generates a duty not just on the vendor but on everyone to refrain from using it without my permission.

The example of Lockean private property rights, then, shows that the distinction between rights *in personam* and rights *in rem* is not co-extensive with the distinction between rights arising out of contingent events and transactions and rights which the bearers are conceived to have *ab initio*. Almost all the rights we shall be concerned with in this work are rights against the world. So in the rest of this chapter, I want to concentrate on the latter distinction—the distinction between what I have called special and general rights.

2. SPECIAL RIGHTS AND CONTINGENT EVENTS

Rights arising out of contracts and promises are the most familiar cases of special rights. They are rights we have because of what has happened—because of the occurrence of some events, apart from which we would not have the rights in question. That any particular promise has been made or contract entered into is a contingent event, one that need not have happened. The parties to a promise or a contract might still have existed and the promise or contract not have occurred. Accordingly, a world is conceivable inhabited by beings just like ourselves in which no promises or contracts were ever entered into and no rights of this sort ever arose. Rousseau postulated the existence of such a world in man's primitive condition before the moralizing possibilities and corrupting effects of society arose. By and large, he suggested, human beings got by for millennia with almost no interpersonal dealings or relations.[9] But we do not have to accept Rousseau's anthropology

---

[8] Nozick, *Anarchy, State, and Utopia*, p. 238.
[9] Rousseau, *Discourse on the Origin of Inequality*, Pt. I.

in order to see that this is possible. All of us get along some of the time without relying on promises; we just have to imagine a world in which we all got along like that all of the time. Certainly in such a world we would all have the moral power to create rights and obligations by making promises; but we can imagine a world in which beings with that power never decided to exercise it.

An analogy may help here. In a game of rugby, the players begin with certain rights: they have the right to kick or carry the ball forward, to pass it backwards, and so on. These we may say are their general rights: they are rights which they have *qua* rugby players throughout the game from start to finish. In addition, during the course of the game, they may acquire other rights: to put the ball into a scrum, to determine the length of a line-out, to restart play with a drop kick from the 22-metre line, to attempt a kick at goal, and so on. These rights, we may say, are their special rights. Whether or not the players get to have any special rights depends entirely on what happens during the game: i.e. it depends on whether there are infringements by players on the other side, whether the ball goes out of play having been touched last by their opponents, whether the ball rolls dead, and so on. Now events leading to scrums, lineouts, drop-outs, and so on in a game of rugby (like promises and contracts in life) are very common and it may be difficult to imagine a game without them. But such a game is entirely possible within the rules of rugby—though tiring it would be very exciting!—and, if it took place, it would be true to say of the teams that throughout the game they had only their general and none of the special rights.

The analogy is helpful because it enables us to see two different sorts of relation that a right may have to a system of rules and to the form of life constituted by that system of rules. Some rights are defined for individuals directly by the rules which constitute that form of life, whereas other rights are provided for in those rules by their reference to certain specified contingencies which, according to the rules, will generate them. The broad rules of morality, for example, define certain rights directly for individuals: the right not to be killed, the right to certain sorts of freedom and well-being and so on. In a sense, these rules indicate what it is to be a player in the moral game of life; it is, among other things, to be endowed with these rights. But other moral rules are important in a different way: they indicate the possibility of having certain rights not merely on the basis that one is a moral being but rather on the basis of the moral importance of certain contingencies. Of course, being a person who is to acquire such rights on the occurrence of such contingencies is itself part of what it takes to be a moral 'player', but actually having the rights in question is not.

The situation is complicated somewhat by the rather flexible way in which philosophers have deployed the concept of a form of life. Sometimes it has been suggested that, say, promising itself could be regarded as a form of life with its own constitutive rules.[10] That suggestion may be important for certain philosophical purposes, but it is misleading in the present context. Promising is not a form of life in itself any more than scrummaging is a game on its own account; rather it is a moral institution which makes sense only against a certain background, and in particular against a background of other rights and duties which do not arise contingently but which are constituted directly by moral rules.

In the previous chapter, I suggested that the best way to understand the idea of *a right* was in terms of the moral importance accorded to an individual interest. The points I have been making can be restated in this idiom. Some moral rules are concerned directly with the importance of certain individual interests. The rule against homicide, for example, is concerned directly with the moral importance of each individual's interest in staying alive; that interest is deemed to have a particular importance for each individual just because of the sort of interest it is. But other rules point to interests which acquire moral importance on this scale only on account of the occurrence of certain contingent events. For example, there is a sense in which almost everyone has an interest in having his lawn mowed by his neighbour. But, in most theories of rights, that interest only becomes important enough to generate duties or obligations on other people when it has been made the subject matter of an agreement or promise. The event of the promise invests the interest with a *moral* significance that it would not otherwise have. The same is true of Lockean private property rights. Perhaps almost everyone has an interest of some sort in having the exclusive control of any given field; certainly many people would benefit from such control. But that interest by itself is not sufficient to count as a right; that is, it is not sufficient by itself to generate duties of exclusion on others. The interest becomes

[10] e.g. Rawls, 'Two Concepts of Rules', pp. 153 ff.

morally important only on account of the contingent event of someone's exercising his labour on the resource; once that happens, the labourer's interest in controlling the resource takes on an importance sufficient to enable us to describe him as having ownership rights over it. The basis on which importance is accorded to this sort of interest, then, differs markedly from the basis on which importance is accorded to the fundamental Lockean interests in life and liberty. The latter are taken to be morally important in themselves in the case of each individual, and that importance generates certain duties on everyone else, irrespective of contingent events. (So far, of course, I am merely outlining the Lockean position; detailed evaluation of this sort of view must await our discussion in Part II of the book.)

We have defined special rights in terms of contingent events: a special right is a right which a person is conceived to have by virtue of the occurrence of some contingent event or transaction. This definition raises one or two technical questions which must be dealt with briefly.

(i) Contingency and Choice

In Hart's analysis, the events giving rise to special rights were all the results of human choice. But it seems possible that an event may be contingent and give rise to rights whilst being accidental or inadvertent so far as all the parties are concerned.[11] If I accidentally spill claret on your rug, you acquire a right to an apology and perhaps even a new rug from me, even if no choice was involved.

A somewhat more important point, which arises directly out of our splitting the special/general distinction away from the *in personam/in rem* distinction, is that the persons juridically affected by the emergence of a special right are not confined to those who have chosen to be involved in its generation. In the case of promissory rights, the person constrained by the right is the person who chose to create it. But if we accept anything like Locke's account of the generation of private property rights, we will have to say that though these rights are created by the person who is to have them, they impose duties on others who played no part in their creation at all. In Chapter 7, I shall argue that this is a reason for entertaining grave suspicions about the Lockean approach to

---

[11] See e.g. Kocourek, *Jural Relations*, pp. 206–7.

property. But that approach should not be ruled out by definitional fiat.

(ii) The Existence of Persons

In a sense, my having any of my rights is contingent on the fact that I have come into and have remained in existence. But it goes without saying that this is not the sort of contingency that is involved in the definition of special rights. This sort of contingency has more the character of a *presupposition* of a rights statement than of a basis from which a right might be deemed to arise.[12]

(iii) Special Relationships

In his discussion of special rights, Hart mentions not only rights that arise out of transactions between individuals, but also rights that arise 'out of some special relationship in which they stand to each other', for example, 'where the parties have a special natural relationship, as in the case of parent and child'.[13] John Locke maintains, for example, that children have 'a Right to be nourish'd and maintained by their Parents' and that parents, in turn, have 'a perpetual right to respect, reverence, support, and compliance'.[14] Like Hart, I shall not discuss rights of this sort at any length. They do not really concern us here, and though they share some features in common with the special rights I want to discuss, there may be one or two disanalogies as well. (For example, what we said in the previous paragraph about the existence of persons means that rights arising out of the parent–child relationship cannot be described straightforwardly as rights arising out of a contingency.)

(iv) Newly Created Rights

Imagine a society where until 1980 there was no universal right in law to elementary education. Then as a result of legislation, such a right came into existence. Since the act of legislation is itself a contingent event, are we to regard the right which results as a special right?

[12] 'Presupposition' in the sense used in Strawson, 'On Referring'. Unfortunately the situation is not quite as simple as this: there are also the cases, discussed in Parfit, *Reasons and Persons*, Chs. 16–17, in which an individual (say, a handicapped child) may claim his rights were violated by bringing him into existence. I cannot discuss these cases here.

[13] Hart, 'Are There Any Natural Rights?', p. 87.

[14] Locke, *Two Treatises*, I, sects. 88–90 and II, sects. 67–71.

This, on my view, would be a serious misunderstanding. We must distinguish between contingent changes in the rules of a system and the contingencies which the rules of the system at any given time make morally important. Only the latter generate special rights. What we should say, then, in the case postulated is that the background rules of the system have been changed so that *now* individuals are deemed to have a *general* right to education. The rules of the system do not make that right dependent on the occurrence of any contingency (and certainly the rules would not normally refer to the contingency that they themselves are thus-and-so); they provide that everyone is to be educated, irrespective of the contingent events and transactions that he may have been involved in. (Indeed, if we imagine that education in the society was a matter of private arrangement in the period prior to 1980, then we should say that the effect of the legislation is to introduce a general right into an area of life previously dominated by special rights.) Of course, rules concerning special rights can also be legislatively introduced. For example, a society may legislate to the effect that certain promises given without consideration will henceforth be regarded as legally binding. My point is simply to insist that the contingency of the act of legislation is not sufficient by itself to make the rights introduced by legislation into special rights.

One other point may be relevant here. Some political philosophers have suggested that an act of legislation is rather like a promise. Because one of the functions of law is to provide a stable and predictable framework around which individuals can organize their expectations, we may say that the legislator who introduces the universal right to education in 1980 makes an implicit promise with his subjects at that time that this law will not quickly be repealed.[15] This complicates but does not undermine my account. If we take this view, we should say (a) that the legislation creates a *general* right in law, namely the right to education, and (b) that the act of legislation also generates a *special* moral right, namely the moral right that the legal right referred to in (a) should not quickly be repealed. (Depending on our background legal and constitutional theory, the second right may also be a legal right. The important point is that its existence complements and does not replace the generality of the first.)

---

[15] Cf. Bentham, 'Principles of the Civil Code', p. 113.

(v) Forfeiture and Abrogation

Many theories of rights provide for the possibility that individuals may forfeit their rights by performing certain actions and also for the possibility that certain rights may justifiably be abrogated in the event of certain contingencies. In Locke's theory, for example, an individual forfeits his right to life by attacking the life of any innocent person.[16] And in American constitutional theory, civil rights, such as the right to freedom of speech, may be abrogated in times of general emergency, for example, when there is a clear and present danger of war. How are we to understand these cases? Do they indicate that the rights in question are really *special* rights because they are contingent on the non-occurrence of aggression and emergency respectively?[17]

I am inclined to think not. The contingencies which give rise to abrogation and forfeiture seem to be of a different order, or to operate at a different level, from the contingencies out of which special rights are deemed to arise. It may be better to regard them as affecting the enjoyment or exercise of rights rather than the existence of the rights themselves.[18] This approach would have the merit of enabling us to distinguish between the abrogation or forfeiture of special rights (the abrogation or forfeiture of property or commercial rights, for example) and the abrogation or forfeiture of general rights (such as civil rights), instead of having to say that the possibilities of abrogation and forfeiture convert all rights indiscriminately into special rights.

3. SPECIAL- AND GENERAL-RIGHT-BASED ARGUMENTS

Having defined the sense in which we can talk about special and general rights, I want now to apply that distinction to the categorization of right-based arguments. A right-based argument for private property is, as we have said, an argument which takes an individual interest to be sufficiently important in itself to justify holding others (especially the government) to be under duties to create, secure, maintain, or respect an institution of private property.

---

[16] Locke, *Two Treatises*, II, sects. 8–13 and 17–18.
[17] I am obliged to Ronald Dworkin for this objection.
[18] In the sense indicated by Austin in the passages quoted in sect. 4(ii), below.

A *special-right-based argument* (or SR-based argument, for short) is an argument which takes an interest to have this importance not in itself but on account of the occurrence of some contingent event or transaction. A *general-right-based argument* (or GR-based argument, for short) is one which does not take the importance of such an interest to depend on the occurrence of some contingent event or transaction, but attributes that importance to the interest itself, in virtue of its qualitative character.

Now, as we saw in Chapter 3, the concept of interests is a contested one. Certainly it is not clear how interests are to be individuated. Consider this example. Every man in a society has an interest in being the owner of Whiteacre (because it is a lush and profitable piece of land). Smith is one of these men and he has this interest: call his interest 'Interest A'. Most theories do not regard interests such as interest A to be, by themselves, sufficient to justify holding others to be under duties to serve them. But suppose Smith takes the initiative and becomes the first person to enclose and cultivate Whiteacre. On Locke's account, he now has an interest in owning Whiteacre which *is* of sufficient importance to justify holding others to be under a duty.[19] Call this interest B. The question is: are interest A and interest B identical? It depends on how we individuate interests. If we individuate them in terms of their content—in terms of what they are interests in—then they are identical: they are both interests in owning Whiteacre. Here we can say straightforwardly that the Lockean account is SR-based, because it shows how a contingent event invests a certain interest with a moral importance that *it* did not previously have. But suppose we individuate interests in terms of the features which make them morally important (perhaps *inter alia*). Then we have to say that, on cultivating Whiteacre, Smith acquires a new interest, B, over and above the interest A that he shares in common with all his fellow men. Some of what Locke says suggests that this is his view: interest A is an interest in Whiteacre itself, whereas interest B is (partly) an interest in Smith's labour. The point is that if we say B is different from A, then there is a difficulty applying our terms 'SR-based' and 'GR-based'. Though interest B is created by a contingency, its importance is inherent: an argument based on its importance therefore looks like a GR-based argument, on the definition I have given. To avoid this unwelcome conclusion, I shall offer an *ad hoc* reformulation of the definition:

[19] Locke, *Two Treatises*, II, sect. 32.

An argument for private property is *SR-Based* if and only if it is right-based and *either* (i) the interest which it takes to be important arises out of some contingent event or transaction, *or* (ii) the particular importance of the interest in question arose out of some contingent event or transaction.

When I refer back to this definition in what follows, I shall, for brevity, omit clause (i). But in every case, the definition can be expanded, if necessary, to include it.

It is the thesis of this book that GR-based arguments for private property have quite a different character and quite different implications—particularly distributive implications—from SR-based arguments for private property.

4. ALTERNATIVE REPRESENTATIONS OF SPECIAL RIGHTS

(i) The 'Conditional' Reformulation

I want finally to consider an objection to the idea that there is an important distinction in principle between special and general rights. The objection goes as follows.

It is possible to redescribe every special right as a general right, albeit a general right which is conditional in its content. Thus consider the paradigm case of B's right to be paid £5, arising out of A's promise. I have regarded this as a special right, since B's having it is conceived to depend on the contingent event of the promise that A made to him. But surely we can say that B had the following general right all along, even before the promise was made—namely, the right to be paid £5 by A if A promised to pay him £5. This is indeed a conditional right, but it is a right which B, in common with everyone else, has *ab initio* as a direct consequence of the moral rule about promises.

Put in this form, the objection leads to the conclusion that each of us has an infinity of these general but conditional rights. I have a right to be paid £1 by A if A promises to pay £1; I have a right to be paid £2 by A if A promises to pay £2; . . . and so on. And I have a right to be paid £1 by B if *B* promises to pay £1 . . . and so on, to infinity, accounting for all possible promisors and all possible promisable benefits. But this point need not detain us. The objection can easily be stated in a more general form using quantifiers: each person has a (general) right that, for all persons *x* and promisable benefits y, if x promises to give him y, he receive y from x. Or, less pedantically, each person has a right that promises made to him should be kept.

The objection seems important because it can be turned against the main distinction I want to draw—the distinction between SR-based and GR-based arguments for private property. It will be said that, from an analytical point of view, there is no difference between these types of argument, and that the difference is purely one of content. The Lockean theory makes the general human right to property conditional, whereas the Hegelian theory makes it unconditional. But both theories suppose that the right to property is a right which all men have. How, then, are we to deal with this objection?

My inclination is to dismiss it as a purely verbal manœuvre. Nothing much is lost by reformulating my distinction in terms of conditional and unconditional rights. We might say that a person has an *unconditional* right if some interest of his is in itself morally so important as to justify holding others to be under duties to perform actions promoting it as it stands. And we may say that a person has a *conditional* right if some interest of his, though not sufficiently important in itself to justify holding others to be under duties to promote it, may nevertheless on the fulfilment of some condition acquire sufficient moral importance to justify conclusions of this sort. *Ab initio* we each have an interest of this second kind in the benefits that might be secured for us by the promises that other people could possibly make, and we each have an interest of this kind in the goods that might possibly be secured for us by, for example, Lockean acts of appropriation. It does not seem important whether we say that these interests form the basis of rights (though conditional rights) as they stand, or whether we say that they form the basis of (special) rights only when the condition is fulfilled. Perhaps indeed we can say both: a special right just is a conditional right whose conditions have been fulfilled. This preserves the distinction between special and general rights, for a general right can be described as a right which is not and never was subject to any condition. The distinction between the two kinds of right-based argument for private property in which I am interested could therefore be preserved.

My main reason for preferring to avoid talk of conditional rights has to do with the logical problems that arise when we want to detach special rights from them.

Suppose A has promised to pay B £5. Then B, surely, has the right *tout court* to be paid £5 by A. Thus even if B has all along the conditional right which the objection attributes to him (the right to be paid £5 if A promises it to him), he now also has this unconditional right as a result of what has happened. But clearly it would be a mistake to regard the unconditional right as just another right which B has; on the contrary, the unconditional right is intimately related to the conditional right attributed to him by the objection. The basis for attributing the unconditional right to B must be his possession of the conditional right together with the fact that the condition has been fulfilled. The trouble is, however, that such an inference cannot easily be elucidated using the traditional *modus ponens* device. Let me explain the difficulty.

From the statement

(1) B has a right to be paid £5 by A if A promises to pay B £5

together with

(2) A promises to pay B £5,

we want to be able to infer

(3) B has a right to be paid £5 by A.

Now, if (1) is understood along the lines of

(1a) If A promises to pay B £5, then B has a right to be paid £5 by A,

then that inference is transparent. (1a) and (2) clearly imply (3), by *modus ponens*. However, if (1) is understood along the lines of

(1b) B has a right to [be-paid-£5-by-A-if-A-promises-to-pay-B-£5],

then the inference will not go through. The conditional looks as though it is sealed into the context governed by the operator 'has a right to [. . .]', and it is not clear how *modus ponens* can detach it from that context. Just as we cannot infer

(4) It will rain

from the statement

(5) John believes that it will rain if Grandad's leg hurts

together with

(6) Grandad's leg hurts,

so we cannot infer (3) from (1b) and (2). The 'has a right to [. . .]' context in (1b), like the 'believes that . . .' context in (5) seems opaque and resistant to truth functional operations on its contents from the outside.

Since it is, I believe, undeniable that (1) and (2) entail (3), it appears to follow that (1) must be understood along the lines of (1a) rather than (1b). But (1a), as it stands, does not attribute a general right—or a right of any sort—to B or anyone else; rather, it states a condition under which B will come to have a certain right. It is clear (1a) can be true in a world in which B does not have any rights at all, since it states only that *if* a certain event happens, then B will acquire a certain right. In other words (1a) expresses perfectly my idea of a *special* right. On the other hand (1b) does purport to describe a general right which all men have even in advance of particular promises being made to them. But, as I have argued, it is a very unsatisfactory description of the moral situation, since it leaves the logical connection between (1), (2), and (3) unexplained. My hunch, then, is that we need the concept of a special right, the concept exemplified in (1a), as distinct from a general right, to explain the way in which rights are generated by promises.

A similar point can be made about the general principle that people have a right to have promises that are made to them kept. Again there are two possible formulations. One is:

(7a)   For all persons x and y and goods z (if y promises to give z to x, then x has a right to get z from y).

The other is:

(7b)   For all persons x and y and goods z, (x has a right to [get-z-from-y-if-y-promises-to-give-z-to-x]).

Despite the fact that both are universally quantified sentences, only (7b) purports to attribute a right to all men. (7a) asserts that all men, when a certain condition is satisfied, come to have a certain right. We may even say (if we want to talk loosely) that (7a) attributes a certain right conditionally to all men. But there is a difference between attributing conditionally a right to all men and attributing a conditional right to all men. The former in itself is not the attribution of a right at all.

Let us apply this briefly now to property. The Lockean position, I have said, is that natural rights to private property are special rights; they are not rights which all men have *ab initio* but rather rights they acquire as a result of the occurrence of certain events. The Lockean position is expressed initially in a principle along the lines of

(8)   A person has the right to exclusive control of the goods he has laboured on.

I suggest we should understand that as having a form like this:

(8a)   For all persons x and goods y (if x is the first to labour on y, then x has the right to exclusive control of y).

This formulation has the advantage that, from it together with

(9)   P is the first to labour on Q,

we get the conclusion that

(10)   P has the right to exclusive control of Q.

The alternative formulation of (8), envisaged in the objection, would involve the attribution to all men of a general but conditional right along the following lines:

(8b)   For all persons x and goods y (x has the right to [exclusive-control-of-y-if-x-is-the-first-to-labour-on-y]).

But, because the conditional corresponding to (9) is sealed into the context dominated by the right-operator, the inference using *modus ponens* from (8b) and (9) to (10) is not available. Lockean man on that approach is left with conditional property rights but he never seems to get any unconditional ones!

So (8a) seems the more felicitous rendering of the Lockean principle. It has the advantage of highlighting the crucial difference between the Lockean approach and what I shall later argue is the Hegelian approach. On the Hegelian approach, property is a general right in the very strong sense that everyone has a right to some property, i.e.

(11)   For all persons x (x has a right to [the existence of some good y such that x has exclusive control of y]).

As I said, I find this line of argument in favour of formulations (1a), (7a) and (8a), and against formulations (1b), (7b) and (8b), quite persuasive.[20] It may not be a conclusive argument, however, for two reasons. First, it is not crystal clear that the operator 'has a

---

[20] For details of the way in which these issues have been handled in deontic logic, reference should be made to e.g. Hintikka, 'Main Problems of Deontic Logic', pp. 87 ff. (Hintikka's attempt to merge the discussion of conditional obligation with that of prima-facie obligations does not strike me as helpful.) My discussion of the issues here, though inadequate, is much clearer as a result of Ronald Dworkin's penetrating criticisms.

right that . . .' *does* introduce a truth-functionally opaque context like 'believes that . . .'. Someone who thinks it is transparent in this regard will see no problem in deriving, say, (10) from (8b) and (9), or (3) from (1b) and (2). Secondly, what I have said entails a particular approach to rights of a different sort—what jurists have called *contingent* rights—which we may find difficult to accept.

(ii) Vested and Contingent Rights

There is a contrast in traditional jurisprudence between contingent rights and vested rights. Austin defined two senses of contingency: one 'large and vague', the other 'more strict and definite'.

Suppose that the right to R is a special right in my sense— inasmuch as an individual has it only on account of the occurrence of some event E. Then before E occurs, someone may want to say that a person A has a *contingent* right to R (in the sense that if E occurs he will get the right to R). Austin is intolerant of this usage:

> In [this] large and vague sense, *any* right to which *any* body (now in being or hereafter to be) may *any* how become entitled is a contingent right. It is possible, for example, that I or you, or anybody now in being or hereafter to be, may become owner or proprietor of A's house, or, more generally still, of any house whatever.[21]

(Austin suggests that so-called *spes successionis* fall into this category.[22]) Strictly speaking, he says, such a contingent right is not a right at all, but rather 'a present *chance*, or a present *possibility*, that *a right* may hereafter arise.'[23]

The other sense of contingent rights is stricter and more definite. Suppose I promise you today that I will give you a lift to Glasgow if my car is repaired tomorrow. Today, your right arising out of this promise is contingent inasmuch as it depends for its realization on the occurrence of a contingent event (the repair of my car). Such a right Austin also describes as an 'inchoate' right: your having the right to a lift to Glasgow depends on the occurrence of two events only one of which has so far occurred. He is inclined to insist that inchoate rights also are not properly species of right but only of the possibility of a right.[24] In law, a familiar example of an inchoate right is the following:

---

[21] Austin, *Lectures on Jurisprudence*, Vol. II, Lect. liii, p. 866.
[22] Ibid. 867.
[23] Ibid. 856.
[24] Ibid.

If land be given to A for his life, and, in case B (a person now existing) shall survive A, to B in fee, the right which is determined by the gift to B and his heirs general is presently a contingent right. For . . . the title . . . whereon the right is to arise, is presently inchoate only, and perhaps never will be consummate. Before it can be consummate, and the right determined to B can vest or come into existence, A must die, leaving B surviving him: which event, forming part of the entire complex title, has not yet occurred: and possibly may never occur.[25]

A *vested* right, on the other hand, is one not subject to contingency in this way. It is a right for the acquisition of which all the requisite events have occurred. Now, of course, such a right may still be a special right: *sub specie aeternitatis* it is subject to contingency in the sense that it vests in the individual who has it on account of the occurrence of contingent event(s). Another way of putting this is to say that the notion of a vested right is time-relative: a right is vested when the requisite contingencies have occurred; until that time it is merely contingent or inchoate. So the distinction between special and general rights and the distinction between vested and contingent rights cut across one another, for the latter is time-relative while the former is not.

For completeness, I should also mention Austin's distinction, among vested rights, between those 'which are coupled with a present right to enjoyment' and those which are not. Consider the following case:

[I]f a legacy be given to an infant, but with a direction in the will that the legacy shall not be paid to him till he come of age, he has a present or perfect right to the legacy, although he cannot touch it before he shall become adult. For if he should die before he come of age, the legacy would not lapse (or the gift would not be inoperative), but the legacy would pass to the successors of the legatee and not to those of the testator. It is not a gift *conditional* to take effect *in case* the infant shall come of age, but an *absolute* gift with a direction suspending the payment to him until he shall come of age.[26]

Arguably this is a feature shared by certain general rights. For example, a constitution may provide that everyone over eighteen years old shall have the right to vote. I think it would be a mistake to regard this as a special right (arising out of the event of a young person's reaching the age of eighteen). It is better to regard it as a

<hr/>

[25] Ibid. 860.
[26] Ibid. 858.

general right which every citizen is deemed to have *ab initio,* though one whose enjoyment or exercise is postponed until they reach a certain age. (Certainly, the conditionality involved here is quite different from that involved in the rights arising, for example, out of a promise.)

Now if we take the hard-line Austinian approach to contingency, the line of argument developed at the end of section 4(i) poses no difficulties. Just as B's right to be paid £5 if A promises to pay him £5 is represented as (1a) and not (1b), so your promised right to a lift to Glasgow if my car is repaired tomorrow is represented as

> (12a)   If my car is repaired tomorrow, you have a right to a lift to Glasgow

rather than as

> (12b)   You have a right to [a-lift-to-Glasgow-tomorrow-if-my-car-is-repaired].

The trouble is that in this case (12b) does seem to capture better our intuitive sense of the right you have arising out of my promise to take you to Glasgow if my car is repaired. I feel uneasy about formulating your right in terms of (12a). If we trust this hunch, then we have to find a way around the *modus ponens* problem anyway, since, on either account we want it to follow if my car is repaired, then you have a right *tout court* to a lift to Glasgow. But if we have to solve the modus ponens problem here for (12b), why can we not solve it also in the same way for (1b), (7b) and (8b)?

My conclusion, then, is that no watertight knockdown argument can be given against recasting what I have called special rights as general rights which are conditional in their content. But, as I have indicated, what is important is that the distinction be recognized— whether it is called a distinction between special and general rights, or between conditional and unconditional rights—and its import- ance understood in the realm of right-based arguments for property. In the chapters that follow, I shall show that, in the justification of private property, a GR-based argument (or an argument based on unconditional rights) has a radically different character from an SR-based argument (or an argument based on conditional rights).

PART II

THE ARGUMENTS

5

Arguing for Property

In the first part of the book, I discussed the concept of private property, the idea of a right-based argument, and the distinction between general and special rights. That discussion was largely analytic in character. In the second part, I want to use that analytical apparatus as a framework for considering the accounts of private property given in the theories of John Locke, G. W. F. Hegel, and Robert Nozick.

My aim in this part is twofold. I want to achieve the best possible understanding of the theories of property developed by Locke and Hegel in the *Second Treatise* and the *Philosophy of Right*, respectively. But I also want to use them as examples for the purpose of exploring the implications of the distinction between SR-based arguments for private property and GR-based arguments for private property.

In Chapter 6, I shall expound Locke's theory of property in some detail. I shall argue that Locke's case for private property centres around a particular SR-based argument: the argument about the *mixing of labour* with resources. But there are also several other strands of argument in his account—some hints of a theory of desert, some hints of a utilitarian theory—and I shall try to show how these relate to what I take to be the core of the Lockean argument. Partly because of these other strands, but also for a much deeper reason, Locke's argument cannot be regarded as a pure specimen of SR-based argument in the way that, say, Nozick's can. I shall show that Locke embraces the idea of there being certain general human rights in the material sphere: for example, he recognizes that everyone has a claim-right against all the world (or at any rate against anyone with goods surplus to his own needs) to a basic minimum subsistence. But there are no general rights to private property, on Locke's account. He attempts in one or two places to derive the existence of special rights of private property from the general right to subsistence; I shall argue that this attempt is unsuccessful. But the general right to subsistence remains in the background of his theory as a broad overarching constraint on the operation of his SR-based argument for private property.

I shall not undertake any systematic exposition of Nozick's theory, but rather use his account to expose what I take to be the deep structure of the SR-based approach to private property. In *Anarchy, State, and Utopia*, Nozick sketches what is almost a pure SR-based argument. Socialism and the redistributive welfare state are wrong, on Nozick's account, not just because they offend against general human rights (such as a putative general right to liberty), but because any attempt to realize them in practice would involve the violation of special rights which individuals, in the course of history, have contingently acquired. These entitlements are for Nozick the rock-bottom of the case for private property. Even if a private property economy is against the general interest, even if it can be shown that it does not generate the economic prosperity that is often claimed for it, even if the possession of property answers to no deep human need and does not contribute to the ethical development of the individual—indeed, even if private property does not in the end maximize individual liberty— still, Nozick claims, it must be upheld and protected as the upshot of our respect for a host of special rights that particular individuals have acquired over particular things. Jones has a right to the exclusive control and disposition of Whiteacre; Susan has a right to the exclusive control and disposition of her Porsche; and so on. That is why there should be a private property element in the economy. According to Nozick, it would be a serious mistake to argue the case for private property the other way round: that is, it would be a mistake on his view to say, first, that a private property system is desirable, and *therefore* that Jones (or someone) should have a right to control Whiteacre, and Susan (or someone) should have a right to control that Porsche. The specific rights that individuals have in relation to specific things take precedence over, and provide what Nozick takes to be the morally conclusive foundation for, the abstract case for private property. In Chapter 7, I shall examine this view and criticize the idea that individuals can acquire exclusive property rights that are strong enough to rebut all other material claims.

In Chapters 8 through 12, I shall consider the subject of GR-based arguments for private property. The main theory I want to consider here is the theory presented by Hegel in the *Philosophy of Right*. Hegel's theory of property (like much of his work) is philosophically very difficult and stylistically very obscure. In my opinion, no satisfactory exposition of the theory exists (at least in English) in the voluminous literature on Hegel. Most commentators are content to repeat or paraphrase what appear to be the crucial phrases in Hegel's presentation of his argument, without attempting to explain what that argument actually involves.[1] This is a particular problem for those who approach the *Philosophy of Right* on the basis of a mildly sceptical interest in property, as opposed to an enthusiastic interest in the Hegelian dialectic. My intention is partly to fill that gap. I believe that Hegel's argument for private property is in fact a very interesting one, and that it is worth expounding it in detail so that it can be set alongside and compared and contrasted with an equally detailed account of the Lockean approach.

The contrast is important because the essence of Hegel's case is, as I shall argue, GR-based. Hegel believes that private property is something that each individual needs, something indeed which it is imperative for each individual to have if he is to go through the stages of ethical growth and development sketched out in the *Philosophy of Right*. On Hegel's account, the ethically important interest which a person has in being an owner is not the contingent interest which arises out of the fact that he has actually acquired some object in a certain way. Nor is it merely an interest in the *use* of the property object—for example, the need to derive sustenance or enjoyment from it—since that interest could be served, as I have already said, in a non-private property regime. Hegel is concerned rather with a person's moral or spiritual interest in being in control of or responsible for some external object connected essentially with his well-being. This control and responsibility help to stablize the willing of the individual concerned, and give some concrete substance to his abstract freedom. It is an essential preliminary to the growth of his substantial freedom.

I shall precede my detailed account of Hegel's theory with a broader discussion of arguments of this type. Many writers have

[1] Ryan's discussion in *Property and Political Theory* is a notable and welcome exception.

suggested that *being an owner* is ethically important to individuals over and above the material benefits that they may derive from the use and control of a resource. (In some cases, these arguments are used to establish an ethical connection between private property and the prerequisites of citizenship.) To those who take such a view, the ethical argument for property matters much more than any consideration of the material prosperity of a capitalist economy (though it is fair to say that on many of these accounts the two considerations are not entirely unconnected), and it matters more also than any considerations of contingent entitlement. The case that they make is based on the relation between private property and individual freedom (understood on some 'positive' conception). They are prepared to confront head-on the moral basis of socialism: where a socialist sees private property ownership as corrupting, degrading, and alienating, they see it as ennobling, fulfilling, and liberating; and where a historical materialist sees individual private property as a transient phenomenon, an essentially bourgeois or petit-bourgeois idea connected necessarily to the early and middle stages of capitalist construction, these basically idealist thinkers see it as a transcendent necessity for the formation and the integration of individual human autonomy, connected with the satisfaction of some of the deepest and morally most important human needs.

In Chapter 11, I shall examine a position which is sometimes adopted by liberals as a sort of a 'half-way house' between an SR-based and a GR-based argument for private property. The position is that people do have a general right to private property, but that this right amounts only to a right to an *opportunity* to acquire property. In other words, the right generates a duty not to exclude anyone from the class of those who *may* own property, but it does not generate any duty to see to it that everybody *does* have property. Whether or not a particular person actually owns property depends, on this account, on whether he has gone through the procedures specified in an SR-based theory. I shall argue that this position is unsatisfactory—mainly because it is difficult to find arguments which lend it support but which do not also support the stronger view that (in Hegel's words) 'everyone must have property'.[2] If that is so, then it is disingenuous on the part of those who believe that an unequal distribution is justified to cite GR-

---

[2] Hegel, *Philosophy of Right*, sect. 49A, p. 237.

based arguments for private property to legitimate that position.

On the whole, then, as I indicated in Chapter 1, I am interested in exploring the broadly egalitarian implications of the GR-based arguments. If private property rights are something that each person needs for the satisfactory development of his autonomy, then it should be a matter of deep concern if the distribution of these rights is such that some people end up with none. So far as *their* ethical development is concerned, it is as though private property did not exist at all. This has important implications for the various theories we are considering. Sometimes Nozick and other thinkers on the New Right seem to want to invoke GR-based considerations to strengthen their essentially SR-based arguments. That, I shall argue in Chapter 9, is a move not normally open to them; at the very least, it introduces deep tensions into their discussion. From an SR-based point of view, it is *not* a matter of concern if an individual owns no property. If he has not engaged in any of the contingent actions or transactions that give rise to these rights, he simply does not have any of the rights that an SR-based theorist is sworn to uphold. Just as the proponent of '*pacta sunt servanda*' is unconcerned with the fate of the man who has not entered into any contracts, so Nozick and Locke are unconcerned with the plight of those who, as a matter of history, have not become entitled to anything. (Locke may be concerned lest that person starve, but he will not be concerned with his propertyless-ness as such. Nozick is troubled by neither concern.) But on a GR-based account, their predicament *is* a matter of concern. Their ethical development is blocked: they cannot, for example, go on to the stages of civic participation which presuppose that one has acquired the maturity that owning property introduces into one's life; and so on. A GR-based element, then, in a theory like Nozick's might provide an ethical basis for violating the very entitlements which, on his SR-based account, are said to be inviolable. If Nozick really wants to maintain the latter position, he must do so in all its starkness, without any of the rhetorical or justificatory advantages that he could derive from aligning himself with the deeper GR-based tradition.

Equally, I think the egalitarian implications of GR-based arguments mean that it is not open to their proponents to invoke a theory of historical entitlement as a way of mapping their abstract theory of property into the justification of any actual distribution of resources. It is, I shall claim, not open to Hegel to argue (as in fact he does): private property is justifiable on GR-based grounds, therefore individual appropriation and transfer on the Locke/ Nozick model is justified.

This, then, will be my main conclusion. GR-based arguments and SR-based arguments for private property are not, in general, capable of supporting one another. To the extent that they are combined together in a single theory of property, the coherence of that theory is put in question. In a final chapter, I shall say something about the objection that private property for some necessarily involves—sooner or later—propertylessness for a great many others. If this is true, a GR-based argument for private property is hopeless, since it puts forward as one of the rights of man something which cannot possibly be realized on a universal basis. Sometimes (as in Marx's work) this objection is based on a particular view about the direction of history. But often it is based as much on a particular view of what the exercise of private property rights themselves involves. There is no room here to enter into any detailed discussion of historical determinism, but in Chapter 12 I shall try and refute the point so far as the conception of private property is concerned.

2. INTERPRETING THE ARGUMENTS

The terms 'SR-based' and 'GR-based' denote *ideal types* of argument (in the sense defined by Weber).[3] The same can be said of 'right-based', 'goal-based', and 'duty-based'. When we come to examine the arguments that have actually been influential in the defence of private property, we are unlikely to come across pure instances of any of these types. The theories we shall be examining are complex and multi-faceted. In each case all sorts of consider-ations are adduced in relation to private property, and sometimes, as I have indicated, they are not even internally consistent. Certainly, I will be doing less than justice to these theories by trying to cram them into this ideal-typic framework. Where the fit is less than perfect, I shall try to indicate why this is so. But the value of a set of ideal types lies entirely in what is done with it, in what we want to typify theories *for*. I believe that my framework has some

[3] See Weber, *Economy and Society*, Vol. I, pp. 9 ff.

value, and, indeed, that it is arguably more valuable for a grasp of complex and impure cases than it would be for pure cases of the categories it sets up. It helps us to expose and understand certain tensions in the material we are reading. It helps explain our often ambiguous response to these arguments for private property: often, one feels compelled by the argument but cheated somehow in the upshot, as though something had been slipped into the picture behind one's back. And it gives us, I believe, some sort of analytically rigorous grip on the *strangeness* of the idea that private property—this regime dependent as it is, in the real world, on the arbitrary contingencies of fortune and endowment—could some-how be regarded by theorists in the Enlightenment tradition as one of the fundamental and imprescriptible rights of man.

There is a further problem about the application of my categories to the arguments I shall be considering. In our use of a common framework, it may seem as though we are attempting to treat the various theories as though they were on a par, as though they all had the same point, and as though each was engaged in the fulfilment of the same task or the success of the same campaign. But can we assume that Locke in the fifth chapter of the *Second Treatise* was engaged in the same enterprise as Hegel was, a hundred and forty years later and in a quite different philosophical and political environment, in the *Philosophy of Right*, or that either of them was involved in doing what Nozick was doing in Part II of *Anarchy, State, and Utopia*? The slightest acquaintance with recent work and recent controversies in the historiography of political theory indicates that this would be a very dangerous assumption indeed.[4] From the point of view of the history of ideas, it may seem crazy to suggest that there is a single enterprise—defending private prop-erty—which unites these theorists, and somehow bridges the gap of history and problematic between Berlin in 1821 and Harvard in 1974, or between the Exclusion Crisis in seventeenth-century England and the resurgence of conservative libertarianism in modern America. A sensitive historian of ideas might want to say that Locke was up to one thing (tailoring the implications of revolutionary constitutionalism to fit the economic predilections of his well-heeled audience), Hegel another (educating civil servants for their role in a conservative Prussian state), and Nozick yet

---

[4] For modern approaches to the historiography of political thought, see, e.g, Skinner, 'Meaning and Understanding'. There is a useful critique of this approach in Boucher, 'New Histories of Political Thought'.

another (providing an intellectual basis for political resistance to the claims of the left–liberal ideology of social justice). If there is no single task uniting these three thinkers, how is it possible to apply a common framework of categories to their disparate arguments— categories which are supposed to represent different ways of doing essentially the same thing?

Three points may be made in relation to this difficulty. First, it is easy to exaggerate the relativity of concerns, tasks, meanings, and problematics in the history of political thought. No doubt it *is* necessary to read each theory in relation to the intellectual (and historical, cultural, political, and biographical) context in which it was written; no doubt we do ourselves a grave disservice in treating chapters from Locke, Hegel, and Nozick as though they had appeared as a symposium in the latest issue of *Philosophy and Public Affairs*. But it cannot be maintained that all theories are utterly and irrevocably context-relative, and that it is impossible to understand them unless one is (or was) a participant in the milieu that brought them forth. If that were true, *any* sort of understanding would be out of the question. We could not even relate individual words and phrases, in Locke's text, for example, to modern meanings or modern understandings; the text would be literally indecipherable.[5] If, on the other hand, something less than this austere relativism is true—if, for example, it is possible for us to grasp and explicate the meanings of at least individual phrases and propositions in an historical text by bringing them into relation with phrases and propositions that *we* use and are familiar with— then why say that there is anything in principle stopping us from grasping and explicating whole theories by bringing them into relation with other theories that *we* are disposed to put forward? To be sure, this must be done sensitively and carefully; but something more than a vague unease about contextual relativity is necessary to show that it cannot be done at all in a particular case.

Secondly, we must remember that none of these theories was written or conceived in a static or theoretically isolated context. Each of these philosophers wrote with one eye on his intellectual predecessors—the others who had grappled with what he, at any rate, took to be the same or similar problems—and with the other eye on his successors—those whom he expected to read and

---

[5] The problem would be one of 'radical translation': see Quine, *Word and Object*; Davidson, *Truth and Interpretation*, Chs. 9–16; and Blackburn, *Spreading the Word*, pp. 57 ff.

criticize his arguments and propose alternatives to them. Nor need these have been only his immediate predecessors and his immediate successors: each referred and related his own discussion to a *tradition* of argumentation on what he took to be, again, substantially the same problem. (Thus Hegel addresses the arguments of Plato concerning private property, and Nozick those of Locke.) We must not let the excitement of discovering the immediate and personal problematic of each writer—With whom must he curry favour? What threat of censorship does he face? Will he get tenure? Which book, among those recently published, cries out for an answer? Where is the next meal coming from? and so on—blind us to the fact that they were all conscious of considering a common problem which they believed had been since ancient times one of the constitutive themes of the tradition of Western political philosophy.[6]

Thirdly, it is necessary to emphasize that the concerns of the working political theorist are bound to be different from those of the historian of ideas. The historian of ideas is interested in tracing the growth and development of thought about politics presumably in the context of a wider attempt to grasp and understand the flow of life and thought in the past. But the working political theorist is primarily interested in modern political problems—issues like how the economy should be organized, how social structures should be judged, what forms of political life are consonant with what we value, and so on. The context of our concerns, in this work, is the modern debate about the fundamentals of economic life and economic institutions. It is an issue which is still best expressed for us in Aristotle's question: 'What are the best arrangements to make about property, if a state is to be as well constituted as it is possible to make it? Is property to be held in common or not?'[7] Now, whether the historian of ideas likes it or not (and whether or not it is 'fair' to the historical figure whose work and individuality he cherishes—whatever that means), each of the theories we are examining is now used as a resource in the modern debate about the defensibility of private property. For the most pressing and urgent practical reasons, we want to know what (if anything) is to be said on behalf of this institution whose worth and justice is now so much in dispute. Theories such as the ones we are considering provide a rich fund of insight, reminder, and argument which can and should be drawn on in the modern debate. I am not saying that we should simply plunder these resources, grabbing a phrase here and a snatch of argument there to suit our current polemical preoccupations.[8] But there is some value in considering, for each of these theories, what is the best case—the most coherent and compelling—that could be made out on behalf of private property using these materials.[9] That may not guarantee the most accurate interpretation (if accuracy is to be conceived in terms of fidelity to the author's intentions), though I suspect we may do better for accuracy working along these lines than at first appears. But at any rate it may be the best way to interpret the theory we are studying, in the familiar sense of the way that does us, as opposed to the dead author, the most good.[10]

If we were to eschew this approach as 'anachronistic, as Quentin Skinner and others sometimes seem to suggest, our political theory would be impoverished and emasculated beyond belief. On the one hand, we would have to foresake any hope of a critical understanding of past theories— for a critical understanding is an understanding which evaluates arguments, and which can do so only from some perspective associated with the evaluator's own concerns. (But if we abandon critical understanding, what other modes of—histori-cal?—understanding does that leave?) On the other hand, we would have to purge our modern thinking about political issues of any reference to the thought and writing of past philosophers, for all such references would be condemned as anachronistic on the Skinner approach. I cannot believe that anyone seriously thinks that would be desirable. The only sense I can make of Skinner's strictures is that they are intended as a hermeneutic for the historian alone. As for the working political theorist, it is hard to imagine what sort of *mistake* he could possibly be accused of making if he were to make use of historical materials—like the works of Locke, Hegel, and Nozick—in a modern debate about property.

[8] Cf. Foucault, *Power/Knowledge*, pp. 53–4: 'The only valid tribute to thought such as Nietzsche's is precisely to use it, to deform it, to make it groan and protest. And if commentators then say I am being faithful or unfaithful to Nietzsche, that is of absolutely no interest.'

[9] I adopt this formulation from Ronald Dworkin, *Law's Empire*.

[10] See also Ryan, *Property and Political Theory*, 'Introduction'.

6

Locke's Discussion of Property

I. INTRODUCTION

In this chapter I shall discuss in some detail the theory of property presented in John Locke's *Two Treatises of Government*. I shall argue that Locke's account, though it has some utilitarian and GR-based strands in it, is to be regarded as fundamentally an SR-based justification of private property.

Locke was anxious to establish that the royal government of Stuart England—and indeed *any* government—had a duty to respect existing property rights. 'The Supream Power,' he wrote, 'cannot take from any Man any part of his Property without his own consent. . . . [I]t is a mistake to think, that the Supream or Legislative Power of any Commonwealth, can do what it will, and dispose of the Estate of the Subject arbitrarily, or take any part of them at pleasure' (II. 138).[1] He wants to argue that violation of this duty is a legitimate ground for violent and even revolutionary resistance to the powers that be: 'Whenever the Legislators endeavour to take away, and destroy the Property of the People, . . . they put themselves into a state of War with the People, who are thereupon absolved from any further Obedience, and are left to the common Refuge, which God hath provided for all Men, against Force and Violence' (II. 222). The basis of this extreme position, I want to argue, is not that the existence of private property serves the public good (though Locke certainly believed that), but rather that rights of private property are among the rights that men bring with them into political society and for whose protection political society is set up:

For the preservation of Property being the end of Government, and that for which Men enter into society, it necessarily supposes and requires, that the People should have Property, without which they must be suppos'd to lose

---

[1] Parenthical references in the text of this chapter are to John Locke's *Two Treatises of Government*, by treatise and section number.

that by entring into Society, which was the end for which they entered into it, too gross an absurdity for any man to own. (II. 138)

These private property rights, according to Locke, are *natural* rights— not in the sense that men are born with them—but in the sense that, though they are acquired rights, they are acquired as a result of actions and transactions that men undertake on their own initiative and not by virtue of the operation of any civil framework of positive rules vesting those rights in them. The account of how and why these special rights of private property arise out of such actions and transactions is the basis of Locke's account of the moral importance of the duty to respect property holdings; and therefore, indirectly, it is the basis of the main argument that a Lockean can offer against any attempt to set up alternative systems of property in a society previously characterized by private ownership.

Another way of putting this is to say that Locke's theory of property is like the theory outlined by Robert Nozick:[2] it is a theory of *historical entitlement*. Ownership rights are established contingently and historically as the upshot of what individuals have done; therefore it is not open to us to abrogate or reorder them on the basis of what *we* think *society* ought to do. So far as justice is concerned, the task of the state is to protect those private holdings whose historical pedigree can be established, to rectify historical injustice where it has occurred, but not to assert any more substantial jurisdiction over privately held resources than is necessary to discharge those tasks. The government—even a government acting with enthusiastic popular support— is constrained by the independently established rights of the individuals subject to it: 'Individuals have rights, and there are things no person or group may do to them (without violating these rights).'[3] The ownership of particular resources, even socially significant resources, is among the rights which define and limit the space available for governments to act.

Though their theories share this basic shape, there are a number of important differences between Locke's account of property and the theory sketched out by Nozick. I shall point these out as we go along. But there is one overriding difference that has a bearing on my overall characterization of Locke's view, so I should mention it immediately.

[2] Nozick, *Anarchy, State, and Utopia*, Ch. 7.
[3] Ibid. p. ix.

According to Locke, not only is government action constrained by special rights of private property, but those rights are themselves constrained by a deeper and, in the last resort, more powerful *general* right which each man has to the material necessities for his survival. This forms the basis of what one might refer to as entitlements of charity in Locke's system (see I. 42). Because it constrains the rights which constrain the activities of governments, it could be argued that its effect is to extend the realm of legitimate state action and to provide a justifying ground for redistributive activism in the economic sphere.[4] Occasionally, Locke tries to argue that, given the circumstances of human life, this general right to subsistence actually generates the moral basis of particular private property rights. In section 6, I shall criticize this strand of Locke's argument. But it raises the question: why, if this *general* right lies at the basis of Locke's theory, do we describe it still as presenting a *special*-right-based argument for private property? The answer is that the general right has nothing to do with private property as such: it is simply a right to the material wherewithal for survival and that might be provided on the basis of any type of property regime. Subsistence is the basis of a general right in Locke's theory, but subsistence organized on the basis of private ownership is not. The justification of private property, as such, is SR-based: rights of private property are not God-given to the individuals who have them. Of course, Locke believed that private property was favoured by God, and that He created the world and its resources with the intention that individuals should acquire rights over it in this way. But there is nothing in Locke to support the proposition that private property is something which all persons have a general right to; his position is that provided each person's subsistence is taken care of there is no cause for moral concern if anybody happens not to have acquired any resources as his own private property.

Now I would feel less secure about all this if Locke had been anything more than half-hearted in his attempt to derive special rights of ownership from the general right to subsistence, or if that

---

[4] Of course, Locke had difficulty believing that there were in fact people in this sort of extreme need. His biographer quotes from a Board of Trade memorandum indicating that in Locke's view most so-called poverty was more the result of idleness and corruption than of real want: Cranston, *John Locke*, pp. 424–5. See also Waldron, 'Locke's Account of Inheritance', pp. 44–5, and 'Turfs My Servant Has Cut', p. 14.

attempt had shown substantial signs of success. But the main argument for private property, though conducted against the background of the general right we are considering, is in fact independent of it: it is the argument based on the idea that when a man labours on a resource, he puts something of himself into it, something which gives him (roughly) the same sort of entitlement to the resource as he had originally in respect of his self, his person, and his actions. I shall argue that in the end this argument too is unacceptable. But the key to my characterization of Locke as an SR-based defender of private property lies in my attribution of this to him as the main argument for his claim that no derogations may be made from the private property of individuals by the state.

There has been an immense amount written about Locke's theory of property in recent years. This is partly because of the general revival of interest in Lockean political theory and partly because of the connection between Locke's theory of property and modern discussions of justice and capitalism. The interpretative work that has kindled most controversy is C. B. Macpherson's book, *The Political Theory of Possessive Individualism*, with its claim that Locke is trying to provide a justification for early modern capitalism and a legitimating basis for a society where political as well as economic rights are to be allocated along strict class lines. I shall not say a great deal about Macpherson's interpretation; though his work remains important, the class-based side of his interpretation has, I think, been decisively refuted.[5] Recently, however, a substantial new work on Locke's theory of property has been written: James Tully's *A Discourse on Property: John Locke and his Adversaries*. Tully's book involves a far more radical rereading of Locke than Macpherson's did; briefly, his thesis appears to be that, far from providing a legitimation for capitalism, Locke denied that there could be private property in the state of nature, insisting that private property was only the creature of civil society and could always be rearranged or redistributed for the public good. The book contains a number of fresh insights, and the author's acquaintance with sixteenth- and seventeenth-century theories of property is formidable. But the theory which Tully attributes to Locke is simply *not Locke's theory*; and the attribution is based on what can only be described as a very

---

[5] See Ryan, 'Locke and the Dictatorship of Bourgeoisie'. But for the lingering influence of Macpherson's view among anti-liberal writers, see Arblaster, *Rise and Decline of Western Liberalism*, p. 165.

seriously defective reading of the *Two Treatises*. Because I think that Tully's mistakes are instructive, and because the interpretation of Locke which he wants to reject is considerably more interesting, for our purposes and in general, than his own interpretation, I shall take the opportunity at a number of places in this chapter to indicate where the mistakes in Tully's analysis lie.

2. THE THEOLOGICAL PREMISSES

John Locke's account of ownership in the *Two Treatises of Government* has a theological dimension which is lacking in the modern discussion of property and justice. We are told in Locke's writings that the natural resources of the world are the subject of the original donation from God to man described in the early chapters of Genesis: 'The Earth, and all that is therein, is given to Men for the Support and Comfort of their being' (II. 26). Resources are seen by Locke not merely (as we have defined them) as material objects *capable* of satisfying human wants and needs, but as created objects *intended* for human use.

God . . . made Man, . . . and furnished the World with things fit for Food and Rayment and other Necessaries of Life, Subservient to his design, that Man should live and abide for some time upon the Face of the Earth, and not that so curious and wonderful a piece of Workmanship by . . . want of Necessaries, should perish again, presently after a few moments continuance . . . (I. 86)

Opinions differ as to the importance of this theological dimension. Certainly, it distinguishes the premisses of Locke's account from some of the other theories we shall be looking at; but does it distinguish them in terms of their implications? Some commentators insist that it makes a great deal of difference. Locke's theory of property, they say, cannot be restated adequately in secular terms; it is theological through and through.[6] (One philosopher has even suggested that the Lockean doctrine is not fit to be taught in the public schools of America as the First Amendment is currently understood![7]) It has been suggested too that this is a factor which distinguishes Locke's view from the

---

[6] See Dunn, *Political Thought of John Locke*, Ch. 8 *et passim*.
[7] Alasdair MacIntyre, in the Carlyle Lectures given at Oxford, Trinity Term 1982.

superficially similar account of property in Nozick's *Anarchy, State, and Utopia*, and that it is the lack of any theological premisses which explains the comparative inhumanity of Nozick's theory.[8]

This is not a question that can be discussed at any length here. It does seem to me that parts of Locke's political philosophy are difficult to restate in secular terms. His argument for the juridical equality of persons (II. 4–6) and his account of the inalienability and imprescriptibility of certain human rights (II. 23) are the most prominent examples. Moreover, these positions are so fundamental to Locke's political philosophy that they give the whole thing an undeniably theological flavour. But other aspects of Locke's political philosophy— for example, his argument from the existence of natural rights to a natural power of punishment (II. 7)— could be accepted by philosophers who wanted no truck with theistic or creationist hypotheses. The wide appeal of Locke's theory, even given his own undoubted Christian commitments, is helped by the fact that his theology is not wholly voluntaristic. Though the *ipsissima verba* of Holy Writ matter for Locke (particularly in the *First Treatise*), still he shares the view held by most thinkers in the natural law tradition that there is no gaping divergence between faith and reason, and that much if not all of what God requires of us could be inferred as a matter of reason and common sense anyway. (The project of demonstrating that this is the case was, as John Dunn and others have pointed out, the driving force of all Locke's philosophical work, though one that remained uncompleted.[9]) So, while we will not discuss in any detail the question of whether the premisses of Locke's theory of property can be represented in secular terms, we should bear in mind his own insistence that the same truths can be grounded in different ways. Typical of this approach is the following passage, where Locke seems to be suggesting that, in the economic sphere, what we are told by revelation accords not only with reason but even with the promptings of impulse and instinct:

God . . . having made Man and the World thus, spoke to him, (that is) directed him by his Senses and Reason . . . to the use of those things that were serviceable for his Subsistence and given him as means of his

---

[8] See e.g. Held, 'John Locke on Robert Nozick'.
[9] Dunn, *Locke*, pp. 65–70; Ryan, *Property and Political Theory*, pp. 22 ff.

Preservation. And therefore I doubt not, but before these words were pronounced, I *Gen.* 28, 29 (if they must be understood literally to have been spoken) and without any such Verbal Donation, Man had a right to the use of the Creatures, by the Will or Grant of God. For the strong desire of Preserving his Life and Being having been Planted in him, . . . Reason . . . could not but teach him and assure him, that pursuing that natural Inclination he had to preserve his Being, he followed the Will of his Maker, and therefore had a right to the use of those Creatures, which by his Reason or Senses he could discover to be serviceable thereunto. (I. 86)

This is quite common in Locke's discussion of property. What God is supposed to have commanded, what reason tells us, and what our instincts incline us to do, amount more or less to the same thing. There is no serious divergence between our nature as creatures, our nature as animals, and our nature as thinking things.

For Locke, the theory of property has four main premises that are expressed initially in theological terms. They are: (1) the doctrine that the world was intended by its creator for human use; (2) the doctrine that, being all creatures of the same rank or status, we are not to be used for one another's purposes as the lower animals etc. are for ours; (3) the doctrine that God intends as many of us as possible to survive and requires us to carry out that purpose; and (4) the doctrine that God has commanded us to labour for our subsistence. I will briefly discuss each of them.

(1) *The Use of Resources.* The first doctrine is regarded as both a revealed and a self-evident truth (I. 28 and 86, respectively). As creatures with needs and appetites finding themselves in a world of resources capable of satisfying them, none of us can be criticized, at least in general, for making use of what is evidently useful. As we have seen, the task of a theory of property is to determine, when there are disputes, who is to make use of what; but the starting point of any but the most fanatically ascetic theory must be that useful objects are there to be used for the support and comfort of human life.[10]

(2) *Equality and Non-Subordination.* The second doctrine consists of two parts: first, that there are morally important differences between human beings and members of other species that justify the subordination of the latter to the former; and, secondly, that there are no such differences between man and man.

---

[10] This is Kant's 'juridical postulate of practical reason': see Kant, *Metaphysical Elements of Justice*, Ladd trans., p. 52 (Prussian Academy Edn. VI, 246).

Sometimes the first part of the proposition is defended voluntarist-
ically: Locke notes, for example, that the lion was created before
Adam and suggests that God *might* have chosen to subordinate
humans to the king of the beasts rather than the other way round,
thus appearing to indicate that only the contingency of God's
express appointment makes the difference here (I. 15). But
elsewhere he defends the subordination of animals in a more
naturalistic way. Man, he says, is 'an intellectual creature, and so
capable of Dominion', and this 'intellectual Nature . . . belonged to
the whole Species, and enabled them to have Dominion over the
inferiour Creatures' (I. 30). He notes the instinctive rather than
intellectual character of animal nature (I. 56), and the animals'
natural fear and dread of man, which shows, he says, that they were
made to be dominated by us (I. 34).

The second part is more difficult, and it was the crux of Locke's
case against Robert Filmer, the theorist of patriarchalism and royal
absolutism, against whom Locke's *Treatises* were mainly directed.[11]
According to Filmer, God gave the world and its resources
(including the lower animals) not to all men, but to Adam and his
line by natural inheritance. Adam's property in the world and all its
resources was coupled with (and anyway in effect amounted to) a
grant of absolute dominion over all mankind. Since he had the right
to exclusive control over everything that anyone needed, it was for
him to lay down the terms on which others lived and died. This,
Filmer argued, was the original prototype of the absolute regal
power which he urged for England; and, indeed, he suggested that
the authority of the Stuart monarchs could be traced back through
to the Adamite line. The last claim, of course, was the easiest for
Locke to ridicule (see I. 104–69).[12] But he also wanted to attack the
premisses of Filmer's position. The terms of the original donation
set out in Genesis, Locke argued, establish 'nothing but the giving
to Man, the whole Species of Man, as the chief Inhabitant, who is
the image of his Maker, the Dominion over the other Creatures' (I.
40). Neither reason nor revelation indicates that any man has been
favoured with peculiar authority from God over his fellows,

there being nothing more evident, than that Creatures of the same species

[11] Filmer, *Patriarcha*. See also Laslett, 'Introduction' to Locke, *Two Treatises*,
Pts. 2–3.
[12] Cf. Ryan, *Property and Political Theory*, pp. 14–15: 'Locke's negative
arguments against Filmer strike most later readers as a simple, if unnecessarily
prolonged knockout of a wholly inept target.'

and rank promiscuously born to all the same advantages of Nature, and the use of the same faculties, should also be equal one amongst another . . . unless the Lord and Master of them all, should by any manifest Declaration of his Will set one above another, and confer on him by an evident and clear appointment an undoubted right to Dominion and Sovereignty. (II. 4)

Locke was not the first—nor certainly the last—philosopher to argue from some basic 'Community of Nature' (II. 6) among human beings to a doctrine of equal authority and non-subordination.[13] Of course, he recognized that there were and should be certain inequalities among men (II. 54): inequalities of strength or wisdom might license inequalities of political power; inequalities of effort, acquisition, and opportunity might license inequalities of property. But these connections would be established in the body of Locke's political theory not in its premisses. It is not the point of the contractarian theory that the wisest should rule; though in a Lockean society, we should expect wisdom to be a distinguishing mark of the responsible and successful magistrate. Similarly, it is not, as we shall see, the point of the Lockean theory of property that 'the Industrious and Rational' should inherit the earth, though if the problem of allocation is solved along Lockean lines many of the first generation of owners, at least, will be industrious and rational men. In its starting point, at any rate, the Lockean theory of property, like the theory of politics, is egalitarian.

(3) *The Duty to Preserve Human Life.* The basis of the third doctrine is regarded by Locke as more or less self-evident, like the first. From a God's eye point of view, each act of creating a human is purposeful: it would be self-defeating to create a being about whose survival one was indifferent (I. 86). From the point of view of each human, however, his own survival is paramount, both as a right and as a responsibility. (I suspect that Locke, if pressed, would have adduced some sort of limited psychological egoism as evidence of God's will in this regard.) So though 'the Fundamental Law of Nature' is 'Man being to be preserved, as much as possible' (II. 16 *et passim*), the law that each man is under is this: 'Every one as he is bound to preserve himself, and not to quit his Station wilfully; so by the like reason when his own Preservation comes not in

---

[13] For a more recent attempt, see Williams 'The Idea of Equality', pp. 112 ff. and 120 ff.; Williams adopts a 'presumptivist' approach to equality surprisingly similar to Locke's in *Two Treatises*, II, sect. 6.

competition, ought he, as much as he can, to preserve the rest of Mankind . . .' (II. 6).[14] One's own preservation comes first, but the preservation of others comes second, and that is important. The duty to preserve others has priority over all egoistic interests of one's own (save one's bare survival); it has priority, for instance, over the desire for luxury, enjoyment, and the accumulation of power.

Does the doctrine impose positive duties to come to the assistance of others? Initially, it is glossed in terms of a negative duty—a man 'may not unless it be to do Justice to an Offender, take away, or impair the life, or what tends to the Preservation of the Life, Liberty, Health, Limb or Goods of another' (II. 6). But Locke quickly makes it clear that the duty has a positive side to it as well. When it is put together with premisses (1) and (2), it generates the following claim-right as the substantive basis of the Lockean theory of property: 'Men, being once born, have a right to their Preservation, and consequently to Meat and Drink, and such other things, as Nature affords for their Subsistence' (II. 25). That this doctrine imposes positive duties on men to satisfy others' needs (or at least stand aside while the needy make use of property acquired by those who are not needy), and that these duties are correlative to the *rights* of the needy, is emphasized in the following important and often-overlooked passage from the *First Treatise*:

God the Lord and Father of all, has given no one of his Children such a Property, in his peculiar portion of the things of this World, but that he has given his needy Brother a Right to the Surplusage of his Goods; so that it cannot justly be denied him, when his pressing wants call for it. . . . As Justice gives every Man a Title to the product of his honest Industry, . . . so Charity gives every Man a Title to so much out of another's Plenty, as will keep him from extream want, where he has no means to subsist otherwise. (I. 42)

(We should perhaps note the context of this assertion. It is used in the *First Treatise* as a second line of defence against Filmer's position: to show that even if God had given Adam all the world, still it would have been unjust of him to threaten to withold resources from others unless his political dominion was acknow-ledged (I. 41–3). Locke, in other words, is not prepared to concede absolute rights to *any* owner, no matter how respectable the

---

[14] For the importance of this ordering, see Waldron, 'Enough and as Good', pp. 325 ff.

pedigree of his endowment. I have taken the liberty of reading the account of property in the *Second Treatise* as though it incorporated this doctrine, despite the fact that entitlements of charity are never referred to there and that its explicit invocation in the *First Treatise* is purely *ad hominem*. But the resulting theory is consistent and not unattractive, and I do not think this reading poses any serious exegetical problems.)

(4) *The Duty to Labour.* The fourth theological premiss of Locke's account is that God has commanded man to labour for his subsistence. Once again, this is put forward both as revelation and as common sense: 'God Commanded, and his Wants forced him to labour' (II. 35). Manna-from-heaven and loaves-and-fishes incidents are few and far between in biblical history; the normal situation is one in which it is apparent both that created nature provides the wherewithal for the satisfaction of our needs and that we must work to derive that satisfaction from it. In his argument against Filmer, Locke noted wryly that if God had intended to make Adam ruler of all the world, he 'made him but a very poor Monarch': 'God sets him to work for his living, and seems rather to give him a Spade into his hand, to subdue the earth, than a Scepter to Rule over its Inhabitants. In the sweat of thy Face thou shalt eat thy Bread, says God to him . . . ' (I. 45). Moreover, it appears from Locke's discussion that God requires us to do more than gain a bare subsistence from the resources He has provided: 'God gave the World to Men . . . for their benefit, and the greatest Conveniencies of Life they were capable to draw from it, it cannot be supposed he meant it should always remain . . . uncultivated' (II. 34). Productive labour, then, is virtuous and God-fearing; while idleness is sinful as well as anti-social.

We should note, though, that Locke does not connect the duty to labour with any idea of a natural impulse to carry it out. Labour is an irksome curse: there is, on his account, nothing corresponding to the later view (found, for example, in Marx's writings) that work can be a fulfilling form of self-expression. Its importance for Locke is purely instrumental and the basis of our secular recognition of its importance lies, not in our finding fulfilment in it, but in our commonsense realization that we *have to* work in order to survive and flourish.[15]

---

[15] For an excellent discussion, see Ryan, *Property and Political Theory*, pp. 5–12.

3. ORIGINAL COMMUNISM

The starting point of Locke's discussion of property is the difficulty which arises out of his insistence that, although the world was created for mankind, no part of it was allocated initially to any particular man for his exclusive use. Since the world and its resources were given 'to Adam and his posterity in common' (II. 25), some further explanation is necessary to show how particular resources could be held legitimately as private property. The view that God gave the world originally to man or to a particular man as *private* property was defended, as we have seen, by Robert Filmer, who linked it with his theory of natural inequality and the divine right of kings. Private property for Adam and his descendants was, on Filmer's account, natural and primeval, while private property for anyone else was the creature of political sovereignty. As the king was the fount of all law, so also he was the origin of all the property rights that his subjects had; it followed that it was absurd for a subject to assert his own rights of property in the face of the king and his fiscal prerogative.

Since the point of writing the *Two Treatises* was to challenge the Stuart appeal to the royal prerogative, Locke would have nothing to do with Filmerian conventionalism about subjects' property. But though he rejected Filmer's theory, his own position of original communism was itself unsatisfactory from an ideological point of view. A revolutionary theory of politics is difficult enough to sell at the best of times, and Locke's intended audience—Whig merchants and the wavering rural squirearchy[16]—were unlikely to be convinced by a theory of political revolution if it also threatened to undermine the moral basis of their material wealth and security. Filmer was aware of this potential embarrassment in the theories of his opponents. He has argued that theories of natural right were thrown into confusion and contradiction by the fundmental 'error which the heathens taught, that all things at first were common, and that all men were equal'.[17] With potentially devastating effects for revolutionary constitutionalism, he pointed out that theories based on this premiss faced a dilemma. Either they entailed something like the Levellers' conclusion that private property was illegitimate and a usurpation of common rights; or they required

[16] There has been a lot of recent work on Locke's intended audience. See e.g. Laslett, 'Introduction' to Locke, *Two Treatises*; Dunn, *Political Thought of John Locke*, Chs. 5–6; and Goldie, 'John Locke and Anglican Royalism'.

[17] Filmer, *Patriarcha*, p. 262.

that the law of nature and the terms of God's donation could be varied after the fact by human convention. The price of the former alternative would be an unpopular and practically unacceptable political theory, while the cost of the latter would be a theory that was intellectually disreputable. Locke's task, then, was to dissolve this dilemma and to indicate how the legitimacy of private property flowed naturally and without inconsistency from the claims about equality and common endowment which he needed as premises for his attack on royal absolutism.

The way in which the original community of goods was understood would clearly make a difference to the solution of this problem. It is easy to imagine an extreme version of original communism, from which no plausible theory of private property could be developed. Suppose each individual were conceived to have an inseverable, inalienable, and imprescriptible claim-right in common with the rest of mankind to the use of each and every resource. Then everyone would have a right to use all resources in common with others, but no one could ever be excluded by any means from the use of anything. To allow for the development of a theory of private property, the rights involved in original communism have to be something less than these rigid claim-rights. Two possibilities suggest themselves. First, perhaps the common rights could be thought of as *alienable* rights, opening the way for the possibility of the establishments of private property by universal consent. Or, secondly, perhaps original communism could be thought of as a system of pure liberties, involving no claim-rights at all: if, for example, original communism meant nothing more than an absence of private property rights in resources when they were created, then the problem would be reduced to one of explaining how private property could be generated *ex nihilo*—a considerably easier proposition than explaining its establishment in the face of pre-existing common rights. Those are two possibilities. For various reasons, Locke did not want to take either approach, though his own solution has rather more in common with the second than the first.

(i) Consent

The first option—alienation of original common rights by consent—was the solution favoured by Locke's predecessors in the natural law tradition, Hugo Grotius and Samuel Pufendorf. Since

Pufendorf's theory went further in this direction than that of Grotius, a brief outline of it will serve as a useful point of contrast with Locke's theory.

Pufendorf denied that first taking was sufficient to establish a right to exclusive possession and use. On his view, since a right of exclusive possession would affect the moral situation of others, it could not be based simply on the unilateral action of the possessor: '[W]e can not apprehend how a bare corporal Act, such as seizure is, should be able to prejudice the Right and Power of others, unless their consent be added to confirm it; that is, unless a covenant intervene.'[18] What unilateral seizure generated, on Pufendorf's view, were not *rights* to exclusive possession but *quarrels* about exclusive possession. These quarrels led in turn to the establishment of a universal agreement on the principle that first taking should generate a right to the unhampered use of any object in one's possession. He recognized, however, that a principle of first taking had its limitations (even when based on consent); he saw that quarrels would still break out because people remained at libery to use the fruits of others' labour when the producers were not personally in possession of them. He therefore postulated a gradual succession of agreements, quarrels, and further agreements, in a series of conventions whose upshot was the establishment of private property in land and in movable resources. Private property was seen, in short, as a conventional basis for the settlement and prevention of the conflicts which arise naturally out of what we have called the problem of allocation. Pufendorf capped this theory of private property by maintaining that, though the institution was conventional, the instituted obligations acquired the force of natural law. Though God did not give the world to man *as* private property, He gave it nevertheless *for* private property: that is, He intended that it should eventually be divided up by convention among men. To this end, He placed us under a natural obligation to refrain from using what belonged to another, and He established the obligation to refrain from the use of another's body (i.e. that which pertains naturally to him—his *suum*) as the natural prototype of this obligation. The effect of the conventional distribution of resources, then, was to bring a man's conventionally allocated property within the scope of his natural *suum* so that the

---

[18] Pufendorf, *Of the Law of Nature*, Bk. IV, Ch. iv, sect. 5 (p. 322).

natural obligation to refrain from what is another's applied now to the external resources too.[19]

Filmer put forward two connected objections to the consent theory of property. First, it was absurd because it made the law of nature 'changeable' and 'contrary to itself'. Secondly, as a practical matter, it was inconceivable that the requisite universal consent could ever have been secured.[20] On its own, the first objection is not valid. To answer it, one need only deny that the rights and privileges of original communism are inalienable. If original rights are not inalienable, the moral position of individuals can change without there being any variation in the content of natural law principles themselves. But this reply shifts the issue decisively to the second objection. For now it must be the case that everyone's agreement really has been secured, otherwise rights have not been alienated in the establishment of private property, but rather abrogated or violated.

Locke was inclined to acknowledge the force of Filmer's second objection. After all, the belief that it was 'possible for all Mankind to meet in one place to give consent' to the establishment of property seemed scarcely plausible. As Filmer remarked sarcastically, 'Certainly it was a rare felicity, that all the men in the world at one instant of time should agree together in one mind to change the natural community of all things into private dominion; for without such a unanimous consent, it was not possible for community to be altered.'[21] And what did people eat in the meantime?, asked the practical Locke: 'If such a consent as that was necessary, Man had starved, notwithstanding the Plenty God had given him' (II. 28). But if, for practical or other reasons, something less than unanimous consent was secured, then it must have been the case that someone was robbed. If so, failing an adequate theory of rectification, all subsequent private titles must be deemed illegitimate.

A conventionalist might attempt various manœuvres to avoid these difficulties. Perhaps he might have recourse to the familiar expedient of tacit or presumptive consent: though the commoners have not consented explicitly to the introduction of private property, they have benefited from or acquiesced in its establishment in such a way as to preclude them from any legitimate

[19] Ibid. sects. 6 ff. (pp. 322 ff.). See also Tully, *A Discourse on Property*, pp. 72–7 and 86–91.
[20] Filmer, *Patriarcha*, pp. 262–74.
[21] Ibid. 273.

objection. But such manœuvres are likely to run foul of equally familiar objections. How can we deem a natural right to have been alienated in the face of the erstwhile right-holder's explicit assertion that all along he had wanted nothing more than to be left enjoying it? The defender of private property must, if his case is complete, have an answer to give to people who claim to have been prejudiced by its institution and who insist that they at least were better off without it; and to say simply that they can be deemed to have accepted what they have always objected to does not satisfy that requirement.

A somewhat more promising approach would be to deny that universal consent was necessary and say instead that the institution of private property took place first on a local basis. As men settled into communities, it became possible for them to make conventional arrangements for the division of the resources in their vicinity which would be valid and binding at least as between the members of each community. In principle, these would be purely *in personam* promissory arrangements and would not generate any rights *in rem*. The arrangements would leave the rights and privileges of outsiders unaffected, for they could not be bound by agreements to which they were not parties. A man coming into a community from abroad, then, would have no obligation to refrain from using resources which members of that community had divided among themselves. He would be within his rights to act as though those goods were still held by all men in common. Now that situation might well lead to quarrels and conflicts between members of various communities. So we might imagine a further set of agreements by which the different communities would agree to recognize one another's dominion over the resources in their respective vicinities and to abide by one another's conventional property rules. In this way, each individual would eventually acquire a conventional obligation, owed in the first instance to other members of his own community, to respect the property conventions of other communities as though he were a party to them. This is quite close to the view adopted by Pufendorf, and it seems a plausible and attractive version of the consent theory of property.

Locke, however, has a reason for wanting to avoid consent theories. It was, at bottom, the same reason that made the Filmerian theory repugnant to him: if an individual's property rights were conventional, then they would be vulnerable in principle to the claim that the demands which the magistrate made upon them in fact fairly reflected the terms of their conventional establishment. In itself, conventionalism provides no defence against oppression or absolutism except for the highly contestable claim that, *as a matter of fact*, those arrangements were not the ones that were entered into.

In his book, *A Discourse on Property*, James Tully attributes something along the lines of Pufendorf's account to Locke. Locke, says Tully, 'subscribes to the view of Grotius and Pufendorf . . . that property in political society is conventional and based on consent'.[22] Certainly, there are important conventionalist strands in Locke's discussion—in his account of the invention of money, of the preservation of commons, and of the regulation of property relations under civil government. However, when we come to look at these issues, I shall argue that the main thrust of Tulley's thesis is completely mistaken, and that, for all these conventionalist strands in his thought, Locke nevertheless committed himself firmly to the position that private property rights could be established in a non-conventionalist way.

(ii) Negative Communism

If the consent theory is rejected, another way of generating individual property rights out of original communism would be to conceive of original communism in a purely negative way. Perhaps the original community of goods does not actually involve any *claim-rights* at all which might stand in the way of private appropriation, but only and at most Hohfeldian privileges, such as the privilege of making use of the resources God has provided. On this account, each individual would be at liberty to use any resources, in the sense that he would have no duty not to do so, but nobody (at least initially) would be conceived to have any rights capable of generating duties on others to refrain from using resources in which they were interested.

If this conception is not developed any further, it amounts, more or less, to Hobbes's account of human rights over resources in the state of nature. In Hobbes's theory, original communism (so understood) was ended by the institution of a political sovereign

[22] Tully, *A Discourse on Property*, p. 98.

and by the conventional forms of property which that sovereign set up.[23] But one might also couple the negative communism view with a theory of unilateral acquisition. If we say that men have *ab initio* no claim-rights over natural resources, but that they may acquire such rights by labour, first use, or occupation, then we have what amounts to a pure version of what I have called an SR-based theory of ownership. All property rights are special rights. Duty-generating rights over resources are established by what happens; they are not established as general rights by the terms of God's endowment of mankind. The only rights which might be described as general are the general privileges associated with negative communism. Since no one has any initial claim-right to the resources of the world, no one is wronged and therefore nobody does any wrong to another by appropriating resources as his property. (This, I think, is quite close to the sort of theory Nozick is interested in; I will pursue that discussion in Chapter Seven.)

The concept of negative communism was defended by Pufendorf and Grotius. According to Pufendorf,

[T]hings are said to be negatively common, as consider'd before any human Act or Agreement had declared them to belong to one rather than to another. In the same sense, things thus consider'd are said to be *No Body's*, rather negatively than privatively, i.e. that they are not yet assigned to any particular Person, not that they are incapable of being so assigned.[24]

As we have seen, Pufendorf did not believe that this rights-vacuum could be filled by acts of unilateral acquisition. Grotius, on the other hand, believed that men in the state of nature could at least acquire rights of exclusive possession by taking things up and beginning to use them. Briefly, by taking something into one's possession and using it, one acquired a right to withold it from others and they acquired a duty to refrain from using it, so long as it was retained in one's possession. This could be done without prejudice to the rights of others, since the original community of resources was understood in a purely negative way. As Tully notes, Grotius made use of Cicero's famous simile of the theatre to illustrate this point:

'Tho' the Theatre is common for any Body that comes, yet the place that everyone sits in is properly his own.' The people who first take their seats

[23] Hobbes, *De Cive* (Epistle to the Reader), and *Leviathan*, Ch. 13, p. 188 and Ch. 24, pp. 295 ff. See also Lopata, 'Property Theory in Hobbes'.
[24] Pufendorf, *Of the Law of Nature*, BK. IV, Ch. iv, sect. 2 (p. 318).

have an exclusive right in their use, and this correlates with a negative duty on the part of others not to occupy it at the same time. But if the theatre fills to capacity, those excluded have no right to demand a seat.[25]

The excluded have in common with all mankind the privilege of occupying an empty seat. If they do so they acquire a special right to its exclusive occupation. But if they do not or cannot, they have no general right to be seated in the theatre, or (to drop the image) no general claim on the resources that others are using.

Locke's conception of original communism has certain similarities to the negative version I have outlined. He did not believe that God's original gift to man established inalienable and imprescriptible common rights in relation to every use that could be made of every resource. He believed, on the contrary, that it was possible for an individual by his actions 'to *exclude* the common right of other men' (II. 27; my emphasis) in relation to particular resources. But though negative communism captures Locke's view of private property rights, it does not accurately express his view of all human rights over resources. We saw in the previous section that Locke has, among the foundations of his account, the doctrine that all individuals have a natural right to sustenance and to the use of whatever resources are necessary for their survival. This forms the basis of his view that men are endowed with the privilege of using the resources God has created, and he attempts to use it later in his account as part of the justification of private appropriation. But it also establishes a primeval claim-right which each man has against every other—a right which entails a duty to make available whatever resources are necessary for another's survival (if they are surplus to the exigencies of one's own).

Locke, therefore, did not believe that original communism should be thought of as nothing but a rights-vacuum awaiting the acts of acquisition that would establish exclusive rights. He believed that men were endowed in common from birth with certain determinate claim-rights over resources, and he did his best to connect his account of the development of private property with his conception of these original and enduring common rights. Whether he succeeded in that attempt is something we will have to explore.

In the discussion so far I have assumed that individuals cannot

---

[25] Tully, *A Discourse on Property*, p. 71. See Grotius, *Rights of War and Peace*, Bk. II, Ch. ii (p. 86), and Cicero, *De Finibus*, Bk. III, Ch. xx.

acquire exclusive rights to make use of resources without some abrogation of original communism. As part of the argument already referred to, however, James Tully denies that this is the case. The point of individual appropriation in the state of nature, he says, is not to abrogate original communism by establishing non-communal property rights; it is rather to *realize* or *consummate* original common property in human use. Tully claims that Locke stresses this fact 'by pointing out that the agent with an exclusive right still remains "a Tenant in common".'[26] But the passage Tully cites to support this claim provides no support whatsoever for his interpretation; its meaning is seriously misconstrued by being taken out of context. What Locke actually says is this:

The Fruit, or Venison, which nourishes the wild Indian, *who knows no Inclosure, and is still a Tenant in common*, must be his, and so his, i.e. a part of him, that another can no longer have any right to it, before it can do him any good for the support of his Life. (II. 26; my emphasis)

The phrase I have emphasized refers to the Indian's relation to the *land* where he roams not to the fruit and venison that he eats. (Fruit and venison are not possible subjects for 'Inclosure' in Locke's sense; that term is never used by him except to refer to land.) Thus the exclusive right and the tenancy in common refer to *different things*: the first to the fruit and venison, the second to the land where it was obtained. Tully very seriously misleads us by suggesting that on Locke's view the Indian remain a tenant in common of the goods he has appropriated.

That passage apart, there is evidence on both sides in this question. With regard to 'Commons, which remain so by Compact', Locke says that appropriation of some sort is necessary, for without it 'the Common is of no use' (II. 28). Applied to natural resources, that supports Tully's view. On the other hand, Locke also says 'that the Property of Labour should be able to over-balance the Community of Land' (II. 40), and that seems more compatible with the usual interpretation that appropriation abrogates rather than consummates original communism. The consideration which seems to me decisive, however, is this. To anticipate slightly the discussion in the following sections, Locke maintains that an appropriator acquires the same sort of exclusive right over his resources as he has already in relation to his own person and his own labour. Since the

[26] Tully, *A Discourse on Property*, p. 105.

latter rights are regarded by Locke as the polar opposite of common rights, it would seem that their introduction into the world of external resources must be conceived to bring an end to, rather than consummate or realize, the original common property of mankind.

4. LOCKE'S CONCEPTION OF PRIVATE PROPERTY

I have noted already Tully's claim that individual property rights in Locke's state of nature do not amount to *private* property, in the sense in which that is nowadays understood. The sense Tully has in mind is given by C. B. Macpherson's definition of private property: '[I]t is a right to dispose of, or alienate, as well as to use; and it is a right which is not conditional on the owner's performance of any social function.'[27] Tully also suggests that private property would be defined by the fact that an owner has the right to 'abuse' the resources that he owns and the right to exclude others from their use. He suggests that Lockean property rights fail to satisfy these definitions in two respects. (1) They are not rights of abuse; on the contrary, a man 'has not the Liberty to destroy . . . so much as any Creature in his Possession, but where some nobler use, than its bare preservation calls for it' (II. 6). (2) They are not independent of social function: Locke, according to Tully, 'holds the belief that any kind of property is not only conditional on the owner's perform-ance of a social function, but is held specifically for the sake of the performance of a social function: to preserve mankind.'[28]

Point (1) is valid but (2) is suspect. On Locke's account, property is held by an individual primarily for the sake of the performance of that individual's duty of *self*-preservation (I. 88) and secondly, for the support, comfort, and convenience of his being (II. 34 and 36–7). Locke makes it clear in a number of places that property is not held by an individual for the benefit of others: 'Property, whose Original is from the Right a Man has to use any of the Inferior Creatures for the Subsistence and Comfort of his Life, is for the benefit and sole Advantage of the Proprietor' (I. 92)—and, we may add, his family (I. 97). No doubt the result of a lot of people holding property on these terms is that a social function gets

---

[27] Macpherson, *Democratic Theory*, p. 126, and Tully, *A Discourse on Property*, p. 99.
[28] Tully, *A Discourse on Property*, p. 99.

performed—namely, the preservation of a lot of people. But it is silly to suggest that an individual holds property in order that *he* can perform this social function: he holds it, on Locke's account, to satisfy his own wants and needs. There is, of course, the further point, which we have already discussed, that a proprietor must not withold his surplus resources from a desperately needy man. But I doubt whether this proviso, which in Locke's view is unlikely to be invoked very often (I. 41), amounts to the doctrine of a social function in Macpherson's sense. If it does, then very few theories satisfy Macpherson's definition of private property: Nozick's perhaps and Filmer's, but certainly not the theories of Grotius, Pufendorf, Hume, Smith, Bentham, Mill, and so on.

Even if Locke's individual property rights do not fit Tully's rather narrow definition of private property, they may still fall under the somewhat more generous concept which we have provided. In Chapter 2 private property was understood in terms of the concept of the allocation of a resource to a particular person on the basis that it would be for that person to determine how, by whom, and on what terms the resource was to be used. An object is mine if it is for me rather than for anyone else to say what is to be done with it. How does Locke's concept stand in relation to this definition?

We should note, first, that Locke used 'property' in a very wide sense, so that it covered rights of all sorts, including personal rights of life, liberty, and security, as well as rights in relation to resources. Tully points out that it is a mistake to say that Locke's use of the term is ambiguous on the ground that it sometimes means 'Estate' and sometimes 'Life, Liberty and Estate': to say that is to confuse the sense of the term with its reference.[29] The sense of Locke's term 'property' is always the same: its nature is 'that without a Man's own consent it cannot be taken from him' (II. 193). This definition may be applied quite consistently and unambiguously to all imprescriptible individual rights.

But in this sense, it follows that a man may have *property in* a resource even though he does not have *private* property (in our sense). As Locke points out, a tenant for life has property in the land which is let to him to the extent that is specified in the original grant, because what he gets from the grant are rights in relation to the land which cannot be taken away from him without his consent

[29] Tully, *A Discourse on Property*, pp. 112–16, esp. p. 116.

(II. 194). So, certainly something more than his use of the term 'property' is necessary to show that Locke believed in private property in the state of nature.

If we look closely, we find that the term 'property *in*' is used as a general term to characterize rights of all sorts relating to resources, whether they are limited rights, common rights, or private and exclusive rights. A tenant for life is said to have a property *in* his land (II. 194); Eve is said to have property *in* the creatures of the earth together with Adam (I. 29); and a man is said to have property *in* the hundred bushels of apples he has gathered (II. 46). This is Locke's most general usage. But he reserves another terminology specifically for the case of exclusive individual rights in a resource: this is the usage in which an object is described as 'the property *of*' an individual. The difference is this. To say that A has property *in* X is consistent with (though it does not entail) someone else, B, having property in X as well. But to say that X is the property *of* A is to deny that anyone else has property in X: it is to indicate that the rights of others have somehow been excluded. Thus, for example, when Locke says 'every Man has a Property in his own Person. This nobody has any right to but himself' (II. 27), the second sentence is not a redundant repetition of the first. Rather it distinguishes the sort of property that a man has in his person and makes it appropriate for Locke to refer later in the same passage to a man's labour as 'the unquestionable Property *of* the Labourer'.

Similarly, though Locke sometimes refers to private appropriation as fixing or beginning a property *in* an object (using terminology that could also describe a man's original common right in the object), he often stresses the more exclusive usage:

[T]he Grass that my Horse has bit; the Turfs my Servant has cut; and the Ore I have digg'd in any place where I have a right to them in common with others, become *my Property*, without the assignation or consent of anybody. (II. 28; my emphasis)

As much land as a Man Tills, Plants, Improves, Cultivates, and can use the Product of, so much is *his Property*. He by his labour does as it were enclose it from the Common. (II. 32; my emphasis)

The more specific usage—'property' with a possessive pronoun (equivalent to 'property of')—tells us what sort of property in an object an appropriator acquires when he appropriates it.

A number of writers—notably Bentham and, more recently,

Macpherson —have pointed out that strictly speaking it is a misusage to apply the word 'property' to things.[30] We should describe *rights* not things as property, and we should regard sentences like 'That Porsche is your property' as, at best, misleading figures of speech. But Macpherson also perceives that the tendency to describe things as property is linked historically to the growth of private property in a capitalist economy.[31] Since more or less all the rights that there could be in relation to a given thing could now be held together and exchanged together in a single transaction by a single individual, and as this sort of transaction became the most common way of dealing with resources in the marketplace, there was no point in distinguishing between the thing itself and the various rights in it that were being dealt with. The abbreviated (and, in theory, figurative) usage served as a quite satisfactory indication of what was going on. No doubt Macpherson has exaggerated the role that Locke played in the legitimation of early English capitalism, but his account of the connection between the property-as-thing usage and private property describes accurately what is going on in Locke's discussion. If I have property *in* an object, what cannot be taken away from me without my own consent is the particular right I have. But if the object is *my property*, then it is the thing itself which cannot be taken away from me, since my right now excludes any entitlement which anyone else might have to use or otherwise deal with it against my will.

We now need to add to this Locke's views about the content of property rights. The view expressed in the *First Treatise* is that property in an object always amounts to some sort of privilege of using it: 'What other Property Man can have in the Creatures, but the Liberty of using them, is hard to be understood' (I. 39). So if several people have property in the same resource, then they all have some sort of right to use it, whereas if the resource is the property of someone in particular then he alone has a right to make use of it. Locke maintains that 'the utmost Property Man is capable of . . . is to have a right to destroy any thing by using it' (I. 39). In this case, if a man has 'utmost Property' in a thing, then the thing must be his property, for otherwise his right to destroy it would be inconsistent with someone else's liberty to use it.

[30] See Bentham, *Introduction to Principles of Morals and Legislation*, p. 211 n; and Macpherson, 'Meaning of Property'.
[31] Macpherson, 'Meaning of Property', pp. 3 ff.

Locke, as we shall see, does not limit use to physical consumption. His early examples in Chapter 5 are all cases of food—cases indeed of individuals destroying things by using them. But later he says that giving things away rather than consuming them oneself, and exchanging them for other things, are ways of making use of them, and he also suggests that some objects may be kept for aesthetic reasons rather than for the satisfaction of bodily needs (II. 46). This indicates that a given object may have a range of possible uses so that there are decisions to be made about when, how, and by whom, the object is to be used. Are these nuts to be eaten now, or tomorrow, or stored for the winter? Are they to be eaten at all, or put on the mantelpiece for decoration? Are they to be sold today for a certain price or witheld from the market till prices improve (Locke refers to the owner's right to barter)? If more than one person has property in the nuts, then some fair way must be found for taking these decisions. But if the nuts are someone's property— that is, if one individual has all the rights which individuals can have in relation to them—then Locke implies that it is for him to decide what to do with the nuts and that no one else has any right to impugn his decision or to enforce a contrary view by putting the nuts to some other use.

There are three important qualifications to this account. First, though Locke's concept of use is very wide, it does not comprehend wasteful or negligent destruction. An owner is not entitled to decide to allow his goods to perish uselessly in his possession (II. 46). In Locke's view, such a decision is tantamount to an abandonment of exclusive property in the goods. But what counts as use and what counts as useless destruction is for *the owner* to decide: briefly, anything he takes to be useful to himself counts as a use of the object however wasteful it may seem to someone else. We shall discuss this further in section 14.

Secondly, as we have noted, all of this is subject to Locke's insistence that the demands of a desperately needy man take precedence over the ordinary decisions of a property owner. But since such cases will be rare in a flourishing private property economy, the account we have given will cover the normal run of cases.

Thirdly, Locke insists from time to time that a proprietor has a duty to look to the benefit of his family, as well as to his own benefit: 'Men are not Proprietors of what they have meerly for themselves, their Children have a Title to part of it, and have their kind of Right joyn'd with their Parents . . . .' (I. 88).[32] Still, this is not incompatible with the idea of private property, in the sense that Lockean rights are not dependent on the discharge of any function which cannot be related to the private affairs of the proprietor.

5. THE STATE OF NATURE

Locke is concerned to show that private property rights are possible apart from government and positive law. He wants to show that there are principles of natural justice which govern property-holdings and that these can be deployed critically against any government that threatens to interfere with or redistribute the property of its citizens. To this end, he argues that property-owning got under way at a time when there was no government, and that the function or 'end' of government is to protect property holdings that it has not itself constituted.[33]

We shall discuss the details of this theory in the sections that follow. But first let us deal with a preliminary objection. A common objection to Locke's theory is that rights of private ownership, properly understood, are inconceivable apart from positive law. Without settled institutions of positive law, there cannot be either the precision and certainty or the security and confidence which we take for granted in modern property relations. Precision and certainty are guaranteed by the settled and determinate rights and procedures of civil law. An owner in our society has a whole cluster of rights, privileges, powers, liabilities, duties, and immunities, but each of them is minutely defined by the law of the land. The objects of property are defined precisely by standardized surveying and specified boundaries, and there are established systems of title, encumbrance, and conveyancing to ensure that uncertainty about entitlement is kept to a minimum. An owner's security and confidence are similarly constituted by positive law. Each incident

---

[32] See also *Two Treatises*, I, sects. 87–90 and II, sects. 182–3. This, by the way, makes nonsense of J. P. Day's criticism that Locke fails to account for the moral rights of an Indian's wife and children to eat some of the apples he has gathered: Day, 'Locke on Property', pp. 208–9. See also Plamenatz, *Man and Society*, Vol. I, pp. 244 ff.

[33] *Two Treatises*, II, sects. 3, 124, 134, 136, *et passim*. See also Waldron, 'Locke, Tully, and the Regulation of Property', p. 98.

of ownership is related to specific procedures for enforcement, and the owner knows or can find out exactly what social force he can call on in given circumstances to uphold his legitimate claims. He has a reasonable expectation that by and large other citizens will abide by the settled rules of property. But he does not need to base this on any optimistic view of their moral character; he places his faith rather in the recourse he can have (and which they know he can have) to the apparatus of writs, courts, bailiffs, and policemen to uphold his rights. Since none of this is available in a state of nature, why should we accept Locke's view that there can be private property—or indeed any sort of property—in that situation?

The two points, precision and security, need to be dealt with separately.

Locke, I think, would acknowledge that property in the state of nature cannot be as precisely or as clearly determined as in civil society. A couple of examples will suffice. Powers of bequest and inheritance may be primitive and inchoate in the state of nature whereas they are bound to be clearly and precisely defined in civil society to avoid economic chaos every time somebody dies.[34] Also, objects of property may be defined very loosely in the state of nature (e.g. X is the owner of 'the field by the old oak tree') whereas they will be defined with precision in civil society (X is the owner of a piece of land of so many rods and perches with such-and-such surveyed boundaries etc.). But this does not mean that the state of nature can have no property system at all. X's natural exclusive property right in an object is, as it were, the *concept* of a private property right in that object: it amounts to little more than the abstract principle that it is for X to decide what to do with the object (loosely and naturally defined). Although such a rule is imprecise, it can nevertheless be followed in the ordinary course of things. It is like most moral principles: we know what counts as respecting it and violating it in normal cases and we can adjust our behaviour accordingly; difficulties arise only in the marginal cases that its rather vaguely understood borders generate from time to time.

The point of moving to civil society is to tighten matters up so that *all* the cases of the application of the principle can be dealt with. The function of civil law is to pin down more precisely the

---

[34] I have discussed this further in Waldron, 'Locke's Account of Inheritance'. (See also sect. 19, below.)

rules and distributions that already exist in a rough and ready form. As Locke puts it, 'The Obligations of the Law of Nature, cease not in Society but only in many cases are *drawn closer . . .*' (II. 135; my emphasis). To put it another way, the move from natural to civil law involves a shift from private property as a concept to a particular settled conception of private property. (An analogy may help. In exactly the same way, the transition to civil society will involve a shift from a situation governed by the moral concept of murder—that is, the vague and abstract idea that it is wrong deliberately to kill people—to a situation governed by a precisely defined legal conception of homicide. The fact that eventually we need to pin things down to such a precise conception does not show that there could not be, or that people could not follow, a moral rule against murder before that.)

However, the second point (the point about confidence and security) reveals a worrying tension in Locke's theory. On the one hand, he believes that because of its simplicity and abstraction, the law of nature 'is easier to be understood than the Phansies and intricate Contrivances of Men' (II. 12). Natural man, he says, finds it easier to follow and obey principles of natural reason than detailed and often counter-intuitive principles of custom and municipal law (I. 58). But he also insists that 'the greater part [of men are] no strict Observers of Equity and Justice' and that therefore 'the enjoyment of . . . property . . . in this state [of nature] is very unsafe, very insecure' (II. 123).[35] This is the reason men seek out and are willing to join civil societies. Now if, as a matter of course, most people do not respect property, it is difficult to see how anyone could ever acquire the sort of expectations and the reasonable degree of settled confidence which property relations, on most accounts, essentially involve. The law of nature may make something mine from a God's-eye point of view; but if most of the people have not internalized the corresponding rule, it is difficult to see how this can make any difference to human affairs.[36] The point is that property is so much a matter of the interplay of expectations that it cannot be imagined in circumstances where the expectations in question are unrealistic, ungrounded, or even non-existent. This is a dangerous point for Locke, for it seems to imply that the rules set up and enforced in a civil society may be the first real rules of property in any practical sense.

[35] See the discussion in Ashcraft, 'Locke's State of Nature'.
[36] For the internal aspect of rules, see Hart, *Concept of Law*, pp. 55–6.

Perhaps the two positions can be reconciled historically. In a number of places in the *Second Treatise*, Locke contrasts a 'Golden Age' of rough equality and native virtue with more recent times in which men's minds have been corrupted by 'vain Ambition, and amor sceleratus habendi, evil Concupiscence' (II. III). In the earlier time, 'there were but few Trespasses and few Offenders' and so there was no need for any apparatus of enforcement: 'The equality of a simple poor way of living confineing their desires within the narrow bounds of each mans small propertie made few controversies and so no need of any laws to decide them' (II. 107). In these circumstances, private property rights could be more or less universally respected and property rules sufficiently internalized to allow us to speak of a natural property system. The later phase—the age of corruption—is linked with the introduction of a money economy and the emergence of larger and more unequal possessions which it makes possible (II. 36–7). In these circumstances men acquire acquisitive and aggressive dispositions and the state of nature takes on a more Hobbesian complexion. But it is distinguished from Hobbes's natural condition by this fact at least: that instead of being a moral vacuum, it is tainted by a nostalgic awareness that property rights were once respected, that the rules are still in a sense there, and that it is probably possible even now to determine who owns what if only we had the leisure and security to do it. Thus men may disregard property rules; but they will have in the back of their minds a vague and guilty awareness that there are rules of property which they are disregarding. The age of corruption, then, will be an age in which men are vaguely conscious of their wickedness rather than one in which they are morally agnostic. This would link Locke's account more closely to the image of the Fall, and provide an important point of contrast with Hobbes, who, as far as I know, avoids this imagery in his characterization of the state of nature. I think that if this contrast can be sustained, it enables Locke to avoid the conventionalist (and therefore potentially absolutist) implications of Hobbes's acount of property.[37]

I find this an attractive and plausible solution to Locke's problem. It faces a slight difficulty inasmuch as Locke, in various places, insisted on indicating a role for government (of a sort) even in the 'Golden Age', and often associated the age of corruption not

---

[37] See Hobbes, *Leviathan*, Ch. 13, p. 188, Ch. 15, pp. 202–3, and Ch. 18, p. 234.

with a later phase of the state of nature but with a more advanced—and corrupt— phase of politics (II. 111). But this complication generates in turn a more sophisticated and, if anything, an even more attractive reconstruction of the Lockean position.

In the paragraphs with which we are concerned here(II. 105–12 and also 74–6), Locke presents a gradualist anthropological account of the development of political society, tracing the evolution of institutions of government out of the informal institutions of parenthood and warlordism. Men tended to trust implicitly in all their affairs the determinations of those who had had any sort of natural or even temporary authority over them. But with the growth in the use of money and the increase in population which indirectly that made possible, possessions gradually expanded, inequality increased, and quarrels and covetousness grew with it. Political power (the power to determine disputes and punish infractions) assumed a greater importance in social life, and became at the same time more complicated and more liable to abuse. At that stage, as Locke put it, 'Men found it necessary to examine more carefully the Original and Rights of Government' (II. 111), to begin thinking critically about politics, and to set up more explicit and articulated political institutions. They found it necessary to be clear about the distinction between father and ruler, and to make explicit the terms of the trust which had hitherto defined implicitly the role of leader and judge among them.

This gradualist account of human politicization and the growth of political self-consciousness is in marked contrast to the simple periodization of Locke's abstract theory of politics. On the one hand, we have the story of a family or a few families living together in conditions in which politics over the centuries became increasingly though perhaps imperceptibly more important so that the 'Family by degrees grew up into a Commonwealth' (II. 110); while on the other hand, we have the theory of a clear break between a stateless state of nature and civil society, with the social contract as the decisive turning point. The two stories are not, of course, inconsistent, nor is it inconsistent of Locke to concede the gist of Filmer's argument about the intimate historical connection between fatherhood and kingship while rejecting such a connection absolutely at the level of political philosophy.[38] Rather, the second story

[38] See *Two Treatises*, II, sects. 2, 64–71, 170–1.

provides a set of moral categories for a critical understanding of the first (which Locke takes to be the literal history of the matter). Just as Locke's tribesmen, in the later stages of the world, found it necessary to consider more carefully what had been going on, so the historical data need to be interpreted using the concepts of Locke's abstract theory (the concepts of original freedom, consent, trust, etc.) before it is applied normatively to the modern situation.[39]

Confusion will certainly arise if we think that the abstract story must match the historical account period for period and event for event. We will get into difficulty, for example, if we ask exactly when in the development of patriarchal leadership the social contract occurred, or exactly when the state of nature came to an end. Those categories should be used for interpreting, not for dating the historical material.[40]

This, I think, is the source of the apparent tension in Locke's account of the security of property in the state of nature. If we understand the state of nature as a specific historical period, we feel inclined to insist that it must have been one thing or the other: either it was harmonious and peaceful, affording a secure basis for property relations (in which case, why were people impelled to foresake it?); or it was Hobbesian in character, disorderly and chaotic, making property relations impossible (in which case, how can we speak of natural property rights?). But the truth is that the concept of the state of nature ranges analytically over a period of human history in which disorder and insecurity were increasing and property relations becoming gradually more perilous. Since this historical period was also one in which, 'by an insensible change' (II. 76), categories of politics, law, and leadership were assuming a greater role in human affairs and were becoming more and more significant as bulwarks of property relations, the tension in Locke's theory disappears. From a historical point of view, property was always fairly secure, though the source of the security changed somewhat over time. But from an abstract point of view, property relations are both secure and insecure in the state of nature, and civil society both makes property relations possible now and responds to them as natural relations that already exist.

[39] See also, Locke, *Essay*, Bk. IV, Ch. xvi, sect. 11 (Vol. 2, p. 258). Richard Ashcraft also cites material from Locke's journal that is relevant here: see Ashcraft, op. cit. p. 899 n.

[40] These paragraphs compress a much longer argument which I have developed in Waldron, 'John Locke: Social Contract versus Political Anthropology'.

6. PRIVATE PROPERTY AS THE SATISFACTION OF NEED

Locke's task is to 'to shew, how Men might come to have a property in several parts of that which God gave to Mankind in common, and that without any express Compact of all the Commoners' (II. 25).

The first move he makes is to suggest that private property is necessary if any human needs are to be satisfied by natural resources. 'Though the earth and all its fruits belong to men in common, yet being given for the use of Men, there must of necessity be a means to appropriate them some way or other before they can be of any use, or at all beneficial to any particular Man' (II. 26.) A natural resource cannot be made use of at all, Locke claims, unless it is appropriated to the exclusive use of one particular individual. The example he uses to support the point is that of food:

The Fruit, or Venison, which nourishes the wild Indian . . . must be his, and so his, i.e. a part of him, that another can no longer have any right to it, before it can do him any good for the support of his Life. (II. 26)

He that is nourished by the Acorns he pickt up under an Oak, or the Apples he gathered from the Trees in the Wood, has certainly appropriated them to himself. No Body can deny but the nourishment is his. (II. 28)

In the case of food, the point is plausible enough. We may be endowed in common, but nourishment is, biologically speaking, an individual matter. As Locke claims, there must come a point in the gathering/cooking/eating/digesting process when a particular piece of food becomes useful to one individual alone to the exclusion of all others. By the time his gastric juices go to work on it (barring the possibility of regurgitation) the common right of others to be nourished by that morsel must have been excluded.

But the argument is a very weak one, on two counts. First, the individual property that it establishes does not involve any right to choose which of a number of possible uses shall be made of a food object. People could be nourished and the fruits of the earth used without anybody having that sort of discretion. The argument goes no way towards establishing, for example, that they have a right to store food objects for their later use or to make exclusive decisions about when to sell them and so on. It does not, in other words, establish private property in the sense we have defined.

Secondly, even to the limited extent that it does establish *exclusive* individual rights, the argument establishes them only for the case of food (and perhaps items of clothing and personal furniture). It does not establish any necessity for exclusive rights in such things as housing, for example, because a house may be useful to one individual without there being any necessity that others be excluded from its use.[41] Locke claims that 'the condition of Humane Life, which requires Labour and Materials to work on, necessarily introduces private Possessions' (II. 35). But this is wrong. Men can labour and obey God's command to subdue the earth, without requiring that their means of production or their raw material should be held as the exclusive property of individuals. A field may be cultivated by a whole tribe and decisions about the use of ploughs and oxen, etc. made on a community-wide basis. Private enclosure and cultivation by individuals for individuals are certainly not necessary for land to be made useful to humans. (Locke implicitly concedes this at a later stage of the chapter on property. He notes that, although in early times pastoral tribes derived undoubted benefits from the land, 'yet it was commonly without any fix'd property in the ground they made use of' (II. 38). At this point, he seems to have abandoned any suggestion that private possessions are necessarily introduced by the sheer fact of human use of common resources.) Of course, it is true that a group or a community cannot use resources without excluding the common rights of mankind as a whole. To that extent, Locke's argument expresses an important point. But it will not give him the conclusion he wants—namely, exclusive rights which can be asserted against one's community as well as against all the rest of mankind.

Perhaps, however, the argument from need can be given a slightly different interpretation. Although strictly speaking it is possible for humans to use land without individually enclosing it, such a use may be thought of as uneconomic and so as a violation of the spirit of God's command to make use of what he has given us. He requires us not just to survive but to 'Be Fruitful, and Multiply, and Replenish the Earth' (I. 33). If Locke believes, with many ancient as well as modern economists, that communal use of land is less efficient than private use, to this extent he may be justified in saying that 'The Law Man was under, was rather for *appropriating*' (II. 36.)

---

[41] Both Laslett and Tully have noted Locke's earlier view that 'Victuals, clothes, ornaments, riches, and all other good things of this life are provided from *common use*'—*Essays on the Law of Nature*, p. 212: see Laslett's footnote to Locke, *Two Treatises*, II, sect. 26, and Tully, *A Discourse on Property*, p. 103. But it may be straining the meaning of the emphasized passage here to infer a direct contradiction between this theory and Locke's view in the *Two Treatises*.

Certainly Locke sometimes leans in the direction of such a view. He points out that a man who appropriates land for himself by private enclosure 'does not lessen but increase the common stock of mankind' (II. 37). By his industry and efforts he 'has increased the stock of Corn, which [people] wanted' (II. 36). Even if he keeps all the corn he has produced for himself, he nevertheless reduces the pressure on other common resources because he feeds himself now from the use of a much smaller piece of land than that which he roamed over before. So others who continue to use common land have per capita more land to roam over than they had before his enclosure (II. 37). (Locke is mistaken, though, in thinking that this argument depends on the fact that the encloser derives a higher level of utility—'a greater plenty of the conveniencys of life'—now than he derived as a commoner. Even if the utility he derives is the same, the land he needs to use in order to derive it on an exclusive basis is likely to be considerably smaller than the area of originally common land divided by the original number of commoners.) On this basis, Locke claims that, in economic terms, societies where most resources have been appropriated privately are more prosperous for *all* their inhabitants (even if some of them are not appropriators) than societies where resources remain common. This is the reason for the famous remark that 'a King of a large fruitful Territory' in America, where land remained common among the Indians, 'feeds, lodges, and is clad worse than a day labourer in England' (II. 41).

But although Locke inclines in this direction, it is worth noting that his economic arguments are much more about the importance of cultivation as such than about the importance of *private* cultivation. The contrast is always between societies where land has been privately enclosed and societies where it has not been cultivated at all. Thus, when Locke asks rhetorically, 'whether in the wild woods and uncultivated waste of America left to Nature, without any improvement, tillage or husbandry, a thousand acres will yield the needy and wretched inhabitants as many conveniences of life as ten acres of equally fertile land doe in Devonshire where they are well cultivated?' (II. 37), the question highlights the utility of cultivated land,, but does not distinguish between the respective economies of private and communist cultivation. We find a similar lacuna in the famous 'Industrious and Rational' passage:

God gave the World to Man in Common; but since he gave it them for their benefit, and the greatest Conveniences of Life they were capable to draw from it, it cannot be supposed he meant it should always remain common and uncultivated. He gave it to use of the Industrious and Rational (and Labour was to be his Title to it); . . . (II. 34)

Locke has not here considered the possibility that a piece of land may be both common *and* cultivated; nor has he considered the possibility that the 'Industrious and Rational' cultivators may be whole communities working together rather than individuals working on their own initiative. Because these points have not been considered, it is, I think, anachronistic to attribute to him any argument about the comparative economic merits of private and communist modes of production.

In any case, though Locke extols the prosperity wrought by intensive cultivation, he does not view it unambiguously as a good thing. On the contrary, the sort of intensive and extensive cultivation that is spurred by the introduction of money on Locke's account is linked with the growth of corruption and covetousness in human affairs. When he talks about 'The equality of a simple poor way of liveing' in the early ages of the world (II. 107), there is no sense at all that these souls are being castigated for their failure to pursue a more enthusiastic agriculture! On the contrary, the very Indians whose economy is ridiculed in the chapter on property are presented in an almost Rousseauesque light in other sections of the *Treatises*.[42] The fact is, as we shall see, that Locke's attitude towards the modernization of the economy is a profoundly ambiguous one.

7. APPROPRIATION BY LABOUR

Since exclusive possession is not on the whole necessary for human subsistence and production, we must imagine the Lockean appropriator not as any ordinary person struggling along with others to wrest a living from nature, but rather as the peculiarly resourceful and opportunistic character portrayed, for example, by Rousseau in the opening lines of Part Two of the *Second Discourse*. He is the individual who sees personal advantage in rupturing what might

---

[42] See Locke, *Two Treatises*, I, sect. 58; II, sects. 36, 107–8, 111. But see also the discussion in sect. 16, below. Cf. Rousseau, *Discourse on the Origin of Inequality*, Pt. I.

have been a previously satisfactory mode of subsistence by enclosing land and seizing materials for himself. He is the man who announces that these goods are now to be regarded as his exclusively, and, in Rousseau's wry phrase, finds 'people simple enough to believe him'.[43] This person is the true founder of private property; and this is the sort of economic opportunism that a Lockean theory takes it upon itself to vindicate.

The question Locke must answer is this: what distinguishes the appropriator from the rest of mankind, who originally had common rights in the resources he has appropriated? Of all the actions that are performed in the process of opportunistic appropriation—selecting an object, planning how to get hold of it, seizing it, marking it out as one's own, defending it, modifying it, using it, destroying it even, securing acquiescence of others in one's exclusive title to it—of all these actions, which are the *crucial* ones on which the moral title of the appropriator is based? If appropriation is vindicated, then everyone's moral position has been altered: the appropriator acquires rights and powers, and everyone else duties, that they did not have before.[44] So something that has been done must have made a big moral difference. What and how?

Locke poses this problem explicitly in the course of his discussion of the nourishment theory. At some point, the food that a man eats must become *his* in the sense that his use of it is necessarily incompatible with others' common rights. But at which point? 'When did they begin to be his? When he digested? Or when he eat? Or when he boiled? Or when he brought them home? Or when he pickt them up?' (II. 28) The answer dictated by the logic of the nourishment theory (the answer based on physically necessary individuation) is the first or the second of the points Locke mentions. But the answer he opts for now is the last: 'And 'tis plain, if the first gathering made them not his, nothing else could. That labour put a distinction between them and common' (II. 28). The food, Locke says, was 'produced by the spontaneous hand of Nature' (II. 26), but in going out and gathering it for himself the man takes the initiative from nature and 'removes it out of the common state Nature left it in' (II. 30). His energetic initiative identifies the object peculiarly with himself and his purposes, and

[43] Rousseau, *Discourse on the Origin of Inequality*, Pt. 2 (p. 76).
[44] See below, Ch. 7, sect. 4, n. 22.

distinguishes it from other resources which are identified with human purposes only in the general sort of way established by the terms of God's donation. There is now something about the object—something in its history, if you like— which associates it naturally with him.

This Labour Theory of Appropriation is sometimes contrasted with theories of 'First Taking' or 'First Occupancy', but the contrast is not really important for the early examples Locke uses. Gathering nuts from the ground, picking an apple from a tree, and killing a deer can be regarded equally as forms of taking resources or as forms of labouring on them. With regard to the fruits and animals of the earth, Locke's theory is more or less coextensive with what any plausible theory of First Occupancy would entail. (One possible exception: Locke suggests (II. 30) that a hunter is entitled to the rabbit he is chasing even before he catches it; this is not what a First Occupancy Theory would entail and, indeed, it represents almost a Fichtean extreme of the application of the Labour Theory.) However, the contrast between labour and mere taking or occupancy *is* important in the case of land. The idea of occupying a piece of land is not entirely straightforward: strictly speaking all that one occupies is the space taken up by one's body.[45] But occupation has traditionally been understood as marking a piece of land off as one's own by enclosure or some other physical act which brings one's person into relation with the whole area of land in question. Locke insists that this is not sufficient. A man must *work* on land in order to appropriate it: 'As much Land as a man Tills, Plants, Improves, Cultivates and can use the Product of, so much is his Property. He by his Labour does, as it were, inclose it from the Common' (II. 32). If land is fenced off without cultivation then, Locke tells us, 'this part of the Earth, notwithstanding his Inclosure, was still to be looked on as Waste, and might be the Possession of any other' (II. 38).[46]

This leaves a slight lacuna in Locke's account which critics like Hume and Kant have been quick to exploit. Before a man can cultivate a piece of ground, he must take it into his possession and exclude others from its use; otherwise their exercise of common rights might make his cultivation impossible. On this basis, Hume

[45] See Becker, *Property Rights*, Ch. 3.
[46] Olivecrona claims that enclosure, although not sufficient for Lockean appropriation, is certainly necessary: Olivecrona, 'Locke's Theory of Appropriation', p. 228.

and Kant attempt to set up a dilemma for Locke. Either the would-be appropriator is entitled to exclude others from the land for the purpose of cultivating it or he is not. If he is, then something other than cultivation must give rise to exclusive rights. If he is not, then his cultivation is based on robbery and can establish no right. The Labour Theory, then, is either redundant or inadequate. Hume and Kant are right to note that Locke did not deal with this point.[47] Because he tended to identify cultivation with individual cultivation, he did not (as we have already seen) face squarely the problem that might be posed by the clash of different modes of production in the same area.

There are two possible ways around the difficulty. Locke might insist toughmindedly that the land remains common until it is actually cultivated; if a would-be appropriator is unlucky enough to pick a field where people are picnicking, he must either plough around them and take title to the field minus the patch in the middle where they are sitting or else abandon his enterprise for the time being and get up earlier than the picnickers the next day.

A second way out is suggested by Olivecrona. He maintains that enclosure is a necessary (though not a sufficient) condition for appropriation. So if enclosure precedes cultivation, we may say that it generates some sort of conditional right—i.e. a right subject to a condition subsequent, that the land be cultivated by the encloser as soon as practically possible.[48] (In terms of the terminology I developed in Chapter 4, Lockean property rights would be doubly conditional.) I suspect that this second view is the one Locke would favour: it makes a sort of concession to the Occupancy Theory but retains the ultimate importance of labour. But both ways out are consistent with what he says.

So far we have noted only the terms of the theory Locke is going to defend. We have said nothing about his defence of it. Certainly, Labour Theories of Appropriation are quite common in the history of philosophical thought about property.[49] Even positivistic philosophers like Hobbes and Bentham, who maintain that property rights are entirely a matter of convention justified if at all by their

[47] See Hume, *Treatise*, Bk. III, Pt. ii, sect. 3, p. 505 n. 1. Kant, *Philosophy of Law*, Pt. I, sects. 15–17 (Hastie's translation of *Metaphysical Elements of Justice*, pp. 92–7). I do not have the Prussian Academy reference for this passage.

[48] Olivecrona, 'Locke's Theory of Appropriation', p. 228.

[49] See Ryan's acerbic comments about 'grandmother egg-sucking instructions' in 'Property, Liberty, and *On Liberty*', p. 226.

utility, drop their guard from time to time and say that the natural function of positive law is to secure to every man the fruits of his labour.[50] Locke himself notes that appropriation by labour is regarded favourably by all contemporary systems of law: it is the basis, for example, of a fisherman's legal as well as his natural right to the fish he has taken from the ocean and it is the basis of squatters' rights and rights of prescription in many legal systems (II. 36). In other contexts, Locke claims that where a 'practice is Universal, 'tis reasonable to think the cause is Natural' (I. 88).[51] But he never regards this as an excuse for avoiding the task of justification. In the present case, justification is very important, for the implications of the Labour Theory are considerable and, from some points of view, oppressive. It may be worth pausing to review some of these implications so that we can see the extent of the justificatory task that Locke faces.

Locke's theory purports to give a certain moral priority over the rest of mankind to those who appropriate resources. Everyone, of course, remains entitled to the means of survival—appropriation does not affect that—but an appropriator is alone entitled to derive comfort and enjoyment from the resources he has taken. He has a liberty to *use and enjoy* those resources, and this is now a liberty which, by virtue of his appropriation, others lack. Their situation has been changed by his action to one of duty: they are now morally required individually and collectively to refrain from taking or using the resources without his consent. Much as they would like to eat his apples, and even if they could derive greater pleasure from them than he could, they are obliged to leave them alone. They cannot even call on his resources for urgent common or public purposes without his consent; if he or his representatives refuse to contribute anything, for example, to the cost of supporting a government (once governments are instituted), there is nothing anyone can do (II. 140).[52] Appropriation, therefore, wreaks a drastic change in the position of non-appropriators. From being tenants-in-common of God's largesse, they are now placed in the

[50] e.g. Hobbes, *Leviathan*, Ch. 13, pp. 186 and 188; Bentham, 'Principles of the Civil Code', p. 98.

[51] But cf. Locke, *Essay*, Bk. I, Ch. iii, sect. 4: 'There cannot any one moral rule be proposed whereof a man may not justly demand a reason.'

[52] It has to be admitted that Locke slides around a bit on this point, shifting from a requirement of individual consent to taxation to a requirement of a majority of representatives' consent: Locke, *Two Treatises*, II, sects. 140–2.

position of moral dependence, for everything but bare survival, on the say-so of individual property-owners.

Another way of putting this, of course, is to say that Locke's property rights are, in the terms we have used, *special* rights. They arise contingently out of the actions of individual appropriators— indeed out of the actions of the very people who stand to benefit from the obligations they impose.[53] They cut across all but the most basic of the general rights and powers with which men were endowed originally by God. So Locke faces the challenge which, as we saw earlier, was posed by Samuel Pufendorf: he has to explain 'how a bare corporal Act' such as labouring on an object 'should be able to prejudice the right and power of others' without their consent.[54]

To make matters worse, Locke cannot rely on the importance or virtue of labour itself to justify the generation of these special rights, for it is not the case that *any* labour on a resource is going to be taken as creating an entitlement. In the sense in which the theory of occupancy is known as *First* Occupancy Theory, Locke's is a theory of *First* Labour. Only the first person to take or labour on a resource gets to be its owner; subsequent labourers work on the resource only under the terms imposed by the owner and usually for his benefit more than their own. Strictly speaking, though, the ordinal term is redundant. These theories are, respectively, Occupancy and Labour Theories of *Appropriation*: they explain how previously common goods become the property of someone in particular. Apart from exceptional cases where a resource reverts back to the common state,[55] this happens only once in the history of each resource. Thereafter it is always dealt with as private property. Since the *second* occupier or the *second* labourer is not dealing with common goods, he cannot commit an act of appropriation in the same sense. When he purports to take the goods or work on them without the owner's consent, his action is to be understood as a way of violating property rights rather than as a way of acquiring them.[56]

So that is the conclusion that must be justified. How does Locke try to justify it? The theory he puts forward attempts to connect a

---

[53] For further elaboration of this point, see Ch. 7, sect. 4.
[54] Pufendorf, *Of The Law of Nature*, Bk. IV, Ch. iv, sect. 5 (p. 322).
[55] See Locke, *Two Treatises*, I, sect. 85, and II, sect. 38.
[56] Cf. Hegel, *Philosophy of Right*, sect. 50A.

man's right to the resources he has appropriated with the rights that he has in relation to himself and his actions.

> Though the Earth and all inferior Creatures be common to all Men, yet every Man has a Property in his own Person. This no Body has any Right to but himself. The Labour of his Body, and the Work of his Hands, we may say, are properly his. Whatsoever then he removes out of the State that Nature hath provided, . . . he hath mixed his Labour with, and joyned to it something that is his own, and thereby makes it his Property. It being by him removed from the common state Nature placed it in, hath by this labour something annexed to it, that excludes the common right of other Men. (II. 27)

This is the core of Locke's theory of appropriation. It is not, as is often thought, *equivalent* to the Labour Theory; rather it is Locke's *justification* of the Labour Theory. The Labour Theory does not stand or fall with this argument. It may survive (provided that it can be defended in some other way) even if we conclude (as we shall) that this particular line of justification is hopeless.

The justification proceeds in two parts. First, Locke expounds a theory of self-ownership: a man has exclusive property in his person, his actions, his labour. Secondly, there is an account of how the force of this property right is transferred to the appropriated resources: this is Locke's theory of *mixing* one's labour. I shall examine these parts in the two following sections.

8. SELF-OWNERSHIP

Are Locke's views on self-ownership consistent with what he says elsewhere in the *Two Treatises*? Here he maintains that every man is his own property. But elsewhere he says that men are 'all the Workmanship of one Omnipotent, and infinitely wise Maker' and that they are therefore 'his Property, whose Workmanship they are, made to last during his, not one anothers Pleasure' (II. 6). Because he is God's property, a man has no rightful power over his own life and commits a trespass if he tries to kill or enslave himself (II. 23 and 135). However, I think any imputation of inconsistency in this context would be mistaken.

First, we should note that Locke draws a clear distinction between the property rights that men have *vis-à-vis* one another and the property they have in relation to God (I. 39, lines 54–60).

The prohibitions on suicide and voluntary enslavement concern the latter while the claims about self-ownership involve only a man's right against other men. Even if my body is ultimately God's property, still no other *humans* apart from me have any sort of rights over it. This is all Locke needs for the purposes of his theory of appropriation, since appropriation is intended to establish only rights against mankind not Promethean rights against God.

Secondly, and more importantly, Locke does not say or require in his theory of appropriation that we should have property rights in our bodies. The term he uses is *'person'*: 'every man has a Property in his own Person. This no Body has any Right to but himself' (II. 27). The significance of this has been amply demonstrated by Tully.[57] 'Person' in Locke's philosophy is a technical term and, in the account of personal identity in the *Essay* is given a meaning quite distinct from 'man' or 'body'. It is possible, on Locke's account, for A to be the same man as B and to have the same body as B without having or being the same *person* as B.[58] Now perhaps it is straining things somewhat to try and establish tight connections between Locke's terminology in the *Treatises* and the more rigorous philosophical arguments of the *Essay*; Peter Laslett, for example, has claimed that there are no connections between the two works and that the *Treatises* were not written as works of philosophy.[59] Still, the use of 'person' rather than 'body' does seem to be deliberate. Locke repeats it in at least four places in the *Second Treatise* when he refers to a man's rights over himself (II. 44, 123, 173, and 190), and he refrains from following Grotius in describing a man's life, body, and limbs as his own.[60] It would be uncharitable not to read the term with the author's own technical meaning, especially when that meaning generates a more consistent and sophisticated theory of self-ownership than one which equated *person* with *body* in this context.

There is an interesting connection between this person–body contrast and the doctrine that an absolute right can be acquired over a thing by creating it. Locke certainly accepts that doctrine and maintains that a creator acquires 'the utmost property' (I. 39) in what he creates. But he denies that any human has this sort of power in relation to his own or anyone else's body. The point is

---

[57] Tully, *A Discourse on Property*, pp. 105 ff.
[58] Locke, *Essay*, Bk. II, Ch. xxvii, sect. 7 (Vol. I, p. 278), *et passim*.
[59] Laslett, 'Introduction' to Locke, *Two Treatises*, pp. 92–105.
[60] Cf. Tully, *A Discourse on Property*, p. 80.

made specifically in relation to Filmer's claim that 'Fathers have a power over the Lives of their Children, because they gave them Life and Being' (I. 52):

> If anyone thinks himself an Artist at this, let him number up the parts of his Childs body, which he hath made, tell me their Uses and Operations, and when the living and rational Soul began to inhabit this curious Structure, when Sense began, and how this Engine which he has framed Thinks and Reasons: if he made it, let him, when it is out of order, mend it, at least tell wherein the defects lie. (I. 53)

Since even the most skilled anatomists (of whom in his day Locke was one) confess their ignorance in this regard, no one is capable of the sort of craftsmanship which the creation of a human body (and the consequent generation of absolute rights over it) would require.

Humans, then, do not have creators' rights over their bodies. But they can be regarded in this strong sense as the creators of their own actions (and *a fortiori* of their work and labour).[61] A free agent, on Locke's account, has the power to perform or forbear any action by his own deliberate choice. He considers the actions open to him, deliberates, and determines upon one of them rather than the others. In so doing he is the initiator of a set of events in the world. Since he could by a contrary determination have avoided them, it is because of what *he* did (not anyone else, not even God) that those events took place. He, then, is the creator of these events. The immediate upshot is that the agent must accept responsibility for his actions. He answers to God for them and his responsibility cannot be shifted to, nor can it affect, anyone else.[62] This is where Locke's notion of the *person* comes in. 'Person,' he says, 'is a Forensick Term appropriating actions and their merit.'[63] A person is a being constituted by the consciousness of free and responsible action: 'as far as any intelligent Being can repeat the Idea of any past Action with the same consciousness it had of it at first, and with the same consciousness it has of any present Action, so far it is the same personal self.'[64] A person 'owns and imputes to itself past Actions' by the persistence in it of the consciousness with which those actions were performed. Personality, therefore, is constituted by the creative activity of a free and conscious agent. We do not

---

[61] For the following summary I have drawn on Tully's account, ibid. 106–8.
[62] Locke, *Letter Concerning Toleration*, pp. 153–4.
[63] Locke, *Essay*, Bk. II, Ch. xxvii, sect. 16 (Vol. I, p. 291).
[64] Ibid. sect. 10 (Vol. I, pp. 281–2).

have to go any further into Locke's theory of the self to see that, given the general character of his position, it is much more plausible for him to say that a man has creator's rights over his person than that he has them over his body.

There is, however, another more serious problem with Locke's claim that every man has a property in his own person and in his actions. A property right is a right that may not be taken from me without my consent. But in this context what would count as taking my property from me without my consent? What would count as violating my rights over my person? If we cannot answer this question, talk of property rights is empty or redundant.

J.P. Day has argued that 'A owns A' is ill-formed on the ground that ownership is an *irreflexive* relation.[65] As it stands, this criticism is inadequate: surely the irreflexivity of ownership is precisely the point at issue. Day's criticism is also made in ignorance of the subtleties of Locke's theory of the self; does 'the *man* A owns the *person* A' involve a reflexive use of 'ownership'? But what lies behind Day's criticism, I think, is a sense that property relations are above all normative relations: they regulate behaviour and indicate obligations. Now it is conceivable that an individual may have obligations to himself but unlikely that these would be expressed as obligations to respect property. If, however, the obligations apply to others, we need to have some idea of what their content might be. We need to know which actions are required or prohibited by the property rights which it would have been permissible for people to perform or omit if the property rights in question had not existed.

If Lockean self-ownership was just property in one's body, then this would be straightforward enough. There are actions which other people *could* perform with my body which my property rights in it forbid them to perform. These include things like cannibalism, rape, enslavement as a beast of burden, plundering my body for transplant organs, and so on. But this is not adequate for Locke's purposes, because, however one reads the 'mixing labour' argument, it is not going to involve the claim that any part of my *body* becomes annexed to the goods I work on. What Locke needs is some intelligible sense for the idea of property rights in the *work* of one's body, in one's *actions* and one's *labour*. (This is an additional

---

[65] Day, 'Locke on Property', p. 212.

reason for preferring the technical reading of 'person' in II. 27—it has a tighter internal relation to action than 'body' does.)

Can an action be the subject-matter of a property right? Day maintains that 'action' is of the wrong logical type to go with 'ownership': 'although activities can be engaged in, performed or done, they cannot be owned'. True, Locke says that a person 'owns and imputes to itself' certain actions which it has performed.[66] But this is merely an attributive usage: to own an action in this sense is nothing more than to acknowledge responsibility for it. It has perhaps some minimal normative force: it is wrong to 'own' the actions which others in fact performed.[67] But this is too weak for Locke's purposes in the chapter on property. Transferred to objects, it would entail only that a thief should refrain from claiming credit for another's production; but he can discharge this obligation and still take the product away from its owner.

A more promising suggestion is that self-ownership and the ownership of actions amount for Locke to a right to personal liberty. Locke connects a man's property in his person with his 'being Master of himself' (II. 44): every man is born with 'a Right of Freedom to his Person, which no other Man has a Power over, but the free Disposal of it lies in himself' (II. 190; see also II. 123). This satisfies our requirement that the notion of property in one's self and one's actions must have a clear normative sense. This is a sense which it has had in some recent discussions of property, which we shall discuss in Chapter 11. But in this context it will not do. A right to liberty is the right to perform actions without obstruction. But logically that right is distinct from any right that an agent may have over or in respect of his actions once they *have been* performed or created. In general, I cannot be said to have a right to liberty *now* in relation to actions I have *already* freely performed. Liberty rights take us no further than the time of the performance of the action.[68]

Day explores a number of other possible senses of labour and work that Locke might have had in mind when he said these could be subjects for ownership. Besides (1) labour in the sense of action or activity, he considers: (2) labour as a capacity or ability to labour

---

[66] Locke, *Essay*, Bk. II, Ch. xxvii, sect. 10 (Vol. I, pp. 281–2).
[67] I owe this point to Gwen Taylor.
[68] Waldron, 'Two Worries', p. 44. See also Waldron, 'Turfs my Servant has Cut', p. 17.

(Marx's 'labour-power'); (3) labour meaning a person or type of person (e.g. 'the legitimate claims of labour'); (4) work in the sense of the concrete product of labour (e.g. 'the works of Michelangelo'); (5) labour as a task to be performed (e.g. 'the labours of Hercules'); and (6) work in the technical sense of a physical quantity of energy (e.g. 'This process involves more work than that one'). In each case it is appropriate to use the genitive case to indicate an attributive relation between labour and an individual. But Day denies that there is here any sense of property or ownership that could be useful to Locke for the purposes of the present argument.[69] Let us go through them one by one.

(1) has already been dealt with.

(2) We do talk, following Marx, of the sale and purchase of labour power and therefore as if labour, in this sense, could be owned.[70] But this sense of owning one's labour is not much use to Locke, because it cannot be transferred to objects to create an entitlement. Someone may take an object I have laboured on, but still leave me with my capacity to labour.

(3) Clearly, labour (meaning labourers) can be owned—in a system of slavery. Locke would insist that a person owns himself (as against all other men) in this sense. But this too is not a sense of 'owning labour' that can readily be transferred to the goods one labours on. Locke wants the labour, not the labourer, to be mixed with the object he produces.

(4) The products of labour can of course be owned. That is the whole point of Locke's account. But just because of that it will not do as an account of 'owning one's labour' at this stage, since that would leave Locke without an *argument* to support his claim about appropriation.

(5) Perhaps labour in the sense of tasks, jobs, or employment can be the subject-matter of rights.[71] People say they have been 'given' a job and they complain when their jobs have been 'stolen'. Still, this will not do for Locke's purposes, first because it is not evident that a Lockean appropriator 'owns' the task he sets himself, and secondly because there is no natural or plausible sense in which a *task* can be said to be mixed with or annexed to the object of the task.

(6) The final meaning is an interesting one. Work in the

---

[69] Day, 'Locke on Property', pp. 208–15.
[70] Marx, *Capital*, Vol. I.
[71] Cf. Reich, 'The New Property'.

physicist's sense of 'the product of a force and the distance through which it acts'[72] cannot itself be owned: it is an adverbial rather than a substantive quantity. But *energy* is a more promising candidate. Energy is involved in ordinary labouring (we talk of 'the expenditure of energy'); it can be the subject-matter of property rights (we purchase energy from the electricity authorities); and, in the case of the energy involved in labouring, it may arguably be regarded as the property of the labourer in the first instance. When we add to that the fact that in our modern understanding energy is convertible into mass, it seems to fit the specifications of Locke's argument.[73] Its main disadvantage for Locke's purposes is that it is quite remote from self-ownership in the sense of his idea of the ownership of one's autonomously created person. But in charitably reconstituting a theory as problematic as Locke's doctrine of self-ownership, we cannot expect to have everything.

One final point of explanation. Day's critique of Locke's theory and my own have been very analytic in character. We have subjected the precise terms of Locke's view to minute scrutiny, rejecting any meaning which seems to involve a logical confusion or a category mistake. It may be objected that this approach is anachronistic and unfair. Instead of focusing on the detail of Locke's interpretation, we should focus on the broad picture he has been painting and the contemporary views he is alluding to. Like his predecessors in the natural law tradition, Locke is working with the notion of the *suum* (as in '*suum cuique tribuere*')— the sphere of inviolable personality defined, in the first instance, by the boundaries of one's body but extendable to comprehend the objects one has appropriated. No doubt, as Karl Olivecrona has argued, this concept is very important for an understanding of Locke (though curiously the philosopher himself never refers to it).[74] But we must do more than note its importance. The claim that the *suum* can be extended by unilateral appropriation is controversial: both Filmer and Pufendorf deny it. Locke's claim that one has property in one's own person and actions is supposed to be the first step in an *argument* to this effect, so we do him no injustice by considering and criticizing it as such. If it is vitiated by incoherence, confusion, or equivocation, then the normative task of legitimizing appropriation has not been adequately completed.

[72] Day, 'Locke on Property', p. 209.
[73] I owe this suggestion to Hillel Steiner.
[74] Olivecrona, 'Locke's Theory of Appropriation', pp. 222–4.

9. MIXING ONE'S LABOUR

Locke claims that when an individual takes objects from their natural state or cultivates previously uncultivated land, he mixes something with those resources 'that excludes the common right of other men' (II. 27) and marks them out as 'his Property, which another had no Title to, nor could without injury take from him' (II. 32). If there is an argument here, it must go something like this:

(1) A man who labours on an object mixes his labour with that object.

(2) But that man owns the labour which he mixes with the object.

(3) So the object which has been laboured on contains something which the labourer owns.

(4) So taking the object out of the labourer's control without his consent is a way of taking his labour from him without his consent; it therefore amounts to a violation of the right referred to in (2).

(5) Therefore no one may take the object from the labourer without his consent.

(6) Therefore the object is the labourer's property.[75]

In this way an entitlement to an object is generated out of the prior entitlement to one's labour on the basis that recognizing the former is the only way of upholding and maintaining respect for the latter once the mixing has taken place. The force of one's entitlement to the labour has been transferred to the object by the action of labouring on it. Once the labour has become embodied in the object, the labourer acquires an interest in the object—an interest as important as his interest in his labour—which he did not have before.

The idea that labour is literally *mixed with* an object is crucial to this argument. Without it we cannot explain how the force of the labour entitlement is transferred to the product of one's labour. With this in mind, let us examine the idea of mixing one's labour with an object in a literal way to see whether or not it makes sense. For the purposes of this discussion, we shall assume charitably that the difficulties in the notion of owning one's actions, discussed in the previous section, do not exist. (The only interpretation of

---

[75] What follows is adapted from Waldron, 'Two Worries'.

owning one's labour which survived that discussion—interpretation (6) equating labour with energy—will be considered a little later on.)

On the face of it, the proposition

(P) Individual A mixes his labour with object O

seems to involve a category mistake. Surely the only things that can be mixed with objects are other objects. But labour consists of actions not objects. How can a series of actions be mixed with a physical object? True, some philosophers do purport to quantify over actions and events treating them as entities in their own right.[76] But I do not think that disposes of the difficulty in the present case.

We can see this if we compare (P) with a more straightforward proposition about mixing:

(Q) The cook mixes the egg with the milk.

In (Q), three objects are referred to—the cook, the egg, and the milk. There is also, if you like, the action of mixing the egg into the milk. Now we may treat this action as an entity or we may not. What matters for my criticism is that, entity or not, the action is certainly not identical with any of the other entities involved. It is distinct from the egg, the milk, and the cook. That seems quite straightforward.

Let us try a similar analysis of (P). Again there are at least three entities referred to:

(P1): the labourer, A, who is the analogue of the cook;
(P2): the labour of A, which, like the egg, is (supposedly) the subject of the mixing; and
(P3): the object, O, the analogue of the milk, into which the labour is being mixed.

So far, so good. But where is the fourth element, the analogue of the action of mixing? Perhaps it is the labour of A; after all, the Lockean claim is that *by labouring* the producer mixes his labour with the product. But A's labour figures already in the account we have given as the ingredient (P2) being mixed in. So instead of the four distinct entities we had in the straightforward case of (Q), we have now at most only three. There is the mixer, the thing being mixed in, and the thing into which it is being mixed; but there is no

---

[76] Cf. Davidson, 'Logical Form of Action Sentences'.

distinct action of mixing. Or, if you like, we have the mixer, the action of mixing, and the object into which something is being mixed; but there is nothing which is being mixed in. We have ingredient and mixture but no mixing, or mixing and mixture but no ingredient. Either way, the ordinary notion of mixing seems quite inappropriate to the case Locke is describing. The situation lacks the requisite plurality.[77]

Our original hunch about a category mistake has led us to discover a much deeper flaw. The phrase 'mixing one's labour' is shown to have the logical form of 'mixing one's mixing'. And that just seems defective.

An objection may be made along the following lines to what I have said. Perhaps (P) is being used by Locke in the first premiss of the argument we are examining in a way which distinguishes its logical form from that of (Q). If this is the case, then the fact that (P) does not conform to the logic of (Q) no more makes (P) ill-formed than the difference between, say, 'A has a pain in his foot' and 'A has a growth on his foot' makes the first of these ill-formed. In other words, it may be objected on behalf of the Lockean argument that we are taking the idea of mixing one's labour too literally. There may be another perfectly legitimate sense for (P) which does not require the plurality of elements we find in (Q).

There are two things to say about this objection. First it is not at all clear that one *can* come up with an interpretation of (P) which will both avoid my attack and do the work in Locke's argument that he seems to want the notion of mixing one's labour to do. Remember this notion is supposed to explain and justify the principle of labourers' entitlements. It is no good suggesting for instance that (P) is just a fancy or rhetorical way of saying 'A labours on O'. That leaves premiss (1) of our argument saying limply that a person who labours on an object labours on an object. The notion implicit in (3)—that the object thereby comes to contain something the labourer owns—is left completely mysterious. The question would still remain open: why does labouring on an object generate an entitlement to it? If the argument we are

[77] This view seems to be shared by Olivecrona, who says: 'It would be absurd to contend that the "labour" of killing a deer or picking an acorn from the ground is, in the exact sense of the expression, "mixed" with the deer or the acorn respectively. Locke cannot have meant it so.' (Olivecrona, 'Locke's Theory of Appropriation', p. 226). But that is what Locke says. Olivecrona does not indicate why he thinks it absurd.

considering has any independent force at all, then Locke is using (P) to answer not beg that question. Any reinterpretation of (P) has to be able to fill that role.

Secondly, the criticism I have made applies not only to the expression 'mixing one's labour' but also some of the other expressions used by Locke in the section we are dealing with (II. 27). Labour is said to be 'joyned' and 'annexed' to objects by the labourer. These expressions in their ordinary sense all share the logical form of (Q): that is, they all involve the idea of someone's bringing one thing into relation with another. So they are equally open to the criticism that, in the case of labouring on an object, there are not two things to be brought into relation with one another but only one thing and an action that is performed on it. Just as we do not ordinarily talk of *mixing* actions with objects, so we do not ordinarily talk of *joining* or *annexing* them to objects, and my criticism explains why.

In the previous section, we entertained the possibility that 'owning one's labour' might mean owning the energy that is expended when one labours. Does the mixing idea become any more coherent when it is applied to this case? We do seem to have here the possibility of a real distinction between the thing mixed and the action of mixing which he lacked in the case of labour understood as action: we can say that, by his actions, he mixed his energy with the object. Still there are problems with this interpretation. Although matter and energy are physically interconvertible and therefore in principle talk of a mixture of matter and energy makes sense, it is not true that every act of labouring or appropriation will involve the *addition* of energy to the thing appropriated. Sometimes as in the killing or capturing of a wild beast, it involves the application of energy to oppose or negate the energy that was already there. In this case, labour and energy have been expended on a resource, but on no plausible physical analysis does the tamed resource now *contain* the energy that has been expended. Nozick, in his discussion of the application of Locke's theory, toys with something like the energy interpretation when he asks whether the area of land appropriated by labour is 'the minimal area such that an act decreases entropy in that area, and not elsewhere.'[78] But a similar point can be made about this. Since

---

[78] Nozick, *Anarchy, State, and Utopia*, p. 174: I am grateful to Hillel Steiner for this reference.

entropy is not a concept which is relative to human purposes (the law of entropy is not the doctrine that things are becoming more and more useless!), we cannot assume that every act of labour or even every creative act of labour decreases or is intended to decrease entropy in an area. Some are but others are not: sometimes we want to enhance entropy, to take things apart rather than increase their complexity. So no criterion of the application of energy to this end will do as an account of what labour involves.

Even if these difficulties about the literal meaning of 'mixing' did not exist, there would be other grave problems with Locke's argument.

The argument, as we saw, depends on the claim that if something to which I am entitled (e.g. my labour) becomes mixed with some other object, then the only way to safeguard and maintain my former entitlement is to hold me entitled to the object with which it has been mixed. But we may dispute whether an entitlement to the object is even a way of protecting the former entitlement, let alone the only way. Even if we assume, for the moment, that the idea of mixing labour makes sense, still once the mixing takes place the labour is to all intents and purposes lost in the object. Once mixed, it no longer exists as labour and there is no longer a question of protecting anyone's entitlement to it. There are, as we saw, problems enough with the idea of an entitlement to labour in any case; but what on earth can such an entitlement (considered on its own) amount to once the labour has been lost in the object?

Once again a banal analogy helps to highlight the difficulty. Suppose there is a vat of wet cement lying about which belongs to no one in particular, and I drop the contents of a bottle of tomato juice into it. Before I can retrieve it, the cement hardens into a concrete block. (Or better still: as in Locke's case, the cement is lying about and I *intend* to drop my tomato juice into it, not wanting to retrieve it.) Can I now claim the concrete block in order to protect my entitlement to the tomato juice? Surely the suggestion would be regarded as some sort of joke. My juice has gone; whatever the justice of my claim to the concrete block, it has nothing to do with my claim *still* to be the owner of the tomato juice. An entitlement to an object consists in the right to use, control, and dispose of it. Even if I am allowed to use, control, or dispose of the concrete block, I can do none of these things with regard to the tomato juice.

Of course, things would be different if there were any possibility of recovering the tomato juice from the concrete block. But soft drinks do not usually survive such experiences. Anyway, to put the case on all fours with the one Locke is describing, we have to think of the mixture of juice and cement as irreversible. (Otherwise Locke has no answer to the point that the producer is entitled, at most, to be given back his labour.) So the drink is as good as lost, despite the fact that we know where it is. As something which can be the subject-matter of an on going entitlement, generating other entitlements by its attachment to other things, it no longer exists for us.

No doubt, the concrete block is different from what it would have been if the juice had not been dropped into the cement; presumably it is a little softer and its internal structure is slightly different. But if there is a question raised by this alteration, it is: 'Who is to have rights over the concrete block, altered in this way by the addition of the tomato juice?' That may be an important question. But what has transpired makes the question 'Who now has rights over the tomato juice?' irrelevant to that. Similarly in the case of an object with which labour has been 'mixed'. The fact that the object has been laboured on certainly makes a difference to it. But the question is now: 'Who is to have rights over the object, given that labour has made this difference to it?' In finding an answer to this question or, more important, in finding a justification for the obvious answer, the further question 'Who *now* has rights over the labour that made the difference?' is of no use at all.

Robert Nozick has used a similar example to develop a slightly different line of attack. Assuming again that labour can be owned and that it can be mixed with an object, Nozick asks:

Why isn't mixing what I own with what I don't own a way of losing what I own rather than a way of gaining what I don't? If I own a can of tomato juice and spill it in the sea so that its molecules (made radioactive, so I can check this) mingle evenly throughout the sea, do I thereby come to own the sea, or have I foolishly dissipated my tomato juice?[79]

This is certainly what Locke would want to say about a man who labours on something already owned by another person without the latter's permission. His labour surely gets mixed with the object in the same way the first labourer's did (unless the first labour

[79] Nozick *Anarchy, State, and Utopia*, pp. 174–5.

somehow made the object impermeable to further mixing!), but in his case that counts as losing his labour, and the first labourer gets the benefit of the second man's efforts. Why, then, can we not say the same about the *first* labourer in relation to the common rights of all mankind? He expended his labour on his own initiative and for his own reasons; we did not *ask* him to do this; why then should we be beholden to him for his pains?[80] Alan Ryan thinks this is answered by Locke's invocation of God's command to subdue the earth (II. 32).[81] But at most that explains only why men labour in the first place, why each man is required to 'lay out something upon [the earth] that was his own, his labour'; it does not explain why he continues to be entitled to what he has laid out. Since God often requires sacrifices of us, the mere fact of His command does not indicate that obedience is not a way of losing one's labour. And it does not explain why the benefits of the labour which God has commanded each of us to perform do not accrue in common to everyone who originally had property in the resource.

If Locke wants to insist that mixing one's labour generates an entitlement he faces one further difficulty. Why does the entitlement amount to full and exclusive rights over ('the utmost property in') the object rather than some lesser interest? For example, why, as Nozick puts it, 'should one's entitlement extend to the whole object rather than just to the added value?'[82] The point here is that an exclusive right to the whole of the improved object amounts to something more (and certainly more valuable) than an exclusive entitlement to one's own labour. Since this extra—the value of the raw materials—originally belonged in common to everyone, we may ask why the claims of others are defeated to this additional extent. What I have in mind as an alternative is that the appropriator should acquire a substantial interest in the object he has worked on, roughly proportionate in some sense to the labour he has expended on it, but that this should not be deemed to exclude altogether the common rights of other men. (Of course, in Locke's theory, those rights are not entirely excluded anyway: the basic right to subsistence is imprescriptable. But I am thinking of more substantial concessions than that—the right of continued access, for example, or the right to a share in the produce.) It may

[80] Cf. Proudhon, *What Is Property?*, p. 84.
[81] Ryan, 'Property, Liberty and *On Liberty*', p. 222.
[82] Nozick, *Anarchy, State, and Utopia*, p. 175.

be objected that this sort of sophisticated discrimination between greater and lesser property interests is possible only in a positive legal system, where different estates in the same object can be recognized, distinguished, and upheld in law, and that would not be practicable in a state of nature. But even if this point were valid, it would establish at most that the full and exclusive entitlements acquired by appropriation in the state of nature were to be viewed as provisional. They could not operate as moral constraints on the activity of a subsequently instituted civil society which was determined to strike retrospectively and in rectification of the crudeness of the natural entitlements a fairer balance between the legitimate claims of the appropriator and those of the rest of mankind.[83]

10. THE LABOUR THEORY OF VALUE

Locke might try to answer some of these points by invoking an aspect of his theory we have ignored up till now—the Labour Theory of Value developed in sections 40–3. There he anticipates objections along the lines we have been developing with the claim: 'Nor is it so strange, as perhaps before consideration it may appear, that the Property of labour should be able to over-ballance the Community of Land. For 'tis Labour indeed that puts the difference of value on everything' (II. 40). He goes on to estimate the extent of the difference that labour makes:

I think it will be but a very modest Computation to say, that of the Products of the Earth useful to the Life of Man 9/10 are the effects of labour; nay, if we will rightly estimate things as they come to our use, and cast up the several Expenses about them, what in them is purely owing to Nature and what to Labour, we shall find that in most of them, 99/100 are wholly to be put on the account of labour. (II. 40)

(In II. 43—he revises the estimate, in the case of the produce of land, to 999/1000.)

Historically, this is an important claim. There is no doubt that it had considerable influence on the development of labour theories of value by the Scottish political economist, Adam Smith, and, through him and his successors in the classical tradition, on the

[83] Cf. Ch. 7, sect. 5, below.

eventual development of Karl Marx's theory of value. But there are two very important differences between Locke's theory, on the one hand, and Marx's and Smith's, on the other.

First, Locke's is a theory of *use*-value whereas their theories concern *exchange*-value. Locke makes no assumption about the proportions in which goods will exchange in the market place, and indeed his views about the arbitrariness and conventionality of exchange indicate a scepticism about the possibility of any quantitative theory in this area.[84]

Secondly, Locke's theory concerns the proportion between the natural use-value and the artificially created use-value in each product; it does not concern the value of one product relative to that of another. Thus even if it is true that labour accounts for 9/10 of the value of anything, there need be no assumption that equal quantities of labour generate equal quantities of value. Five minutes' labour might account for 9/10 of the value of an apple while an hour's labour accounts for 9/10 of the value of a wooden staff; but this does not imply, on Locke's account, that the staff is twelve times more useful than the apple. It is not that sort of theory.

Locke wants to put the theory to a different use. He uses it to bolster the claim that appropriation by labour is a legitimate way of excluding the common rights of the rest of mankind. If the usefulness of appropriated resources derived mainly from 'the spontaneous hand of Nature', that would be a difficult task. Why should the minimal expenditure of energy by an opportunist be sufficient to exclude everyone else from the enjoyment of these natural benefits? But if Locke can show that 'labour makes for the greatest part of the value of things' (II. 42), then anyone complaining about exclusion by an appropriator can be accused of desiring almost nothing but 'the benefit of anothers Pains' (II. 34). (This presumably is one of the reasons Locke insisted on cultivation rather than mere enclosure as the basis of legitimate appropriation.) Similarly, if natural resources and land are 'almost worthless Materials, as in themselves' (II. 43) in their natural state, then it does not seem so unjust that an appropriator should acquire exclusive title to the whole of the object he has taken. For there is only a negligible difference between the worth of his labour and the value of the object he now controls.

[84] See Locke, *Two Treatises*, II, sect. 37, lines 1–5; also II, sect. 184. The closest Locke gets to any theorizing of this sort is in his offhand suggestion in II, sect. 50 that labour is the 'measure of value'.

The Labour Theory of Value is perhaps most plausible in the case of land. There is, as Locke notes, a striking difference between the usefulness of a piece of cultivated land and the usefulness, as it stands, of a piece of waste ground (II. 36 and 42–3). It is also plausible in regard to manufactured artifacts: in accounting for the usefulness of a loaf of bread, we must consider not only the efforts of the farmer and the baker but also those who produced the tools without which the cultivation of wheat and the manufacture of flour and bread would have been impossible (II. 43). But the theory is quite implausible in regard to food and other items that have merely been gathered from their natural state. Quantification is difficult in such a case, but do we really want to say that the action of gathering acorns that have fallen on the ground accounts for the greater part of their usefulness? The labour accounts at most for their location on the dinner table; the nourishment they afford is almost entirely intrinsic to the natural objects themselves. Locke appears to concede this when he contrasts the value of acorns, water, and skins, with that of bread, wine, and cloth (II. 42). Paradoxically, then, there seems more room for complaint about the exclusive appropriation of acorns than about the exclusive appropriation of land, on the Lockean Labour Theory.

What is the connection between the claim (intended literally) that labour is *mixed* with a product and the theory that labour accounts for the greater part of its value? No doubt Locke saw a connection here, but it is significant that he expounds the value-theory entirely without reference to the earlier claim. So since the Labour Theory of Value can be expressed independently of the 'mixing one's labour' doctrine, it is not affected by the latter's incoherence; and it can stand by itself (though of course it will not have the same work to do) once the argument based on the mixing idea collapses.

This is important for the evaluation of other labour theories of value. Marx makes very prominent use of the idea that labour comes to be contained in the objects that have been worked on (though needless to say this is not intended as a justification for private appropriation!). In *Capital*, he writes of labour's being 'congealed', 'objectified', 'materialized', 'crystallized', 'contained', 'accumulated', and 'bound up' in an object, so that the object 'absorbs' and 'is soaked in' human labour.[85] (The immediate provenance of these idioms is probably Hegelian; we shall consider

[85] Marx, *Capital*, Vol. I, pp. 128, 129, 131, 143, 287, 296.

Hegel's theory of appropriation in Chapter 10.) These turns of phrase are related to three of Marx's more important theses: first, that labour is the main source of use-value (a thesis he shared with Locke); secondly, that in a market economy products tend to exchange in proportion to the amount of socially necessary labour time that would be involved in their reproduction; and thirdly, the thesis that when certain products take on the character of capital, they confront the workers as 'dead labour' oppressing and alienating that of the living.[86] If the idioms about objects *containing* labour had to be interpreted literally, then all three theses would be suspect. But we can see now that the first thesis certainly, probably the second, and maybe even also the third, can be expressed without recourse to the incoherent idea that objects contain labour in any literal sense. That can be seen as nothing more than a picturesque way of expressing the relation between the condition of an object and the labour that wrought some change in it; if we want to express such a relationship systematically, we may find it helpful to talk as though the labour was *in* the product so that in dealing with the product one could imagine oneself dealing with a certain mathematical quantity. No literal sense need be accorded to this usage: it is purely a heuristic device. This, then, distinguishes Marx's theses from Locke's attempt to justify individual appropriation, to which the literal (and incoherent) sense of 'mixing one's labour' is absolutely indispensable.

11. ALTERNATIVE INTERPRETATIONS: (A) IDENTIFICATION

Interpreted literally, the argument about mixing labour does not provide a coherent justification for the view that appropriators acquire entitlements. Is there any other way Locke's discussion can be read so that, without relying on this argument, it nevertheless supplies a plausible defence of appropriators' entitlements? Several have been suggested. In this section, I discuss the idea that the appropriator identifies himself with his object in such a way that respect for his person demands recognition of his entitlement. In section 12, I consider Tully's interpretation that appropriators' rights are a species of creators' rights. These two interpretations preserve the SR-based character of Locke's argument, though they

[86] See Avineri, *Social and Political Thought of Karl Marx*, p. 120.

differ in their account of the nature of the interest that is generated by appropriation. The third interpretation is the view that Lockean appropriation is based on a principle of moral desert. This is not straightforwardly a right-based argument, but as a common interpretation it needs to be considered.

Olivecrona attributes to Locke the idealist view that personality can somehow be extended by identification to comprehend external objects:

We can have a feeling of things being so intimately connected with ourselves that they are part of our very selves. Being deprived of such objects represents something more than an economic loss. It is experienced as an attack on the personality itself. The feeling of unification with a physical thing varies according to circumstances. It is strongest with regard to things in daily use or dear to us for sentimental reasons. The farmer feels united to the soil on which he works. The town-dweller has a similar feeling for he house that is his own; something of himself sticks in that house where he has been living so long with his family.[87]

He claims this is what Locke is getting at when he uses the (superficially 'absurd') idea of mixing one's labour. By working on an object, a man identifies with it and in a sense makes it part of himself. Once this happens, for us to allow anyone else to use the object without his consent would be to allow them to use a part of his personality. That would imply that the second man 'had a right over another free individual, which is out of the question.'[88]

We might ask all sorts of questions about this view. Does it apply to any case of appropriation? When a man gathers acorns or shoots a rabbit does he necessarily identify himself with these humble objects and extend his personality to comprehend them? If by some psychological quirk he does, is that sufficient to justify the imposition of irksome duties on other people? Is it not more plausible to say that what he identifies himself with is his business but cannot prejudice the moral position of anyone else? Do parents have property in their children to the extent that they identify themselves with them? What about cases where people identify themselves with resources belonging to others—for example, when a man identifies with the house he has been occupying on a monthly lease? Does this generate any entitlement beyond that agreed to by his landlord?

[87] Olivecrona, 'Locke's Theory of Appropriation', p. 224.
[88] Ibid. 225.

The last question can be answered readily enough. Just as second and subsequent occupiers acquire no title under First Occupancy theory, so second and subsequent identifiers acquire no title under this account. The goods in question have already been identified with by somebody else. But when goods are lying around in common and where no one has so far singled out any resource for his particular purposes, then the mere fact that a man forms an affection for an object and regards it as an enduring feature in his personal environment might be accounted sufficient to justify some sort of prohibition on others' taking it from him.

But the other questions are not so easy. They raise general issues about the nature of identification and the circumstances under which it can be expected to occur. Identification seems a very subjective phenomenon; are we to accept that people are entitled to whatever natural goods they *say* they have identified with?

If we look for a more objective test, we run into serious difficulties. Presumably identification arises out of (or at least involves) an expectation that one will be able to continue using the object indefinitely. (Without such an expectation, one's identification with the object would amount to little more than the mere *wish* to keep it—something whose frustration is hardly going to cut one's personality to the quick nor constitute serious disrespect for personality.) Certainly settled expectations play an important part in the structure of personality. As Bentham noted in his discussion of property:

It is hence that we have the power of forming a general plan of conduct; it is hence that the successive instants which compose the duration of life are not like isolated and independent points, but become continuous parts of a whole. *Expectation* is a chain which unites our present existence to our future existence, and which passes beyond us to the generation which is to follow. The sensibility of man extends through all the links of the chain.[89]

But Bentham also saw that expectations of this strength and importance cannot be expected to arise naturally: 'A feeble and momentary expectation may result from time to time from circumstances purely physical: but a strong and permanent expectation can only arise from law.'[90] A man will not expect to keep a deer he has killed or acorns he has gathered in a Hobbesian state of nature; or, if he does, his expectation will not extend

[89] Bentham, 'Principles of the Civil Code', p. 111.
[90] Ibid. 113.

beyond his estimation of his own ability to defend them. Only when he can predict that by and large others will abide by some principle of respect for his acquisitions is he likely to form a settled expectation of keeping them.

Much the same can be said about Hume's argument that first occupancy generates an expectation of continued use by the operation of the psychological mechanism of association on the idea of one's first use.[91] Like his theory of causation, this will rely at some point on the constant conjunction of first use and a subsequent series of uses. (It is true that Hume countenances the possibility of induction from a single case; but only against a background of numerous inductions themselves based on constant conjunction.[92]) But that constant conjunction is unlikely to occur unless the principle of First Occupancy is already being tacitly respected.

Thus the principle of respect for expectations and the concomitant idea of identifying with a property object cannot be the *foundation* of a principle of entitlement; such a principle must already be generally respected before the relevant expectations can come into play. The same applies to Olivecrona's idea of respecting the extension of personality. His examples seem plausible only when viewed in the context of an established system of property which has been generating expectations for ages. Of course, people in our society may identify with the resources whose exclusive use is guaranteed to them by law. But when the very first farmer took it into his head to plough and cultivate a field, was he likely to identify himself with the field? Only if he had reason to believe that he could or should remain in indefinite control of it and reap the products of his labour. But then *that reason*, rather than the expectations it generated, would be the true foundation of property.

As Bentham saw, a principle of respect for the expectations that people happen to have built up concerning the use and control of resources leads only to a conservative requirement to maintain whatever system of property rights is already in force: 'As regards property, security consists in receiving no check, no shock, no derangement to the expectation founded on laws of enjoying such

[91] Hume, *Treatise*, Bk. III, Pt. ii, sect. 3, pp. 503–4 and n. I am grateful to Alan Ryan for making me consider this point.
[92] Ibid., Bk. I, Pt. iii, sect. 8, p. 105; see also Bennett, *Locke, Berkeley, Hume*, p. 293.

and such a portion of good. The legislator owes the greatest respect to this expectation which he has himself produced.'[93] But this will not do for an interpretation of Locke's argument because Locke's account is critical not conservative. He is purporting to tell the legislator what sorts of expectations he ought to produce; such advice cannot itself be based on a principle of respecting established expectations.

12. ALTERNATIVE INTERPRETATIONS: (B) CREATION

Tully denies that Locke's view involved the idea of mixing one's labour 'with a pre-existing object which persists through the activity of labouring'. In Tully's view, Locke 'sees the labourer as making an object out of the material provided by God and so having a property in his product, in a manner similar to that in which God makes the world out of the prior material He created.'[94] Although the labourer does not create the raw material, he does create the object which he composes out of it. Tully cites a number of passages from the *Essay* indicating Locke's view that the identity and existence of an object is a matter of 'the determinate figure of sensible parts.'[95] So a man may 'compound and divide the Materials, which are made to his Hand' and in this way become responsible for the existence of an object that did not exist before.[96]

At first sight, this account seems to fit Locke's theory neatly for, as we have seen, he concedes that God-like creative activity might generate an entitlement (I. 53). He connects our being the property of God with the fact that we are His 'Workmanship' (II. 6). Still there are serious difficulties with Tully's interpretation of property rights as creators' rights.

For one thing, it yields a conclusion which is far too strong. Creator's rights are absolute rights entirely unlimited by any duty of stewardship. Locke talks of a creator's right 'to destroy his own Workmanship' (I. 53) without adding the qualification which he usually indicates for human property—namely, that one has only a right to destroy a thing 'by using it' (I. 39). There would be great

---

[93] Bentham, 'Principles of the Code', pp. 113–4.
[94] Tully, *A Discourse on Property*, pp. 116–17.
[95] e.g. Locke, *Essay*, Bk. III, Ch. vi, sect. 40 (Vol. II, p. 66).
[96] Ibid., Bk. II, Ch. ii, sect. 2 and Ch. xxvi, section 2 (Vol. I, pp. 91 and 271–2).

difficulty explaining the introduction of the spoilation proviso (see section 14 below) and the continued constraint of the universal right to sustenance (see section 15 below) if property rights were understood as creator's rights. 'God-like' creation[97] would give us God-like rights over objects, and that (certainly on Tully's own account) is far too strong for the property rights that human appropriators are supposed to have. True, Locke regards man as a God-like creature, made in God's image.[98] But when he uses this description, Locke is referring to man's intellectual nature not to man as *homo faber* or *homo laborans*. He never once connects man's God-likeness with his productive capacity.

If anything, Locke is at pains to distinguish man and God in this regard. The idea that productive labour involves an act of creation runs into the same sort of difficulty as the idea that the conception of a child is an act of creation by its parents. There Locke's argument was that, since a father does not know how literally to *make* a child, he cannot acquire creator's rights over it (I. 52–3). But, as Nozick notices, the same point can be made about external production: 'By this criterion, people who plant seeds on their land and water them would not own the trees that then grow. Surely most of what most of us do is to intervene in or originate processes whose complete operation we do not understand, yielding a result we could not completely design.'[99] If, on the other hand, Tully regards this as sufficient to count as creation,[100] he leaves Locke without any argument against traductionism.

In fact, as Tully acknowledges, Locke never actually invokes the idea of creator's rights to explain appropriators' entitlements.[101] (This is very odd if, as Tully claims, it is the key to his theory of appropriation.) But he says that Locke uses the word 'make' consistently and repeatedly to indicate man's creative activity. It is, I suppose, pedantic to point out that this last claim is simply false.[102] 'Make' and its cognates are used in three main senses in the chapter on property: (1) 'to make use of something' is the most common usage (II. 31, 36, 38, 43, 45, 46, and 51); (2) 'making

---

[97] This is Tully's phrase—*A Discourse on Property*, p. 59.
[98] Cf. ibid. 110.
[99] Nozick, *Anarchy, State, and Utopia*, p. 288.
[100] Cf. Tully, *A Discourse on Property*, pp. 119 ff.
[101] Ibid. 120.
[102] One of the difficulties with Tully's book is that his repeated misrepresentation of Locke requires this sort of 'nit-picking' refutation. Otherwise his references are too easily taken as read.

something one's property' (and some variations on it) is common in the early paragraphs (II. 25, 27, 28, 30, and 31); and (3) Locke says in several places that labour 'makes up' the greater part of the value of artifacts (II. 40, 42, and 44). I guess this last usage is the closest to the one that Tully wants, but even so it is quite a distance from the idea of making or creating an object. Tully is right to note that Locke describes appropriation as changing natural material into useful goods. But he describes the usefulness not the useful good itself as the effect of labour.[103] Nowhere does Locke give any indication that he wants to connect this labour theory of use-value with any doctrine of creator's entitlement.

It may be worth briefly considering a version of the creation argument recently revived in the modern discussion of property by the economist Israel Kirzner.[104] In the course of a complicated argument about the morality of arbitrage, Kirzner argues in favour of a principle of 'finders-keepers' based on a doctrine of creator's entitlement. (Briefly, 'finders-keepers' is then applied to an arbitrageur's discovery of the new value constituted by discrepancies in the prices of similar goods in different markets.)

In order to introduce plausibility into the notion of finders-keepers, it appears necessary to adopt the view that, until a resource has been discovered, *it has not*, in the sense relevant to the rights of access and common use, *existed at all*. On this view it seems plausible to consider the discoverer . . . as, in the relevant sense, the *creator* of what he has found. It becomes, then, fairly easy to understand how the finder can be held justly entitled to keep that which he has 'created'. . . . The finder-creator has spontaneously generated hitherto non-existent resources, and is seen, therefore, as their natural owner.[105]

The difficulty with this position is that it rests on an *analogy* between finding and making. But an analogy between X and Y transfers moral significance from X to Y only if Y is like X in some morally relevant respect. Now although there are similarities between creating and finding (e.g. in both cases no one had previously seen the resource), it is not clear how their relevance can be determined without a fuller account of the basis of the moral

---

[103] That is unless one reads Locke, *Two Treatises*, II, sect. 40, lines 11–12 as saying that 9 out of 10 useful objects are the effects of labour; but the usual and more plausible reading is that 9/10 of the usefulness of each object is the effect of labour. The former reading would be inconsistent with Locke's gloss in lines 12–17.

[104] Kirzner, 'Entrepreneurship, Entitlement and Economic Justice'.

[105] Ibid. 395–6.

significance of creation. Kirzner asserts that the relevance is there and that the creator is the natural owner of his creation. But assertions do not help much, and nor do our 'intuitions' in a case where our only 'experience' of creation consists in stories we have been told about magic. In Locke's theory, the only example we have of a creator is God, and in modern discussion of property, the only thought-experiments we are asked to consider are those involving the creation of resources *ex nihilo*. Neither of these is a familiar idea; each of them asks us to imagine processes which miraculously violate the laws of nature (such as the conservation of matter) against the backdrop of which our normal 'intuitions' on these issues are formed. To put it bluntly, until we know *what it is* about magic that entitles a magician to the thing he has created (and how could we know that?), we will have difficulty with any moral analogy which tries to assimilate ordinary human enterprise to the magic of miraculous forces.

13. ALTERNATIVE INTERPRETATIONS: (C) DESERT

We spoke earlier of the Lockean appropriator as an opportunist. But according to Locke it is morally good to labour on hitherto common resources. To do so is to obey God's command (II. 32 and 35) and to prove oneself 'Industrious and Rational' (II. 34). So perhaps appropriators *deserve* exclusive entitlements as rewards for their virtue. This is a common interpretation of Locke's theory.[106] It is consistent with a certain view of the spirit of capitalist enterprise—the view which identifies the industry of the producer with rationality, prudence, and self-restraint.[107]

Before evaluating this interpretation, let us note a couple of analytical points about desert. First, 'desert' is being used here in a strong moralistic sense. It does have a weaker sense in ordinary usage in which 'A deserves X' means the same as 'A is entitled to X'. But in the sense involved here, statements of the former type are supposed to be able to operate as *arguments* for statements of the latter type.

Secondly, I am unsure whether a view which bases property

---

[106] See e.g. Miller, 'Justice and Property'; Becker, *Property Rights*, pp. 43 ff.; and Dworkin's lectures on 'Liberalism', delivered at Oxford in 1978–9.

[107] e.g. Weber, *Protestant Ethic*, and Dworkin, 'Liberalism', pp. 137–8.

entitlements on desert should be regarded as a right-based theory. For it to be a right-based theory, on the definition given in Chapter 3, we should have to say that the deserving person had an interest in getting his reward and that this interest was the basis of our concern that it should be given to him. But generally this is not true. We do try to give people as rewards things which it is in their interests to have, but their interests are not usually taken to be the basis of the obligation to reward their virtue. In most cases, the rationale of reward for virtue is found in a duty-based or utilitarian theory. On a duty-based account, we regard ourselves as morally bound to reward those who have acted virtuously (on grounds that have to do more with our obligations than with their rights); moreover, in this tradition, the self-interested expectation of reward is usually seen as vitiating moral virtue. In utilitarian theories—which are by far the most common in this context— the rationale for reward is simply consequentialist. For example: 'Who sees not that whatever is produced or improved by a man's industry ought, for ever, to be secured to him in order to give encouragement to such useful habits and accomplishments.'[108] Here, the obligation to reward is based not on the interests of the recipient alone, but on all the interests that are benefited by his useful habits and accomplishments. Still, although they are not right-based, desert theories of appropriation are sufficiently close to the theories we are examining to be worthy of further discussion.

The claim that an action deserves a reward invites three questions: (1) What makes the action a good action? (2) Why should it be rewarded (as opposed to merely noted, praised or approved)? and (3) What reward is appropriate? These questions provide a useful framework for considering the Desert Theory of appropriators' entitlements.

(1) Why is labouring on common resources meritorious? There are two connected answers that a Lockean theorist can offer. Labouring is an act of direct obedience to God's command (I. 45–6 and II. 32–5) and therefore good in the sense of pious. Also labouring is good because it makes a useful contribution to the wealth and prosperity of mankind (II. 36–7). These points together generate a view, expressed throughout Locke's writings, that labouring is an activity proper to man, as much a part of his nature

---

[108] Hume, *Enquiry*, sect. 3, pt. 2, p. 195.

as, say, procreation. Idleness is therefore unnatural as well as unproductive and disobedient (though, as I have stressed already, Locke does not infer from this that labour is fulfilling or, in any sense, its own reward).[109]

But this leads to a fundamental difficulty. By these criteria, all labour is good whether it is the labour of an appropriator at the dawn of time, the labour of a tenant farmer on someone else's property, or the labour of a worker in modern industry. All these men are obeying God's command, all are contributing to the wealth of mankind (cf. II. 28 and 43), and all are acting in accordance with man's productive nature. Consider the following example:

One year A decides to work a previously uncultivated patch of ground and (assuming for the moment Locke's conclusion) thereby gain full rights of ownership in the land and its products. The following year A employs B to cultivate the same patch of land in the same manner, paying him a wage to do so. . . .[F]rom the point of view of desert, A and B have performed identical activities, and it seems that if ownership rights were the appropriate reward for A in the first year, they must also be for B in the second year.[110]

(It may be objected that the difference is that B's labour lacks the independent initiative of A's. But the example can be adapted to take account of this or to make B's labour deserving in other respects.) The point of the example is that a plausible theory of desert will not discriminate betwen the first labour and the second labour expended on a resource in the hard-and-fast way that a theory of appropriation requires. Since it is concerned with the intrinsic virtue of labouring, it cannot take account of facts such as that A's labour was temporally prior or that B's was done under contract.

It is easy to see why Locke's theory, interpreted in terms of desert, could be mistaken for a socialist theory of property.[111] If goods were to be distributed in accordance with desert and if, in the economic sphere, labouring was to be regarded as the most morally deserving activity, then industrial workers would have a greater claim to the wealth they produced than the subsistence wages they were paid by their (idle) employers. The wealth was produced with their toil, their sweat, and by their virtue, while the employer, who

[109] Ryan, *Property and Political Theory*, pp. 28–9.
[110] Miller, 'Justice and Property', p. 7.
[111] See e.g. Dunn, *Political Thought of John Locke*, p. 6 n. 1, and Tully, *A Discourse on Property*, p. x.

probably inherited the factory, may never have done a decent day's work in his life.

To put the point another way: it is difficult to see how a criterion of moral desert can serve as the basis for an initial distribution of property rights without also being brought into play to assess subsequent patterns of property-holding. If labour counted as deserving in the beginning, why does it not count as deserving now? But if later patterns are assessed (and redistributed in accordance with desert) then the historical entitlement character of the Lockean theory of property is undermined.[112] Locke's idea, then, that *first* labour generates an entitlement cannot easily be interpreted as a theory about the moral goodness of labouring.

(2) Not all morally good or right acts ought to be rewarded (at least on earth). If I fulfil the duty not to kill, I do what is right, but I am not usually regarded as meriting reward on that account. Even praise and approval seem inappropriate for the mere fulfilment of duty; duty is something that can simply be expected of me without further ado. Reward may be appropriate for supererogatory acts; in these cases we want to mark the fact that something has been done above and beyond the ordinary call of duty. But that hardly applies to the case we are considering.

There are two possible grounds for reward in the case of labour. The first is consequentialist: we reward A in order to encourage him and others to act in a similar way in the future. We all benefit when land is privately cultivated, and so we attach artificial pay-offs to acts of cultivation in order to make them attractive to those who undertake them. The second ground is connected with this. As we saw in section 2, though labouring was regarded as virtuous in the tradition Locke drew on, it was also regarded as unpleasant. So there may be almost a compensatory element involved in the reward. The suggestion may be that, unless some such compensation is forthcoming, people will have a motive to avoid onerous labour and try to live instead on the productive efforts of others.

(3) If a case can be established for rewarding meritorious labour, we must turn then to the question of what the reward should be. If the Desert Theory is taken as an interpretation of Locke's theory of property, the reward amounts to full and exclusive property rights in the resources one has worked on.

---

[112] Miller, 'Justice and Property', pp. 7–9; see also Dworkin, 'Equality of Resources', pp. 307–11.

This raises special problems for the utilitarian account of the merit of labour. If the contribution that the labourer has made to the good of mankind just *is* the improved value of the resources he has worked on, then it seems odd to give him the whole of that value (plus the original raw materials) as a reward for his contribution. Mankind as a whole is still better off at the end of this process, but men apart from the appropriator are worse off than they were before. He has added to the prosperity of society, but he gets to keep the extra he has added. Other men, who previously had rights in common over the unimproved resource, now sacrifice those to him as his reward. So he is much better off, and they are slightly worse off. A net gain in general utility, no doubt, but it is difficult to see that it is worth their while to encourage this sort of 'contribution' with this level of reward. The underlying point here is that the putative reward represents a cost to everyone but the person rewarded. His reward just *is* their submitting to the obligation to refrain from using the resources he has worked on. Perhaps people will make sacrifices to reward a particularly meritorious action. But Locke's theory implies something stronger— that this reward *ought* to be given and that the labourer is *entitled* to it. That seems odd in a situation where the sole merit of his deserving action consists in the fact that it benefits himself![113]

Locke does talk of benefits which other people derive from one man's appropriation. We considered earlier the view that they may benefit from decreased pressure on common land (II. 37). But this seems to take us even further away from the logic of reward. The benefit here arises not directly from the action of labouring, but from the action of living exclusively off one piece of land. So the benefit accrues to the others only if the labourer already has exclusive control of the land he has cultivated. Thus instead of being a reward *for* his beneficial action, the man is being 'rewarded' *in order to make* the action beneficial. We would have to distort both Locke's words and the notion of reward to sustain the Desert Theory as an interpretation of this part of his discussion.

I have connected the Desert Theory with the idea of moral virtue: a person deserves a reward roughly in proportion to his overall moral merit. Perhaps that is too strong. Sometimes punishments and rewards are meted out not on the basis of overall desert but on

---

[113] This seems to undermine the suggestions made in Becker, *Property Rights*, pp. 48–56.

the basis of merit internal to the activity within which the punishing and rewarding are taking place. In a game, for example, players are penalized for infractions of the rules irrespective of anything else about them or their character. Similarly, a gold medal is the reward *for* winning the race and nothing else. So, one might say, property entitlements are internally related to appropriation. They are just the reward *for* productive appropriation and they have no connection with moral virtue apart from that.[114] But by itself, this will not do as a justification of the origin of property entitlements. For we want to know *why* production and property should be internally connected in this way. Perhaps the reason lies in a more substantial notion of moral desert, or in the 'mixing labour' theory, or in some arbitrary convention. But the 'internal desert' theory which I have outlined here does not contribute anything to the argument on its own.

In general, the evidence for interpreting Locke's discussion as a theory of desert is very slender. He does regard labour as virtuous and appropriation as justified. But his view seems to be that the latter is necessarily bound up with the former, rather than being a reward connected with it on grounds of moral desert. We are told that 'God, by commanding to subdue, gave Authority so far to appropriate' and that the exigiencies of the human condition necessarily introduce 'Private Possessions' (II. 35). This is not the language of desert but the language of practical necessity. Just as special rights can arise out of a promise without being morally deserved by the promisee so, on Locke's view, exclusive property rights are conceived simply to arise out of individual labour on common resources without being 'awarded' as a response to the moral merit of labouring. It is true that we have not so far been able to find any interpretation of Locke's view which makes that position plausible, but I hope I have said enough about the Desert Theory to deter people from looking for any further assistance in that direction.[115]

Finally, I should mention another desert-based interpretation. Instead of (or as well as) saying that the labourer deserves property rights as a reward, one might say that the idle and the covetous

---

[114] I am grateful to Ronald Dworkin for suggesting this possibility.

[115] Alan Ryan takes the desert element in Locke's theory more seriously than I do: see Ryan, *Property and Political Theory*, p. 44. (See also the brief discussion in Ch. 10, sect. 2, below.)

deserve to forfeit their rights over previously common resources as a punishment for their sloth. This fits roughly with what Locke says in II. 34. But it is, of course, quite incompatible with the fact that the *industrious* cultivator of one patch of ground is excluded, every bit as much as the slothful idler, from the neighbouring patch of ground that someone else has cultivated.

14. THE SPOILATION PROVISO

In Locke's view, property rights can be exclusive without being unqualified. One qualification he imposes is that the appropriated resources must be put to some *use*:

God has given us all things richly, 1 Tim. vi. 17. is the Voice of Reason confirmed by Inspiration. But how far has he given it us? To enjoy. As much as any one can make use of to any advantage in life before it spoils; so much may he by his labour fix a Property in. Whatever is beyond this is more than his share, and belongs to others. (II.31)

Goods which are not used become common again despite someone's labour having been mixed with them. The property of labour cannot outweigh the fact that natural goods were intended by their creator to be used. Locke places particular stress on this with regard to land: '[I]f either the Grass of his Inclosure rotted on the Ground, or the Fruit of his planting perished without gathering, and laying up, this part of the Earth, notwithstanding his Inclosure, was still to be looked on as Waste and might be the Possession of any other' (II. 38).

The proviso, however, is a generous one, because Locke's concept of use is very broad. It is use 'to *any* advantage of life' and therefore is not confined to consumption or production for consumption, but also includes, for example, aesthetic uses and the use of the object as a commodity in exchange (II. 46). As long as 'Support and Comfort' of some sort are derived from it the spoilation proviso is satisfied. We have already seen that Lockean property can be interpreted as a man's exclusive right to determine which of the many uses that an object might have is going to be realized in fact. Once land has been improved by labour, it is for the labourer to decide how it shall be used. His title to make that decision lapses only if he fails to exercise it or exercises it in such a way as to prevent the land from ever being useful in any way to anyone at all.[116].

Locke contrasts the use of a resource with its wasteful destruction. Destruction in itself does not violate the spoilation proviso: often we destroy a thing in using it (I. 39). What Locke means is the negligent or deliberate loss of use-value without use, so that an object becomes useless for any human purpose. If this happens in circumstances where, but for the appropriation of the object, it might have been used by someone else, then the appropriation is retrospectively illegitimate and the appropriator guilty of a grave transgression of natural law. He has prevented an existing object created by God for human use from affording satisfaction to any human need or want.

Sometimes it is in a man's interest to let something perish uselessly in his possession. There is a scene in *The Grapes of Wrath*, in which armed men stand guard over a pile of rotting oranges which are being destroyed by their owners in order to maintain the market price.[117] Though the growers are better off, they have still violated the spoilation proviso. Unless they use the rotting oranges as manure or something like that, they have derived no advantage *from the use* of the fruit. Destroying the oranges is intended purely to bring about a situation in which it is as if they had never been created, as if that fruit had never been capable of satisfying the desires that the growers want to satisfy with the produce that they *do* intend to bring to the marketplace. That is why the armed guards are there—to ensure that the objects are destroyed but not destroyed through human consumption. The case, then, is a classic violation of the proviso.

When the proviso was introduced, Locke presented it as an answer to the objection, 'That if gathering the .. Fruits of the Earth, &c. makes a title to them, then any one may ingross as much as he will' (II. 31). But the proviso does not deal completely with that objection. It does rule out the case in which a man accumulates resources purely to beggar his neighbours, to diminish their ability

---

[116] In this regard, I see no justification for Tully's view that Locke's 'main ideological conclusion' was that 'fixed property in land does not have a natural foundation'. (Tully, *A Discourse on Property*, p. 122.) That interpretation is contradicted directly by Locke in one passage (*Two Treatises*, II, sect. 35, lines 16–17), and the passage Tully cites to support it (II, sect. 38, lines 16–17) refers only to the common practice of certain nomadic tribes.)

[117] Steinbeck, *Grapes of Wrath*, Ch. 25, esp. p. 369.

to satisfy their needs. But it does not generate any quantitative limit to human possessions. The amount a person can appropriate is determined not by this proviso but by the amount of labour he is capable of expending and by the various modes of use and consumption that are open to him. So long as desires are confined within the narrow bounds of 'a simple poor way of living' (II. 107), the appropriated holdings will be small and roughly equal. 'No Mans Labour could subdue, or appropriate all: nor could his Enjoyment consume more than a small part' (II. 36). If he wants to do nothing but eat its produce, a man's desires can be satisfied from a very small holding of land. A change occurs, however, as human desires grow more varied and new modes of satisfying them grow up. The patch of land that previously filled a man's belly with turnips may not satisfy his new aesthetic desires; 'his Enjoyment' now consumes more. With the growth of a money economy, it becomes possible for some men to command the labour of others and thus appropriate for themselves more than they could by their own energies. So the size of holdings increases and rough equality disappears. All this happens without any change in the terms of the spoilation proviso. It is not abrogated or rendered ineffective by the new conditions of economy, as some commentators have argued.[118] What happens is that it loses the quantitative delimiting character that was for a while associated with it as a result of the contingencies of a particular mode of production and exchange. Qualitatively its terms remain the same: appropriate as much as you can with your labour, but do not let anything perish uselessly in your possession.

15. 'ENOUGH AND AS GOOD LEFT IN COMMON FOR OTHERS'

It is commonly thought that Locke recognized a further constraint on legitimate appropriation: when he takes resources by labouring on them, a man must leave behind enough resources of the same quality for others to appropriate.

For this Labour being the unquestionable Property of the Labourer, no Man but he can have a right to what that is once joyned to, at least where there is enough and as good left in common for others. (II. 27) . . .

Nor was this appropriation of any parcel of Land, by improving it, any

[118] e.g. Macpherson, *Possessive Individualism*, p. 208.

prejudice to any other Man, since there was still enough, and as good left; and more than the yet unprovided could use. So that ineffect, there was never the less left for others because of his enclosure for himself. For he that leaves as much as another can make use of, does as good as take nothing at all. (II. 33)

But, on the traditional interpretation, if a man does not leave enough for others, then his appropriation is illegitimate, because exclusive rights for him are acquired at the expense of other people's ability to acquire equal and similar rights. This requirement has been called 'the Sufficiency Limitation'.[119]

I have argued elsewhere that this interpretation is implausible.[120] I will not repeat the textual basis for that argument here, except to say, first, that in the place where the Spoilation Proviso is introduced and discussed (II. 31), it is presented as though it were the only limit on appropriation, and in terms that would be redundant and absurd if the putative Sufficiency Limitation had been introduced a few sections earlier; and, secondly, that to say that appropriation is justified '*at least where*' there is enough left for others is not, on the face of it, to *restrict* appropriation to those circumstances.

The textual evidence in favour of interpreting 'sufficiency' as a restriction is mainly implicit and indirect. First, Locke is at pains to stress that a man who appropriates under conditions of plenty does no injury to anyone else (II. 36). It is tempting to infer that he means that a man who appropriates under conditions of scarcity *does* injure other people. (But of course that inference would be fallacious.)

Secondly, Locke appears to connect the age of plenty with the lack of any need for consent to appropriate and the age of money and scarcity with a suggestion that now, after all, property is based on consent. He says, for example, that there would still be enough land in the world for twice its population, 'had not the Invention of Money, and the tacit Agreement of Men to put a value on it, introduced (by consent) larger Possessions, and a right to them . . .' (II. 36). Perhaps Locke is suggesting here that once there has ceased to be enough left for everybody, unilateral appropriation is no longer a sufficient basis for exclusive property; it must now be underwritten by consent. Tully takes this to mean that 'with the

[119] Macpherson, *Possessive Individualism*, p. 211.
[120] See Waldron, 'Enough and As Good'.

introduction of money, . . . the theory of natural appropriation and use has no application' and that property holdings must now be distributed conventionally.[121] But even if we were to concede the existence of a Sufficiency Limitation, this would be an exaggeration. Locke believes the consent involved in the introduction of money (i.e. the conventional basis of its exchange-value) is quite sufficient to legitimize the 'disproportionate and unequal Possession of the earth' (II. 50) that results from its use. He does not seem to think that anything more is necessary to introduce 'a Right [to] larger Possessions' (II. 36); on the contrary, appropriation can proceed subsequently on the same basis as before. There is no suggestion at all that the resulting distribution of resources must also be agreed to.[122]

Thirdly, in his discussion of the English common, Locke attributes the illegitimacy of unilateral enclosure to two factors. First, since it is a 'common by compact', the commoners must consent to any variation of the terms of their agreement. Secondly, '[T]he remainder, after such inclosure, would not be as good to the rest of the Commoners as the whole was, when they could all make use of the whole: whereas in the beginning and first peopling of the great Common of the world, it was quite otherwise' (II. 35). There is some tension here with the argument in II. 37 (lines 12–32). But this is the passage in the *Treatise* where Locke comes closest to explicit recognition of something like a Sufficiency Proviso.

My interpretation is somewhat different. When Locke does refer to it, the fact of sufficiency for all is spoken of as *an effect* of the early operation of the Spoilation Proviso rather than as a limitation in its own right. Enough and as good left for others is what happens when a small number of people appropriate land, each by his own efforts, to satisfy simple and uniform needs:

The measure of Property, Nature has well set, by the Extent of Mens Labour, and the conveniency of Life: No Mans Labour could subdue, or appropriate all: nor could his Enjoyment consume more than a small part; so that it was impossible for any Man, this way, to intrench upon the right of another, or acquire to himself, a Property, to the Prejudice of his Neighbour, who would still have room, for as good, and as large a Possession (after the other had taken out his) and before it was

<hr>

[121] Tully, *A Discourse on Property*, p. 146.

[122] Does monetarization precede politicization in Locke? (The point is discussed in sect. 16, below.) Certainly for Locke, the former is not in any way dependent on the latter, and the consent involved in each process is quite different.

appropriated. This measure did confine evry Man's Possession, to a very moderate Proportion . . . (II. 36)

So long as these conditions obtained, 'there could be no doubt of right, no room for quarrel' (II. 39): nobody could 'think himself injur'd' by another's appropriation (II. 33). Such grievance would be rationally incomprehensible since there was no way such an appropriation could be said to harm him. (Of course, people would still covet one another's possessions: an abundance of unimproved resources is compatible with a shortage of improved or manufactured goods. So property rights would still have some work to do.) Locke seems to have been in two minds as to whether this situation still obtained at the time he was writing. Sometimes he suggests that it does. If a man cannot find land here to appropriate, 'let him plant in some in-land, vacant places of America, we shall find that the Possessions he could make himself upon the measure we have given, would not be very large, nor even to this day, prejudice the rest of Mankind, or give them reason to complain, or think themselves injured by this Man's Incroachment' (II. 36). But later he notes that with the introduction of money, larger possessions have been introduced, so that men may well now be 'straitned' by one another's acquisitions.

What happens, then, when there are no longer enough resources for everyone to appropriate? At least this: people now begin to have at least a comprehensible concern about other people's appropriations, for their well-being is now affected by them, perhaps for the worse. We can expect disputes over property rights to become more frequent, and we can expect that there will also be an increase in violations of what appropriators take to be their rights. The combination of the 'evil Concupiscence' which money brings with it and the disputes which arise inevitably out of the appropriation of scare resources, means that the primitive judicial procedures which characterized the early ages of the world are no longer satisfactory. This, as we saw, will be the motiviation for the move to civil society (II. 38, 105–111, and 123 ff.).

But, in my interpretation, although the growth of scarcity may undermine respect for and ready recognition of appropriators' rights, it need not be taken to undermine the justifiability of the rights themselves. Indeed, on one reading of the argument for appropriation, it would be inconsistent for Locke to suggest this. As we saw earlier (section 7, above), Locke believed (mistakenly) that any human use of natural resources involved private appropriation, and that needs could not be satisfied nor the duty to labour discharged without the introduction of private possessions. Consider, then, the situation of a man who faces conditions of moderate scarcity. He has the capacity to apppropriate the resources he needs but he knows that in doing so he will be depriving at least some others of the opportunity to make a similar appropriation. What is he to do? If a Sufficiency Proviso is in operation, the man in this situation must sit back and starve, since by feeding himself he would be appropriating resources (II. 28) in violation of natural law. Since everyone else in that situation is in the same position, presumably everyone must starve for the same reason, and all God's human creatures would perish notwithstanding the fact that He had provided resources for the sustenance of at least some of them. Such a result, dictated by the alleged proviso in conditions of scarcity, is absurd in view of Locke's general ethical position. Although the fundamental duty of the law of nature is the preservation of mankind or as much of it as possible (II. 6, 11, 16, 25, 128, 129, 134, 149, 159, 168, and 182), an individual's first moral responsibility in this connection is to himself: 'Every one as he is bound to preserve himself, and not to quit his Station wilfully; so by the like reason *when his own Preservation comes not in competition*, ought he, as much as he can to preserve the rest of mankind' (II. 6; my emphasis). It follows, surely, that he who appropriates the food and shelter he really needs is entitled, even bound, to use them—*irrespective of the needs of others*. (Of course, if he appropriates more than he needs, then 'his own Preservation comes not in competition', and other needy people have a right to be sustained out of his surplus (I. 42).

Thus the 'enough and as good' idea cannot be construed as a restriction on legitimate appropriation without concluding that it is inconsistent with what Locke claimed to be the fundamental law of nature. Locke, indeed, is not a philosopher noted for his consistency (least of all in matters of natural law),[123] but where the imputation of inconsistency is based on a strained reading of the text, and where a more natural reading avoids the inconsistency, then the strained reading should be dropped.

We should note finally the drastic effect that a Sufficiency Limitation would have on Locke's account of property. If such a

---

[123] See e.g. Laslett, 'Introduction' to Locke, *Two Treatises*, pp. 79 ff.

Limitation were imposed, it would not be the sort of thing that could be satisfied at one time (in an age of abundance) but dispensed with later (in time of scarcity), as C. B. Macpherson suggests.[124] The argument to this effect is due to Nozick. Consider the first person X for whom there is not enough and as good left to appropriate. The last person to appropriate, Y, left Z without his previous liberty to act on an object so as to appropriate it, and in that sense did not leave enough for him. So Y's appropriation would not be allowable under the Limitation. Therefore the penultimate appropriator, X, left Y unable to make an appropriation, for he left him in a situation where he, Y, could not appropriate without straitening Z. Therefore X's appropriation would be illegitimate. But then the antepenultimate appropriator, W, ended permissible appropriation, leaving X in this position, and so his appropriation was impermissible. And so on right back to the first person, A, to appropriate a permanent property right.[125] As A. M. Honoré points out: 'However one interprets Locke's requirement that the acquirer must leave enough and as good in common for others ... the intention behind it is not satisfied unless entitlements are adjusted from time to time according to what then remains for others.'[126]

Why would Locke have claimed that such a limitation must be recognized? The most plausible answer is given by Tully. The Sufficiency Limitation is simply the recognition, so far as acquisition is concerned, of everyone's original claim-right to an adequate subsistence from the resources of the world.[127] This is an inalienable and imprescriptible right given by God; it cannot, in Locke's view, be abrogated by someone else's unilateral action. So if someone has appropriated resources in circumstances of such scarcity that others are left in desperate need, the property rights he acquires will be limited by the others' rights to use any resources that are surplus to his survival needs to satisfy their own.

I do not deny that Lockean property was limited in this way. But this limitation is somewhat different from the so-called Sufficiency Limitation. The latter does not give everyone a general claim-right to subsistence, rather it purports to give them a general claim-right to appropriate: everyone has a right that sufficient resources should

[124] Macpherson, *Possessive Individualism*, pp. 211 ff.
[125] Nozick, *Anarchy, State, and Utopia*, p. 176.
[126] Honoré, 'Property, Title, and Redistribution', p. 113 n.
[127] Tully, *A Discourse on Property*, p. 129.

be left in common for him to make an *appropriation* that is as good as anyone else's. It is easy to show that these rights are not equivalent. Allowing an individual access to resources for appropriation may be one way of assuring his subsistence, but there are others. He may survive through gainful employment on the property of others, or through charitable provision.[128] So by enforcing a Sufficiency Limitation, we would be limiting the ways in which we could ensure the survival of others, and we may well limit the number of people we were able to preserve. Suppose there is enough land for some but not all to appropriate a workable patch. Given a Sufficiency Limitation, nobody may appropriate unless everybody can; so in this situation, everyone must try to survive working on common land without any sort of enclosure. But allowing appropriation by a few might well (as Locke believed) increase the net social product (II. 36–7). If so, the operation of the simple principle of charity on this product would allow more people to survive than would survive under the auspices of the Sufficiency Limitation. So, once again the alleged Limitation seems to be in conflict with Locke's fundamental law of nature, which is that as many people should be preserved as possible.

One or two commentators have recognized that it is implausible to attribute to Locke the view that appropriators are required to leave an equal opportunity for others. Nozick suggests a more flexible limitation: an appropriation must not actually *worsen* the situation of anyone else. Now it is true that a person's situation is prima facie made worse by his losing the opportunity to appropriate, but, on the other hand, he may gain from the increased prosperity which another person's appropriation injects into the community. So long as no *net* loss is suffered, Nozick argues, no one may legitimately complain.[129]

Of course, on Nozick's reconstruction, there is a problem, as he says, 'of fixing the baseline': Lockean appropriation makes people no worse off than they would be *how*?[130] Perhaps a plausible answer is: no worse off in point of the satisfaction of their needs than they were immediately before the appropriation. But this is unsatisfactory, at any rate as an interpretation of Locke. Suppose a man is starving at the time of my appropriation because (unlike me)

---

[128] See sect. 17, below.

[129] Nozick, *Anarchy, State, and Utopia*, pp. 175–6.

[130] Ibid. 177. For a slightly different view, see Gauthier, *Morals by Agreement*, Ch. 6; I have not had time to consider Gauthier's argument here.

he does not have the energy to gather any manna. Once I have appropriated some manna, that person is still starving, but he is no *more* starving as a result of my acquiring exclusive rights to the manna than he was as a result of its natural unavailability to him. Nevertheless Locke's doctrine of charity gives him a right to my surplus food once I have made it physically capable of being used by him. My appropriation does not make him worse off, but it does make a difference to him; for now, the only thing standing between him and sustenance is the enforcement of my property rights. For Locke that is significant: since the *raison d'être* of property is human sustenance, property rights must never stand in the way of sustenance. Nozick's reconstruction of the 'Lockean Proviso', then, is too weak for Locke; it does not even live up to the demands of the minimal Lockean requirement of charity.

If we are going to adopt a weaker 'Lockean Proviso', it seems most plausible simply to identify it with the doctrine of charity: property rights, however acquired, do not prevail in the face of desperate need.[131] The weakened Nozickian proviso, then, is at best a special case of this. It is the doctrine of charity applied to appropriation: no appropriation is legitimate if (taking everything into account) it makes the survival of any other person less rather than more likely.

If this much is conceded, is there any reason to *add* to Locke's theory (understood in this way) the more stringent condition—that there be enough and as good left for others *to appropriate*? We have shown that the so-called Sufficiency Proviso must not be allowed to displace the principle of charitable subsistence. But instead of competing with that principle, Sufficiency could be ranked lexically below it, so that others must always be left with an opportunity to make an appropriation if (but only if) this can be done without limiting our capacity to ensure general subsistence.[132] Is there any justification for including the stronger Sufficiency Limitation in this way?

I should say at once that this is an important issue for my interpretation of Locke's theory. On my view, his is mainly an SR-based theory of property (though there is the general right to

---

[131] For my argument for this principle, see Ch. 7.

[132] For lexical ordering, see Rawls, *A Theory of Justice*, sects. 8–9. The idea is not an anachronism in this context, for we already have it implicitly in Locke's theory of natural law: it is exactly the relation between the duties of self-and other-preservation indicated in *Two Treatises*, II, sect. 6.

subsistence in the background). But on the interpretation of the Sufficiency Limitation suggested in the previous paragraph, men would have a *general* right to private property, in the sense that they would have a right, enforceable against others, not to be left in a situation where appropriation was impossible for them. Anyone who wanted to appropriate resources (and so acquire private property rights) and found none around to appropriate could, on this account, claim that his rights were being violated. Even if he had plenty to eat out of the common supply and a job to do, he could say that, nevertheless, he ought to be given access *as an appropriator* to the natural means of subsistence and production. Locke is often regarded as the theorist *par excellence* of 'the natural right to property', and usually this is just a sloppy way of saying that he believed property rights could be acquired in a state of nature.[133] But if we sustain the present interpretation, we are attributing to him the much stronger claim that, prior to particular property rights, each person has the natural right, enforceable against others, to an opportunity to acquire property rights by appropriation. Since this interpretation would change the character of Locke's theory radically so far as my analysis is concerned, it is worth considering whether there is any basis for it.

We have seen already that it is not required by Locke's view that men have a general right to subsistence. That can be satisfied without everyone having to make a private appropriation of natural resources. But what about Locke's views on labour? Since he regarded productive labour as a duty, and since he believed that people generally had a right to be able to carry out their duties, does this not generate a general right to appropriate good by labour? Again the answer is 'No'. Although, on Locke's account, appropriative labour is productive, the converse need not be true. A man may work and fulfil God's command even though he does not own or come to own the resources he is working on. The labour of a servant is productive and virtuous even though he has no property in his means of production and no rights over his product. Similarly there is nothing in Locke's argument to indicate that he thought it morally necessary for people to mix their labour with virgin resources. There is nothing, for example, remotely corresponding to Hegel's view that a person must embody his freedom in an external object and so become an owner in order to develop

---

[133] See the discussion above, in Ch. 1.

ethically as an individual.[134] On Locke's account, some people get
to mix their labour with unowned resources while others do not. If
he refers to the former occasionally as 'the Industrious and
Rational' (II. 34), it is only to provide a basis for his criticism of the
'Quarrelsom and Contentious'—those who groundlessly covet the
property of others, whether they have property themselves or not.

To sum up. There is nothing in Locke's discussion to indicate
that he believed private appropriation satisfied any deep need in
man apart from the physical needs that were satisfied by the
appropriated resources. Since it is possible for those needs to be
satisfied without appropriation, there is no basis for attributing to
Locke the strong Sufficiency Limitation or the general right to
private property that would go along with it.

16. MONEY AND EXCHANGE

Locke contrasts the rough equality of property holdings in the early
ages of the world with the 'disproportionate and unequal Possession of the Earth' (II. 50) that he saw around him in his day. But he
regarded both distributions as legitimate and invoked the fact of the
introduction of money into what was previously a use-and-barter
economy to explain the transition from the one sort of distribution
to the other.

He begins with an account of exchange. Since most useful
resources are perishable, a man may not hoard up too many of
them for fear of violating the Spoilation Proviso. From his earlier
discussion of that Proviso, one might have thought it wrong to
appropriate goods surplus to one's capacity to consume: 'As much
as any one *can make use of* to any advantage of life before it spoils;
so much may he by his Labour fix a Property in. *Whatever is
beyond this, is more than his share* and belongs to others' (II. 31;
my emphasis). This appears to imply that goods become common
property again as soon as it is clear that they are surplus to the
appropriator's personal requirements.

But in II. 46, Locke indicates that this is not his view. The terms
of the Spoilation Proviso, he says, are not breached unless the goods

[134] Cf. Ryan, 'Locke and the Dictatorship of the Bourgeoisie', p. 224: 'According
to Macpherson, Locke holds that capitalists develop their personalities in capitalism;
but Locke says nothing of the sort.'

in question actually perish. Once they do then, retrospectively, their appropriation may be held illegitimate. But until they do, even if they are manifestly surplus to his capacity to make personal use of them, they remain exclusively at the disposal of their appropriator. Locke attempts to reinforce this view by extending the meaning of 'use' to include not only consumption and the satisfaction of personal wants and needs but also giving, bartering, and exchanging:

> If he gave away a part to any body else, so that it perished not uselessly in his Possession, these he also made use of. And if he also bartered away Plums that would have rotted in a week, for Nuts that would last good for his eating a whole Year, he did no injury; he wasted not the common stock; destroyed no part of the portion of Goods that belonged to others, so long as nothing perished uselessly in his hands. (II. 46)

Perhaps, though, this extension of 'use' is unnecessary for Locke's account of exchange. Certainly it has no connection with his underlying view that the world was given to us to use. (The terms of God's donation would not be satisfied if every resource was forever and exclusively circulated as an exchangeable commodity!) The important thing about exchange is not that exchanging things is a way of using them but that the goods eventually get used in the narrower sense, i.e. consumed or applied to human wants. Exchange is simply a mechanism for allocating goods to those who need to make use of them (again in the narrower sense) at any particular time. The situation, then, is that the proprietor has exclusive rights to deal with and control the destiny of the resources he owns. He may use them himself or give them away to someone else to use, on whatever terms he likes. The only limitation is that he must not deal with them in such a way that they perish uselessly while under his control (and the same goes for those to whom he transfers the goods).

One immediate implication of the growth of barter is that it becomes legitimate for men to own and cultivate more land than they can personally consume the produce of. One acre of turnips may suffice for my needs; but if I appropriate ten acres, I can exchange the surplus turnips for objects others have appropriated that are less perishable than my produce. These other objects may be walnuts which last longer and can be used at leisure or exchanged again for more turnips when my reserved supplies run out. Or I may exchange them for 'a piece of Metal' or 'Shells' or 'a sparkling Pebble or a Diamond'—objects whose usefulness to me (in the strict sense of enjoyment) is entirely aesthetic and which can be hoarded indefinitely or exchanged at any time to buy other objects or commodities. Since these objects never perish they can be accumulated by a large landowner as he receives them in exchange for his produce, 'the exceeding of the bounds of his just Property not lying in the largeness of his Possession, but the perishing of anything uselessly in it' (II. 46). Provided a man can find a market for the produce that he cultivates, there is no limit, apart from the amount of the appropriative labour he commands, on the extent of his appropriation.

Tully argues that, on Locke's view, land itself cannot be exchanged.[135] But he offers no evidence for this interpretation apart from the fact that Locke does not mention the exchange of land in II. 46 and 50. The interpretation seems plainly mistaken. Since land, on Locke's account, can be bequeathed (II. 73), given away (II. 193) and rented (II. 194), it is hard to discern any obstacle in the letter or logic of the argument to its being exchanged. Tully's aim is to show (against Macpherson) that neither land nor money can function as capital according to Locke. But in this regard, both Tully and Macpherson are wrong. In the *Two Treatises*, Locke says next to nothing about the use of resources as capital. We cannot infer anything from the silence. The most we can say is that there is nothing in the logic of the rest of Locke's argument to justify Tully's imputation of an underlying hostility to capitalism.

Locke does appear to assume that there is a latent acquisitiveness in human nature which can be expected to surface as soon as it is freed by the introduction of money from the constraints of natural law: 'Find out something that hath the Use and Value of Money amongst his Neighbours, you shall see the same Man will begin presently to enlarge his Possessions' (II. 49). To this extent, Macpherson is correct to relate Locke's conception of human nature, along with Hobbes's, to the spirit of rising capitalism.[136] Both Hobbes and Locke presented views of human nature which made it particularly apt for a dynamic and acquisitive economy. It is true that Locke talked sometimes about the artificiality of much contemporary acquisitiveness. He spoke in the *Essay* of 'the

[135] Tully, *A Discourse on Property*, p. 149.
[136] Macpherson, *Possessive Individualism*.

fantastical *uneasiness* (as itch after *Honour, Power,* or *Riches,* etc) which acquir'd habits by Fashion, Example, and Education have settled in us',[137] and in the *Second Treatise* of the 'vain ambition, and *amor sceleratus habendi*, evil concupiscence' (II. 111) which entered human affairs with the introduction of money. But on his view, human nature was always liable to be so corrupted: 'Nor can it be otherwise in a Creature, whose thoughts are more than the Sands, and wider than the Ocean . . . Their imagination is always restless and suggests variety of thoughts, and the will, reason being laid aside, is ready for every extravagant project' (I. 58). Custom and convention do no more than crystallize these tendencies; all that was lacking in primitive society was the moral opportunity to indulge them in material terms.

It is, moreover, wrong to suggest that Locke was unequivocally enthusiastic about 'the Innocence and Sincerity of that poor but virtuous Age' (II. 110) before human affairs were monetarized; and wrong also to say that all 'the consequences of work and industry which he wishes to endorse accrue to mankind without the use of money'.[138] In that age, there may have been less conflict because there was enough land—indeed, much more than enough—for everyone to cultivate (II. 36–7). But this point also had its bad side. It meant that vast tracts of land lay neglected and uncultivated and that the earth did not bear anything like the number of inhabitants it was capable of sustaining. Man was commanded by God to 'Be fruitful, and multiply, and replenish the Earth' (I. 33 and 41) and Locke regarded underpopulation as a damning indictment of any society (I. 33 and 106). But by definition underpopulation is exactly the condition of a society where there is more than enough land for everyone to appropriate. Unappropriated land is worth very little, on Locke's view—

So little, that even amongst us, Land that is left wholly to Nature, that hath no improvement of Pasturage, Tillage, or Planting, is called, as indeed it is, *wast*; and we shall find the benefit of it amount to little more than nothing. This shews, how much numbers of men are to be preferd to largeness of dominions, and that the increase of lands and the right imploying of them, is the great art of government. (II. 42)

Since Locke adds, a few sections later, that such a waste of land 'can scarce happen amongst that part of Mankind, that have consented

---

[137] Locke, *Essay*, Bk. II, Ch. xxi, sect. 45.
[138] Tully, *A Discourse on Property,* p. 130.

to the use of money' (II. 45), it is clear that he did not regard the monetarization of the primitive economy as altogether a bad thing.

We have seen that the introduction of money, on Locke's account, leads inevitably to an increase in material inequality. It does so initially by exaggerating the differences between men's ability to labour: 'As different degrees of Industry were apt to give Men possessions in different Proportions, so this Invention of Money gave them the opportunity to continue to enlarge them' (II. 46.) An energetic appropriator, with the capacity to exchange his products for durable goods, finds that the sky is the limit so far as appropriation is concerned; while those who either cannot or will not labour so industriously on natural resources soon find that the opportunity for any appropriation at all is rapidly diminishing.

Locke shares our modern suspicion of this sort of inequality. Whether in response to qualms based on something like a Sufficiency Limitation or on the basis of some other concern, he is at pains to stress that this 'inequality of private possessions' (II. 50) has been tacitly consented to and that therefore its legitimacy cannot be doubted. Property relations now involve a conventional element which was not there in pre-monetary times.

Tully has claimed that 'this second phase of Locke's theory occurs after the establishment of government'.[139] But Locke contradicts this: 'This partage of things, in an inequality of private possessions, men have made practicable *out of the bounds of Societie, and without compact*, only by putting a value on gold and silver and tacitly agreeing to the use of Money' (II. 50; my emphasis). If we want to periodize Locke's theory of property, we should talk perhaps of three phases: (1) rough equality under conditions of plenty; (2) unequal possessions, under conditions of scarcity, made legitimate by the introduction of money; and (3) the regulation of property under government. Perhaps (2) leads eventually to (3), on Locke's account, but it is a mistake nevertheless to identify them.

What sort of tacit consent is involved in the introduction of money? Locke relates it to the fact that the value of money is conventional. The 'intrinsick value' of a thing depends only on 'its usefulness to the Life of Man', and in this sense 'a little piece of yellow metal' does not have the value of 'a great piece of Flesh, or a whole heap of Corn'. (II. 37). Such an equivalence can be

[139] Tully, *A Discourse on Property*, pp. 129–30, 152–4, and 165.

established only by 'fancy or Agreement' between men (II. 46), and is, in itself, 'but a Phantastical imaginary value', with no foundation in nature (II. 184). Now it is trivially true that all those who make use of a currency must subscribe at least implicitly to the conventions that establish its value. It is tempting to conclude, then that where monetarization is prevalent, consent to it will have been universal. Sometimes Locke maintains that all mankind have joined in this agreement: 'For *mankind*, having consented to put an imaginary value upon gold and silver, by reason of their durableness, scarcity and not being liable to be counterfeited, have made them by general consent, the common pledges.'[140] But elsewhere he implies that the agreement is regional not universal and he talks of places where the inhabitants have not 'joyned with the rest of Mankind, in the consent of the Use of their Common Money' (II. 45 and 48).

Much later he rests an important argument on this point. The amount of reparations that a conqueror in a just war can claim is limited to the 'intrinsick value' of the goods that have been taken by the defeated aggressor. The aggressor is not liable to make good the exchange-value of the 'Riches and Treasure' he has stolen, because the duty of reparation is natural and nature knows nothing of the conventional value of these objects (II. 184). Now either this is an appallingly bad argument or it rests on the possibility that conqueror and aggressor might not have been parties to the same monetary conventions. If they were not, it would be unfair to impose the conqueror's estimation of the value of his loss on the liabilities of the aggressor. But if they were, surely the natural obligation to abide by the conventions one has entered into (II. 14) would oblige the vanquished party to recognize and make good the value of the treasure he has stolen on the basis of his own prior agreement as to the worth of objects of that sort. A charitable interpretation of this argument, then, requires us to question the universality of the consent to the introduction of money in Locke's account.

But once this is admitted, the argument that Locke bases on monetary consent begins to crumble. Not *everyone* needs to agree to put a value on gold and silver before monetarization gets under way: it is sufficient if only those who are going to be parties to

[140] Locke, *Considerations of the Lowering of Interest and Raising the Value of Money*, p. 15.

monetary transactions agree. As Nozick and others have pointed out, provided only that those who are going to do business in a monetarized market can reach a point of co-ordination in their dealings, no express or universal agreement will be necessary even among them.[141] Now, consider a man who has made no appropriation of land and who has taken from nature only the goods that he personally needs. He will have no occasion to go to market or engage in any money transactions; he lives on the basis of a domestic subsistence mode of production and has no surplus to exchange.[142] But he above all will be prejudiced by the increased appropriations of those who are more energetic than he is, once money is introduced, and by the unequal and disproportionate possession of the earth that results. Locke then has made a terrible mistake in thinking that the conventional basis of monetarization implies universal consent to the resulting inequality. Those who benefit from the inequality must certainly consent to the intro- duction of money that made it possible; but those who are most gravely prejudiced by it are likely to have had no say in the matter.

There is also another obvious objection to Locke's argument. Is consent to the introduction of money the same as consent to the consequences of the introduction of money? If I engage in one small monetary transaction, am I then acting in bad faith and going back on my (implicit) word if I subsequently complain about the unequal distribution of land or about the fact that I have been left with little or nothing? Perhaps there is an argument in Locke's theory for saying that I have no legitimate ground for my complaint, but it has nothing to do with my consent to the introduction of money. The argument would be that I can have no objection in any case to others' entering into voluntary transactions that allow them to avoid the force of the Spoilation Proviso. But if we were inclined to deny this, that is, if we thought nevertheless that I do have some ground for complaint (perhaps on the basis of some version of the Sufficiency Proviso), then it is difficult to see that the mere fact of my acquiescence in the use of money would change our minds in this respect.

My conclusion, then, is that the consent involved in the introduction of money makes no difference to the legitimacy of the

---

[141] Nozick, *Anarchy, State, and Utopia*, p. 18.
[142] For domestic subsistence mode of production, see Taylor, *Community, Anarchy, and Liberty*, pp. 105–7.

resulting inequality. Locke must choose: either inequality is illegitimate, or its legitimacy in the state of nature has nothing to do with consent.

17. MASTERS AND SERVANTS

Discussion of Locke's theory of money and inequality leads naturally to a consideration of his view of wages and of the relationship between master and servant. Here as elsewhere, the claims put forward by Tully provide a useful point of departure.[143]

One of the the things Tully is concerned to do in *A Discourse on Property* is to rebut the suggestion, made popular by C. B. Macpherson[144], that Locke's 'state of nature' exhibits many of the features of a capitalist economy including, most importantly, the wage relation. For Macpherson's claim to be sustained, it would have to be shown that a proletariat could exist in Locke's state of nature; in other words, it would have to be the case that many people would have no access to the means of production except by selling their labour power to landowners or the owners of industrial resources in return for money wages. That Locke took this for granted as a feature of the seventeenth-century English economy is clear and well-documented.[145] The introduction of money makes possible the development of larger and more unequal acquisitions which leave some people 'straitn'd' by the possessions of others (II. 36). But the evidence for attributing any view to him about the actual legitimacy of the wage relation in the state of nature is a little scanty.

The clearest hint that we have comes in this passage in Locke's elaboration of the Labour Theory of initial acquisition:

Thus the Grass my Horse has bit; the Turfs my Servant has cut; and the Ore I have digg'd in any place where I have a right to them in common with others, become my Property, without the assignation or consent of any body. The labour that was mine, removing them out of that common state they were in, hath fixed my Property in them. (II. 28)

It is the reference to the servant that is crucial. The implication seems to be that the labour performed by my servant counts as

---

[143] This section is adapted from my paper, 'The Turfs My Servant has Cut'
[144] Macpherson, *Possessive Individualism*, Ch. 5.
[145] See Macpherson's discussion and references, ibid., pp. 216 ff.

'mine'. So it must be possible, on Locke's view, for the labour—not just the products of the labour, but the labour itself—of one person to become the property of another.

There is a question as to how conclusive this passage is. Although it occurs early in Locke's discussion of property, when he is talking about property in the state of nature, its specific context is an analogy between acquisition in the state of nature and acquisition by individuals 'in *Commons*, which remain so by Compact' (II. 28). The two situations are supposed to be on a par inasmuch as they both involve acquisition of goods by labour 'in any place where I have a right to them in common with others'; and clearly Locke intended acquisition in commons to throw some light on acquisition in the state of nature. Macpherson believes we can simply take Locke's bland asssumption of the wage-relation in regard to commons, and 'read it back' into the state of nature with which commons, in this passage, were being compared.[146] And, on the face of it, there does not seem to be any obstacle to this approach.

Tully, however, offers two arguments against the proposition that capitalist relations are already enshrined in Locke's state of nature. In the first place, he argues that Locke imposes a general prohibition on coercive exploitation which makes capitalist relations in the state of nature morally impossible. And, secondly, he argues that Locke's *other* comments on the master–servant relation, if read carefully, show that it does not involve the sale and transfer of labour power but only an agreement by the labourer to perform a specific task for the benefit of another. In fact, both these arguments seem dubious.

Tully begins by insisting that the relation between master and servant, like other relations in the state of nature, is taken by Locke to be a voluntary one. But Tully's views on what counts as voluntariness are completely at odds with Locke's conception of these relationships. Compare the following two passages. First, Tully:

Since it is a freeman who makes himself a servant, the agreement must presuppose that the choice not to become a servant is available to him . . . If, for some reason, there is no alternative, then the man is not free and the master–servant relation cannot arise. . . . If a man is driven by necessity to work for another, then the necessity is based on force . . . [147]

---

[146] Macpherson, *Possessive Individualism*, p. 217.
[147] Tully, *A Discourse on Property*, p. 137.

And now, Locke:

> God having made Man such a Creature, that, in his own Judgement, it was not good for him to be alone, put him under strong Obligations of Necessity, Convenience, and Inclination to drive him into Society, as well as fitted him with Understanding and Language to continue and enjoy it. The first Society was between Man and Wife, which gave beginning to that between Parents and Children; to which, in time, that between Master and Servant came to be added . . . (II. 77).

Only if we drive a wedge between the talk here about 'Obligations of Necessity' and the mention of master and servant can we regard Locke's conception of the latter as *voluntary* in Tully's sense. Of course, 'Convenience' and 'Inclination' must be taken into account too. But the important point is that Locke assumes that the element of 'Necessity' will be present and does not take the view that it detracts from the legitimacy of the relationships in question. It is significant, I think, that Tully in his discussion of master and servant makes no mention of this passage at all, nor of the passages in the *Essay Concerning Human Understanding* in which Locke suggests that 'the greatest part of mankind . . . are given up to labour and enslaved to the necessity of their mean condition, whose lives are worn out only in the provisions for living', adding that this is 'the natural and unalterable state of things in this world and the constitution of human affairs.'[148]

Instead, Tully relies on the following passage from the *First Treatise*:[149]

> a Man can no more justly make use of another's necessity, to force him to become his Vassal, by withholding that Relief, God requires him to afford to the wants of his Brother, than he that has more strength can seize upon a weaker, master him to his Obedience, and with a dagger at his Throat offer him Death or Slavery. (I. 42)

Now this passage, together with the rest of sections 41–3 of the *First Treatise*, is, as we have seen, undoubtedly very important. But it does not yield the conclusion that Tully wants. Locke is talking here about forcing someone to become one's vassal. His argument against Filmer at this point is that the exclusive property in land which Filmer supposes Adam to have cannot give him 'Power over the Life of another' (I. 41 and 42) or 'Soveraign Arbitrary

[148] Locke, *Essay*, Bk. IV, Ch. ii sect. 20. (p. 297).
[149] Tully, *A Discourse on Property*, p. 137.

Authority' (I. 41). But as Locke himself insists (II. 2), this is not the sort of power claimed by a master; so the argument that this *despotic* power cannot be acquired under conditions of the weaker party's necessity leaves untouched the view that the master–servant relation *can* be established under these conditions.

Indeed, elsewhere Locke denies that 'Soveraign Arbitrary Authority' can be created voluntarily at all; since men have no legitimate power over their own lives, they cannot transfer it to another (II. 23). So even if a man were not under strong obligations of material necessity, the sort of relationship Locke is describing in this passage could not be established legitimately. Therefore we cannot extrapolate from the passage in question any general requirement of voluntariness, in Tully's sense, for these relationships.

The most that follows from the passage Tully quotes is that the capitalist has a duty to relieve the dire needs of the propertyless worker 'where he had no means to subsist otherwise' (I. 42). He must not let him starve. But if the capitalist offers the needy man employment, then it is no longer the case that he has 'no means to subsist otherwise', and the doctrine of charity—including the doctrine that in circumstances of true need the propertyless person has a *right* to others' goods—is no longer in play.

Perhaps Tully can take up a slightly stronger position. Surely if there are moral objections to even the voluntary establishment of the vassal relationship, because of the sort of relationship it is, so also there may be moral objections to the wage relationship just because of the sort of relationship *it* is. This seems to be his position in the following passage:

In purchasing an agent's power to labour and in directing it, the capitalist destroys the autonomy of the person. For Locke, this would be to destroy his very humanity; that combination of concept and execution which makes a human agent like God. In this respect, the agent who is directed in his activity is like the slave or vassal, the very relation to which Locke's servant is contrasted.[150]

Now today it is the case that everyone shares Tully's concern about alienated labour. But attributing it to Locke may be an anachronism. Consider, for example, another distinction Locke made, which Tully overlooks, between *slavery* and *drudgery*:

I confess, we find among the Jews, as well as other Nations, that Men did

---

[150] Tully, *A Discourse on Property*, p. 141.

sell themselves; but, 'tis plain, this was only to Drudgery, not to Slavery. For, it is evident, the Person sold was not under an Absolute, Arbitrary, Despotical Power. For the Master could not have power to kill him, at any time, whom, at a certain time, he was obliged to let go free out of his Service . . . (II. 24)

Clearly, Locke regards drudgery with some distaste. But he explicitly refrains from articulating that distaste in terms of a moral prohibition. There is in this section—which is, after all, the place where Locke rehearses various natural law constraints on the sorts of relations that can be entered into—no moral objection to the relation between master and drudge. But drudgery here does involve the sale of labour power for a given period of time under alienative conditions. Indeed, the nature of the drudgery contract, which Locke is prepared to accept, may go far beyond what full-scale capitalism, with daily or weekly wages, normally requires.

In a subsequent response to this point, Tully has insisted that drudgery, on this conception, is still 'in fact incompatible with the master–servant relation' and that it is an anachronism to identify the two.[151] But elsewhere Locke seems quite happy to identify drudgery with labour in the contemporary economy. In the *Essay* he says that it is part of the 'natural and unalterable state of things' that

It is not to be expected that a man, who *drudges* on all his life in a laborious trade, should be more knowing in the variety of things done in the world than a packhorse, who is driven constantly forwards and backwards in a narrow lane and dirty road only to market, should be skilled in the geography of the country. [my emphasis][152]

Passages like these should make us very cautious about infiltrating modern assumptions about autonomy and alienation into our interpretations of Locke's thought.

The second main argument that Tully puts forward is that there is an important passage in which Locke describes the master–servant relation in terms which do not involve the sale of labour power.[153] Locke says:

a Free-man makes himself a Servant to another, by selling him for a certain time, the Service he undertakes to do, in exchange for Wages he is to

---

[151] Tully, 'Reply to Waldron and Baldwin', p. 45.
[152] Locke, *Essay*, Bk. IV, Ch. ii sect. 20. (p. 297).
[153] Tully, *A Discourse on Property*, pp. 138–42.

receive: And though this commonly puts him into the Family of his Master, and under the ordinary Discipline thereof; yet it gives the Master but a Temporary Power over him, and no greater, than what is contained in the Contract between 'em. (II. 85)

Tully places great stress here on the proposition that what is sold is 'the Service he undertakes to do', that is, a complete task, specified in advance in the contract. On Tully's interpretation, the servant does not contract to put himself at the disposal of the master for a given period of time to perform actions for the master's benefit and under his instructions as and when he is required to do so. Instead, he agrees to perform a certain task: to cut certain turfs, to serve the food at a given dinner party, or to spin a given amount of yarn, and so on. How he does the task, with what implements, and how long it takes him, are matters entirely for the servant. He retains, in Tully's phrase, 'sovereignty . . . over his own labour activity'.[154]

Two things strike me immediately as odd about this interpretation. First, if it was Locke's view that the servant sold to the master only a complete task which he performed, as it were, *in his own time*, why did Locke bother to say that the servant sells the service 'for a certain time'? Secondly, why the stress on the 'Temporary Power' of the master? If all that is involved is the performance of a given task to specifications in return for what amounts to a fee, the master–servant relationship need no more involve 'Discipline' or 'Power' than the relationship between a property developer and a tenderer or a sub-contractor.

Tully stresses that, in any case, 'it is logically impossible for an agent to alienate *his* labour'.[155]. But this is either false or unhelpful. Of course, nothing that an agent does, by way of contract, submission or otherwise, can alter the fact that actions performed by him are actions performed by him. But what follows from this? Certainly not that actions performed by him cannot become the *property* of another; that would follow only on account of a very elementary equivocation on 'his'. Perhaps Tully is suggesting that, in order for actions to count as *being performed by X*—that is, in order for them to count as *his actions*—X must have greater autonomous control over his activity than the capitalist wage relationship would allow. Perhaps he is right about this. Certainly in more modern industry it becomes very difficult to regard the

[154] Tully, *A Discourse on Property*, p. 141.
[155] Ibid. 138.

individual worker as the performer of actions, as opposed to mere movements, at all. As Marx suggests in *Capital*, the only real agent involved in, say, an assembly-line factory process is 'the collective worker, formed out of the combination of individual specialised workers'.[156] The wage relation, then, in its advanced industrial forms, may involve a very serious diminution of human agency. But, obviously, this aspect of industrial capitalism was not something with which Locke, in late seventeenth-century England, was particularly familiar. Tully may be correct in his speculation that most servants and labourers were in possession of their own implements, and in control of their own conditions of production, 'until at least the late eighteenth century'; in any case, I do not want to dispute that here.[157] The crucial question is not whether Locke was aware of industrial alienation, but whether he offers any moral basis in his political philosophy for criticizing it.

However distasteful it seems, I think we have to return a negative answer to the latter question. As we have seen, Locke already had the category of *drudgery*—an unpleasant but legitimate form of economic exploitation—which could be applied to characterize the plight of the industrial proletariat. And his view that the master–servant relation was entered into under 'strong Obligations of Necessity' seems perfectly at harmony with more recent characterizations of class relations under capitalism.

It is true that Locke placed great value on autonomous unalienated labour; it was, for him, 'the great Foundation of Property' (II. 44). But it is a confusion to infer from this that alienated labour relations are prohibited by Locke. It follows only that alienated or heteronomous labour is not valued very highly; but that is not incompatible with its forming the basis for a legitimate economic relationship. There is, however, one important point that may be drawn from this. In one part of his argument, Locke attempts to show that it is labour which is responsible for the wealth and prosperity of modern societies, and that explains why it is legitimate to take labour as a basis for property entitlements. But we know that if, indeed, it is labour which creates modern prosperity, it is the unpleasant and alienated drudgery of the proletariat, not the autonomous and self-possessed activity of Lockean farmers. This means that under modern conditions it is

[156] Marx, *Capital*, Vol. I, Ch. 14 (p. 468).
[157] Tully, *A Discourse on Property*, p. 140.

impossible for a Lockean to establish the connection between the autonomy and natural rights side of his Labour Theory of property and the more utilitarian wealth-creating side which he needs to round off his argument. The two parts of the argument come drastically apart; who knows which part Locke would have followed if he had realized this?

18. THE TRANSITION TO CIVIL SOCIETY

We have seen that Locke claims that individual property rights are possible in a state of nature and that they are based, in the first instance, not on the consent of mankind but on the unilateral appropriative acts of individual proprietors. They are, in our terminology, *special* rights. Subsequently, according to Locke, many if not all of the individuals who have these rights become by their own consent members of a political society, subject to positive law. So the question arises: what happens in this transition to the special rights of those individuals? Are they retained intact in civil society or are they now subject to conventional review and redistribution?[158]

At first sight, it seems as if Locke favours the former alternative. Time and again, he stresses that man enters civil society 'to preserve his property' (where 'property' includes estate as well as life and liberty).[159] The government, he argues, 'is obliged to secure every ones property by providing against those . . . defects . . . that made the State of Nature so unsafe and uneasie' (II. 131). It is hard to see how we can make sense of these passages unless we say that the property entitlements which are to be secured under government are the same as the property entitlements whose enforcement was so insecure in the state of nature. The logic of the idea of preservation seems to indicate a continuation of natural entitlements into civil society. Otherwise, what would men be entering civil society to preserve?

While this is the most obvious reading of Locke's argument, it is far from uncontroversial. Tully, for example, attributes to Locke what he calls 'the remarkable conclusion that property in political society is a creation of that society',[160] and that when he enters civil

---

[158] This section is adapted from my paper, 'Locke, Tully, and the Regulation of Property'.

[159] See Locke, *Two Treatises*, II, sects. 87, 94, 123–4, 127, 131, 137–8, 171, 199, 201, 226, and 229.   [160] Tully, *A Discourse on Property*, p. 98.

society, '[a]ll the possessions a man has in the state of nature . . . become the possessions of the community'[161] so that 'the distribution of property is now conventional.'[162] According to this interpretation, man in civil society has no other property entitlements than those vouchsafed to him by the positive law of his community.[163]

It is a matter of some importance which is the correct interpretation—Tully's or the more traditional view outlined above. If Tully is right, there are limits on the extent to which a Lockean theory of property can provide a basis for a theory of constrained or limited government of the sort discussed by Nozick. Since property rights are conventional after the formation of society, since they do not retain their natural priority to politics, it can no longer be maintained that these rights constrain the state 'leaving no room' for welfarist concern or redistributive intervention on the part of government.[164] For the government, having called in whatever property rights existed in the state of nature, may now decide in the public interest, to establish a new set of rights, which are understood from the beginning to be susceptible to review, limitation, and, if need be, redistribution from time to time. The setting up of such a system of property would be no injustice, given Tully's interpretation, nor could subsequent intervention be regarded as oppressive if those who held the rights had taken them on that understanding.[165] Admittedly, for all this to follow from the Tully interpretation, it would have to be shown that not merely Locke's *ipsissima verba* but also the logic of his theory committed him to this position. Otherwise it would be open to theorists like Nozick to reject Locke's suggestions to this effect as a (typical) inconsistent deviation in his thought, which may be overlooked in modern reconstructions of Lockean theory.[166] In what follows, then, I shall consider not only what Tully claims to

[161] Ibid. 164.

[162] Ibid. 165.

[163] Ibid. In this regard, Tully cites Kendall, *John Locke and the Doctrine of Majority Rule*, p. 104. Other interpretations of Locke along these lines include: Olivecrona, 'Locke's Theory of Appropriation', p. 231; Nozick, *Anarchy, State, and Utopia*, p. 350; Scanlon, 'Nozick on Rights', p. 126. Recently Tully has claimed that this interpretation is now to be regarded as 'the standard account': 'A Reply to Waldron and Baldwin', p. 37.

[164] Nozick, *Anarchy, State, and Utopia*, p. 238.

[165] This possibility is suggested in Ryan, 'Yours, Mine, and Ours', at pp. 329 ff.

[166] Cf. Nozick, *Anarchy, State, and Utopia*, p. 350 n. 9: 'Locke shifts *illegitimately* from someone's wanting society to secure and protect his property to his allowing it complete jurisdiction over his property' (my emphasis).

derive from the text of *Two Treatises*, but also how he understands his interpretation to be related to the overall direction and logic of Locke's political theory.

It is possible to regard property rights in Locke's state of nature as 'transitional' or 'provisional' without subscribing to Tully's view. We might instead interpret Locke as holding a view similar to Kant's: that the property rights acquired in the state of nature are provisonal and require eventual ratification by the laws of civil society; but that the requirement of positive ratification does not involve any possibility of abrogation or substantial derogation. Every provisional property right has an irrefutable claim to ratification; and although civil society may set the terms on which property is *subsequently* acquired, it can do nothing in the way of redistributing those rights that have been acquired already.[167]

But Tully wants something much stronger than this. He says that when Locke's civil society is instituted, previously acquired goods become community goods. They are then distributed on a basis that is only obliquely related to their initial apropriation. 'The society Locke envisages,' says Tully, is one in which 'the share of the goods of the community belonging to each is determined by the labour of each for the public good.'[168] In particular, everyone must have 'the means necessary for *comfortable* subsistence' (my emphasis) and sufficient access to the means of production to enable him 'to labour in, and enjoy the fruits of, his calling in a manner appropriate to man, and analogous to God's activity as a maker'. These, Tully says, 'are the explicit premises of the argument and the normative framework in terms of which a system of property relations is assessed.'[169] On Tully's view, this normative framework involves no essential reference back to 'the necessity of preserving men in the possession of what honest industry has *already* acquired';[170] it is an entirely forward-looking framework.

Tully relies for this interpretation on half a dozen passages which have always posed difficulties for the traditional view:

(1) In II. 30 Locke suggests that 'the Civiliz'd part of Mankind ... have made and multiplied positive Laws to determine Property'.

---

[167] Kant, *Metaphysical Elements of Justice*, Ladd trans., pp. 64 ff. (Prussian Academy Edn., VI, 255 ff.).

[168] Tully, *A Discourse on Property*, p. 168.   [169] Ibid. 169.

[170] Locke, *Letter Concerning Toleration*, p. 83.

(2) In II. 35, Locke indicates that in a country 'where there is Plenty of People under Government, who have money and commerce', consensual arrangments may be made to preserve certain pieces of land as 'common by Compact'.

(3) In II. 38 Locke says when nomadic herdsmen settled into cities, 'by consent, they came in time, to set out the bounds of their distinct Territories, and agree on limits between them and their Neighbours, and by Laws within themselves, setled the Properties of those of the same Society'.

(4) A similar suggestion is found in II. 45. Once land became scarce, 'the several Communities settled the Bounds of their distinct Territories, and by Laws within themselves, regulated the Properties of the private Men of their Society, and so, by Compact and Agreement, settled the Property which Labour and Industry began'. Similarly, the 'several States and Kingdoms' by the 'Leagues' that they have made 'have, by positive agreement, settled a Property amongst themselves, in distinct Parts and parcels of the Earth'.

(5) In II. 50 Locke says bluntly that 'in Governments the Laws regulate the right of property, and the possession of land is determined by positive constitutions'.

(6) Finally, much later, in II. 120, Locke asserts that when anyone joins a civil society by consent, he necessarily 'submits to the Community those Possessions, which he has or shall acquire, that do not already belong to any other Government.'

That is the evidence for Tully's interpretation.

The first thing to say about these passages is that, apart from (6), they are all comments which Locke interpolates into his discussion, *by the way*; each is parenthetical to the main argument of the section in which it appears.[171] By itself that does not show that Tully's reliance on them is mistaken. But the doctrine he wants to attribute to Locke on the basis of this evidence is, as he says, a 'remarkable' one.[172] One would have thought that if in fact Locke held this view, he would have devoted more than a few scattered sentences to its exposition. Once we begin a close examination of these passages, the dangers of relying on this scattered evidence, abstracted from its context, become apparent.

In order to see what Locke means in these passages, we must bear

---

[171] For amplification of this point, see Waldron, 'Locke, Tully and the Regulation of Property', p. 101.
[172] Tully, *A Discourse on Property*, p. 98.

in mind two important and related distinctions. The first is between resources which have been appropriated by individuals at the time civil society has been set up and those that have not. The second is between the property rights of individuals and the territorial jurisdiction of various states.

Nothing in the argument about natural entitlement implies that at the time when civil society is set up, all the resources in the area will have been appropriated. Locke suggests, in passage (3), that nomadic herdsmen will have found it unnecessary to cultivate and thereby appropriate the land over which they roam. So when they settled down into political society, the land in their vicinity may still be held in common.[173] So how is a newly formed civil society to deal with the unappropriated resources in its vicinity? This question, interesting though it is, must be distinguished from the question (with which we are concerned) of how it is to deal with the resources that its citizens *had* appropriated before they entered civil society. It seems on the face of it unlikely that they will admit of the same answer. In various places, Locke suggests a number of answers to the former question. Sometimes, as he indicates in passage (2), the new civil society may establish a 'common by Compact' so that common access to the so far unappropriated land is now guaranteed by positive law (II. 35). Sometimes, by contrast, the unappropriated resources may be left available for unilateral appropriation as before (which the state will then recognize); this, Locke suggests, is what happens with regard to fish in the ocean, ambergris, and game, even in the most civilized and law-governed societies (I. 30). Or, thirdly, resources which have no 'natural' owner may 'come into the Hands of the Public Magistrate' to be dealt with in the way Tully suggests, on the basis of what best serves the interests of the community (I. 90).[174]

These, then, are the main ways in which governments may deal with hitherto unappropriated resources. They provide, I think, an adequate explanation of what Locke is getting at in passage (2), and part of what he is getting at in passages (1), (3), (4), and (5). But none of this so far entails that the government has any right to redistribute resources that had been appropriated by its citizens *before* the civil society came into existence.

---

[173] Note that this does not amount to the suggestion, which Tully attributes to Locke, that land *may not be appropriated*—Tully, *A Discourse on Property*, pp. 99 and 189. That would be to read 'commonly' as 'necessarily', and to fly in the face of Locke's explicit assertions to the contrary in *Two Treatises*, II, sects. 32–3.

[174] See the discussion in sect. 19, below.

The second distinction, between property rights and territorial jurisdiction, is related to the first. It has been suggested above that a political society may deal in various ways with resources in its vicinity. But Lockean political society is a matter of relations of consent and trust between persons; how can it be said to have a location or *vicinity*? Initially, a political society acquires a territorial dimension in relation to the accumulated cluster of pieces of land appropriated already by its individual members. When they join the society, they 'submit' their possessions to the community, and this means at least (though Tully thinks it means a lot more) that the government of the community acquires a territorial jurisdiction over the land which its citizens own. But if some land has *not* been appropriated, the question of *which government* (if any) has the right to deal with it (in the ways I outlined above) becomes problematic. *This* is the question which Locke, in passages (3) and (4), envisages being settled by treaty between the various civil societies.[175]

Now it is obviously important to distinguish this *inter*-societal process, which is necessarily conventional in character, from the processes, whatever they are, that take place *intra*-societally with regard to the property relations of citizens one with another. Certainly, Locke talks of them both in the same breath in the passages we are examining. But that is no excuse for confusing them. Unfortunately, Tully seems to want to blur the distinction. He quotes the following extract from II. 45 (passage (4) above)— 'by positive agreement, [they] settled a Property amongst themselves, in distinct Parts and parcels of the Earth'[176]—to support his view that Locke believed property *within* civil society was conventional. But he fails to indicate that the subject of the quoted sentence (the referent of his interpolated 'they') is 'several States and Kingdoms', or maybe 'the Leagues that have been made between several States and Kingdoms' (the grammar is not entirely clear), but certainly not at this point in the passage 'individual citizens within the same society'. The effect is to mislead the reader as to the force of the quoted passage, certainly in terms of the distinction we have just drawn.

Once we have attended to these distinctions, what is left in the six passages I quoted from Locke to support Tully's interpretation? There is, first of all, the claim in passages (1) and (5) that, in

[175] See also Waldron, 'Locke's Account of Inheritance', p. 50.
[176] Tully, *A Discourse on Property*, p. 98.

civilized societies, the possession of property is '*determined*' by positive law. There is, secondly, the claim in passage (4) that the positive law of a community '*regulates*' the property of its citizens. Thirdly, there is the idea, in passages (3) and (4), that the effect of positive law is to '*settle*' the property which labour and industry began. Our understanding of these functions of the Lockean government, to *determine*, *regulate*, and *settle* property relations among its citizens, will give us our understanding of what Locke means in passage (6) when he says that citizens must '*submit*' their possessions to the community.

The concept of *determination* is the most straightforward. To determine a person's rights is to find out what they are. It is not to (re-)create them or (re-)constitute them. Determination, for Locke is the characteristic function of a judge: 'In the State of Nature there wants a known and indifferent Judge with Authority to determine all differences according to the established law' (II. 125). Such a judge in the state of nature would resolve disputes not by inventing rights *ex nihilo* but by applying the established law of that condition (i.e. the law of nature) to find out which if any of the disputants has the rights he claims. By analogy, to suggest that a political society has positive laws to determine property rights is to say—at least with respect to resources that have already been appropriated—that the function of law is to settle once and for all the disputes that are likely to arise continually in the state of nature as to who is entitled to what. In making this determination, the legislature will not draw up new entitlements on the basis of what seems to it to be the public interest, but will rather endeavour to ascertain natural entitlements, state them precisely, and 'annex' to them, known penalties to enforce their observation (II. 13). [177]

The *regulation* of property relations is likewise not conceived by Locke as a creative process. Locke takes great pains to distinguish the regulation of property from its confiscation or redistribution:

But Government into whatsoever hand it is put, being as I have before shew'd, intrusted with this condition, and for this end, that Men might have and secure their Properties, the Prince or Senate, however it may have power to make laws for the regulating of Property between the Subjects one amongst another, yet can never have a Power to take themselves the whole or any part of the subjects Property, without their own consent. For this would in effect be to leave them no Property at all. (II. 139)

---

[177] See also the discussion in sect. 5, above.

To suppose otherwise, Locke suggests, would be to embroil oneself in the contradiction that men 'must be suppos'd to lose that by entring into Society, which was the end for which they entered into it' (II. 138).

It is important to see that Locke's contrast here is between regulation of property by the legislature and its confiscation again *by the legislature*. The former is a proper discharge of legislative power; the latter, Locke suggests can never be legitimate. This makes a nonsense of Tully's suggested interpretation of these passages. He reads them as follows. When a man enters society he surrenders the property he has acquired to the community. The community then, by legislative processes, redistributes these resources on the basis of the general good. In respect of these redistributed holdings, the community then falls under an obligation of natural law not subsequently to disturb them.[178] This interpretation is strained and implausible. It seems to indicate that the Lockean legislature is under fewer constraints of natural law in respect of its dealings with natural rights than it is in respect of its dealings with conventional entitlements. Natural entitlements, according to Tully, may be redistributed as the legislature sees fit, whereas conventional entitlements acquire all the protection of natural law. If this sort of contrivance is the cost of Tully's reading of Locke, clearly the traditional reading is preferable.

The third function referred to in the passages we are examining is the *settlement* of property by the legislature. There is a sense of 'settlement' which if applied here might support the Tully interpretation. This is the sense in which a testator has the power to 'settle' his estate as he pleases (II. 116). But it is difficult to apply this sense to the term in passages (3) and (4).[179] A more plausible reading takes the 'settlement' of a system of property entitlements to be the provision of the conditions necessary for it to become a permanent and stable basis of economic relations: the drawing up of precise boundaries, the setting up of a system of titles that will in large measure eliminate needless disputes, and the establishment of judicial, executive, and administrative agencies to resolve any difficulties that remain and to secure entitlements effectively against violation. To be sure, these forms of regulation may involve a certain degree of modification of natural entitlements. Whereas in

---

[178] Tully, *A Discourse on Property*, pp. 164–72.

[179] I am indebted to Andrew Reeve for discussion of this point: see also Reeve, 'Political Obligation and Strict Settlement'.

the state of nature a farmer may have conceived of himself as being entitled to 'that field over there', he will now be conceived of as entitled to a particular piece of land whose location and boundaries are strictly, precisely, and publicly defined. However, this will not involve the wholesale abrogation of natural property rights, but merely their subjection to the conditions necessary for their effective protection by positive law.

Bearing all this in mind, we can see now what Locke means when he suggests in passage (6) that anyone joining a political society must 'submit' his possessions to the community. Tully's interpretation of the passage is as follows: 'All the possessions a man has in the state of nature, or shall acquire in his commonwealth, become the possessions of the community.'[180] But there is nothing in Locke to support that reading. The correct interpretation is stated by Locke a few sentences later: 'By the same act therefoere, whereby any one unites his Person, which was before free, to any Commonwealth; by the same he unites his Possessions, which were before free to it also; and they become both of them, Person and Possession, subject to the Government and Dominion of that Commonwealth . . . ' (II. 120). Unless Tully wants to suggest that the citizen's own *person* also becomes 'the possession of the community', to be dealt with as the legislature sees fit, his interpretation is hopeless, for Locke is suggesting here that person and property are subject to the community to exactly the same extent. The extent of that subjection is made perfectly clear elsewhere in the *Treatise*: both in his own actions and in the use and enjoyment of his property, the citizen is to be governed by the legitimate laws of his community. And one of the conditions of the legitimacy of those laws is that the legislature 'cannot take from any Man any part of his Property without his own consent' (II. 138–40).

My conclusion then is that Tully has presented no convincing evidence to challenge the traditional interpretation of Locke's view on property in civil society. Certainly the six passages we have examined are not straightforward; they have always posed problems for the exegesis of Locke's theory of property. By selective quotation and by abstraction from their context, Tully tries to make it appear as though Locke were wholly conventionalist about property relations in civil society. But more careful scrutiny

---

[180] Tully, *A Discourse on Property*, p. 164.

together with an understanding of the basic distinctions I outlined dispels that appearance.

One final point. To maintain that Locke believed that natural entitlements survive the transition to civil society is not to suggest that he regarded private property in civil society as absolute or unlimited. We have already seen that, in Locke's view, all property rights, whether natural or conventional, are subject at all times to the general right of every man to a basic subsistence when his survival is threatened. That general right—the primeval natural right of Lockean communism—remains in the background of the whole of the theory that we have been discussing in this chapter, and it qualifies all of the special rights whose existence Locke has been attempting to argue for. So there is no need to make property rights conventional or put them at the mercy of a civil legislature in order to bring this limitation into play. Since it applies already to natural entitlements, it is *a fortiori* one of the natural duties that civil authorities may legitimately enforce in the discharge of their function of upholding natural rights.

19. INHERITANCE AND BEQUEST

The final question I want to consider in my discussion of Locke concerns his views on inheritance and bequest.

What happens to the property of a Lockean appropriator when he dies? Do his goods revert to their natural state, so that they become once again available for appropriation by others? Or do they pass to his family or to his nominated heirs? Locke's views on this matter are far from straightforward.[181]

In the *First Treatise*, Locke wrote:

But if any one had begun and made himself a Property in any particular thing, (which how he, or any one else, could do, shall be shewn in another place) that thing, that possession, if he disposed not otherwise of it by his positive Grant, descended Naturally to his Children, and they had a right to succeed to it, and possess it. (I. 87)

The parenthetical reference is, of course, to Chapter 5 of the *Second Treatise* which contains the gist of Locke's theory of acquisition and exchange. Surprisingly perhaps, that chapter contains nothing

---

[181] This section is adapted from my paper, 'Locke's Account of Inheritance'.

at all about inheritance and bequest. Locke's comments on those matters in the *Second Treatise* are confined to remarks about the way in which a father gains a degree of power over his children by his Lear-like liberty to bestow his estate on those who please him best (II. 72), an insistence that an heir succeeds to his inheritance on the same terms of civil law as his predecessor held it (II. 73), and the claim that a lawful conqueror in a just war does not obtain a right to the property of the defeated aggressor inasmuch as the property vests naturally in the aggressor's dependents, with whom the conqueror has no quarrel (II. 182–3).[182].

In even these scattered fragments of a theory, we see the beginnings of a problem. In his discussion of conquest in the *Second Treatise*, and in his lengthy account of inheritance (intended as an attack on Filmer's theory) in the *First*, Locke talks of the natural right of a proprietor's dependants to possess his goods when he dies or forfeits his life. But other comments in both treatises suggest that Locke believed a proprietor should have a degree of testamentary freedom, even to disinherit members of his family if he wanted to. The question then arises: which is to prevail—the testator's liberty to bequeath his property or his dependants' natural right to their inheritance?[183]

The answer suggested by the passage quoted above is that bequest prevails over inheritance; Locke says the natural right of the children is contingent on the absence of any 'positive Grant' to the contrary. But what is the justification for this view? We need to ask (1) what is the justification for *any* system of succession by another to a dead man's property? and (2) what is the justification for ranking bequest ahead of inheritance in such a system?

That Locke recognized a need to justify *any* system of succession is clear from his attack on Robert Filmer's theory of property. Filmer's position was that the earth and its fruits were given to Adam by God and descended naturally down Adam's line to his eldest son. We have already seen how Locke criticized the first part of this position. But the second part is also dubious: what is the justification for the inheritance of Adam's eldest son?

---

[182] For an interesting discussion of these passages, see Gauthier, 'The Role of Inheritance'.

[183] Commentators disagree about what to infer from this ambivalence. Gough observes that Locke does not 'pretend that testamentary bequest is a natural right' (*John Locke's Political Philosophy*, p. 86 n). But in introducing his account of the English legislation in this area, Tyler insists that Locke saw free testation as 'a natural right—a necessary incident of property' (*Family Provision*, p. 1).

Now in all Inheritance, if the Heir succeed not to the reason, upon which his Father's Right was founded, he cannot succeed to the Right which followeth from it: For Example, Adam had a Right of Property in the Creatures, upon the Donation and Grant of God Almighty, . . . yet upon his Death his Heir can have no Title to them, no such Right of Property in them, unless the same reason, viz. God's Donation, vested a right in the Heir too. For if Adam could have had no Property in, nor use of, the Creatures without this positive Donation from God, and this Donation were only personally to Adam, his Heir could have no right by it, but upon his death, it must revert to God the Lord and Owner again: for positive Grants give no Title farther than the express words convey it, and by which only it is held. (I. 85)

But a similar problem can be posed for Locke's own account of succession. The Labour theory of Acquisition appears to establish only *personal* entitlements, that is, entitlements peculiar to the person whose labour has been mixed with the resource in question. It is *my* labour that is mixed there, and that is why *I* am entitled to it. How then are the *multipersonal* entitlements involved in any system of succession to be established? In Locke's own words, 'it might reasonably be asked here, how come Children by this right of possessing, before any other, the properties of their Parents upon their Decease, For it being personally the Parents, when they dye, without actually Transferring their Right to another, why does it not return again to the common stock of Mankind?' (I. 88). The point is that property in Locke's state of nature is never *res nullius*. If an individual ceases to own a certain resource and if no one else is entitled to it, the property is held again by mankind as a whole. If mankind as a whole ceases to exist, there is still the original proprietor, God, waiting in the wings to resume His original title. There is, therefore, always a 'natural' alternative to any of the artificial succession systems dreamed up by men. If either bequest or inheritance is to have any real ethical foundation, a justification must be adduced that is sufficient to displace the available alternatives.

As far as bequest is concerned, no explicit justification appears in either treatise. However, both the *First Treatise* and to a lesser extent the *Second* contain powerful defences of the natural right of children to inherit their parents' property. The difficulty is that the justification seems considerably more powerful than the rather qualified proposition that Locke seems to want to justify. That proposition is, as we saw earlier, that children have a natural right to succeed to their father's property 'if he dispos'd not otherwise of it by his positive Grant' (I. 87). But the argument Locke adduces appears to support the stronger proposition that children have an almost absolute right to succeed no matter what alternative arrangements the father may have made. Locke's argument for inheritance, in other words, seems to preclude any argument for bequest.

The justification of inheritance is as follows. God implanted in men first and foremost a principle of self-preservation, and it is this principle, applied rationally to the world that they see around them that gives rise to the natural law of private property. But he also made them subject to a principle of propagation—the natural urge to bring children into the world—and as a corollary imposed an obligation on the parent to preserve what he had begotten (II. 56).

This gives Children a Title, to share in the Property of their Parents, and a Right to Inherit their Possessions. Men are not Proprietors of what they have meerly for themselves, their Children have a Title to part of it, and have their Kind of Right joyn'd with their Parents, in the Possession which comes to be wholly theirs, when death having put an end to their Parents use of it, hath taken them from their Possessions, and this we call Inheritance. Men being by a like Obligation bound to preserve what they have begotten, as to preserve themselves, their Issue come to have a Right in the Goods they are possessed of. (I. 88)

It turns out, then, that a parent does not acquire an indefeasible personal title to property simply by the investment of labour. The goods that he appropriates are his subject to the joint rights of his dependants. While he lives, his children share a title with him. When he dies, they acquire the whole of his property by survivorship.

Locke uses this argument to attack Filmer's doctrine of primogeniture. If the rationale for inheritance is the parental obligation to preserve offspring, there can be no distinction between first-and last-born offspring (let alone between male and female, on which Filmer also relied). This by itself is sufficient to dispose of Filmer's contention that all the property in the world is vested in a single line (I. 91). (Locke adds that if any one child *is* to have precedence it should be the last-born, since it is he who is likely to be in most need of sustenance at his parents' death.)

The position of a wife is a little more complex. Locke nowhere talks of a wife as a dependant. Any entitlement she has to her husband's estate arises, first, out of her contribution to it (II. 183), secondly, out of the matrimonial contract whose terms are negotiated freely between the intended couple subject to any restrictions of domestic positive law (I. 47; II. 78, 83 and 183), and thirdly, out of her joint responsibility for the nurture of the children (II. 52).[184]

In Locke's view, the parents' duty is correlative to the children's rights. He develops this into a slightly stronger position, maintaining that these rights are not merely *in personam*, against the parents, but rights *in rem*, against all the world. On this basis he insists that a wrongdoer's property can never be forfeit so long as he has innocent dependants. The life of a defeated aggressor is at the mercy of his lawful conqueror, but only his life:

> His goods, which Nature, that willeth the preservation of all Mankind as much as is possible, hath made to belong to the Children to keep them from perishing, do still continue to belong to his Children. For supposing them not to have joyn'd in the War, either through Infancy, absence, or choice, they have done nothing to forfeit them: nor has the Conqueror any right to take them away . . . (II. 182)

Now if, as Locke says here, a parent cannot forfeit his property by his misconduct, is there any reason to suppose that he should be able to alienate his property from his family deliberately by gift or bequest? Surely the answer must be 'No'. The child's title to his father's property is not a mere privilege dependent on the will of the father but a right, and the father's liberty to alienate his property is curtailed by the corresponding duty. *A fortiori*, a gratuitous legatee or donee has no right, as against the dependants of the father, to keep the goods he has been given. The property is *owned* in part by the child. Without his consent it cannot be given away. And if it is really necessary for the sustenance of the child, then the child is precluded by natural law from giving this consent, since no one may voluntarily forgo what is necessary for his survival (II. 23).

What explanation, then, can be given for Locke's ranking bequest ahead of inheritance in the *First Treatise*?

A possible explanation is that he was refering to the disposal of wealth surplus to the requirements of the dead man's dependants. In the case of a wealthy man or one whose children are able to fend for themselves, some of his good may not be required for the posthumous fulfilment of his parental obligations. It may be argued

---

[184] For a fuller discussion of Locke's views on the economic status of women, see Clarke, 'Who Owns the Apples?', pp. 713 ff.

then that the proprietor has an absolute rather than a qualified title to those goods (so far as his children are concerned) and can dispose of them as he pleases. The dependants' rights, on this approach, are treated like any other debt owed by a deceased at the time of his death: they are a charge on his estate. Once all the charges have been satisfied, then the legacies in his will can be executed. Admittedly it may be hard to determine the precise point at which parental obligations are fulfilled and any further provisions for offspring becomes unnecessary; at one point, Locke suggests that children have 'a right only to a bare Subsistence, but to the convenience and comforts of Life, as far as the conditions of their Parents can afford it' (I. 89). But in principle there ought to be a point at which we would cease to blame a parent for not providing any further for his children.

In two passages in the *Second Treatise*, Locke seems to take an approach along these lines:

A Father may dispose of his own Possessions as he pleases, when his Children are out of danger of perishing for want . . . (II. 65)

The Possession of the Father being the Expectation and Inheritance of the Children ordinarily in certain proportions, according to the Law and Custom of each Country; yet it is commonly in the Father's power to bestow it with a more sparing or liberal hand, according as the behaviour of this or that Child hath comported with his Will or Humour. (II. 72)

The idea seems to be that each child is entitled to a minimum level of inheritance, but that the final proportions are in the discretion of the father. Thus, the right of the children to inherit what they need and the liberty of the parent to bequeath as he wishes are not incompatible, since they do not necessarily relate to the same property.

On this account, then, the priority as between bequest and inheritance is exactly opposite to that asserted in the *First Treatise*. There Locke maintained that the father's property 'if he dispos'd not otherwise of it by his positive Grant, descended naturally to his Children' (I. 87); but now we are interpreting him to say that the children's right to inherit comes first, and the operation of the father's grant comes second. I think the latter intepretation is to be preferred since it is, as I have pointed out, more consistent with the argument that Locke puts forward in *both Treatises*.[185]

[185] Using the general heuristic that we should interpret Locke's argument to make it the best it can be.

(I have said that bequest comes second to inheritance. But the situation may be even more complex. Presumably the children's right to inherit will also come third, if goods they do not need are not disposed of in their father's will. And if there are no children to inherit, then, as Locke puts it, 'the Possessions of a Private Man revert to the Community . . . [or] . . . in the State of Nature become again perfectly common, no body having a right to inherit them . . .' (I. 90).)

We have established the priority of inheritance to bequest, but we have still not established any independent justification for bequest. If a deceased man's goods are surplus to the needs of his dependants, why do they not automatically become common goods again, liable to be appropriated by anyone? Why should a proprietor be able to control the destiny of the goods he used to own after his death?

We have already seen, in our discussion of the Spoilation Proviso, that Locke was quite happy with the idea of a usable surplus reverting to common ownership: 'As much as any one can make use of to any advantage of life before it spoils; so much he may by his labour fix a Property in. Whatever is beyond this, is more than his share, and belongs to others' (II. 31).[186] But we have also seen that (for this purpose) Locke was not prepared to count as surplus, goods that an appropriator was able to dispose of by gift or exchange (II. 46). Can disposition by bequest be handled in the same way?

There are two possible approaches to this. We may want to lay stress on Locke's insistence that a man should have exclusive control only over the goods that he 'can make use of to any advantage *in life*'. Now perhaps giving something away or selling it may bring joy to the donor or be of some advantage to the vendor. But when a bequest takes effect, the testator is dead, and can derive no advantage from his act. As the jurist W. G. Miller has noted, 'there is an essential difference between an unconditional convey-ance by a man in health and vigour and a conveyance by a man who lets a thing drop from his fingers because he can no longer hold it'.[187] We may have doubts, then, about whether even Locke's very wide conception of *use* can be extended to cover this case.

The alternative, however, is to recognize (as I argued in section 16) that Locke's account of powers of exchange and alienation does

---

[186] See the discussion in sects. 14 and 16, above.
[187] Miller, *Lectures on Philosophy of Law*, p. 255.

not really need to rely on an extension of the meaning of use at all. All Locke requires, in the Spoilation Proviso, is that goods should not be exclusively appropriated in such a way that they are of no use to anyone at all. (The example I gave of a clear violation was the case where a man allows the fruit he has appropriated to perish uselessly while refusing anyone else permission to use it, on any terms.) Passing surplus goods on by bequest ensures that they will continue to be used after their initial appropriator has died. So, on this ground, there is nothing to choose between a system of bequest and a system which allows goods surplus to the needs of a testator's dependants to lapse into common ownership.[188]

In addition, there may be considerations of social peace and positive law which count against allowing deceased estates simply to become common goods, liable to be appropriated by anybody, when the dependents of the deceased have no need of them. We know that, on Locke's scheme of things, positive law may not abrogate natural law, for 'the Law of Nature stands as an Eternal Rule to all Men, legislators as well as others' (II. 135). But within these bounds of natural law, civil society may enact laws to regulate (though not violate) ongoing property entitlements. Is the legislature, then, permitted to make laws regulating the disposal of that part of a deceased's estate which is surplus to the needs of his dependants? Would a legislature be violating the terms of its trust by setting up positive institutions of its own to govern succession?

Consider a concrete situation. A wealthy merchant dies. His children have all grown up to become wealthy merchants in their own right, and his widow is already well provided for. His estate, then, is surplus property, and he has bequeathed it to a friend. But before that bequest can be put into effect, a fortune hunter (who has read the first few sections of Chapter 5 of the *Second Treatise*) comes along to the dead man's house, mixes his labour with the goods in the estate (digging the garden or whatever), and calls the property his own. When challenged by the dead man's executor and his friend, the fortune hunter informs them that the surplus resources reverted to the common stock of mankind as soon as it became clear that they could be of no further use to the merchant, and that they are therefore up for appropriation just as if they had never been taken out of their natural state in the first place. Obviously, in the absence of any law regulating the matter, the man

---

[188] Cf. Bentham, 'Supply Without Burthern'.

would have a case. The property no longer belongs to the deceased, nor is it needed by his dependants. If his friend wants any of it, he had better get down to the estate pretty smartly and mix his labour with whatever he can get his hands on, for otherwise he will have no entitlement over the rest of mankind.

But suppose that long ago the legislature in that country, worried by the disorder occasioned by thousands of eager fortune hunters, scouring the obituaries in the newspapers and scrambling over each other to appropriate any available estate, instituted a system whereby property would pass on death according to the expressed will of the deceased, or, failing that, to members of his family. Would this be sufficient to defeat the claims of our fortune hunter?

I think it would. The fortune hunter might object that by instituting and administering such a system, the legislature was depriving him of the opportunity to appropriate goods from the common stock of mankind and that this opportunity was something that he, as a human being, had a natural right to. A powerful argument, however, can be brought against the proposition that there is any such natural right. The argument is in the form of a *reductio*.

Assume there is a natural right to an *opportunity* to make an appropriation from the common stock of mankind. Any such right must surely be an *equal* right, that is, a right to an equal opportunity, for we cannot suppose such a right greater in some men than in others. But if everyone has an equal right to an opportunity to appropriate goods and land from the common stock of mankind, it is easy to show that no one has a right to take advantage of that opportunity. The first person who makes an appropriation (especially if it is an appropriation of land) necessarily by that very act deprives those who follow him of an opportunity equal to his own. As Locke pointed out in his earlier *Essays on the Law of Nature*, 'When any man snatches for himself as much as he can, he takes away from another man's heap the amount he adds to his own, and it is impossible for anyone to grow rich except at the expense of someone else.'[189] Of course, subsequent appropriations may be equal in value, or even greater, but the *opportunity* will never be the same. Thus insistence that the opportunity to appropriate must remain equal precludes the right

[189] Locke, *Essays on the Law of Nature*, p. 211; cf. Nozick, *Anarchy, State, and Utopia*, pp. 175–6.

of anyone to make any appropriation at all. But if no one has any right actually to make an appropriation, then the consequence will be that talk of an opportunity to appropriate is empty. So the fortune hunter's claim would land us in contradiction. We must conclude that his claim is false, and that the interest of every man in the common stock of resources does not extend so far as to guarantee him an opportunity to appropriate. All it guarantees him is a title to possess whatever he does, in fact, appropriate from goods that are available for appropriation.

The legislature, therefore, deprives no one of any natural right by preventing surplus property from falling back into the common stock of mankind. Indeed, Locke seems to be convinced that once civil government is set up, there will be only very limited scope for the direct acquisition of property by mixing one's labour. Fishing, hunting, and the discovery of minerals are the main areas in which appropriation will continue to give rise to entitlement (II. 30). In general, as we saw in the previous section, the acquisition and transfer of property come under the jurisdiction of positive law once property holders enter society (II. 50 and 120). The contrast between the disposal of surplus wealth in the state of nature and its disposal in civil society is drawn quite sharply by Locke in a passage in the *First Treatise*. Discussing the possibility that a person may die leaving no will and no eligible heirs, Locke writes: 'But where there are no such to be found, i.e., no Kindred, there we see the Possessions of a Private Man revert to the Community, and so in Politic Societies come into the Hands of the Public Magistrate: but in the state of Nature become again perfectly common, no body having a right to Inherit them ... (I. 90). Exercising this jurisdiction, the community may decide to recognize and allow processes of testamentary disposition on grounds of social convenience.

Of course, if bequest and succession rights are made a matter of civil law in this way, it needs to be remembered that the legislature may alter the civil law whenever it seems prudent and in the public interest to do so. Provided the legislature is acting within the terms of its trust (promoting the common good and not violating natural law), it may, for instance, abolish bequest altogether and vest surplus property permanently in 'the hands of the Public Magistrate', along the lines of Locke's suggestion mentioned above (I. 90), or it may demand that a proportion of the estate be paid into public coffers before any bequests are put into effect. In practice, most governments do this by means of graduated estate duties. No one's rights are violated and no one's consent is needed, since no one has any expectations of the property apart from the expectations to which legislative action itself gives rise. No doubt there are many good utilitarian arguments supporting the proposition that estate duties should not be too high. But these will be considered by the legislature in the course of weighing up the general good of the public, not as individual constraints of natural right.

20. CONCLUSION

We have completed our rather lengthy survey of John Locke's discussion of property, and it may be worth pausing briefly to review our main conclusion.

The core of Locke's theory, I argued, is an SR-based argument for private property: by labouring on resources in the state of nature a man acquires an interest in them which is sufficiently important from a moral point of view to support the proposition that others (including governments) have a duty not to take those resources away from him without his consent. But Lockean man has no general right to acquire such an interest: he has no general right to appropriate, or to be given an opportunity to appropriate. The only general right that he has, in the area, is to be guaranteed a subsistence if he cannot find it for himself. *In extremis*, this may justify him taking the surplus goods of others for his own use. But on the whole, Locke believed (perhaps a little too optimistically) that the general right to subsistence and the whole business of bringing special rights into existence through appropriation would point in the same direction: a prosperous society with considerable inequality but in which, nevertheless, everyone would be better provided with an opportunity, through appropriation or employment, to earn a decent living.

We saw that Locke did not believe the introduction of civil society made much difference to the overall shape of this fabric of rights. It was, of course, the government's function to provide for the security of people's rights in the economic field as elsewhere, and to regulate them in detail to the extent necessary to perform that function. In addition, the legislature could act interstitially in a number of areas—settling boundaries with other societies, providing rules to govern resources not already taken into private ownership, setting up institutions of succession to fill the gaps left by natural law entitlements, and so on. But in general, governments and legislatures were to regard themselves as constrained in their actions by an array of rights (special property rights and general subsistence rights) whose justification proceeded quite independently of any considerations of positive law.

That, I have argued, is the shape of Locke's account. I also looked closely at the particular argument he put forward for saying that labouring on a resource in the state of nature created an entitlement over it. He gave two arguments, and both were very weak. The first was that private appropriation is the only way to meet human needs; but that is simply false, particularly so far as the use of land is concerned. It may be the most efficient way, but it is not the only way, and so the argument can hardly support a conclusion of right. The other argument was the one about 'mixing one's labour'. This idea, I argued, is simply incoherent as it stands, and none of the familiar ways of rescuing it— in terms of desert, creation *ex nihilo*, or psychological identification— holds much water either. So the best-known SR-based theory fails to provide an adequate defence of private property.

In the next chapter, we shall mount a more general attack. Using the theory of Robert Nozick as our paradigm, we shall argue that no adequate SR-based theory of private property—or at least, none except a very heavily qualified one—could possibly be made acceptable.

Historical Entitlement: Some Difficulties

1. FROM CONTENT TO FORM: THE CASE OF NOZICK[1]

I want to turn now from the evaluation of a particular SR-based theory to some discussion of the very idea of justifying private property in this sort of way. Locke attempts to convince us that a man's interest in the exclusive control of a resource acquires a special moral importance as a result of his having laboured on it. We found his argument far from convincing. The idea of mixing one's labour seemed incoherent and that incoherence vitiated the strategy of somehow transferring the force of a man's entitlement to his own person onto the objects of his labour. None of the other ideas commonly associated with the Labour Theory of acquisition—desert, creator's rights, and psychological identification — seemed sufficiently substantial to justify the claim that rights of private property could be acquired in this way. They fail to establish that the individuals in question have a right to the exclusive control of the resources they have been working on.

In this chapter, I want to explore some more general difficulties with this sort of argument. They have to do not with the details of any particular SR-based defence of private property, but with the overall structure of the SR-based approach. Briefly, I want to give some general reasons for thinking that the idea that individuals can, by their own unilateral actions, impose moral duties on others to refrain from using certain resources and that the moral force of these duties can be transmitted by processes like exchange and inheritance, is a very difficult idea to defend in an unqualified form.

Although my focus is more abstract than it was in the previous chapter, it is helpful, nevertheless, to concentrate on a particular theory. Robert Nozick's theory of historical entitlement, though

---

[1] Parenthical references in the text of this chapter are to pages in Nozick's *Anarchy, State, and Utopia.*

seriously incomplete as a full discussion of private property, fits the bill for two reasons.

First, the sort of historical entitlement theory that Nozick wants to outline is almost a pure case of an SR-based argument for private property. On Nozick's account, nobody has any right to hold resources as private property—*or indeed to make any use of them at all*—unless they have acquired such rights over particular resources through the performance of particular actions or trans-actions. A Nozickian theory would specify in detail the actions and transactions that give rise to rights over resources. Rights arising out of these specified actions and transactions define (almost) all the rights there are in relation to the use and control of material resources;[2] as he puts it, they 'leave no room' for any general rights in relation to people's material condition (p. 238). Unlike Locke, Nozick concedes no general right to elementary material subsist-ence to modify the special rights of private property that he wants to argue for. Moreover, Nozick does not purport to offer any general account of the importance of private property. It is not defended on utilitarian grounds nor on the grounds of any connection with the conditions of ethical development, human flourishing, or (despite appearances) individual liberty. (Nozick does offer some libertarian arguments against certain egalitarian and socialist theories; but these are almost wholly negative in character.) The case for private property, in Nozick's view, is simply the case that can be made out for saying that certain contingent circumstances give rise to certain special rights in relation to particular resources for particular individuals.

Secondly and ironically, Nozick's work is useful to us here just because of its theoretical incompleteness. It is notorious that Nozick presents not a theory of historical entitlement but the bare bones of a theory. We are told that according to such a theory there are certain conditions under which people acquire rights of private property and certain other conditions under which these rights are transferred from one person to another, but we are not told what these conditions are. What is missing, Nozick says, is a 'complic-ated truth . . . which we shall not formulate here' (p. 150). He acknowledges that he has provided no more than 'the general outlines' of a theory of justice.

---

[2] Except in so far as Nozick's weak 'Lockean proviso' can be thought of as generating rights: see sect. 6, below.

Many critics regard it as a failing of Nozick's book that he does not specify a content for his principles.[3] Nozick, however, insists that it is possible to make headway in political philosophy at a more abstract level. His main aim, as Jeffrey Paul points out, is 'to carve out a place for a theory of distributive justice that would be the antithesis of the prevailing views on the subject.'[4] His concern is that recent theories of economic justice and equality (such as John Rawls's) have ignored *the very idea* of historical entitlement, not that they have ignored his own favoured conception of it.

[W]e do not need any *particular* developed historical-entitlement theory as a basis from which to criticize Rawls' construction. If *any* such fundamental historical entitlement view is correct, then Rawls's theory is not. . . . We would be ill advised to accept Rawls' theory . . . unless we were sure that no adequate historical entitlement theory was to be gotten. (pp. 202–3)

A little later, he restates the point emphatically:

I am as well aware as anyone of how sketchy my discussion of the entitlement conception of justice in holdings has been. But I no more believe we need to have formulated a complete alternative theory in order to reject Rawls' undeniably great advance over utilitarianism, than Rawls needed a complete alternative theory before he could reject utilitarianism. What more does one need or can one have, in order to begin progressing toward a better theory, than a sketch of a plausible alternative view, which from its very different perspective highlights the inadequacies of the best existing well-worked-out theory? (p. 230)

Leaving aside the fact that the incompleteness of Nozick's theory is orders of magnitude greater than that of Rawls's, the point seems a fair one. It is reasonable to ask sometimes, modestly, what an adequate theory of justice and property would be *like*, rather than postponing all discussion until we are sure we have settled all the details of what such a theory actually *is*.

It is interesting that Nozick is unwilling to do what he did in Part 1 of his book—namely, appeal to Locke's theory of natural rights for the substance that is missing from his own.[5] There has been some confusion about this. Onora O'Neill suggests that Nozick's

---

[3] e.g. Wolff, 'Nozick's Derivation of the Minimal State', p. 101. See also Griffin, 'Towards a Substantive Theory of Rights', pp. 137–8.
[4] Paul (ed.), *Reading Nozick*, 'Introduction', p. 5.
[5] See Nozick, *Anarchy, State, and Utopia*, pp. ix, 9–12, 17–18, and 137–8.

principle of acquisition, at any rate, is the 'principle sketched in Locke's chapter on Property in the *Second Treatise*'.[6] Certainly she is right to the extent that Nozick's theory is Lockean in inspiration; just as Locke has inspired, in one way or another, most recent writing on property.[7] But it is simply not true that Nozick adopts Locke's approach to appropriation. When he considers Locke's argument for the Labour Theory (the argument based on 'mixing' one's labour), Nozick rejects it completely (pp. 174–5), and it is not clear whether he even wants to hang onto the idea that *labouring* rather than, say, mere *occupation* is the basis on which property entitlements are established. He says that it is important to hold onto 'the notions of earning, producing, entitlement, desert, and so forth' (p. 155) and this might suggest a Lockean preoccupation with industriousness. But there are ways of articulating these notions in a theory whose shape is the same, but whose substance is quite different from Locke's. As we shall see, Nozick believes any theory of acquisition should be qualified by what he calls a 'Lockean proviso' (pp. 175–82)—a requirement that an acquisition must not worsen anyone else's situation, inspired by Locke's suggestion that initial acquisition leaves 'enough and as good' for others. But this too is inconclusive, since in Locke as in Nozick that proviso (if it exists) has nothing specifically to do with the Labour Theory and could be used to qualify *any* principle of justice in acquisition.

For our purposes, the fact that Nozick's discussion is at the same time uncompromising and insubstantial is ideal. For it means, we can concentrate our attention on *the idea of an SR-based argument for property* without being distracted by any considerations of content. We can see in a stark and exposed form what sort of position the SR-based defender of private property is arguing towards, and what the difficulties in that sort of position are.

2. HISTORICAL ENTITLEMENT THEORIES

Nozick is interested in what he calls 'historical entitlement theories' of justice: that is, theories which account for the justice or injustice of distributions of resources, not in terms of structural features of

---

[6] O'Neill, 'Nozick's Entitlements', pp. 311–12.
[7] See Ryan, *Property and Political Theory*, p. 14.

the distributive outcomes in question (such as whether the holdings are equal, or proportionate to the distribution of something else, like need or moral desert), but rather in terms of the procedures by which the distribution was arrived at. (It is a system of pure procedural justice.[8]) Among all the various ways in which it is in fact possible for individuals to acquire control over resources, such a theory will pick out those procedures which are *just*. This specification of just procedures will be captured, Nozick suggests, in an inductive definition of '*entitlement*', along the following lines:

(1) A person who acquires a holding in accordance with the principle of justice in acquisition is entitled to that holding.

(2) A person who acquires a holding in accordance with the principle of justice in transfer from someone else entitled to the holding is entitled to the holding.

(3) No one is entitled to a holding except by (repeated) applications of (1) and (2). (p. 151)

It is, on Nozick's account, a sufficient condition for the justice of a distribution that everyone is *entitled* (in this sense) to the holding assigned to him under that distribution. It is sufficient but not necessary, because of the role Nozick indicates for a principle of the rectification of past injustice, though it is unclear whether or not rectification is supposed to yield full-blooded moral *entitlements* (pp. 152–3).

Clearly the principle of justice in acquisition (hereafter PJA) occupies a crucial role in any historical entitlement theory. The principle of justice in transfer (the PJT) cannot do its work until someone gets to be entitled to a resource by means other than the PJT: the PJT operates on material provided in the first instance by the PJA. The PJA is concerned with the initial 'appropriation of unheld things': 'This includes the issue of how unheld things come to be held, the process or processes by which unheld things may come to be held, the things that may come to be held by these processes, the extent of what comes to be held by a particular process and so on' (p. 150). But Nozick does not tell us what his favoured PJA is; that is, he does not himself embark on the task of specifying which procedures for acquiring control over resources from their natural state are just and which unjust.[9]

---

[8] For the notion of pure procedural justice, see Rawls, *A Theory of Justice*, p. 85, and Nozick's discussion in *Anarchy, State, and Utopia*, pp. 207–9.

[9] No further elaboration is offered in Nozick's recent book, *Philosophical Explanations*.

He also fails to tell us what his favoured principle of transfer is; but from various hints elsewhere in the book it is possible to reconstruct a PJT which we can plausibly attribute to him. Presumably, it will legitimize the sort of transactions described in the famous Wilt Chamberlain example (pp. 160–4), and also familiar procedures like sale and purchase, gift, donation, and bequest; it will legitimize what we regard broadly as market transactions; and it will have something to say about thorny topics like fraud, negotiability, formal requirements of deed and contract, implied warranties and conditions, and so on.[10] One expects that the favoured PJT will reflect something like the received wisdom of the common law of property and contract on these matters (though it is worth noting that this body of law is by no means fixed and its underlying principles are far from clear or straightforward.)[11]

It is easy to talk about justice in transfer, for most of us are familiar with the transfer of privately owned resources (though as we shall see shortly it is less easy to justify a PJT in the context of an entitlement theory). The trouble is, that in specifying a PJA, we cannot derive the sort of guidance from common practice and legal principle that we can derive in the case of justice in transfer. The transfer of holdings is a topic which is familiar and mundane: most of us engage in it several times each week. But considerations of justice in acquisition are bound to be obscure and recondite even for those who take historical entitlement theories seriously. The reason is simple. Almost all the resources of the world have, on any such account, been initially appropriated long ago. They are already covered by legitimate entitlements (or entitlements based on rectification) and they are not up for legitimate appropriation by us. Appropriation of unheld resources is, therefore, not a concept we have to employ much in everyday life. Knowing what a valid PJA is would have little direct effect on our lives: its direct effect is confined to the time, centuries ago, when there were significant unheld resources to appropriate.[12] The ethical importance of a PJA to us is indirect, inasmuch as it functions to secure the basis of a system of historical entitlements that is supposed to have got under way long ago but which continues to constrain us today.

[10] See, e.g., Nozick, *Anarchy, State, and Utopia*, pp. 157–9, 167–8, 235–6, and 262–8.

[11] Cf. the interesting discussion in Atiyah, *Rise and Fall of Freedom of Contract*.

[12] Locke insisted that his PJA still had direct consequences for his time: see *Two Treatises*, II, sects. 30 (fish etc.) and 36 (land in Andalusia and America).

This leaves the PJA in a curious and almost anomalous position. As a principle it has to be valid, first, in respect of those whose actions it is supposed to constrain directly (our ancestors long ago), and, secondly, in respect of those whom it is supposed to constrain indirectly (us today, when we are tempted to meddle with the system of entitlements). One does not have to be an ethical relativist to see the difficulties here. What were conditions like when resources were first taken into ownership? How well developed was moral consciousness? Were those to whom the principle was supposed to apply capable of implementing it properly? Could it conceivably have been a principle which they held and abided by explicitly? Or in any way? If we turn from ancient to modern capabilities, how can *we* make sense *now* of principles whose only direct application was hundreds or perhaps thousands of years ago? If we cannot, does that not deprive such a principle of any right to be regarded as the generating basis of a system of entitlements that is to continue to constrain us today? These are exciting but very difficult questions, and they have yet to be explored by moral philosophers. They pose serious problems for a theory which has the shape of Nozick's; certainly it is not surprising that he shied away from them.[13]

I have said that the PJA specifies the actions that must be performed before the acquisition of private property rights in a particular object can be deemed to have taken place. Out of the various ways in which a person may act on or handle a natural resource, the PJA will indicate which of them is to be regarded as conferring exclusive rights on that person and duties or obligations on others.

In a theory like this, the justice of acquisition will be understood in a right-based way. Briefly, a defender of a PJA must show that the performance of the specified acquisitive actions invests with some particular moral importance the agent's interest in retaining exclusive control over the object on which he has been acting. (In Locke's theory, for example, this interest is invested with special importance deriving from the fact—if it is one—that the agent's labour has come to be 'mixed with' the object.) That is a difficult enough task.

A much more difficult task is the following. Even if he can establish that an appropriator acquires an interest that has some

---

[13] I am grateful to Leslie Green for stimulating these thoughts.

special claim to be respected, the theorist of historical entitlement must also go on to show that when the original appropriator transfers the holding to another, in accordance with the PJT, the other person acquires an interest of exactly the same degree of moral importance in retaining the object that has been transferred to him. The function of the PJT is to indicate that the strength of the original entitlement is preserved in the hands of a succession of transferees once the appropriated holding has been sold, given away, or bequeathed by the original appropriator, so that, even if we are not all original appropriators, still our private property rights continue to constrain the activities of the state. So a defence of the PJT component of a theory of historical entitlement is a matter of showing that a transferee's interest in the exclusive control of the holding is morally just as important and commands the same respect as the original appropriator's interest in retaining control of the object he had just appropriated. Otherwise transfer will have the effect of *watering down* entitlements progressively as they pass from hand to hand, so that the further we get from the original appropriator the less compelling an owner's interest in not being expropriated will be.

That is the task facing anyone who wants to defend the transfer element in a theory of historical entitlement. It is important to realize that this task is *not* discharged merely by demonstrating that the appropriator's rights include a power to pass on all the rights, liberties, and powers that he has acquired.[14] It is, indeed, difficult enough to show *that*, inasmuch as a theory of appropriation need not yield a conception of ownership which involves a power of alienation, and will do so only if it can be shown that the act of appropriation makes it important for appropriators to be able to trade things as well as to have the exclusive use of them. But even if an appropriator acquires a power of alienation, that does not establish that those in whose favour he exercises it acquire an interest in the holding passed on to them which is as compelling as his own was. It would be quite consistent to maintain, for example, that an appropriator has a right to bequeath his property, but that the legatees who receive it are *less* entitled to it than he was just because they got it as a result of bequest rather than on the basis of their own labour. ('Less entitled' may mean, for example, that it is easier for other moral considerations, such as need or social utility,

[14] Cf. Dworkin, 'Equality of Resources', p. 310.

to prevail over their rights.) If on the other hand, we insist that the original appropriator's power of alienation does involve a power to pass on the full moral force of his own entitlement to another, then it will be correspondingly more difficult to establish that such a power should be included in the package of rights he acquires in his original appropriation.

How, then, is this task to be performed? I can think of only three possible lines of argument, and they all face considerable difficulty.

First, perhaps we can argue that the person to whom the appropriator first transfers his holding must himself have given value for the transfer, and that he is therefore entitled to receive back in exchange rights which are at least as strong as those he has given away. The goods which the transferee has alienated in the transaction may be resources to which he too was originally entitled as a result of an appropriation. It would be odd if two appropriators, exchanging their holdings, were both to end up with entitlements that were morally weaker than those they began with. But there are several difficulties with this argument. It works only in cases where goods have been transferred for consideration; and it suggests that entitlements *may* be watered down when transfer involves gift, bequest, or inheritance. But this is not what historical entitlement theorists want to maintain (cf. pp. 167 ff.). Moreover, even in cases where the transfer has been reciprocated, *is* it so odd that each party ends up with a weaker entitlement? After all, on most PJAs, original appropriation involves the establishment of a special relationship between a particular person and a particular object (for example, on Locke's account, *it* comes to 'contain' *his* labour). If, in spite of this special relationship, a person finds it convenient to swap control over the object for control over another one to which he is not related in this particular way, that is his business. The fact is that, if he does this, the object which he then has an interest in controlling is no longer an object with which he has established the relationship which a theory of justice in acquisition deems to be of such special moral importance.

A second line of argument looks at it more from the point of view of the transferor. If he is not in a position to pass onto others an entitlement at least as strong as his own, then his ways of dealing with the object and the advantages he can derive from it will be limited. But distressing though this is from his point of view, it is hardly compelling for the rest of us. We do not assume that when a person acquires an object he should acquire an absolutely unlimited right to derive whatever advantage could conceivably be derived from dealing with that object. On any account, there will be some limitations. So there can be no a priori argument to the effect that he *must* have a power to pass on an entitlement as compelling as his own simply on the ground that that would be a jolly useful thing to have.

Thirdly, perhaps it could be argued that the transfer process itself invests the transferee's interest in controlling the object with a special importance analogous to that with which the appropriation process invests the appropriator's interest. But how would such an argument go? Are we to imagine a situation like that in which a child watches a toy in a shop window day after day as he saves up for it, so that by the time he finally purchases it he has identified with it so strongly as to make it already a part of himself? What if he fails to save up enough money? Does he still have a claim to the object? Anyway, are run-of-the-mill cases of transfer sufficiently like this to warrant saying that this is the *general* sort of consideration justifying a PJT? I cannot think how these questions could be answered.

I have not provided a knock-down argument against the PJT component in a theory of historical entitlement. But I hope to have indicated the nature of the difficulties that the justification of this component is likely to involve.

For the rest of this chapter, I shall mainly ignore the issue of transfer and concentrate on original acquisition. It is the PJA that introduces the idea of special right into a theory of historical entitlement, and gets the whole 'recursion' (p. 151) under way. If it does not work, or if it faces serious difficulties, then doubt is cast on the whole SR-based approach to the defence of private property.

3. ACQUISITION

A PJA is a principle indicating the possibility of a certain sort of change in the moral world. It states conditions under which material resources which hitherto have not been owned by anyone in particular can, at a certain time after certain events, become the private property of some individual. It explains, in other words, how private property entitlements in material resources are possible and how a system of such entitlements gets under way.

But this is not sufficient to explain what a PJA is. There are many ways in which a system of private property might get established. For example, maybe everyone in the world or in a certain territory got together and agreed to divide all available resources into individual holdings and to distribute those holdings among the parties to the agreement.[15] There might then be a principle indicating that anyone who received a holding as a result of such a distribution would be entitled to the resources in that holding. But that would not be a PJA. It would lack the special character that distinguishes principles of justice in *acquisition* from other sorts of distributive principle. What is special about a PJA is this: it indicates that the transition to the private ownership of a resource can be effected by the unilateral action of the individual who is to be the owner. That is, a PJA stipulates an action or set of actions A, such that anyone who performs A with respect to some resource *ipso facto* becomes the owner of that resource.[16]

We might as well make this schema precise so that it can be a fixed point in what follows. A PJA will have the following form:

For all x and for all r, if x does A with respect to r, then x becomes the owner of r.

That is the *form* of a PJA. To specify a particular PJA is to indicate the range of 'r' and the act-description which is to replace 'A'.

A word about the term 'with respect to' in the antecedent of the conditional above. I take it that this links up with the action A to ensure that x's performance of A bears some *intentional* relation to the resource r.

Various intentional relations are possible here. One possibility is that, in performing A, x intends to *affect* r in some way. This is characteristic of Labour Theories of acquisition, such as Locke's theory. The acquisitive action A, on the Lockean view, is the action of labouring on the resource: one removes something out of its natural state by hunting and killing it, or by gathering it, or, in the case of a piece of land, by tilling, planting, cultivating, or otherwise improving it.[17] In all these instances some physical change is wrought in the object. (Locke's example of the hare, which is to be

---

[15] Cf. the theory developed in Pufendorf, *Of the Law of Nature* Bk. IV, discussed in Tully, *A Discourse on Property*, pp. 72–7. More recently, see the accounts of Dworkin, 'Equality of Resources'; and Ackerman, *Social Justice*, Chs. 2 and 6.

[16] I owe this formulation to Lloyd-Thomas, 'Liberty, Equality and Property', p. 186.

[17] Locke, *Two Treatises*, II, sects. 27–32.

the property of its pursuer even before he catches it, is an exception to the general character of his theory in this respect.)[18]

Other PJAs that have been sugggested have not required so much. 'First Occupancy' theories, for example, require only that x should act so as to bring about a certain change in his relation to r. To *occupy* a piece of land is to bring it about intentionally that one stands in a specified geographical relation to the land that one did not stand in before.

Sometimes it has even been suggested that A need not involve any physical action at all—that the mere intentional direction of one's will upon an object is sufficient to appropriate it. This suggestion is considered and rejected by Kant (apparently on the grounds that some connection between the agent and the object under conditions of time and space is necessary to make one's relation to the object known to others and to avoid the unpleasant possibility that someone might unilaterally appropriate all the resources in the world by a mere act of will).[19] It is sometimes suggested that Hegel's theory of appropriation was of this kind; that objects can be appropriated by mere acts of will.[20] This is a mistaken intepretation. Hegel's view was that the appropriation of objects *involves* an act of will, and that it is important because of its ramifications for the will; but he insisted that the act of will must be 'actualized' with respect to an external object by physical occupancy, the taking of physical possession, or, at the very least, by the marking of the object.[21] (This misinterpretation mistakes Hegel's account of the importance of acquisition—embodiment of the will in the object—for an account of the *mechanics* of acquisition.) I believe, however, that the pure mental act theory of acquisition (or something rather like it) was held by Fichte.[22]

In any case, although most writers do not regard a mere intention to appropriate a resource as sufficient, most of them take it to be necessary (Kant, Hegel, and Fichte explicitly; Locke, I think, implicitly). So that whatever the action A turns out to be, its performance must involve the intention to acquire rights of ownership in the resource—although it may often, as in the case of Lockean labouring, involve other intentions as well. This, as we shall see, is quite important.

[18] Locke, *Two Treatises*, II, sect. 30.
[19] See the discussion in Gregor, *Laws of Freedom*, p. 53.
[20] See e.g. Stillman, 'Property, Freedom and Individuality', p. 133.
[21] Hegel, *Philosophy of Right*, sects. 41–58. See below Ch. 10.
[22] Fichte, *Science of Rights*, pp. 166–7.

The other notion that needs to be cleared up before we can make progress is, of course, the notion of *ownership*. We have already examined the difficulties involved in reaching a definition of ownership. To simplify the argument in the rest of this chapter, I want to work with a slightly simplistic conception of ownership which concentrates attention on what is distinctive and controversial about a PJA. The interesting and controversial thing about ownership, as it is supposed to feature in a PJA, is that it is an *exclusive* right against all the world. What is crucial—and controversial—about an act of acquisition is that, if it is successful, others are excluded from access to and use of the resource in question. Thenceforth they have a duty, owed to the appropriator, to keep off the land he has acquired or to refrain from eating the chestnuts he has gathered. Of course, this right of exclusion is not all there is to ownership: a PJA can hardly take its place in a theory of historical entitlement if the rights it generates are not also rights that can be alienated in favour of others. The conception of ownership involved in such a theory includes a power of alienation; and that, as we have seen, poses problems. But for the sake of the present argument, we will define ownership as involving the right of exclusion *at least*: so that a person counts as the owner of *r only if* he has a right to the exclusive use of *r*, i.e. *only if* others have a duty (which he alone can waive) to refrain from using *r*. This simplification is a concession to the position we are going to attack: as we shall see, it is hard enough to defend the view that rights of exclusive use can be generated through unilateral acquisition, let alone the view that the exclusive rights so generated are also unilaterally *transferable*!

We can put this partial definition of ownership together with our schema for a PJA to get the following more complex schema:

> For all *x* and for all *r*, if *x* does A with respect to *r*, then, for all other individuals *y*, *x* acquires a right that *y* refrain from using *r*.

The argument I am going to present in the rest of the chapter has two parts. In the first part (section 4), I want to expose the radical unfamiliarity of a PJA. When we look at it closely we find that it is something which is so unlike any other ethical idea that it cannot simply be regarded as an intuitive or self-evident truth (whatever that means). On the face of it, it seems unfamiliar and repugnant; certainly it cries out for justification. In section 5 I confront the issue of justification more directly. I want to claim that a PJA could never form part of a contractarian theory of justice, unless it were heavily qualified by a very strong Lockean proviso—a proviso much stronger than the one Nozick is prepared to concede. Now that, of course, looks unsurprising: after all, one of Nozick's main claims is that contractarianism is inadequate precisely because it leaves no place for considerations of historical entitlement. But I shall argue that this claim is based on an evident mistake on Nozick's part. My conclusion will be that the idea of an unqualified PJA should be rejected on the contractarian ground that no such principle could possibly be made acceptable to all of those whose behaviour it is supposed to constrain.

4. CONTINGENT RIGHTS

My first misgiving about the very idea of a PJA can perhaps best be introduced by quoting a passage from Kant's discussion of property in *The Metaphysical Elements of Justice*: 'When I declare (by word or deed), "I will that an external thing shall be mine", I thereby declare it obligatory for everyone else to refrain from using the object of my will. This is an obligation that no-one would have apart from this juridical act of mine.'[23] Now this is the interesting thing about a PJA. It indicates a way in which rights and obligations can be created—a way in which duties can be brought into existence where they did not exist before.

The idea of an obligation's coming into existence as a result of contingent occurrences is not entirely unfamiliar in moral life. We are familiar with the idea in relation to promises and contracts. If I promise to read a paper to a seminar, I acquire at the moment of the uptake of that promise an obligation which I did not have before— an obligation which I would not have apart from this contingent event of promising. A new obligation has been brought into existence.

Someone might object that I did have an obligation before I made the promise: namely the general obligation to keep my promises from which my particular obligation to read a paper to the seminar derives. It may be thought, in other words, that I have, at all times and for all actions *a*, an obligation to do *a* if I have promised to do *a*. This is in effect the suggestion we explored towards the end of Chapter 4; but as we saw there, there are difficulties with the

<hr />

[23] Kant, *Metaphysical Elements of Justice*, Ladd trans., p. 64 (VI, 255).

derivation of the particular obligation from the more general principle. But the point can as easily be expressed the other way. By promising, I bring into existence an unconditional obligation which I did not have before (for all that I may have had a conditional obligation to do the same thing). And similarly with acquisition. A PJA shows how by performing the action A, I can bring into existence unconditional obligations (for others) that they did not have before (for all that they may be thought to have had conditional obligations under the principle).

A PJA, then, has in common with the promising principle that it indicates a way in which obligations and duties can come into existence where no such obligations or duties existed before. But if this similarity is obvious, the main dissimilarity betwen promising and obligation is even more striking. In the case of promising, the obligation is brought into existence by the person who is to be bound by it. To promise is to put *oneself* under an obligation. A PJA, on the other hand, indicates a way in which, by performing the acquisitive act A, an individual can put not himself but *everybody else* under an obligation. By his act, he acquires not duties but rights, and thousands of other people, including people he has never spoken with, people he has never met, people who have never even heard of him, suddenly find themselves labouring under obligations which they did not have before.

This, I guess, should be an obvious point. But it is often overlooked. People assume that acquisition gives rise mainly to a new relation between the appropriator and his object. But property relations do not exist between persons and objects; they exist between persons and other persons. For a property relation to come into existence, therefore, is necessarily for the normative positions of untold individuals to be altered.

This unilateral creation of a new universal obligation would not be of very great concern if the obligations created were not onerous ones. But the obligations correlative to property rights *are* onerous. They concern our access to and use of resources which are scarce relative to the demands which human wants place on them. And these demands are urgent because, in many cases, the use of material resources is a matter of life and death. So what we are being asked to accept, when a PJA is put forward is this: that there are actions which individuals can perform whose moral effect is to place millions of others under obligations whose discharge may require them to place their own survival in jeopardy. Furthermore, it is not only survival that may be threatened, but also their ability to discharge whatever duties and obligations they have to see to the welfare of others. A parent may have a duty to see that his child is fed; but his ability to discharge this duty will be undermined if the resources which the child needs have been put 'off-limits' by the appropriation of somebody else. This is to say nothing of our more far-reaching obligations to save the lives of anyone who is starving or to guarantee some material basis for the survival of future generations.

I am not suggesting that unilateral acts of acquisition are directly harmful. (Whether we are in fact harmed will depend on whether we do what we are said by such a principle to be obliged to do.) My worry is about the *moral* effect of the appropriation: if some PJA is true, then individuals are in a position to make it morally difficult or morally impossible for others to secure their own survival or discharge their other responsibilities; they may make it impossible for others to do these things without doing wrong. (This point survives, in an attenuated form, even if we say that the duties generated by acquisition are only *prima facie* duties which may be outweighed by other duties: even if this is so, the acquisition may make it difficult for us to discharge the latter duties without compunction.)[24]

Now it is equally true that the obligations which arise out of promises may also place one's welfare or survival in jeopardy (if, for example, one has promised to do something dangerous), and that they too may cut across the other obligations that we have. But the difference is that, in the promising case, the new (and possibly dangerous) obligation has been created by the person who is to bear it: if it is my promise then it is I who have introduced this new factor into my moral life. It seems reasonable to say that each person has a responsibility to keep his own moral life (the set of his obligations and duties etc.) in order as far as he can, and that taking care in the assumption of promissory obligations is part of the discharge of that responsibility.[25] (Perhaps it is this point, rather than any deep concern about liberty, that lies behind our estimation of the importance of voluntariness in contract and market transactions.) But in the case of acquisition, we simply fall under obligations as a result of other people's acts: it is not our fault that

[24] See Ross, *The Right and the Good*, Ch. 2; see also Melden, *Rights and Persons*, pp. 4 ff.

[25] This point owes a lot to Walzer, *Obligations*, esp. Chs. 1 and 9.

these complications enter our moral lives nor could it plausibly be claimed that it is our responsibility to avoid them.

There is, then, this radical difference between contingent obligations based on promises and contingent obligations based on acquisition. But maybe there are other analogies to help the proponent of a PJA. What he needs in order to familiarize us with his proposition is some sort of widely acknowledged moral duty with the following features:

(1) the duty is owed to and benefits some individual x;
(2) the duty comes into existence as a result of some action a by x;
(3) discharging the duty may be dangerous or morally embarrassing to those who have it; and
(4) those who have the duty have not consented to being put in that position.

Are we familiar with any duties of this sort?

Perhaps the most familiar case is something along the lines of our duty to rescue or come to the aid of someone who has injured himself or put himself in danger. This seems to satisfy conditions (1)–(4). But even here there is a disanalogy. As I mentioned in section 3, the acquisition of resources has this further feature: that the appropriator not only intends to perform the acquisitive act A, but also (and I think necessarily) intends to perform it *as* an acquisitive act. That is, he performs the act with the intention of acquiring the rights that it gives rise to. But to perform an act with the intention of acquiring rights is necessarily to perform it with the intention of imposing duties on other people. So for an accurate specification, we require this further feature:

(5) the action a is performed by x with the intention of imposing the duty described in (1)–(4).

Even after we have added this further feature, we do not entirely lose our grip on the analogy with the case of rescue. We have to imagine not only an individual whose actions have got him into danger from which we are obliged (at considerable risk to ourselves) to rescue him, but also an individual whose intention in putting himself in this position was precisely to impose this obligation on us. I guess the 'cry for help' suicide attempt is something along these lines.

But one feels very queasy about obligations of this sort; one thinks that those who have such obligations thrust upon them are entitled to feel some resentment towards the individual they are thus obliged to help. We feel something of the exasperation one encounters in dealing with a child, who is experimenting with moral relations to find out what he has to do in order to oblige his parent to help him. Moreover, even if we do recognize an obligation in such a case, we do so, I think, despite features (2) and (5), rather than because of them. We feel an obligation to rescue these people because we recognize a more general obligation to come to the aid of those in danger however they got there. Our readiness to rescue those who have deliberately endangered themselves and their potential rescuers is very much a derivative and peripheral application of this principle.[26] But in the case of a PJA, we are asked to accept that the deliberate act of acquisition is itself the sole and intrinsic basis of the obligation to respect the agent's control over the resource. We are to have this onerous duty thrust upon us, not as a derivative special case of some duty with which we feel more comfortable, but because and *simply* because he has decided to impose it.

(There may, however, be other features of the acquisitive act which bring into play other more familiar duties. Our duty not to knock the food out of the hand of someone who is eating it is derivative from the general duty not to assault. But such duties fall far short of duties to respect *property* rights. As Kant saw, and as a number of philosophers have argued recently, these duties would at most protect *de facto* physical possession. They would not be sufficient to establish ownership entitlements.)[27]

What I have shown so far is that a PJA would be an unfamiliar, and maybe unwelcome, addition to a morality just like our own. It would lead to the imposition of duties in a way which is quite unlike the imposition of any other duties with which we are happy or familiar. But, of course, by itself, this is not an argument against the inclusion of a PJA in an acceptable morality. Maybe there are moral facts which simply *are* unfamiliar, *sui generis*, and unpalatable. Many natural facts are unpleasant to face, but, if they are facts, that is all there is to it. And the situation may be the same in

---

[26] In the same way, our obligation of gratitude to those who have thrust benefits on us with the *intention* of imposing this obligation (e.g. rulers who want to take advantage of Socrates' theory of political obligation) is a derivative, peripheral, and, I think, highly problematic application of the general and more familiar obligation of gratitude for benefits received. I am grateful to Robert Durrant for suggesting this example to me.

[27] Kant, *Metaphysical Elements of Justice*, Ladd trans., p. 54 (VI, 248); see also Scanlon, 'Nozick on Rights', pp. 124 ff.

moral reality. Nevertheless, I think I have done enough to show that the inclusion of a PJA in our morality is not to be taken for granted or regarded as in any sense self-evident. Because it is so unfamiliar, we should not be surprised if people refuse to 'see' it. The proponent of a PJA should not be surprised to be told that any such principle cries out for a justification, and he should have something to say to discharge that justificatory obligation.

5. ACQUISITION AS A SUBJECT FOR CONSENT

For the reasons I have mentioned, many people will baulk at the idea that any of the demands of justice are properly captured in a PJA. What can the proponent of a PJA say to convince them?

Can he perhaps make an appeal to moral intuition? Suppose he claims that the truth of some PJA is simply evident to him, and that it ought to be evident to others if they are 'seeing' things clearly. It is sometimes thought that this was Nozick's approach: that the reason he did not explicitly state or argue for a specific set of principles of justice was that he thought them self-evident and argument unnecessary.[28] But that is a mistaken interpretation. First, as we have seen, Nozick has other good reasons for not specifying a favoured PJA. And secondly, early in the book he does make gestures in the direction of moral argument concerning justice and rights (pp. 48–51). True, the account he gives is very sketchy (though tantalizingly attractive). He promises to address the issue more fully on another occasion, and the fact that he has yet to deliver on that promise does not by itself indicate that he takes its fulfilment to be theoretically unnecessary.[29] But, Nozick aside, what are we to say to a genuine intuitionist proponent of a PJA?

I think there are very good reasons, which John Rawls must take the credit for bringing to our attention, for refusing to be satisfied with an intuitive approach to political morality.[30] The reasons have to do with the liberal conception of the function of political philosophy. One of the functions of political philosophy is to show

[28] See e.g. Nagel, 'Libertarianism Without Foundations', p. 195.
[29] Nozick, *Anarchy, State, and Utopia*, p. 51; cf. Nozick, *Philosophical Explanations*, Ch. 5. (The latter work contains a discussion of rights, but nothing to fill out the connections between the considerations alluded to in *Anarchy, State, and Utopia* and any set of particular principles of entitlement.)
[30] Rawls, 'Kantian Constructivism', esp. pp. 517–19 and 557–90.

how (or whether) political and legal arrangements which are on the face of them coercive can nevertheless be reconciled with the principle of the autonomy of the individual moral agent. One way of doing this is to show that the arrangements in question embody standards and principles (or procedures for determining standards and principles) which all citizens actually accept. If this is true, then, in accepting them, the citizens have already condemned in themselves the offences to which state coercion is a response; they have cut away the ground from under their own feet in complaining that the coercion violates their autonomy.[31] But we are unlikely to get very far with this in the case of a PJA because, as a matter of fact, there is no unanimous agreement among citizens on standards and principles of justice.[32] Certainly, we must assume that there is no PJA which is actually accepted by everyone whom it is liable to constrain.

If there is no actual consensus, is there any other way of reconciling individual autonomy with the coercion that the operation of any system of justice inevitably involves? A move is sometimes made in the direction of hypothetical consent. The citizen is told that under certain counterfactual conditions he *would have consented* to a particular principle of justice (to which *in fact* he has not explicitly subscribed), so that *to this extent* the enforcement of the principle is not incompatible with respect for his autonomy. Now clearly the stronger and less plausible the counterfactual hypothesis, the greater the gap between the justificatory theory and the actual operation of the coercive rules we are trying to legitimize. The individual to whom we are addressing the justificatory argument may not be able to recognize himself in the hypothetical situation we are describing if the counterfactual is very strong, and so he may deny that there is any important connection between the consent that would have been given there and his own consent.[33] But if the counterfactual is weak, then the features which distinguish the actual situation from the one in which it is suggested that consent would have been given may be so trivial or morally unimportant that no self-respecting agent will want to rest his complaint about coercion on those differences. Rawls's attempt to derive a positive and detailed account of justice on this sort of basis

[31] This is the approach taken in Rousseau, *Social Contract*, Bk. I, Chs. 7–8 and Bk. II, Ch. 4.
[32] Cf. Hayek, *Mirage of Social Justice*, Chs. 9 and 12.
[33] Cf. Dworkin, *Taking Rights Seriously*, Ch. 6, esp. pp. 150–4.

is well known: according to Rawls, fair principles of justice are those that would command the unanimous consent of the citizens they are to constrain bargaining behind a 'veil of ignorance' as to their individual talents, endowments, and conceptions of the good life.[34] The strength and plausibility of the counterfactual hypothesis involved in Rawls's 'original position', and indeed the claim that his detailed conception of justice would be adopted therein, both remain the subjects of intense controversy. We cannot go into that here.

But perhaps a less ambitious scheme might work in a negative way. Instead of trying positively to *derive* a conception of justice, perhaps we can at least *rule out* some possible conceptions using a contractarian hypothesis. Perhaps, in other words, we can show that a suggested principle of justice is *un*acceptable by showing that there is no remotely plausible or coherent counterfactual hypothesis under which that principle would command the universal consent of citizens.

This is the approach taken by Kant in his political philosophy. The assumption of a social contract, according to Kant,

is in fact merely an idea of reason, which nonetheless has undoubted practical reality; for it can oblige every legislator to frame his laws in such a way that they could have been produced by the united will of a whole nation. . . .This is the test of the rightfulness of every public law. For if the law is such that a whole people could not *possibly* agree to it (for example, if it stated that a certain class of *subjects* must be privileged as a hereditary *ruling class*), it is unjust.[35]

This is also, in my view, one of the most important aspects of John Locke's political philosophy. Time and again, Locke argues (against various permutations of royalist absolutism) *not* that the people have not in fact consented to these arrangements, but rather that the arrangements are such that rational consent to them is *unthinkable*. Claims like 'No rational Creature can be supposed to change his condition with an intention to be worse' and 'A Man . . . cannot subject himself to the Arbitrary Power of another' illustrate the strand of negative hypothetical contractarianism in Locke's thought.[36]

---

[34] Rawls claims that the Veil of Ignorance rules out knowledge of features of real life that are 'arbitrary' from a moral point of view: *A Theory of Justice*, pp. 12, 18–19, and 140–1.

[35] Kant, 'Theory and Practice', p. 79.

[36] See Locke, *Two Treatises*, II, sects. 131 and 134–41.

The force of this negative approach is evident. If there is no plausible story we can tell in which a suggested political principle *would have been* accepted by the people, then there is no hope at all of reconciling the coercive enforcement of that principle with the liberal requirement of respect for the dignity and autonomy of individual citizens. The search for actual consent is redundant; the negative hypothesis precludes it. Thus a conclusive way of showing the unacceptability of a PJA as the foundation of a theory of justice would be to show why no principle of this sort could command unanimous consent in the 'original position' of any plausible social contract story.

So imagine now that the parties in a hypothetical 'original position' of the Rawlsian sort were asked to consider whether they accept a PJA. It does not matter whether it is a particular specified PJA or just the idea of a PJA, as I have outlined it. Presumably in the course of their deliberations the parties would consider the way in which PJAs operate. They would be aware of the points made in the previous section: that a PJA puts individuals in a position unilaterally to impose far-reaching, dangerous, and morally embarrassing obligations on other people—obligations whose discharge would diminish the latter's life-chances and may imperil their survival. They would be aware that the resources over which a PJA was to operate would be scarce relative to human demand (otherwise why have rules of property at all?) so that the effect of its operation would be to secure the satisfaction of some demands at the expense of others. They would be aware that the unilateral character of acquisition would mean that duties might be imposed on them without regard to their social distribution. If a PJA were to operate, everyone would have a motive to perform the acquisitive act A with respect to some useful resource; but not everyone who was so motivated would succeed in doing so because there would soon come a point at which there were few resources left. Their awareness of all this would lead them to look closely at the suggested acquisitive action A. In the nature of things, the specification of A would be the specification of an action which some people were more adept at performing than others. Some would be very good at A-ing—they could do A quickly and easily—whereas others (handicapped in this regard) might be altogether incapable of A-ing or be capable of it only with the greatest difficulty. These advantages and handicaps would not all be intrinsic to the people concerned. Even if A were an action that everyone could perform more or less equally well, still it would be only the *first* person to perform A with regard to a given resource who got to be its owner. (His ownership then would impose a duty on others to refrain from A-ing with regard to his resource.) So those who turned out to be closest in time and space to unappropriated resources would benefit unequally from the operation of such a principle.

The parties in the original position, then, would be aware not only that a PJA provides a basis for the unilateral acquisition of rights and imposition of duties, but also that these rights would be distributed unequally. They would know that those who, on account of handicap or situation, were least good at A-ing would have all of the onerous duties and few or none of the rights which acquisition generated. In terms of their survival and life-chances, they would be entirely at the mercy of those who were better than they at A-ing.

The parties would be aware of these points. Before considering what they would conclude from them, two general considerations are important.

First, a point that may seem trivial but is in fact very important. I assume that a PJA does have practical consequences in the sense that its operation would make a difference to the actions of those who accept it. In other words, I asssume that it is *practical*, not *redundant*. A principle of justice is redundant if the actions it forbids are actions which could not or would not have been performed anyway (and *mutatis mutandis* for the actions it requires). A principle of justice is practical just to the extent that it forbids actions that the agents have no other reason not to perform and enjoins actions that they have no other reason to perform, apart from the reasons given and appealed to in the theory of justice itself. Thus, from a practical point of view, a non-redundant PJA will require individuals to refrain from using resources in circumstances where, apart from that prohibition, the use of those resources would be a viable and perhaps attractive option for them. Now, no doubt, many of those who appropriated resources would erect fences and build safes so as to make it impossible for their newly-won property to be interfered with. But that is contingent and, from the point of view of justice, irrelevant. We are to understand that, in the cases where it applies, the PJA is to be the sole obstacle to the performance of the actions it forbids.[37]

Secondly, the parties are understood to be considering the PJA under the assumption that, were they to accept it, they would be bound by it. They are understood to be bargaining, as Rawls puts it, in good faith.[38] If the principle they accepted required them to refrain from some action in certain circumstances, then they would be committing themselves to refrain from that action in those circumstances. So if a PJA requires a person to refrain from using resources that he needs when they have been acquired by someone else, then any agreement to that principle would require that person to refrain from satisfying his needs in that way. The parties must bargain, in other words, as though there were no room for reneging or evading this commitment once entered into. As Rawls puts it, they must 'weigh with care whether they will be able to stick by their commitment in all circumstances'.[39] If they are doubtful on this score, they should avoid entering into that commitment and therefore reject the proposed principle.

The effect of all this is that the parties would know that by agreeing to a PJA at least some of them would be committing themselves to refrain from using resources to satisfy their pressing physical needs in circumstances where it would otherwise be open and perhaps sensible for them to do so. It seems to me that this is not a commitment that anyone can enter into in good faith. We need to imagine what it is like to starve to death or perish from cold when food and shelter 'owned' by someone else are, in a purely physical sense, available.[40] No one surely is entitled to assume in himself the sort of stoic fortitude that would enable him to resist the overwhelming temptation to 'theft' or 'trespass' in these circumstances. Remember that, for present purposes, the sanctions with which a theory of justice would be defended in real life are

---

[37] See Rawls, *A Theory of Justice*, p. 145. (Cf. the approach taken in Ackerman, *Social Justice*, where it is assumed for the purposes of 'ideal' theory that we can have a 'perfect technology of justice' which makes it impossible for whatever rules of justice are chosen to be violated. In my view, Ackerman's assumption, even at the level of ideal theory, runs profoundly against the grain of liberal political philosophy, abandoning as it does the need for continuing consent and compliance, and one of the most important 'circumstances of justice'—mutual vulnerability.)

[38] Rawls, *A Theory of Justice*, sect. 29.

[39] Ibid. 176.

[40] For an eloquent description, see Honderich, *Violence for Equality*, pp. 16–22.

irrelevant. All sorts of unjust principles could be made viable in social and political life by the use of coercive sanctions. But the test of justice and moral legitimacy (the test of the justifiability of using sanctions!) is whether the arrangements could, in principle, command their own support in all the circumstances in which they were to operate.

For these reasons, it seems unlikely that a PJA could secure unanimous acceptance in advance from those who were to be bound by it. Moreover, this conclusion stands whether or not the parties are considering its acceptance behind a Rawlsian 'veil of ignorance' as to who is good and who is bad at performing the acquisitive action A. Of course, those who have reason to believe that they are good at A-ing may sign up for it. But anyone who has reason to believe that he is (or may turn out to be) relatively bad at A-ing knows that he is putting his very survival at risk by consenting to a PJA. He would prefer to take his chances in a Hobbesian state of nature where he could at least 'grab' in order to survive rather than commit himself to a PJA.

It may be objected to this conclusion that a person who was bad at A-ing and who would therefore do badly under a PJA might believe himself to be even worse at doing what was necessary to gain the use of resources in a Hobbesian state of nature. He may have reason to believe that he is even worse at grabbing things when he needs them than he is at A-ing![41] But I do not think this hunch gives him a reason to opt for a PJA. His being worse, on the whole at grabbing things than at A-ing does not preclude the possibility that, *in some cases*, the practical force of a PJA would put him on his honour not to grab things which he could otherwise grab to satisfy his pressing needs. In those cases, then, the principle would make impossible demands on him, and that is sufficient for our conclusion that he could not agree in advance in good faith to abide by it.

It may be true, nevertheless, that everyone, even the acquisitively handicapped, would do better for themselves under the system of property entitlements established by a PJA than they would in a Hobbesian state of nature. After all, once a secure set of entitlements has been established, agriculture, industry, and commerce can get under way with the resulting benefits for

---

[41] I owe this objection to R. M. Hare and other members of the All Souls Moral and Political Philosophy Group.

everyone that that involves. This position has been at the heart of capitalist liberalism ever since Locke's famous assertion that 'a King of a large fruitful Territory' in contemporary America, where land had not been taken into private ownership, 'there feeds, lodges, and is clad worse than a day Labourer in England.'[42] But this consideration, if true, does not favour a PJA as such. The point about the prosperity of a secure and established system of property obtains no matter what its basis and structure. If the economy were founded on an initial egalitarian distribution of resources, the same point would still obtain. As Jeremy Bentham noted in his writings on property, the important thing so far as security and prosperity are concerned is not the principle on which the economy is organized but a conservative respect for its organization no matter what the content of its principles.[43]

So it looks as though a PJA—any PJA—will fail the negative test of hypothetical consent that we have been considering. It is, to use Kant's words, a principle 'such that a whole people could not possibly agree to it'. To this extent, the implementation of a law or a structure of institutions based on a PJA is bound to be irretrievably coercive. It follows that as long as there are more plausible alternatives, a system of historical entitlements is indefensible in the liberal tradition.

6. NOZICK AND 'MANNA FROM HEAVEN'

As I indicated earlier, none of this is very surprising. Nozick himself readily concedes that no historical entitlement theory (and therefore no PJA) would be chosen in Rawls's 'original position' (pp. 198 ff.). He blames this on the Rawlsian 'veil of ignorance' (p. 203). But this is a mistake. A 'veil of ignorance' perhaps ensures that *nobody* votes for a PJA, since nobody is prepared to take the risks which accepting a PJA involves. But lifting the veil makes no difference to the fact that *not everybody* would vote for a PJA. We have to remember that unanimity is required: one cannot be voted into a social contract by a majority.[44] The principle must be justified in relation to all those against whom it might be enforced.

[42] Locke, *Two Treatises*, II, sect. 41.
[43] Bentham, 'Principles of the Civil Code', p. 119.
[44] Cf. Dworkin, *Taking Rights Seriously*, Ch. 6; though see the bizarre comment on Locke's theory in Arblaster, *Rise and Decline of Western Liberalism*, p. 165.

Nozick thinks that the Rawlsian (and presumably also our Kantian) enterprise is fundamentally misconceived. These approaches, he claims, 'treat objects as if they appeared from nowhere, out of nothing' (p. 160)—as if they 'fell from heaven like manna' (p. 198). But this, he insists, is not the case: 'The situation is *not* one of something's getting made, and there being an open question of who is to get it. Things come into the world already attached to people having entitlements over them' (p. 160). Nozick concedes that if things *did* fall like manna from heaven, maybe the Rawlsian approach or something like it would be an appropriate solution to the problem of distribution (p. 198). But he thinks we can ignore that possibility because it is not the situation we face.

This is an obvious mistake. As far as a principle of justice in *initial acquisition* is concerned, material resources are exactly like manna from heaven. Consider the earliest human act of production that an entitlement theory is required to take into account. Before he began producing, the person concerned faced a world of resources, of raw materials, that was simply there. Nobody produced it, nobody (except, in some stories, God) created it. If ever there was a time when resources ought to have been treated as though they fell like manna from heaven, this was that time. On Nozick's own account, the PJA is concerned with 'the appropriation of unheld things' (p. 150), things to which nobody so far had any entitlement. In a word, a PJA is a principle for dealing with the problem of manna.[45]

Of course, our ancestors who made the first appropriations did not ask themselves Rawlsian questions. They were cold and hungry, and if they had paused to ponder these intricate questions of social justice, they would have starved notwithstanding the plenty that had been provided for them.[46] They had to take what

[45] There is a view that appropriators in some sense 'create' the resources they discover—before they discovered it, it was *as though* the resource did not exist: see e.g. Kirzner, 'Entrepreneurship, Entitlement and Economic Justice'. But: (a) this is not Nozick's view; (b) it is not true in any literal sense, and it is not clear that the idea of creation can do the work Kirzner and others want it to do unless it is true in a literal sense; and (c) it is certainly not true in *any* sense for those resources such as land in which individual appropriation involves a change in the mode of use rather than first use or discovery (see Locke, *Two Treatises*, II, sects. 32 and 38). I suppose Kirzner's point applies best to 'intellectual property' and perhaps (by metaphorical extension) to the discovery of buried minerals. For further discussion of this idea in the context of Locke's theory, see above, Ch. 6, sect. 12. (I am grateful to Susan Sterett for pressing this point.)

[46] Cf. Locke, *Two Treatises*, II, sect. 28.

they could get. But the fact that *they* were incapable of dividing
resources on a fair basis (and therefore had no obligation to do so)
does not show that their acquisitions acquire the status of full-
blown moral constraints on subsequent social possibilities. At best,
their entitlements to keep what they have seized were based on the
assumption that the mechanisms for a fairer distribution were not
available. When that assumption failed, when those mechanisms
did become available, then the entitlements founded on the
assumption of their absence could not prevail. They were revealed
then as *provisional* entitlements not as the enduring foundations of
a system of justice that could continue to constrain us today in our
thinking and action on the matter.[47] The issue *we* face is whether
we—who *are* capable of responding to the demands of justice—are
to be constrained in our efforts to do so by a system of entitlements
arising out of the appropriations of those who were incapable of
responding (or unwilling to respond) to those demands. In
resolving this issue, the question of the justice of their acquisitions
is crucial for us in a way that it could not have been crucial for
them.[48] And since they were facing resources to which, at that
stage, nobody was initially entitled, the Rawlsian or the Kantian
approach seems a perfectly appropriate way of answering that
question.

7. LOCKEAN PROVISOS

I have so far said nothing about the so-called 'Lockean proviso'
with which Nozick qualifies his PJA (pp. 175 ff.). Locke is widely
believed (though I think mistakenly) to have qualified his Labour
Theory of acquisition with the proviso that an appropriation, to be
legitimate, must leave 'enough and as good . . . in common for
others'.[49] On this account, my cultivation of a previously unowned
field would generate a private property entitlement only if there
were other land available for improvement by anyone who claimed

[47] For the idea of a provisional entitlement, see Kant, *Metaphysical Elements of
Justice*, Ladd trans., pp. 64–78 (VI, 255–313). Tully suggests that Locke's view had
a similar shape: *A Discourse on Property*, Pt. III.
[48] For an account of the importance of questioning the idea of justice-in-
acquisition from a socialist point of view, see Cohen, 'Freedom, Justice and
Capitalism', esp. pp. 11–16.
[49] Locke, *Two Treatises*, II, sects. 27 and 33. See the discussion in Waldron,
'Enough and as Good' and in Ch. 6, sect. 15, above.

to be prejudiced by my acquisition. Nozick sees quickly that if this proviso were applied literally under conditions of immediate or even eventual scarcity, it would have the result that no acquisitions at all could be regarded as legitimate. For this reason, perhaps, he modifies the proviso so that it requires only that the situation of others should not be *worsened* by the acquisition taking everything into account including the indirect benefits that they might eventually derive from my appropriation. If their situation is worsened, I must either compensate them or else give up my claim to the resource I have taken.

We must be clear, though, about what worsening a person's situation means in this context. A person's situation is worsened if he suffers materially from someone else's use and consumption of resources that he might otherwise be inclined to use or consume. But it is also worsened if he is deprived of the moral liberty to use and consume such resources whether or not they have been made physically unavailable by someone else. The possibility that his situation may be worsened in this way with regard to resources that on some occasion he may need, either for his own subsistence or to discharge his responsibility for others', is, I have argued, conclusive against the acceptability of any PJA in a Rawlsian 'original position'. To avoid that argument, a Lockean proviso would have to make the entitlements generated by a PJA continually sensitive to the needs of others. It would not be enough to indicate *net* benefit or to show that *on the whole and in the long run* the situation of the people affected by acquisitions would not be worsened. An adequate Lockean proviso must require that the effect of the PJA it qualifies is *never* to require those whom it constrains to choose between compliance and the exigencies of their own survival. To repeat: if a PJA, whether qualified or unqualified, is such as to require a person to refrain from 'helping himself' to the resources he needs for his own subsistence or that of others for whom he is responsible, then it is not a principle which is capable of unanimous acceptance in good faith by those who are to be governed by it.

I suspect that the 'strong' proviso traditionally attributed to Locke (the proviso which Nozick rejects) will satisfy this test. By requiring that an appropriator should leave enough resources of similar quality available in the state of nature for others to take if they want to, a Lockean PJA is never open to the charge that it requires people to choose between compliance with its terms and starvation. There is always a third possibility—to take the resources that one needs in order to survive from the common stock that has been left by the last appropriator.[50]

But this is no more than an instance of the much broader requirement in Locke's theory that everyone has a natural claim-right to the use of the resources that he needs for his basic subsistence. 'The preservation of all, as much as may be' is described by Locke in several places as the fundamental duty of the law of nature. (Its fundamental character is shown, for example, by the fact that it prevails even over considerations of retributive justice.)[51] At the beginning of the chapter on property, the requirement is stated in terms of a natural right: '[N]atural Reason ... tells us that Men, being once born, have a right to their Preservation, and consequently to Meat and Drink, and such other things, as Nature affords for their Subsistence ... '[52] It is made clear that this is the framework within which the Labour Theory of acquisition operates. The justification of individual appropriation, in Locke's theory, is connected so intimately with this general right to subsistence that it is impossible to imagine that the property rights generated by the former could ever have priority over the demands of abject need generated by the latter.

As if that were not clear enough from the logic of the argument of the *Second Treatise*, the point is made explicit in the *First*:

God the Lord and Father of all, has given no one of his Children such a Property, in his peculiar Portion of the things of this World, but that he has given his needy Brother a Right to the Surplusage of his Goods; so that it cannot justly be denied him, when his pressing Wants call for it.[53]

With this over arching proviso, Locke's PJA escapes our argument. It is not postulated as the first principle of a theory of justice; it is arguably derivative from and certainly subordinate to a more general principle of need.

But the situation is quite otherwise with the sort of theory Nozick is toying with. According to him, the main objection to any talk of rights to life or subsistence is that

these 'rights' require a substructure of things and materials and actions; and *other* people may have rights and entitlements over these. No one has a right to something whose realization requires certain uses of things and

---

[50] Cf. Locke, *Two Treatises*, II, sects. 33–4.
[51] See above, Ch. 6, sect. 2.
[52] Locke, *Two Treatises*, II, sect. 25.
[53] Ibid. I, sect. 42.

activities that other people have rights and entitlements over. . . . The particular rights over things fill the space of rights, leaving no room for general rights to be in a certain material condition. The reverse theory would place only such universally held general 'rights to' . . . be in a certain material condition into its substructure so as to determine all else; to my knowledge no serious attempt has been made to state this 'reverse' theory. (p. 238)

(We will leave aside the fact that the last point is made in ignorance not only, as we have seen, of the theory of John Locke, but also of much of the most interesting recent work in distributive theory, from Rawls to Walzer.)[54] What emerges clearly from this passage is that, in a Nozickian theory, the entitlements generated in the first instance by a PJA are expected to dominate and determine all other considerations of economic justice and, in particular, considerations based on the sort of abject need that would normally impel men of good will to violate them. Against this background, the tacking on of a very weak Lockean proviso represents, at best, a confused eclecticism, or, at worst, the half-hearted indulgence of bad conscience about the ultimate unacceptability of a principle of justice in acquisition.

Of course, no actual property system can include among its legal rules a right that anyone may take from the holdings of another what he needs to survive. Necessity in our law is no defence to theft or trespass.[55] Elsewhere, however, I have shown how this constraint can be turned into the basis of an argument for a redistributive welfare state— a system which, by ensuring that the situation of desperate need never arises for anybody, effectively guarantees that property rights never have to be asserted and enforced in the face of such need.[56].

[54] Apart from Rawls, *A Theory of Justice*, see also e.g. Dworkin, 'Equality of Resources'; Gewirth, *Human Rights*, Ch. 8; and Walzer, *Spheres of Justice*, Chs. 3–4.

[55] For the common law rule, see *R. v. Dudley and Stephens* (1884) 14 Q B D 273 and *Southwark L B C v. Williams* [1971] Ch. 734 at 744. see also Smith, *Law of Theft*, p. 59.

[56] See Waldron, 'Welfare and the Images of Charity'.

8

General-Right-Based Arguments for Private Property

Theories of historical entitlement are quite common. But it is rare to find them standing on their own, and in this respect Nozick's theory is something of an exception. Usually they are supported by some more general account of the importance of private property to man.

It is important to see that when I talk about a *general* justification of private property, I am not talking merely about a universally quantified version of Locke's theory, of a Nozickian theory, or of whatever other account is given of the generation of special property rights. In an SR-based argument for private property, there will be a story about why, for all individuals and all resources, an individual who does action A to a resource gets to be its owner. That is a 'general' account in the sense that it is universal but it is not what I mean by a general justification of private property. A general justification of private property is one which shows why private ownership is important, i.e. why it is important in general that individuals should have rights of this sort. It does not base this account on the importance of the particular relations which particular individuals might enter into with particular things.

Often this more general account is utilitarian in character, drawing on the sort of considerations I sketched out at the beginning of Chapter 1. This is true, for example, of the theories of David Hume and Jeremy Bentham: first, there is an explanation of why it is good for a society to have a settled system of private property; then there is an account of how particular resources may be appropriated by individuals on the basis of First Occupancy to get such a system underway.[1] In this sort of theory, the special

[1] See Bentham, 'Principles of the Civil Code', pp. 158 ff.; Hume, *Treatise*, Bk. III, Ch. ii, sect. 3, pp. 505 ff. But cf. Ryan, *Property and Political Theory*, pp. 99 ff.

rights of property—the rights generated by occupancy—do not stand on their own. The justification of the claim that such a right has arisen refers to and gains the support of the more general argument about the utilitarian importance of private property. In other words, the account given of the particular event or transaction in which a resource was appropriated does not have to bear all the weight of justification; the general theory takes up some of the burden of justifying the claim that so-and-so is entitled to be the owner of such-and-such. (Much the same is true of theories about the rights that arise out of promises. As well as an account of the way in which particular transactions generate obligations, there is characteristically a general argument about the importance of the institution of promising as a whole.[2] Once again, the account of the circumstances of the individual promise does not have to bear the full weight of justification for the claim that the promisor has an obligation. Part of that burden is taken up by the more general and often utilitarian argument.)

The need for a general theory can be illustrated by referring to the difficulties faced by theories of First Occupancy when they are treated as purely SR-based accounts.

I have not given the idea of First Occupancy any sustained discussion in this work, because it seems to me that the bare idea of occupancy—of taking possession of a resource—cannot seriously be regarded as carrying much justificatory weight on its own. Asking 'Who had it first?' may be a natural enough way of resolving disputes about the ownership of a resource once we have established that it is a good idea that resources should be privately owned.[3] But it goes no way to advance the case in favour of private property as against other possible types of property system. (The Lockean argument about 'mixing one's labour', by contrast, did promise to bring some genuinely justificatory considerations—the idea of self-ownership—to bear on that issue.)

Maybe the idea of First Occupancy is a way of presenting an elementary libertarian justification for the view that the sheer physical possession of goods by individuals ought not to be disturbed: the *first* person to take possession of a resource does so, *ex hypothesi*, without pushing others aside, and, unless he

---

[2] See Rawls, 'Two Concepts of Rules', and Hart, *Punishment and Responsibility*, Ch. 1.

[3] See Becker, *Property Rights*, pp. 30–1. See also Rousseau, *Social Contract*, Bk. I, Ch. 9.

voluntarily relinquishes that possession, he is the one who must be pushed aside by second and subsequent occupiers. But this, as Kant and others have noted, is an argument at most for a principle of negative liberty in the economic sphere: people must not physically interfere with one another's actual use of material resources. It falls far short of a justification of private property, if that is understood as an institution which accords individuals rights to exclude others even when the object in question is not under their physical control.[4]

Another gloss on First Occupancy is the idea, put about by Hume and Bentham, that the man who first takes a resource into his possession will hope and expect to continue in that possession and to be able to use and enjoy the resource on a long-term basis,[5] and that this natural expectation ought to be respected. I have already expressed my doubts about this (see section 11 of Chapter 6). Briefly, if we accept the line that Bentham, at any rate, also wants to run—that expectation is the child of law and that 'natural' expectations in a lawless state of nature are likely to be very weak indeed—then this argument presupposes the existence in some form of the very rules and institutions it purports to justify and thus begs the question of their ultimate justification.[6]

Theories of First Occupancy have always been troubled by the problem of defining 'occupancy'. What counts as occupying a piece of land? Do I occupy anything more than the ground beneath my feet? If the answer is 'Yes', how is that area delimited? Is it enough for me to point to the area I am appropriating? Or is something else necessary like enclosure or cultivation? [7] It seems to me that those versions of First Occupancy which do not turn out to be covert versions of the Labour Theory reduce eventually to something like the following claim: the first person who *acts as though he is the owner* of a resource gets to *be* its owner. That is what I think First Occupancy amounts to in the end. But when it is stated in that rather bland way, it is evident that theories of this sort, taken on

---

[4] This point is stressed in Kant, *Metaphysical Elements of Justice*, Ladd trans., p. 54 (Prussian Academy edn., VI, 238). See also the discussion in Gibbard, 'Natural Property Rights' and in Scanlon, 'Nozick on Rights', pp. 126 ff.

[5] See esp. Hume, op. cit. 503–4 and n.

[6] For the idea of 'natural expectation', see Bentham, op. cit. pp. 112 and 149–50. These passages contradict the view, also expressed by Bentham, that expectations not created by positive law are likely to be 'feeble and momentary'—ibid. 113.

[7] Cf. Becker, op. cit. 26–8.

their own, cannot possibly conclude the argument about what sort of property system to have. They work only if private property has already been argued for. (Otherwise why would one think that *acting like an owner* was a way of acquiring any rights at all?) In other words, they presuppose a prior account of why private property is important, and they draw most of their justificatory force from that general background argument. At best, what they add is nothing more than a distinctive view about how private property rights are to be distributed, once it has been decided that private property rights are good things to have.

When an SR-based account of particular actions and transactions is supported by a general theory in this way, it becomes important to consider the relation between the general and the special parts of the theory. Can our general justification of private property be entirely independent of our account of the particular transactions? Or does the former place limits on what can be offered in the way of the latter? These issues will be considered in Chapter 9.

In the theories I examine in this chapter and the next, the function of providing a general background argument is performed by right-based considerations rather than by the utilitarian arguments I mentioned a page or two ago. Instead of saying that it is good for the general welfare that we should have a system of private property, it is argued that individual men and women have a *right* that such an institution should exist—that the existence of a system of private property fulfils an individual need or serves some individual interest which is considered of sufficient moral importance to generate duties for the society as a whole.

Sometimes this sort of right-based argument may be an instrumental one. The existence of a system of private property may contribute to the promotion of other goods—such as political freedom or a certain level of personal welfare—to which individuals are conceived to have a right. These are what may be called *indirect* GR-based arguments for private property.[8] They are distinguished by the fact that the rights in question need not (though they may) be held by those who hold the property. Often these are very important arguments. However, in this book I shall concern myself with arguments which proceed on the basis that the institution of private property serves certain general individual

---

[8] For an example of an argument linking capitalist property and political freedom, see Friedman, *Capitalism and Freedom*, Ch. 1.

rights *directly*—in other words, arguments to the effect that our society ought to uphold and maintain an institution of private property (rather than any other sort of property system) because individuals have, to put it crudely, a general right to own things. (I hope to discuss indirect libertarian arguments for property in more detail elsewhere.)

Whether it is utilitarian or right-based, a general background argument for private property can do justificatory work that a purely SR-based argument (like Nozick's) cannot do. Two artificial examples will illustrate.

(a) Imagine a hunter-gatherer society in which it has never occurred to anyone to make an individual appropriation of a piece of land (perhaps the society alluded to in section 38 of Locke's *Second Treatise*). Suppose now that the members of this society get together to decide on what basis land use should be controlled and allocated. Those members who believe in an SR-based theory of private property will have no basis whatsoever for urging a private ownership solution. Their theory aims to protect only the special rights of private property that individuals have actually acquired; so far as its foundations are concerned, it is indifferent to whether any such rights are in fact generated or not. If they are, it wants them protected; but if they are not, it has nothing to say. So if the weight of opinion is in favour of a communist solution to the problem of the allocation of land, the SR-based theorist of private property has no basis for any objection. By contrast, a utilitarian or GR-based theorist may have grounds for sounding a note of warning. On his account it may be important for individuals, either aggregatively or severally, that land should be privately owned rather than commonly or collectively held. A theory like his can provide general reasons for instituting private property in land which, in this situation, a theory based exclusively on contingent individual entitlements cannot do.

(b) Imagine a society (say the Soviet Union 150 years hence) emerging from a confused and disastrous period of communism. As the society reconstructs itself and tries to put its tangled economic past behind it, the question arises of what system of property it should now institute. In principle, assuming that once long ago there had been private property in that society, an SR-based theory of historical entitlement should be able to provide an answer based on its principle of the rectification of injustice: presumably resources should be vested now as private goods in the hands of the successors-in-title to those from whom they were unjustly expropriated by the *ancien régime communiste* a couple of centuries earlier. As Nozick puts it, such a society should make use of the 'best estimate of subjunctive information about what would have occurred . . . if the injustice had not taken place'.[9] But, of course, it is very likely that no such information is available, and that we cannot make even probabilistic estimations about what would have happened if the scourge of communism had not afflicted the society for 200 years. In these circumstances, Nozick concedes that a plausible principle of rectification may permit, as a second best solution, the redistribution of resources on the basis of the sort of considerations of equality and social justice which he excoriates elsewhere in his work: perhaps even a theory like Rawls's has a role to play in these circumstances.[10] The important point for our purposes is that, once the subjunctive calculation of individual entitlement has failed, an SR-based theory like Nozick's offers no basis whatever for arguing that the society should now have a private rather than a collective or a common system of property. In theories of this sort, the case for private property is exhausted by the account of the particular entitlements specified individuals have to specified things. If no such entitlements can be established, no case for private property remains, so far as an SR-based theory is concerned.

It may be thought that, when the demands of justice are unknown, *any* distribution of resources as private property has a fractionally greater chance of being just than any non-private distribution—namely, the tiny probability that the former may happen to coincide with the distribution of individual holdings which (if only we knew) justice-as-entitlement actually requires. But this is not the case. If communism had not been forced on this society, still the individual proprietors might voluntarily have chosen to exchange and mutually modify and combine their entitlements into a system that happens to match exactly any communist alternative now being proposed in the reconstruction

[9] Nozick, *Anarchy, State, and Utopia*, pp. 152–3.
[10] Ibid. 230–1. For difficulties with Nozick's account of rectification, see Davis, 'Nozick's Entitlement Theory', pp. 348 ff.

phase. The improbability of this is no greater than that of any particular private property distribution matching what justice-as-entitlement actually requires.

A general argument for private property, on the other hand, is not beset by these handicaps. Even if it is impossible to establish who is historically entitled to own what, still, on the basis of a general theory, it can be argued that it is desirable to have some sort of private property system. A general theory of private property—whether it is utilitarian or right-based—allows us to say what is important about private property systems without having to refer in the first instance to specified individuals' ownership of specified things.

2. RIGHTS, LIBERTY, AND PROPERTY

Very few GR-based theories of private property have been worked out to the extent that Hegel's is—we shall examine his theory in a later chapter—and his theory, as we shall see, is far from fully articulated. In this chapter, however, I want to draw attention to the main considerations which have been invoked by defenders of private property in this tradition, and explore in a general sort of way some of the implications and shortcomings of their arguments.

In Hegel's theory and in almost all of the theories we are going to discuss here, a connection is asserted between the existence of private property and the promotion of individual *liberty*. To put it crudely, it is maintained on various grounds that men have a general right to private property because being the owner of something is in some sense constitutive of freedom. Before we go on to see what these grounds are, let me say something about the connection between rights and liberty and the various conceptions of freedom that are involved here.

As we saw in Chapter 3 it has sometimes been claimed that there is a special connection between talk of rights and the value of individual freedom. Some say that freedom constitutes the only appropriate subject-matter for human rights—and that talk of rights to material well-being or to certain sorts of services is a distortion of the language of rights except to the extent that those goods can themselves be regarded as involving aspects of individual freedom.[11] Others maintain that even if there are rights to goods other than freedom, still the underlying *point* of rights-discourse is to maintain a certain pattern or distribution of human freedom,— so that for example we cannot understand what it is for someone to have a right except by grasping the way in which he is permitted to abrogate the freedom of another. At least one philosopher who has held this view—Hart in his early articles on rights—also maintained that the fundamental general right, presupposed by all other rights-discourse, was the equal right of all men to be free. An element of freedom, he said, was built into the very concept of a right, in the sense that a right-bearer was necessarily someone who was free to waive, or to insist on, the performance of the duty correlative to his right.[12] In Chapter 3 we saw that tight analytic connections like these between rights and freedom have become increasingly unpopular among right-based theorists: good reasons have been given for wanting to talk about inalienable rights, about rights derived from fundamental values like equality rather than liberty, and about both fundamental and derivative rights to be passively recipient of services and assistance from others. So I refrained from insisting on any tight connection between rights and freedom in my account of what constituted a right-based theory.

The definition given in Chapter 3 was that a person has a *right* if the promotion of some interest of his is morally so important as to justify, without further ado, holding others to be under a duty to him in this regard. A full theory of rights will provide a basis, usually rooted in a conception of human nature, for picking out the important individual interests which satisfy this formula and for distinguishing them from what we might describe as the mundane human interests whose promotion does not in itself warrant the imposition of duties on others in this manner. Now while this schema does not *commit* the right-based theorist to any obsession with freedom, it is nevertheless capable of accommodating the claim that interests in freedom are important enough to constitute the basis of some individual rights, and it is quite compatible too with the more restrictive idea that interests in freedom are the only

[11] e.g. Cranston, 'Human Rights: Real and Supposed', and Flew, *Politics of Procrustes*, pp. 38 ff.

[12] Hart, 'Are There Any Natural Rights?'; see the discussion in Ch. 3, sect. 6 (i) above.

interests whose promotion has this degree of moral importance. The debate, then, between those who assert some special link between rights and freedom and those who deny the existence or exclusiveness of that connection can be reproduced within the schematic definition of rights that I have proposed; only now it is presented as an issue of moral substance rather than as an analytical issue about the concept of rights.[13]

I know of no theory of rights which maintains that the interest (such as it is) which each individual has in being free to perform any action at all forms the basis of a right. That is, I know of no convincing argument for a human right to freedom in general. But there are three other sorts of theories which make liberty or freedom more plausibly the subject-matter of rights. First, there are theories which maintain that each individual has a right to *the most extensive liberty of action possible*, compatible with an equal liberty of action for everybody else. Secondly, there are theories which maintain that *certain liberties* are important rather than liberty in general—that is, people's interests in being free to perform certain types of action (such as political self-expression or the choice of sexual partners or whatever) matter more than their interests in being free to perform actions of a more mundane sort (such as driving without a seat-belt or walking in a park after nightfall). Thirdly, there are theories which are concerned fundamentally not with freedom of action in general nor with specific freedoms but with *being a free man* in a sense associated with some 'positive' conception of liberty. (The boundaries between these three types of theory are far from impermeable. John Rawls's first principle of justice is a theory of the second kind, but adopts the distributive approach of the first.[14] And many theories of the second kind single out specific liberties as important by virtue of their connection with the third idea, maintaining that there are certain liberties whose possession in some sense constitutes positive freedom.) Let us now relate these three types of theory to the general justification of private property.

A particular libertarian theory of any of these kinds might generate an argument for private property. We are familiar with

---

[13] I have developed this idea a little further in Waldron, 'Critical Notice of Hart, *Essays in Jurisprudence*', Pt. IV.

[14] As Hart points out, this reflects a change from the formulations in Rawls's earlier work: see Hart, 'Rawls on Liberty', p. 228.

arguments to the effect that systems of private property are, either invariably or on the whole, more free than alternative types of property system, or that they make the societies in which they operate more free—in the sense of vouchsafing a more extensive freedom of action to all or most citizens— than societies characterized by alternative types of property system. There may be arguments to the effect that certain liberties associated with private property—such as the freedom to exclude others from a private realm of one's own or the freedom to trade—are particularly important, and indeed important enough to be regarded as individual rights which a society in its design of social and economic institutions ought to respect. It may be argued that being a private owner or having or exercising some of the liberties and responsibilities associated with private ownership is an indispensable part of what it takes to be or become a free man. For example, it may be argued that the discipline involved in being in charge of the resources necessary for one's own material survival makes a unique contribution to the promotion of virtues like foresight, prudence, responsibility, and reliability which are a necessary part of the self-mastery that positive freedom involves.

In the two following sections, I want to say more about these different types of libertarian right-based argument for property, and then in section 5 I shall indicate ways in which these arguments may be evaluated and their implications explored.

3. LIBERTY AND LIBERTIES

Any property system, as we have seen, will involve a complex distribution of freedoms and unfreedoms so far as the use of material resources is concerned. In a system of private property, I am quite at liberty to make use of the resources assigned to me (within very broad limits), but I am not free to use any of the resources assigned to others in any way, at least not without their permission. (If I try to, the others will call the police and I will be dragged away.) In a system of common property, by contrast, my freedom to make use of any resource is not limited by the say-so of anybody else, though it is limited by the fact that others are also at liberty to use it and that its use is regulated on the basis of some fair principle such as 'first come, first served'. One can imagine an argument being made out to the effect that a system of the first sort offers in fact a greater net amount of liberty for everyone (other things being equal) than a system of the second sort, and so that our right to the most extensive liberty of action compatible with a similar liberty for others requires that our property system should be one of private ownership rather than common property. Like G. A. Cohen, who has written extensively about this, I am not at all confident that such an argument can be sustained.[15] At any rate, it would involve coming to grips with the horrendous problem of quantifying negative liberty for the purposes of interpersonal and social comparisons; and it is not clear whether this is a task that can usefully be undertaken.[16] I shall not say any more about this first approach in the present work, though I will be presenting a more complete discussion of the difficulties involved on another occasion.[17]

But perhaps I should go into a little more detail about the connections that might be thought to obtain between private property and certain 'basic liberties' which are thought particularly important.

In a system of private property individuals have, as a matter of course, certain rights and powers over material resources that they are unlikely to have in other property systems. Three are particularly striking: the exclusive right to determine what shall be done with a resource; connected with the first, the right to exclude others from the use of a resource; and, characteristically, the power to alienate one's rights over a resource on whatever terms one thinks appropriate (often loosely called 'the freedom to trade'). It may be argued that these rights protect certain important human liberties. Although freedom as such to perform *any* action is not an important political concern, freedom of choice in the economic sphere and free trade are often regarded as areas of freedom that are of extraordinary importance. One's choices here (how to manage one's land, whether to sell an asset now or later, how to decorate one's front door) concern an area of decision which is of more than mundane concern. Since our material environment is as important to the conduct of our lives as our political environment—we are, after all, embodied beings—free control of and

[15] e.g. Cohen, 'Capitalism, Freedom and the Proletariat'.
[16] For doubts about the quantifiability of freedom, see Dworkin, *Taking Rights Seriously*,, pp. 268 ff., and 'Liberalism', p. 124. For a more optimistic approach, see Steiner, 'How Free?'
[17] Waldron, *Poverty and Freedom*.

freedom to manipulate and rearrange elements of that environment are as important to the human individual as, say, the traditional political freedoms.[18]

The element of exclusive use which property rights involve is often justified on the basis of its connection with freedom and privacy. If every resource is publicly controlled or in principle available for use by all on equal terms—if, for example, every place is a public place— the use of material resources by an individual will in every case count as an 'other-regarding' action (to use the terminology associated with J. S. Mill).[19] And since every action involves the use of some material resources (if only the land to stand on to perform it), it would follow that individuals were answerable to others for each and every action they performed. This, it may be argued, would be intolerable: such complete answerability would be morally exhausting and individually debilitating. If so, it would seem to follow that there must be a realm of private freedom somewhere for each individual—an area where he can make decisions about what to do and how to do it, justifying these decisions if at all only to himself. Again, to the extent that all action involves a material element, it seems to follow that such a realm of private decision would require an individual to have control of a certain material environment (a home, for example) from the use of which the interests and concerns of others and of society generally could be taken to be excluded. Of course, one does not want to insist that the virtue of private property is that it can be used selfishly, without any consideration for others; on the contrary, ownership rights like all rights can be exercised in ways that are morally wrong and objectionable.[20] But—so the argument would go—it is important for individuals to feel that they can make some decisions without treading on the *rights* of others, decisions which, though sensitive to others' interests do not in their nature require that the others in question have to be consulted before they are made.

A second argument links property and privacy in a different sense.

---

[18] Cf. the discussion in Steiner, 'Structure of a Set of Compossible Rights'. It is not clear whether Steiner intends to develop this into an argument specifically for *private* property, or into an argument that a consistent set of rights presupposes *some* sort of property system. I am inclined to doubt whether his arguments can take him very much further than the latter (very weak) conclusion.

[19] Mill, *On Liberty*, Ch. 1.

[20] See Waldron, 'Right to do Wrong'.

Humans need a refuge from the general society of mankind. They
need to have a place where they can be assured of being alone, if
that is what they want, or assured of the conditions of intimacy
with others, where intimacy is called for. This is not just a matter of
having private property in a house, a flat, or a room of one's own;
what is required is what might broadly be called 'a household', that
is, the gathering together of all the resources (furniture, kitchen,
library, bath, bed) necessary for the performance of the tasks which
it might be thought important to be able to perform in private. Of
course, no one will deny that the resources of a household are
necessary for human life, and every humane property system will
seek to make them available for all. What distinguishes the present
argument is the contention that individuals need to have these
resources available to them on a basis which excludes others from
their use: they need to have not just a household, but a household
of their own.[21]

The element of free trade requires a more complex defence, if
only because buying, selling, and giving are not strictly actions
which we can be free or unfree to perform but rather *the exercise of
powers* which are or are not given recognition and effect by the
society. (A society could withold the right to buy and sell goods
without there being any *action* whose performance was actually
prohibited. A could be left free to pass a chattel to B and to receive
another in return; it is just that these actions would have no legal
effect.) For this reason, talk of freedom of trade—like talk of
freedom of contract—belongs in a different logical category from
talk of, for example, freedom of speech or freedom of assembly.

In outline, an argument for the importance of freedom to alienate
property might go like this. Conducting and planning one's life is
not just a matter of what one does by and for oneself; it is also a
matter of the accommodations one reaches with others. This is as
true in the material sphere as it is in, say, the sphere of sexual
relations. In both spheres, people are capable of, and are inclined
to, reach accommodations with others on their own terms and on
their own initiative to satisfy needs or wants that they cannot
satisfy on their own. They will regard these accomodations and the
terms on which they are reached as partly constitutive of their
social being, as establishing a place for themselves in a community

---

[21] An argument along these lines can be found in Arendt, *Human Condition*,
pp. 29 ff. and 61 ff.

of persons. They will resent any political order which treats these accommodations as though they were of no consequence, as though the fact that they were arrived at by individuals coming together on their own initiative meant that they did not matter.[22]

Of course, the analogy between sexual and economic arrangements should not be pushed too far. In the former case, we should place great stress on the element of passion, love, and intimacy in the arrangements that people make, and on the fact that this makes it doubly wrong to disrupt or undermine interpersonal accommodations in this sphere of life. The analogy is not meant to suggest either the Kantian line (which Hegel attacked) that marriage and sexual relations can be analysed as contracts or the equally absurd view that market relations are intimate and affective in character.[23] The real analogy is that in both cases individuals attach importance to the ability to enter freely into arrangements whose shape and character they have determined in interaction with the others whom they want to involve. More abstractly, individuals like to exercise their capacities of deliberation, reflection, and choice in the shaping of the local social environment in which they are to live and act. It is true that not all aspects of a person's social environment can be shaped in this way, and true too that just because it is a *social* environment, no individual can expect that his choice alone will have a conclusive or determining effect. Defenders of private property are sometimes accused of overlooking the social side of human nature. But that is unfair. What may be true is that they have a somewhat different conception of human communality than, say, their socialist opponents. They do not believe that human communality is exhausted by participation in the life and decision-making of a society *taken as a whole*; they insist that respect for this side of human nature also involves respect for what might be called the micro-social arrangements that couples, groups, or clusters of people enter into on their own.[24]

Adam Smith wrote about 'a certain propensity in human nature . . . the propensity to truck, barter and exchange one thing for another'.[25] It was not Smith's intention to argue that every 'natural propensity' in man should be indulged, or that 'naturalness' formed

---

[22] Cf. Nozick, *Anarchy, State, and Utopia*, Pt. III.

[23] Hegel, *Philosophy of Right*, sects. 75R and 163R. See also Waldron, 'When Justice Replaces Affection'.

[24] I am grateful to Zenon Bankowski for the formulation of this point.

[25] Smith, *Wealth of Nations*, Bk. I, Ch. 2, p. 17.

the basis for distinguishing those freedoms which we should regard as rights from those we should not. His argument is more utilitarian in character: the indulgence of this propensity, at least, generates wealth and opulence which benefits everyone. But one might want to make out some sort of right-based argument along the lines I have already indicated. The existence of this propensity in almost every society, no matter what its official property system, is at least prima facie evidence that it corresponds to an interest which ought to be taken seriously in systems of political economy.

In Chapter 2 we noted that an argument for private property was not necessarily an argument for free trade or for vesting individuals with a power of alienation (see section 7 of that chapter). But the sort of argument we have just been considering may have an impact on the case for private property in two ways. First, if we are already convinced that there is a case for private property in the sense of giving individuals rights of exclusive control and decision over particular resources, such an argument may convince us that those rights should be packaged together with a power to buy, sell, and exchange them. Secondly, we may be convinced that private property as such is a good idea purely on the basis of this argument about the right to exchange. That is, if we think it important for individuals to be free to enter into arrangements with others on their own initiative regarding the use and control of material resources, we may conclude that the only way they can have this freedom is if they are accorded rights of exclusive control and decision over the resources that they might want to bring to these accommodations. The case for private property, then, would be derived from the case for freedom of trade, rather than vice versa.

4. PRIVATE PROPERTY AND POSITIVE LIBERTY

In the previous section, I sketched some arguments to the effect that various liberties associated with private property are particularly important for human beings in general. Sometimes, however, the argument is not so much that a particular liberty is important in its own right, as that having it or exercising it is important for establishing oneself *as a free man*. The idea here is that freedom is something like a moral status to be attained through one's efforts and perhaps with the assistance of others. Freedom is not seen in a purely negative light, as the absence of obstacles to action in general or to actions of particularly important types; it is seen rather as something positive— as something distinctive and specific which may or may not exist, or which may or may not be brought into existence, in the space from which the obstacles to choice and action have been cleared away.[26]

We cannot go far into the details of the controversy about 'positive' and 'negative' freedom. There is, however, one point that I wish to stress. In his seminal presentation of that controversy, Isaiah Berlin confused matters a bit by suggesting that the purely negative conception of liberty was opposed by a *single* ideal of positive liberty—an ideal of self-mastery and the 'higher' self which was connected 'by steps which, if not logically valid, are historically and psychologically intelligible' to a doctrine that 'true freedom' involves social identification and social responsibility.[27] In fact if one is doubtful about a strictly negative view of liberty, such as that proposed by Hobbes—'Liberty, or Freedome, signifieth (properly) the absence of Opposition; (by Opposition, I mean externall Impediments of Motion)'[28]—then it is possible to move out from that negative position in one or more of a variety of 'positive' directions, each placing stress on quite different philosophical themes, and yielding a diversity of non-negative conceptions. Each resulting conception has some claim to be regarded as a 'positive' conception of liberty, since each focuses on something specific and distinctively important that may or may not exist in the space that purely negative liberty guarantees. Each indicates that something more than the mere clearing away of external obstacles is required before genuine freedom can come into existence, but they offer different and competing conceptions of what that something is. In other words, the positive critique of negative liberty may involve several different themes, and it is a mistake to suggest, as Berlin appears to, that those themes must always be packaged together. (That this is an important mistake can be seen from the prevalence of 'slippery slope' arguments in the area.)[29]

For our purposes, it is important to see that there is a variety of

---

[26] I owe this formulation to Berki, 'Political Freedom and Hegelian Metaphysics', pp. 366 ff.

[27] Berlin, *Four Essays*, p. 152.

[28] Hobbes, *Leviathan*, Ch. 21, p. 261.

[29] See the discussion in Taylor, 'What's Wrong with Negative Liberty?'.

arguments for (and against) private property based on positive
liberty, derived from these various critical themes.

(i) Liberty and Independence

According to Berlin, 'The "positive" sense of the word "liberty"
derives from the wish on the part of the individual to be his own
master. I wish my life and decisions to depend on myself. . . . I wish
to be the instrument of my own, not of other men's acts of will.'[30]
As it stands, this does not seem far from the negative conception,
since imposing external obstructions to another's behaviour is the
best-known way of making him an instrument of one's will. But
there are also other modes of domination and dependence.

The slavish follower of fashion, the sycophantic retainer, the
bureaucrat who follows orders unreflectively, and the 'masses' who
worried Mill and Tocqueville (who 'like in crowds'), are all free in
the negative sense that their actions are not *blocked* or *compelled*
by others' domineering wills.[31] But they are not masters of
themselves, independent of others' wills: on the contrary, the
exercise of their negative freedom is constantly conditioned by their
perception of the approval and disapproval of wills other than their
own.

Independence as a positive aspect of liberty has often been linked
in the Western tradition with the idea of citizenship. A citizen
should be one who is in a position to bring his *own* judgement to
bear on political issues, rather than one who responds as a member
of a retinue, a slave of political fashion, or the mere representative
of an interest or faction.[32] So the connection (if one exists) between
liberty as independence and the idea of private property helps
explain the view, common until the middle of last century, that the
ownership of property was an indispensable qualification for
citizenship and for the franchise.

Dependence, and hence unfreedom on this conception, may have
many causes. One that is important in the present context is the
association between a readiness to submit one's judgement to
others and relations of *economic* dependence; thus it was widely
believed that a necessary condition for positive liberty in this sense
was some sort of economic independence. Sometimes this is

---

[30] Berlin, *Four Essays*, p. 131.
[31] Mill, *On Liberty*, Ch. 3, paragraph 6, p. 74.
[32] e.g. Rousseau, *Social Contract*, Bk. II, Ch. 3. See also King and Waldron, 'Social Citizenship'.

understood in the sense of rough equality: no one must be rich enough to be able to purchase the dependence of another nor poor enough to be bought in that way.[33] This idea seems to generate a requirement that a free man must have sufficient economic security so that he does not have to depend on others' say-so to satisfy his basic wants and needs. For if he is economically dependent, he will be sensitive to the necessity of not offending and perhaps of pleasing and flattering those on whose say-so he relies. As Mill pointed out, the threat to freedom of thought in modern society comes not so much from the criminal law but from our submission to what we think are the opinions of those we *have* to please:

In respect to all persons but those whose pecuniary circumstances make them independent of the good will of other people, opinion, on this subject, is as efficacious as law: men might as well be imprisoned as excluded from the means of earning their bread. Those whose bread is already secured, and who desire no favors from men in power, or from bodies of men, or from the public, have nothing to fear from the open avowal of opinions but to be ill-thought of and ill-spoken of . . .[34]

Clearly, private property, as we have defined it, offers this security and independence. If a man owns the resources he needs, then he depends for his use of them on the say-so of no one but himself, and so material necessity is unlikely to be transformed into moral or political dependence. There may of course, be other causes of dependence: according to Rousseau, the luxury of modern society corrupts freedom and 'deprives the state of all its citizens by making some the slaves of others and all the slaves of opinion'.[35] And there may conceivably be non-private systems of property which could provide a guaranteed subsistence without opening up the danger of the development of relations of dependence, either of individuals on each other, or of individuals on their rulers, or of individuals on the opinions of the masses. But the broad direction of this argument from positive liberty to private property is evident enough.

(ii) Self-Assertion and Recognition

So far independence has been defined negatively. But conceptions of liberty as independence have sometimes been understood in a more positive and active sense. It is necessary for the free man not only to

[33] See e.g. ibid. Bk. I, Ch. 9; also Rousseau, *Political Economy*, pp. 134 ff.
[34] Mill, *On Liberty*, Ch. 2, paragraph 19, p. 39.
[35] Rousseau, *Social Contract*, Bk. III, Ch. 14.

be independent of others, but actively to assert himself as a free and independent will and to be recognized as such by others. The need for self-assertion is connected with an idea that true freedom is necessarily self-conscious, and so must be made real to the agent by deliberate actions that have the display and assertion of freedom as their *raison d'être*. The need for recognition is connected with a metaphysical doctrine about the relation of self and other: subjectively, at least, and perhaps objectively too, a self has no real being except in its conscious relations and interactions with others.

These philosophical themes form an important part of Hegel's conception of freedom and of the argument for private property that he develops on that basis, and they will be discussed in more detail in Chapter 10. For the present, we should note three main connections that they have with the idea of private property.

First, self-assertion can be understood as a man's assertion of himself against nature. Natural resources by themselves are 'blankly material' with 'no point or purpose of their own; if they are to have a point or purpose they must be given one by being occupied by human goals and purposes'.[36] By investing a natural object with purpose an individual becomes aware of the priority of will in a world composed largely of objects that cannot actively possess it. Thus he ceases to regard himself as a mere animal part of nature and begins to take seriously the special and distinctive features of rationality, purpose, and will. Now strictly this need not require private appropriation on the part of each individual, for it is conceivable that active participation in a collective appropriative enterprise would be enough to make one conscious of the superiority of human will, and *a fortiori* of one's own will, over the natural world. What is necessary is that each human involved in the project must see himself as participating in the *willing, planning, and controlling* aspect of the enterprise, rather than merely being harnessed to somebody else's or to a group's appropriative enterprise as though he were merely a natural force, like a beast of burden or like water-power.

Secondly, self-assertion can be understood as a man's assertion of himself against other men. In the economic sphere, this may be thought to require the possibility of resource use on the basis that his own plans, projects, and preferences count for something, and do not always have to be ratified or agreed to by others before they

---

[36] Ryan, *Property and Political Theory*, p. 122.

can be put into effect. In a more extreme form, the demand for self-assertion may lead to a celebration of competitiveness and even aggressiveness in the economic sphere. Here the link with private property—indeed with a competitive, capitalist market—is evident. It is interesting, however, that the further the self-assertive conception of freedom is pushed in this direction, the less it tends to justify *private property* as a general human right. For it may be that what is important to freedom, on this conception, is not the actual possession and exercise of ownership rights, but the active and competitive endeavour to obtain them. Thus a man who is propertyless may still be free if he is asserting himself continually in the scramble for appropriation. Freedom, on this conception, then, justifies a right to private property only in the third of the four senses that we distinguished in Chapter 1 (section 4): that is, it justifies the claim that everyone should be at least *eligible* to hold property rather than that private property is something that everyone must hold. This distinguishes it from the other arguments in this section which, to the extent that they justify private property at all, justify an individual right to private property in the more substantial sense. I shall say a little more about this in Chapter 11.

Thirdly, the element of recognition may be linked to that of private property in the following way. Since ownership rights impose constraints on the behaviour of others, my having these rights involves others' recognizing me as a source of moral constraint and thus as a locus of respect. They must limit their desires for the sake of *my* freedom, and their willingness to do so gives me a confidence in the social importance of my freedom that I might not have if it remained a purely individual characteristic.[37] However, (to anticipate the discussion in Chapter 10) I have my doubts about this. To be taken seriously by self and others, an individual must, on this Hegelian line, be recognized as a bearer of rights and, to the extent that recognition is important in the economic sphere, as the bearer of rights in relation to external resources. But systems of private property are not unique in investing individuals with rights over external resources: systems of common property do this (e.g. everyone has a right to use the park) and so may systems of collective property (e.g. everyone has a right to participate in collective economic decision-making or to have his

---

[37] See the discussion in Knowles, 'Hegel on Property and Personality'. See also Plamenatz, 'History as the Realization of Freedom', p. 41.

needs and interests taken into account). Thus the argument from recognition moves too quickly from the idea that there should be property rules (which will in many cases confer individual rights) to the idea that those rules should constitute a specifically *private* property regime.

(iii) Coercion and Autonomy

So far, we have concentrated on what may be called external aspects of positive liberty: independence of others, and self-assertion and recognition in the external sphere. But other themes in the positive critique of negative liberty are concerned with the internal character of individual choice and freedom, and with the obstruction and assistance of others to the extent that this affects the internal aspect of freedom.

Aspects of this theme have long been accepted, at least implicitly, in the negative tradition. The core of the negative idea is that freedom is threatened only by external human obstacles to action. But this takes care of only a very small proportion of what even the toughest minded liberal would regard as threats to freedom: cases of actual physical restraint and violent impediment. Most threats to freedom, however, are *coercive* in character, involving the threat of sanctions rather than the imposition of impediments. (Note, however, that coercion may involve both: it is only because the gunman has me in his power that he is able to threaten me.)[38] A threat leaves a victim with a choice: he decides whether to open the safe or let his friend be burned alive, and the person making the threat need pose no obstacle to that choice one way or the other.[39] So in order to explain how coercion threatens freedom, it is necessary to lay stress on the way in which the victim is constrained to make his decision—the mode of his decision-making— rather than on the sheer existence or non-existence of a certain behavioural option. We must look at what threats do to what happens

[38] Ronald Dworkin has suggested to me that all that is wrong with coercion (by threats) is that someone has unjustly interfered with another's life or goods so as to constrain his options. On this account, making the threat and putting the choice problem to the victim are not in themselves unjust; rather, they are, in many cases, the upshot of injustice. This is an interesting view, but there is not space to discuss it any further here. (Perhaps the issue of the injustice of coercion should be separated from the issue of the way in which it undermines freedom.)

[39] Cf. Aristotle's account of voluntariness in *Nicomachean Ethics* 1110[a] (Ross trans., pp. 48–9).

within the space of negative freedom that threateners typically leave clear for their victims' decisions.

The most promising account is that a threat affects my freedom by tying a decision, say, about whether to give money to a certain individual, to a motive or desire which I find it more or less impossible to resist and which I would not normally want to be moved by in decisions of that sort.[40] If we offer this sort of account, we presuppose a conception of freedom involving an ability to distance oneself from the immediate impulsion of desire and to choose what sort of desires to be moved by in various areas of decision-making.[41]

This conception of freedom may be identified with certain elements in the liberal ideal of *autonomy*. Autonomy need not involve, as Kant suggested, the transcendence of desire and the determination of the will by the form of reason alone. But it does involve the ability to stand back from one's occurrent desires, to determine in some way—on the basis of a thought-out conception of the good—which desires and preferences one wants to be motivated by, and thus what is going to count in one's life as a prospect, an opportunity, a practical consideration, a harm, and a set-back. With this done, choice, decision, and action are a matter of responding to those values and to the desires that have been given this reflective precedence, and of restraining the impulse to respond to the immediate pull of each preference as it arises.

Some desires are less amenable to this process and we find it difficult to resist their immediate impulsion. These include our basic needs: the imperatives of our survival and the minimum conditions of our existence as rational and potentially moral beings. In formulating and executing a conception of the good we must take the existence of these desires into account and allow for the satisfaction of basic needs in a way that does not undermine the ethically more important business of distancing, selection, and restraint. So an adequate conception of autonomy will allow a place for the impulsion of need, but will try to draw a distinction between the types of choices and actions most appropriately motivated in this way and those whose motivation should be

---

[40] I draw here on the excellent discussion in Frankfurt, 'Coercion and Moral Responsibility'.

[41] See also Frankfurt, 'Freedom of the Will' and Taylor, 'What's Wrong with Negative Liberty?'

governed autonomously. (This distinction is bound to be controversial. For example, perhaps it is appropriate that the decision whether to work or not should be impelled by the desire for sustenance; but is it appropriate that the choice of a *career* should be determined in this way?) Autonomy is threatened then not in all cases when needs impel behaviour, but when the boundary between actions that are appropriately impelled by need and actions that are not is crossed.[42]

Coercion, as we have seen, is one way of crossing that boundary. Whether or not we should give large sums of money to strangers is not, on any account of autonomy, the sort of decision that should be impelled by the desire not to be burned to death. But the boundary is also crossed when certain desires take on a pathologically impulsive character—when, for example, the desire not to go outdoors or not to talk in front of large groups of people (a desire we would normally want to be able to distance ourselves from and consider whether to be motivated by it) takes on all the compulsiveness of a basic need.[43]

A third threat to autonomy is more relevant to the issue of property. If a person is faced with abject and long-term material deprivation, he will be preoccupied with his most impelling needs and will have neither the opportunity nor the psychological space to consider in general how he wants his life to go. His behaviour will be composed almost entirely of actions impelled by the elementary need to find a subsistence. Immersed in his basic needs, he never has the opportunity to attain the autonomy and control of his desires that we value in human freedom.[44]

This is another basis on which it may be argued that true freedom requires material security. The point is not the familiar banality that it is a mockery to offer civil and political freedom to a starving man; rather it is that being a free man positively requires some degree of material security, since without it one would never have the opportunity to exercise the reflection, restraint, and control that constitutes an autonomous life.

By itself this is not an argument from liberty to private property.

---

[42] I have drawn here on work by Raz in 'Liberalism, Autonomy and Neutral Concern', pp. 110 ff. But my account, I think, develops his suggestions in a rather different direction from that in which he wants to turn them. I am grateful to Joseph Raz for discussion of these points.

[43] See Taylor, 'What's Wrong with Negative Liberty?', p. 185.

[44] Cf. Raz, 'Liberalism, Autonomy, and Neutral Concern', pp. 110–13.

At most it is an argument for universal provision for pressing material needs. Indeed with its welfarist implications, it has been one of the main foundations for the social democratic case *against* private property, at least against private property rights that are unequally distributed and unlimited by any obligation to contribute to social provision.[45] However, when combined with the point about the need for moral, political, and therefore economic independence, considered earlier, it generates a very strong argument for something like the ideal of a property-owning democracy in which material security is guaranteed to all on the basis of resources or sources of income that they *own*.

(iv) Freedom and Moral Duty

There is, in Western thought, a long and venerable association between freedom and morality, in which the requirements of right action and the performance of moral duty are seen not as restrictions on individual freedom but as its fulfilment or culmination. Philosophers as diverse as St Paul, Augustine, Locke, Kant, and Hegel have drawn a distinction between *licence* and *liberty*: between abstract, subjective, and capricious notions of freedom, where freedom is supposed to consist in the ability to do anything at all, and more mature and profound conceptions of freedom, where freedom resides in the choice of *right* action and is problematic in cases of moral evasion or wrongdoing.[46]

Phenomenologically, the basis of this distinction lies in the experience of moral weakness: the familiar sense that in failing to live up to the moral standards we aspire to follow, we are subject to the compulsion and determination of motives and aspects of our character that we would want to repudiate 'if we had the choice'. Philosophically, the position has been expressed in terms of a number of positive themes. First, it is expressed in terms of an ideal of self-mastery. A higher or rational 'real' self is contrasted with, as Berlin puts it, 'my "lower" nature, the pursuit of immediate pleasures, my "empirical" or "heteronomous" self, swept by every

---

[45] See e.g. Plant, *Equality, Markets and the State*.

[46] For a helpful discussion, see Ignatieff, *Needs of Strangers*, Ch. 2. The tension in Kant's philosophy between freedom as duty and the possibility of autonomous wrongdoing is explored in Clarke, 'Beyond "The Banality of Evil"', pp. 422 ff. For Aristotle's view that we are autonomously responsible for bad actions as well as good, see *Nicomachean Ethics* 1113[a] (Ross trans., pp. 59 ff.).

gust of desire and passion, needing to be rigidly disciplined if it is ever to rise to the full height of its "real" nature'.[47] There is an implicit contrast here between passion and reason, between the human and the animal sides of man's nature. Secondly, and connected with that, it is expressed in terms of the ideal of autonomy, where there is thought to be a unique moral solution to the problem of organizing and controlling one's life in accordance with a chosen conception of the good.[48] Thirdly, there is a paternalistic connection between the idea of respect for liberty and respect for persons as rational (or potentially rational) beings. As L. T. Hobhouse put it,

[Liberty] rests not on the claim of A to be let alone by B, but on the duty of B to treat A as a rational being. It is not right to let . . . error alone, but it is imperative to treat . . . the mistaken or the ignorant as beings capable of right or truth, and to lead them on instead of merely beating them down. The rule of liberty is just the application of rational method. It is the opening of the door to the appeal of reason. . . [49]

Fourthly, it can be expressed in terms of virtues like prudence, stability of character, and responsibility, in a normative sense. The free man is not blown hither and yon by following every whim and caprice: he seeks what T. H. Green described as 'a *permanent* good' where the establishment of a character, and the connection between his actions now and his actions in the past and future, are stabilized by an awareness of traditional wisdom and concrete, settled, and determinate goals.[50] Fifthly, to the extent that morality is understood as a *social* system rather than an individual ideal, it can be expressed in terms of the idealist view that only by participating properly in the moral life of his community—only by following what Hegel called 'the duties of the station to which he belongs'—can a man find true and fulfilling freedom. 'Duty,' as Hegel put it, 'is the attainment of our essence, the winning of *positive* freedom.'[51]

I want to take up the last two of these themes in more detail in the sections that follow. But what, in general, are the implications of this 'moralized' conception of liberty for the defence of private property?

[47] See e.g. Berlin, *Four Essays*, p. 132.

[48] Perhaps this point does not depend on the hypothesis of a *unique* solution. As Raz points out in *The Morality of Freedom*, the point would stand, provided only that there are *some* possible conceptions of the good that ought to be rejected.

[49] Hobhouse, *Liberalism*, p. 123.

[50] Green, *Lectures on Political Obligation*, p. 7.

[51] Hegel, *Philosophy of Right*, sect. 142.

A preliminary point to note is this. If liberty (as opposed to licence) comprises only actions which it is reasonable or right for the agent to want to perform,[52] and if standards of rightness or reasonableness make reference to prevailing rules of property, then it will hardly be possible to criticize existing property institutions on the ground that they limit liberty. Equally, however, it will be impossible to defend existing property rules on the basis of this sort of conception of liberty, since the latter presupposes already that those property rules are morally justified. Maybe that justification makes reference to some other conception of liberty; but obviously our justification of private property cannot depend on a conception of liberty that presupposes it already.[53]

However, if we can offer an independent account of the virtues of acquisition or the exercise of private property rights, we may be in a position to offer a libertarian defence of the property-owner against those who claim to be prejudiced by his activities along the following lines. To restrict the owner's activities would be to place restrictions on liberty, since he is performing the morally good actions of bringing land into cultivation and taming natural resources. But his activity, in its appropriative aspect, places no real restrictions on others' liberty since the desires it frustrates are the morally unreasonable desires generated by envy, covetousness, and idleness. We have seen that there are hints of such an argument in Locke,[54] but we also saw its difficulties: it is easy enough to show that the actions involved *in* appropriation are reasonable and morally intelligible; it is much more difficult to show that it is morally reasonable that those actions should involve appropriation. We may want to say instead that the virtue of taming natural resources is *spoiled* by the acquisitiveness that goes along with it. If we say this, then equally we will not find the complaints of the non-industrious unreasonable, nor will we be disposed to say that the 'liberty' which they say is frustrated by property rights is to be regarded as mere licence.

Moreover, even if we can defend private property on the basis of a moralized definition of liberty, there will be serious consequences for the conception of private property that results. On most

[52] For this view, see e.g. Benn and Weinstein, 'Being Free to Act' and Oppenheim, *Political Concepts*, pp. 15–16.

[53] This argument is suggested by Cohen, 'Capitalism, Freedom and the Proletariat'.

[54] Ryan, *Property and Political Theory*, p. 44 takes the theme of moral desert in Locke's theory more seriously than I do.

conceptions, private property gives a man rights which he may exercise rightly or wrongly, reasonably or unreasonably. But if his ownership is defended on the basis of the moral liberty which it involves, then we may have to place restrictions on this. We may want to say, for example, that '[a] man may hold land on condition that it is productively employed, and should lose it if it is not', and impose on owners generally enforceable duties of stewardship and good husbandry.[55] Whether this would leave anything recognizable as private property, or whether it would amount in effect to the substitution of some collective conception, would then be a matter for debate.

(v) Caprice and Responsibility

In the positive liberty tradition, the most powerful argument for private property has been based on the need for stability, discipline, and responsibility in the exercise of free will.

Even if an individual is able to distance himself from and reflect upon his desires, it is easy for his willing to remain at the level of the pursuit of particular whims, where one project is undertaken now, a quite different one tomorrow, and no resolve ever becomes a settled or relatively permanent feature of his intentional life. What is done today in the pursuit of some resolve, need not matter for tomorrow, for by tomorrow some quite different project may have been undertaken, with different, perhaps even opposite, criteria of success and failure. The result is that traditional virtues like prudence and a sense of responsibility become meaningless, and maybe it even becomes difficult to develop a real sense of one's identity as an agent enduring over periods of time.[56] From most moral points of view this is worrying, and it is a worry that may also be expressed in terms of liberty. A person who exercises his negative liberty in this way, living for the projects of the moment with no sense of any 'permanent good', no sense of any enduring commitments which might give unity to his life, is not fully free since he is not exercising his faculties of deliberation, foresight, choice, and decision to their fullest extent.

How might the ownership of private property affect matters? One argument is that if a man's subsistence depends on the

---

[55] Ryan, *Property and Political Theory*, pp. 35–6.
[56] There is an interesting discussion in Hampshire, *Thought and Action*, p. 220.

management of resources over which he has exclusive control and for which he has sole responsibility, then habits of foresight and prudential calculation will develop, as he learns that what he does today may affect his life chances tomorrow. Acts of appropriation and the use of resources takes on a special significance:

[T]hey are not merely a passing employment of such materials as can be laid hands on to satisfy this or that want . . . but reflect the consciousness of a subject which distinguishes itself from its wants; which presents itself to itself as still there and demanding satisfaction when this or that want, or any number of wants, have been satisfied; which thus not merely uses a thing to fill a want, and in so doing at once destroys the thing and for the time removes the want, but says to itself, 'This shall be mine to do as I like with, to satisfy my wants and emotions as they arise.'[57]

In a system of collective or common property, by contrast, the connection between action today and prospects tomorrow may not exist at all. Even if it does, it is likely to be mediated by some collective conception of what that connection ought to be, and perhaps also undermined by the effect on one's prospects of the responsible or irresponsible actions of others. (Notice, by the way, the interesting distributive implications of this argument. It seems to imply that it is important for individuals to own just enough resources to guarantee them a reasonable standard of living if they manage them wisely; to have *more* property than that might undermine the effect by encouraging a more careless attitude.)

A similar argument can be made concerning the productive use of resources.[58] It is often thought important that a system of property should allow individuals to work productively on their own initiative on certain resources and retain the products of their labour. This is not merely because individuals are entitled, as a matter of *special* right to the products of their labour; if it were, there would be no injustice in prohibiting productive labour—and the generation of such entitlements— altogether. Instead, the argument concerns the relation between production and responsibility. To *produce* is to perform actions now which make other actions possible in the future: I take a piece of willow and I make it into a cricket bat so that the action of playing a cover drive becomes possible with that physical object. Contrary to the Marxian

---

[57] Green, *Lectures on Political Obligation*, Lect. N, p. 212.
[58] This paragraph condenses an argument presented in more detail in Waldron, 'Producers' Entitlements'.

conception of production, the intentional object of productive labour is not an image of the finished product but the actions that the productive labour will make possible—actions which are not possible with the resource one is working on as it stands. It is the idea of the actions the labour will make possible, not the image of the finished product, which guides the production process.[59] Now production, in this sense, takes place in all economies, and it is an open question whether those who perform the productive actions will also get to be the ones who perform the actions which the production makes possible. In a system where they do, where the producers and the users of the finished product are the same, production may make an important contribution to one's sense of responsibility and the endurance of oneself over time. Production in its very nature involves action-oriented action, action in the present which looks towards action in the future. When the future action is known at the time of production to be one's own, then the act of production comes to involve an awareness of one's future agency, and one's present actions become permeated with a sense of one's persistence in time. Thus reasons which are essentially future-oriented will be drawn into the intentionality of current acts. In order even to explain reasons for the performance of a present act of production, reference will have to be made to one's future self. In this way a sense develops even in one's most common and mundane actions that the various parts of one's life are linked together and welded into a larger structure.

Another argument concerns the object of ownership itself. If I have worked on some material, it comes to embody the intentions that I had at the time, not in the Lockean sense of literally containing something of mine, but in the sense that the object is now in a condition caused by the fact that I worked on it with those intentions rather than any others. Once that has happened, I may not be able to change my mind—to decide, for example, to make something else using this material—because what I have already done to it places limits on what can be done to it in the future. Once a sculptor begins carving a *pietà* out of a block of marble he may not be able to change his mind and carve a man on horseback instead. The fact that the object registers one's intentions in this way therefore encourages a more careful selection of intention, for

[59] For the view that it is the *idea* of the finished product that is important, see Marx, *Capital*, Vol. I, Ch. 7, p. 284.

the agent knows that he cannot chop and change as he pleases once he embarks upon some project. Again, this effect is more difficult to achieve if resources are not owned privately, for then limits are placed on purpose and intention not only by one's present acts but by the external and unpredictable actions of others. As we shall see, this is one interpretation (I think it is the best interpretation) that can be put on Hegel's account of the ethical importance of property.

(vi) Collective or Political Conceptions

Though the conceptions of liberty we have considered up till now have all been 'positive' in character, all of them have focused on *individual* freedom and have concerned themselves with the quality of individual choice, willing, and action. Some, it is true, have a social element: conceptions which regard recognition as wholly or partly constitutive of personality suggest that it is impossible for an individual to be free if he lives in complete isolation from others. Also, conceptions which identify freedom with duty may have a social element if (but only if) duty is understood in the sense of social responsibility. But it is possible to offer a critique of the negative conception, and to put forward various substantial and positive accounts of what is worth promoting in the space left to individuals once external obstacles have been cleared away, without committing oneself in any way to the view that true freedom consists in the pursuit of collective purposes or in the life or projects of a community.[60] Nevertheless, views of this kind have been put forward, and it is to their connections with private property that we shall now turn our attention.

In English political thought, these views have been associated with idealist and organic conceptions of the relation between the individual and the state, and more recently with the reception of *marxisant* approaches to man and society. Individuals, it is said, cannot develop their freedom by acting on their own, without relation to social ends. As Green put it, 'we rightly refuse to recognize the highest development on the part of an exceptional individual . . . as an advance towards the true freedom of man':

[60] This point is stressed by Taylor, 'What's Wrong with Negative Liberty?', pp. 178 ff.

When we speak of freedom as something to be highly prized, we mean a positive power or capacity of doing or enjoying, and that, too, something that we do or enjoy in common with others. . . . When we measure the progress of a society by its growth in freedom, we measure it by the increasing development and exercise on the whole of these powers of contributing to social good with which we believe the members of the society to be endowed . . .[61]

From this perspective, purely negative conceptions of freedom are attacked on the grounds that they are too individualistic, perhaps even too egoistic. Marx, for example, in his critique of the Declaration of the Rights of Man, wrote:

The freedom in question is that of a man treated as an isolated monad and withdrawn into himself. . . . [T]he right of man to freedom is not based on the union of man with man, but on the separation of man from man. It is the right to this separation, the rights of the limited individual who is limited to himself. . . . Thus none of the so-called rights of man goes beyond egoistic man, man as he is in civil society, namely an individual withdrawn behind his private interests and whims and separated from the community. Far from the rights of man conceiving of man as a species-being, species-life itself, society, appears as a framework exterior to individuals, a limitation of their original self-sufficiency.[62]

In many socialist thinkers inspired by Marx, this attack has led on to a repudiation of the whole idea of individual rights, and the substitution of more explicitly communitarian modes of political discourse.[63] Among the liberal idealists, however, it led to an implicit 'socialization' of the idea of rights: 'A right is a power of acting for his own ends,—for what he conceives to be his good,— secured to the individual by the community, on the supposition that its exercise contributes to the good of the community.'[64] A right to liberty *against* one's society, then, on this sort of account, is 'an impossibility'.[65]

The thesis that liberty has this social side to it must be distinguished from two individualist theses. The first is that the liberty of one man must be made compatible with a like liberty for others. The notion that I cannot claim liberty as a moral right for myself without committing myself to an identical liberty for all is

[61] Green, 'Liberal Legislation', p. 652.
[62] Marx, 'On the Jewish Question', p. 146.
[63] e.g. Pashukanis, *Law and Marxism*, Ch. 4.
[64] Green, *Lectures on Political Obligation*, Lect. M, p. 207.
[65] Ibid. Lect. H, p. 145.

based on simple universalizability, and it characterizes even the most negative conception of freedom. This need involve no socialization of the concept of liberty itself. Secondly, the claim that liberty involves the pursuit of 'a common good' may refer merely to the idea of an individual good which men have in common (in the sense that we all have life, health, and the use of our limbs in common); in this case, the proposition rules out peculiar or idiosyncratic claims of right, and establishes a clear and simple basis for reciprocity. (The ambiguity between this view and a genuinely socialized view of liberty is quite deep-set in Western political theory; it is, for example, crucial to understanding some of the tensions in Rousseau's concept of the general will.[66] In T. H. Green's writings about freedom, all three views are run together without distinction in many places.)[67]

If we turn now to the genuinely socialized conceptions of freedom, we will find that the weakest sort holds that freedom for each individual consists in his participation in the pursuit of the collective purposes and common life of those with whom he lives in society, and that freedom is not to be located in purely personal or private pursuits. A much stronger version has it that freedom cannot really be claimed as a right for *individuals* at all: it is first and foremost a feature of collectives—a free people or a free society—and attributable to individuals only to the extent that they participate in those aspects of the life of the collective on which the attribution of this feature is based. This strong version makes freedom into much more of a social goal than an individual right, in the sense defined in Chapter 3. In what follows, I shall be concerned mainly with those weaker versions which make participation in collective life a condition of true freedom for individuals.

Though these conceptions agree in rejecting a purely personal or private account of what liberty is, they differ in the type of communal involvement which they regard as essential to individual freedom. For writers like Hannah Arendt it is participation in politics, in the public sphere, rather than in economic production or social life.[68] For Marx, on the other hand, political rights capture at most only the collective and participatory *form* of genuine human

---

[66] See Rousseau, *Social Contract*, Bk. II.

[67] See e.g. Green, *Lectures on Political Obligation*; Lect. G, p. 120 and Lect. N, p. 217. See also Green, *Prolegomena*, Bk. III, Ch. 3, pp. 229 ff.

[68] Arendt, *Human Condition*, pp. 43 ff. For her conception of freedom, see Arendt, 'What is Freedom?', and also *On Revolution*, pp. 29–35.

freedom; they neglect its economic *substance*. In political community, man 'is valued as a communal being', but as long as economic life remains privatized, 'real, practical emancipation' will never be achieved:[69]

[I]t is natural necessity, the essential human properties however estranged they may seem to be, and *interest* that holds the members of civil society together; *civil not political life is their real tie*. It is therefore not the state which holds the atoms of civil society together, but the fact that they are atoms only in imagination, in the heaven of their fancy, but in reality tremendously different from atoms, in other words, not divine egoists, but egoistic human beings.[70] [original emphasis]

As one would expect, conceptions which locate individual liberty in the economic life of a collective are hardly going to be favourable to private property, for private property licenses individuals to take decisions about the use of socially important resources without reference to communal purposes. Certainly, a socialized conception of liberty will look unfavourably on exercises of ownership rights which make no contribution to the common good. For example, in the political philosophy of T. H. Green, private property is based on what he calls

freedom in the positive sense: in other words, the liberation of the powers of all men equally for contributions to a common good. No one has a right to do what he will with his own in such a way as to contravene this end. It is only through the guarantee which society gives him that he has any property at all, or, strictly speaking, any right to his possessions. This guarantee is founded on a sense of common interest.[71]

Green believed that there were reasons for not interfering directly with the exercise of rights to secure social or moral ends: as far as possible, restraint on freedom for the sake of the social whole should be 'a self-imposed restraint, a free obedience, to which, though the alternative course is left open to him, the individual submits because he sees it as his true good'.[72] But the social interest may provide a reason for adjusting the basic rules of the property system in a way which fosters the virtuous exercise of property rights. As we have seen, private property is a concept of which there are many conceptions, and an argument for private property based

[69] Marx, 'On the Jewish Question', p. 140.
[70] Marx, 'Critique of Political Economy', p. 504.
[71] Green, 'Liberal Legislation', p. 653.
[72] Green, *Lectures on Political Obligation*, Lect. N, p. 218.

on a socialized conception of freedom is likely to favour some conceptions of private property and provide grounds for rejecting others. For example, one conception of ownership may permit planning or hygiene restrictions while another does not; it seems likely that a conception of liberty which makes reference to a collective social or economic good will tend to favour the former.

In theories which locate 'true liberty' in *political* participation, on the other hand, the situation is likely to be more complicated. The considerations about citizenship that we have already mentioned may come into play here, and generate an argument for private property on the basis of a politically socialized conception of freedom. Similarly, in Arendt's writings we find hints of a claim that political participation requires individuals to have a private base from which they can make their forays into the public political arena:

> What prevented the *polis* from violating the private lives of its citizens and made it hold sacred the boundaries surrounding each property was not respect for private property as we understand it, but the fact that without owning a house a man could not participate in the affairs of the world because he had no location in it which was properly his own.[73]

This is partly a matter of roots, of having a stable sense of one's identity and origins. But it is also a matter of the protection for privacy that we discussed in section 3. In typical Heideggerian fashion, Arendt adduces the importance of political participation as the very thing that generates a need for a place where one can hide from others:

> [T]he four walls of one's private property offer the only reliable hiding place from the common public world, not only from everything that goes on in it but also from its very publicity, from being seen and being heard. A life spent entirely in public, in the presence of others, becomes, as we would say, shallow. While it retains its visibility, it loses the quality of rising into sight from some darker ground which must remain hidden if it is not to lose its depth in a very real, non-subjective sense. The only efficient way to guarantee the darkness of what needs to be hidden against the light of publicity is private property, a privately owned place to hide in.[74]

Though political participation is the essence of freedom, the exercise of freedom is not the totality of life. Arendt's plea for the

---

[73] Arendt, *Human Condition*, pp. 29–30.
[74] Ibid. 71.

private realm, and *a fortiori* for the private property that protects and constitutes it flows from her recognition that humans need some respite from the communal forms of activity in which their freedom consists.

The central thesis of this section could not be illustrated more clearly than by the contrast between the economic and the political views of communal life which socialized conceptions of liberty involve. 'Positive liberty' is not the name of a single political ideal; it is a rubric under which we find clustered many different and competing accounts of human freedom, capable of generating quite disparate conclusions so far as the justification of property systems is concerned. Some of them provide evidence for the commonly held view that positive (as opposed to negative) conceptions of liberty are antithetical to private property. But others—even some of the ones which deny that human liberty consists in purely individual fulfilment—are capable of providing a starting point for GR-based arguments in favour of that institution.

5. EVALUATING GENERAL-RIGHT-BASED ARGUMENTS

It is unfortunate that in the growing literature on property, the lines of argument outlined in the previous section have not been more fully discussed. For example, in Lawrence Becker's *Property Rights: Philosophic Foundations*, though there is a brief discussion of the thesis that since people naturally want to acquire things for themselves it would be politically oppressive for the government to prohibit that, there is no discussion at all of any of the lines of argument we have outlined, and only two dismissive paragraphs devoted to the idea that private property might be necessary for the development of moral virtue.[75] There is, I think, an explanation for this gap in the modern discussion.

The arguments we have been considering are associated very strongly with the tradition of philosophical idealism. Though idealist approaches to political philosophy were dominant in England in the 1880s to 1890s they suffered from the general onslaught on that tradition initiated by Russell and others after the turn of the century. In addition, the later influence of Isaiah Berlin's attack on the positive liberty idea cannot be overestimated. Though

[75] Becker, *Property Rights*, p. 86.

a number of impressive rearguard actions have been fought, Berlin's critique and particularly his insistence that all positive liberty themes come naturally together in one package have made it very difficult to discuss these themes in an atmosphere free of distracting worries about moral totalitarianism. That has made arguments about the economic implications of positive freedom difficult for liberals. Of course, positive conceptions of freedom continue to be popular among socialists. But, on the one hand, they face quite savage opposition on this from many established liberal philosophers.[76] And, on the other hand, socialist philosophers understandably have, on the whole, no great interest in drawing out of these conceptions any ideas which are favourable to institutions like private property.

The result has been not the elimination of these themes from the discussion of property, but their relegation to a sort of shadowy existence in the realm of political rhetoric as opposed to substantial philosophical argument. For example, in 'new right' and libertarian discussions of property, these themes tend to be hinted at or thrown out in passing in the course of an argument in which other considerations such as utility, efficiency, or special historical entitlement are dominant.[77] Equally, themes in the positive liberty tradition which are uncongenial to private property are invoked as a basis for rhetoric rather than argument by those who want to put the case against that institution. We are simply told for example that libertarian arguments for private ownership 'make a mockery of liberty'—without any serious analysis of the basis and implications of the conceptions of liberty that such arguments presuppose.

The arguments I have been outlining should be subject to critical discussion and evaluation at three levels.

First, we should ask: does liberty *really* involve what a particular positive conception says it involves? Or, to put it another way: is the argument based on an adequate or on an impoverished or exaggerated conception of liberty? For example, a GR-based argument for private property may be disputed on the ground that, even if private property is required by some positive conception of liberty, still that conception of liberty is too far-fetched to be taken seriously as a basis for justification. This should not be regarded as

---

[76] See e.g. the clash between B. Gibbs and A. Flew in Philips Griffiths (ed.), *Of Liberty.*

[77] See, e.g. Kohr, 'Property and Freedom'; Wiggins, 'Decline of Private Property'; and Friedman, *Machinery of Freedom*, Ch. 1.

a debate about what the term 'liberty' really means. I can see no point in addressing that issue and have no idea what would count as a way of settling it.[78] A more fruitful approach is the following. If we acknowledge that the term 'liberty' has a certain positive evaluative force, that we use it to appraise institutions and societies and to express certain commitments and concerns, we may ask whether it is appropriate to associate that evaluative force of those commitments and concerns with what, on a given 'positive' account, individual liberty is said *really* to involve. For example, if we believe that the term 'liberty' is characteristically used to express a very high level of positive approbation, and if we believe on independent grounds that the issues highlighted in a putative positive theory are not really all that important, then we may well decide against regarding that theory as an acceptable conception of liberty.

More directly, for our purposes, we may ask simply whether the interest in the development of an individual's will, choice, and moral character that a positive account of liberty picks out is sufficiently important in itself to justify without further ado holding others to be under a duty to serve it. That is, we may bypass the question of whether some positive theory expresses an adequate conception of liberty, and ask simply whether people should be taken to have a right to whatever it is that that theory regards as important.

Secondly, assuming that the basic concern of the argument is a compelling one, whether it is described as a concern for liberty or not, we should ask: does it really require *private* property for individuals, or would some system of common or collective property satisfy that concern just as well? Here the situation is complicated by the fact that, as we saw in Chapter 2, private property is a concept of which there are many conceptions. The aim of a right-based argument for private property is not (or not necessarily) to justify the present institutions of ownership in western capitalist societies, but to justify the adoption or mainten-ance of property institutions *of a certain general type*. For example, some of the positive liberty arguments for private property support

---

[78] For some discussion of some of the problems involved in the definition of liberty, see e.g. Gray, 'On Liberty, Liberalism and Essential Contestability'; Connolly, *Terms of Political Discourse*, Ch. 4; and Miller, 'Linguistic Philosophy and Political Theory'. For a more optimistic approach, see Oppenheim, *Political Concepts*, Chs. 4–5. See also Waldron, *Poverty and Freedom*, Chs. 1 and 3.

the idea of an economy of smallholders, bartering and trading with one another, but not an advanced capitalist economy with assembly-line production and intense division of labour. Arguments like this may raise serious questions of practicability; but they still count as arguments for private property even though they do not support the institutions with which we are familiar. (Moreover, we should note that problems of real-world practicability, utopianism, and reactionary nostalgia are no greater for these arguments in favour of private property than for many of the socialist alternatives that are put forward against it!)

It is often possible to imagine complicated and sophisticated systems of non-private property rules which might, at a scratch, do everything that a given conception of positive liberty requires of a property system. For example, maybe some complicated form of 'market socialism' would foster the settled character and the sense of individual responsibility that a Hegelian conception of liberty takes to be important as well as a private property system would. Does the existence of such possibilities mean that the argument from positive liberty to private property is a bad one? Not quite.

For one thing, we would have to be sure that the imagined system satisfies the other conditions we require of any property system: that it be stable, learnable, and capable of generating its own support.[79] Unless these conditions were satisfied, the imagined system would not be a solution to the problem of allocation. In Chapter 2 some of these conditions were related to the notion of a property system's 'organizing idea': the notion of the main basis on which individuals are conscious of their property system, of its organization, application, and legitimization. It seems reasonable to require not only that the detailed rules of the imagined system should do the work for liberty that we want it to do, but also that the organizing idea should make a contribution in this respect. So, for example, although the rules of a particular conception of collective property may be capable in principle of fostering a stable sense of individual responsibility, we must also take into account the effect on individual responsibility of people going about their daily lives with the idea in their head that, as a basic rule, important resources are reserved for collective rather than individual purposes.

Having said that, it is only fair to add that none of the arguments

[79] See the discussion in Ch. 2, sect. 5(iv), above. See also Rawls, *Theory of Justice*, pp. 145 and 177 ff.

considered in the previous section makes out any cast-iron case for private property. They are much more in the nature of right-based considerations tending to favour private property than knock-down right-based arguments against other forms of property regime. Now, once we are faced with a choice of property systems any of which would in principle satisfy the demands of liberty, other considerations, such as utility or prosperity are likely to come into play. If these end up clinching the case in favour of the private-property conception, then we may say that the right-based consideration, while not conclusive, has nevertheless played a role (for the choice on grounds of utility might have been quite different had the choice set not been constrained by the right-based consideration). There is also a further practical point. If the question we face is not 'What (pure) type of property system are we to institute?' But rather 'What sort of (incremental or substantial) modifications are we to make to the institutions of an already existing mixed economy?',[80] then considerations which are in themselves less than conclusive in answering the former question may nevertheless have a role to play in helping us to answer the latter.

The third and final thing we have to examine is the distributive implications of the argument. Does it justify the sort of uneven distribution of private property that we have at the moment? Or does it require a radical redistribution of property, so that, for example, everyone has a roughly equal share? If it does require redistribution, is that practicable? And is it possible without undermining the very idea of private property that we are trying to introduce? I shall address these issues of redistribution and practicability in Chapters 9 and 12 respectively.

[80] See above, Ch. 2, sect. 5(v).

9

The Proudhon Strategy

1. FROM PROPERTY TO EQUALITY?

In the 'First Memoir' of his book *What is Property?*, Pierre-Joseph Proudhon considers an argument in favour of the institution of private property put forward by one Monsieur Cousin. Cousin's argument is one that we should call GR-based and it is founded on a premiss of liberty:

My liberty, which is sacred, needs for its objective action, an instrument which we call the body: the body participates then in the sacredness of liberty; it is then inviolable. . . . My liberty needs, for its objective action, material to work upon; in other words, property or a thing. This thing or property naturally participates then in the inviolability of my person.[1]

To this, Proudhon offers the following response: 'Well, is it not true, from M. Cousin's point of view, that, if the liberty of man is sacred, it is equally sacred in all individuals; that if it needs property for its objective action, that is, for its life, the appropriation of material is equally necessary for all . . . ?'[2] This response, says Proudhon, is not offered in order to *refute* M. Cousin or those who argue in the way he does: 'I will only prove, by all the arguments with which he justifies the right of property, the principle of equality which kills it. As I have already said, my sole intent is this: to show at the bottom of all these positions that inevitable major, *equality* . . . '[3] Or, to put it more bluntly, 'Every argument which has been invented in behalf of property, *whatever it may be*, always and of necessity leads to equality; that is to the negation of property.'[4] This is Proudhon's strategy in his famous polemic.

In this section, I want to explore the application of this strategy to the GR-based arguments we have been considering. I think

---

[1] Proudhon, *What is Property?*, p. 65. (I have not managed to discover who Cousin was, other than that he was the author of a book, *Moral Philosophy*.)
[2] Proudhon, *What is Property?*, p. 66.
[3] Ibid.
[4] Ibid. 39–40.

Proudhon is mistaken if he believes his strategy is successful against literally all arguments for property. It does not work, at least not necessarily, against utilitarian arguments, nor does it work against SR-based arguments, except to the extent that they incorporate a GR-based element. But it looks a promising strategy when turned against GR-based arguments, for those arguments are articulating a general thesis about what the liberty of man requires and so they ought to generate moral claims that can be made on behalf of *all men*, not just those who happen to have property at present. What I shall do then is, first of all, explore the universalist implications of GR-based arguments; secondly, consider how far that drives us in the direction of equality; and thirdly, discuss the incompatibility between an argument with these implications and the idea of unilateral appropriation. (I shall postpone till Chapter 12 consideration of whether these universalist or egalitarian conclusions amount in fact, as Proudhon suggested, to the death or 'the negation' of property.)

2. UNIVERSALIZABILITY

If I say that my liberty is morally important, and that its importance justifies holding others to be under duties to respect and promote it, I am logically committed to saying liberty is that important, and that it is something which ought to be respected and promoted, in the case of every man. I cannot say that liberty is morally important in the case of me and people like me, but not morally important in the case of people like *them*, unless I am prepared to indicate some morally relevant ground for distinguishing between us and them that could in principle apply to us as well. All this is at the level of the least controversial application of the troubled principle of the universalizability of moral judgements.[5]

If I say that true liberty involves not just freedom from constraint, in general or in certain areas, but some positive element such as self-mastery, the development of autonomy, or active participation in political life, then I seem to be committed to holding that that is true of the liberty of every man. Of course, positive liberty may be something which not everybody happens to

---

[5] For universalizability, see Hare, *Freedom and Reason*; Mackie, *Ethics*, Ch. 4; and Gewirth, *Reason and Morality*, Ch. 4.

have, as things stand; but presumably liberty as a morally important aim, as something which people have an interest in attaining, will be the same for everyone.

Now the following is perhaps a little more controversial. It has been suggested by one or two theorists of positive liberty that true liberty may be something which only the few are fit for, and for which the many show their unfitness precisely by their failure to strive actively to attain it. Mill sometimes implied this about the ideal of positive liberty which he associated with individuality and the higher pleasures.[6] And, in *On Revolution*, Hannah Arendt wrote:

The fact that political 'elites' have always determined the political destinies of the many . . . indicates, on the other [*sic*] hand, the bitter need of the few to protect themselves against the many, or rather to protect the island of freedom they have come to inhabit against the surrounding sea of necessity; and it indicates, on the other hand, the responsibility that falls automatically upon those who care for the fate of those who do not. . . . With respect to the elementary councils that sprang up wherever people lived or worked together, one is tempted to say that they had selected themselves; those who organized themselves were those who cared and those who took the initiative. . . . The joys of public happiness and the responsibilities for public business would then become the share of those few from all walks of life who have a taste for public freedom and cannot be 'happy' without it.[7]

I am probably not alone in finding this suggestion uncongenial. But even if we accept such a 'two level' theory of liberty—positive liberty for those who 'have a taste' for it, negative liberty (at most) for those who do not—there are still universalist implications to be drawn out. The distinction between the two types of people must be stated in terms that are both plausible and universalizable; and it will hardly do, for example, to assert (as Arendt does in one or two passages) that the only way to tell whether someone has the taste for positive liberty is to see whether he has actually managed to attain it. Since liberty, on all these positive accounts, is a developmental notion[8]—something that must be striven for and attained over time—and since much of the normative force of positive liberty ideas is supposed to consist in a requirement that this development and striving should be nurtured and respected, it

[6] Mill, *On Liberty*, Ch. 3.
[7] Arendt, *On Revolution*, pp. 276 and 278.
[8] The Hegelian idea of *bildung* is implicit in them all.

follows that we must not use a pure 'success' criterion for picking out those whose positive liberty is to be a matter of moral concern. If the positive conceptions of liberty are to do the normative work that we expect them to do, they must generate duties to respect the development of liberty in those who have not yet attained it.

The next step in the universalist application of the Proudhon strategy involves the connection between liberty and the rights and opportunities which the development of liberty is said to require. If positive liberty in *my* case requires that I should have and exercise ownership rights over some significant resources, then positive liberty in *everybody's* case (or in the case of everyone who has the taste for it) requires that they should have and exercise such rights. If the requirements of my liberty invest my interest in owning things with enough importance to form the basis of a moral right, then equally the requirements of the liberty of all men invest their interest in owning things with that importance too.

The final step is based on the realization that the owners of property, as things stand, are not the only people who have an interest in owning things. Of course, they do have such an interest, and they may appeal to theories of positive liberty to show why it is morally important that this interest should be respected. But other people—non-owners—have an interest in owning things too. In their case, the interest is less concrete: it may not be related to specified resources, and it is likely to be expressed in terms of general proprietorial aspirations rather than in terms of particular items ('I wish I owned *a car*' or 'I wish I had *a house of my own* to live in' rather than 'I wish my ownership of *this* car or *this* house to be respected'). But if owning things is necessary for the development of positive liberty, and if these are people who show by their striving that they have a taste for positive liberty, then the moral importance of liberty accrues to their rather abstract interest in owning things too. To put it the other way round, if somebody has no private property of his own, then, as far as a GR-based argument is concerned, the existence of an institution of private property does him no good. As T. H. Green put it: 'a man who possesses nothing but his powers of labour and who has to sell these to a capitalist for bare daily maintenance, might as well, in respect of the ethical purposes which the possession of property should serve, be denied rights of property altogether.'[9]

[9] Green, *Lectures on Political Obligation*, Lect. N, p. 219.

It may perhaps be objected that to say this is to ignore the distinction betwen acts and omissions. Maybe it is worse positively to attack existing property rights than to fail to provide them for certain people (in roughly the same way as it is worse to kill someone than to fail to save his life). I find this move unconvincing here for several reasons. The first is a general point. The acts/ omissions distinction is itself a matter of the deepest controversy in moral philosophy: many deny that the distinction carries this sort of moral weight, and cannot understand why, if one is concerned about an interest, one should not be as concerned about the failure to promote it as one is about the positive attempt to impede it.[10]

It is true that belief in the distinction is sometimes associated with a commitment to rights. People sometimes think that it is only utilitarians who are suspicious of the distinction between doing something and failing to prevent it. But though suspicion of the acts/omissions distinction is commonly associated with utilitarianism, it need not be confined to a goal-based approach. I argued in Chapter 3 that reliance on the distinction between actions and omissions, and the agent-relativity that often goes with it, appears better to characterize *duty*-based critiques of utilitarianism than *right*-based ones. A right-based theorist, concerned in an 'agent-neutral' way for the promotion of certain key interests that human individuals have, will not view them as the basis of deontological side-constraints.[11] For him what matters, is that those interests suffer no harm, and it is of secondary importance whether that harm is associated with intentionality or negligence. He will be as concerned, therefore, about a failure to promote them as he is about a positive attempt to undermine them provided that in the two cases the interest he is focusing on suffers to the same extent.

It is no good saying, as people often do, that we recognize general duties not to *act* against other's interests, but that we only recognize duties not to refrain from promoting others' interests in *special* cases. (Thus, people draw attention to the fact that we all have a duty not to kill, but that only those in special relationships—like the relation of parent to child—have duties not to let others starve.) Even if this is true in morals (which I doubt), it only begs the question here. For we are asking: *should* there be a special duty to

---

[10] There are good general discussions of the issues in: Foot, *Virtues and Vices*, Ch. 2; Glover, *Causing Death*, Ch. 7; and Honderich, *Violence for Equality*, Ch. 2.

[11] See above Ch. 3, sect. 3(ii). See also Nagel, 'Limits of Objectivity', pp. 126 ff.

promote the interests in freedom, etc., which property serves? We cannot answer that question adequately simply by assuming in advance that there is not. Moreover, it should be remembered that we are talking here about governments and governments do have special duties; they do stand in a special relation to the interests of their subjects. That is why we set them up. We expect governments to protect people's lives, not just refrain from killing them. Why not, then, also expect them to promote each person's ethical interest in being a property-holder, and not merely refrain from taking the goods of those who are property-holders already?

Another way of putting this is to say that our interest in property is effectively an interest in the political and economic structure of society. The question we began with—Aristotle's question—was: 'What are the best arrangements to make about property, if a state is to be as well constituted as it is possible to make it?'[12] Now, if our answer is that we should have private property, and if our reason for that answer is the interest which everyone has in the ethical benefits of property-ownership, then the arrangements that we make should reflect the full impact of that reasoning. Setting up those arrangements in a way which does not do that is as much an action to the detriment of the interests in question as positively attacking them would be. It is true that, despite our rhetoric, political philosophers are seldom if ever involved in the actual construction of social arrangements—certainly not in the original establishment of a basic structure. A theory of justice and rights is primarily a theory of judgement rather than a blueprint for institutional design. Our immediate aim is to find a basis for evaluating (criticizing, defending) social institutions which grew or were established for reasons quite independent of political philosophy. But we ask ourselves the Aristotelian question because that gives us a good purchase on the task of evaluation. And if we approach evaluation in that spirit, it would be disingenuous to suggest that we should be somehow less severe on what the social structure does not do as on what it does do. That is why it is fatuous to say, as F. A. Hayek and others often do, that a theory of justice should concern itself only with intentional harms, and that it should not, for example, purport to judge the unintended outcomes of market processes.[13] The fact is that there are all sorts of choices

---

[12] Aristotle, *Politics*, Bk. II (Sinclair trans.).
[13] Hayek, *Mirage of Social Justice*.

to be made about market and other institutions, and we know or we have a fair idea of what their consequences may be. If we make one set of choices, whose consequences are worse for people's interest in positive freedom than another set of choices would be, then we must accept responsibility for that outcome. We cannot excuse ourselves by pointing out that the choice was exercised by default, if the default was conscious and the outcome foreseeable.

The final point to be made in this context is that, even if the distinction between acts and omissions can be maintained, it is not straightforwardly applicable in the case of property. If a property-less person grabs something in order to make use of it, the owners of that thing will have to intervene or act positively against him in order to protect their rights. So, because property rights depend on the *positive enforcement* of property rules, keeping people proper-tyless (when they are otherwise inclined to take resources for themselves) is not just a matter of failing to give them something; it is a matter of continual *action*.[14]

The conclusion then is this. Though arguments based on a general right to liberty may be used by those who have private property to rebut attempts to expropriate them or to take the resources that they own into collective ownership, consistency requires that the same arguments be deployed with equal fervour on behalf of those who have no private property to rebut attempts to perpetuate their propertylessness or to perpetuate the situation in which they have to rely either on collective provision or on the goodwill of property-owners for their material well-being. In each case, the moral concern is the same: people need private property for the development and exercise of their liberty; that is why it is wrong to take all of a person's private property away from him, and that is why it is wrong that some individuals should have had no private property at all.

It follows that, in any dispute between proprietors and the propertyless over the morality of the existing distribution, a putative general right to property may figure on either side. Marx put it well in one of his earliest writings on the subject: 'Through my private property do I not exclude a third person from this property? And do I not thus violate his right to property?'[15] And Proudhon made much the same point when he wrote:

---

[14] I have developed this argument further in Waldron, 'Welfare and the Images of Charity'.

[15] Marx, 'Theft of Wood', p. 21.

Under this system, the poor and the rich distrust, and make war upon, each other. but what is the object of the war? Property. So that property is necessarily accompanied by war upon property. . . . The rich man's right of property . . . has to be continually defended against the poor man's desire for property. What a contradiction![16]

(Whether or not this really is a contradiction will be considered in Chapter 12.)

Perhaps we can go even further than this. If anything, our GR-based concern should be greater in the case of the propertyless than in the case of proprietors faced with expropriation. For one thing, the latter have at least had property, and it may already have done the work which, on a right-based argument, it is supposed to do. (This will depend on the details of the particular argument. I have not been able to consider the difficult question of whether particular GR-based arguments require that every individual should have property of his own *at all times*.) For another thing, in the real world, redistributive proposals seldom involve the total expropriation of any individual: what is usually involved is carving off a substantial proportion of someone's wealth, leaving him with just enough property to live on. But the real world predicament of the propertyless is that they have *no property at all*. Thus a concern such as Cousin's that human liberty needs property 'for its objective action' seems to apply much more acutely in their case.

3. JUSTIFICATION AND DISTRIBUTION

The suggestion we are exploring is that the reasons why we think private property is justified might also be reasons which dictate a particular distribution of it.

However, at a general level, that sort of suggestion seems open to question. Does the defence of some institution always involve a commitment to a particular distributive principle? Is justification not one thing and distribution another? The general issue here has been discussed in relation to punishment by H. L. A. Hart. In his book *Punishment and Responsibility*, Hart is anxious to show that 'different principles . . . are relevant at different points in any morally acceptable account of punishment', and that one may be a utilitarian about the general *point* of the institution of punishment

[16] Proudhon, *What is Property?*, p. 48.

without being committed to deciding who ought to be punished and how severely always on utilitarian grounds. Hart argues as follows:

There is, I think, an analogy worth considering between the concept of punishment and that of property. . . . In both cases, we are confronted by a complex institution presenting different inter-related features calling for separate explanation; or, if the morality of the institution is challenged, for separate justification. In both cases failure to distinguish separate questions or attempting to answer them all by reference to a single principle ends in confusion. Thus in the case of property we should distinguish between the question of the *definition* of property, the question why and in what circumstances it is a *good* institution to maintain, and the question in what ways individuals may become *entitled* to acquire property and *how much* they should be allowed to acquire. These we may call questions of *Definition, General Justifying Aim*, and *Distribution*. . . [17]

Hart goes on to observe 'how much darkness is spread by the use of a single notion ("the labour of a man's body and the work of his hands") to answer all these different questions' in Locke's discussion of property. I think that is extraordinarily unfair to Locke. His discussion, as we have seen, is sufficiently complex to offer independent observations on all these questions; certainly he offers quite different answers to the first two. In any case, Hart wants to insist that 'the beginning of wisdom is to distinguish similar questions and confront them separately'.[18]

I am inclined to agree with this general strategy so far as the first two of Hart's questions are concerned. In Chapter 2 we set out explicitly to offer an account of the concept of private property which was independent of any view about how private property could be defended (though, as we saw, this cannot be done with particular conceptions of that concept). But the requirements of wisdom are not nearly so clear in the case of the last two. Whether an account of the General Justifying Aim of an institution generates any implications so far as distribution is concerned depends entirely on the character of the General Justifying Aim and the 'shape', so to speak, of the justification that is being offered. If the General Justifying Aim is goal-based, then it may well be that distributive questions can be dealt with separately. For example, the utilitarian argument that private property is a necessary condition for a free

[17] Hart, *Punishment and Responsibility*, p. 4.
[18] Ibid.

market which is in turn a necessary condition for economic prosperity may generate no distributive conclusions apart from the general requirements that there must not be monopolies and that people with holdings must be free to exchange them more or less as they please. But this is not so in the case of right-based justifications. If I justify representative government, for example, on the ground that people should participate in the making of the laws which are to bind them, I cannot then go on to say that it is an open question, to be confronted separately, how and on what basis the franchise should be distributed. The General Justifying Aim that I have identified *dictates* a conclusion about distribution; and it leaves no further questions open in that regard.

Similarly, in the case of property. If I say that the General Justifying Aim of the institution of private property is to foster the development of individual liberty, then unless I am treating liberty merely as a social goal (e.g. 'It would be a good thing if there were quite a bit of liberty about'), I am committed immediately to a particular approach to distribution. Since I evince a concern that liberty should be regarded as important in the case of each individual, and since I want to argue that the possession of private property is necessary for the development of liberty, I cannot then go on to say that the distribution of property is something to be determined on quite separate grounds which have nothing to do with this General Justifying Aim. To put this another way: in the right-based tradition at least, the justification of an institution like private property just *is* a matter of showing the importance of a certain distribution of goods, liberties, and opportunities for individuals. This is most striking in the case of SR-based justifications: for there the case for private property is nothing more than the case that can be made out for saying that Jones is to be the owner of Whiteacre, Smith is to be the owner of Moorsfield, and so on. But it is true of GR-based arguments as well.

4. EQUALITY?

This leads us to the issue of equality. We have seen that universalizability requires us to take the case for property based on positive freedom equally seriously in the case of all men (or in the case of all who have a taste for freedom). Does that generate (as

Proudhon thought) a requirement that all private property should be equal, and that no one should own more or less resources than anybody else? In section 5 of Chapter 10 we shall see that Hegel presented a cogent case for a negative answer to this question. In the present section, I shall argue to a somewhat similar conclusion using a distinction established by David Miller.

In his article 'Arguments for Equality', Miller sought to distinguish between genuine egalitarian arguments and 'arguments in which equality figures only incidentally'. He located what he called 'entitlement arguments' (not to be confused with historical entitlement arguments) in the latter category: 'These hold that each person is entitled to achieve a certain condition C; when this demand is met, it is in an obvious sense true that all are equal insofar as all have achieved C.'[19] For example, C may be good health or being adequately accommodated or educated. Arguments about the right to liberty are of this type: in these arguments C is *being a free man*. Now C itself may be a point on a scale that extends in both directions: it is possible to be less than C or more than C (or perhaps 'more C'—in better health, better educated, more free, etc.) According to what Miller calls an entitlement argument, if anyone is less than C, that is a matter for grave moral concern: his interest in being at least C is sufficiently important to justify holding others to be under a duty in this regard. But what if someone is above C and could move further above it; does that warrant proportionate moral concern? The answer in most cases will be 'No'. The man may have an interest in rising further on the C-scale, and we may think that interest ought to be taken into account in social decision-making, but it will not necessarily attract the same concern as the increment in well-being necessary to bring someone up to C. Of course, this depends on what sort of condition C is. If it is a threshold or achievement condition, like being literate, or like being a free man according to most positive conceptions of liberty, then improving someone's situation above C will not have anything like the same urgency as bringing somebody up to C. But even if it is not a threshold condition (if, for example, C is like being healthy or being fit), we may expect the intensity of the moral concern to tail off gradually the more one rises on the C-scale. In the latter case, the concern will continue to exhibit a certain egalitarian character: the level of concern that X should be so far up

[19] Miller, 'Arguments for Equality', p. 75.

the C-scale will match exactly the level of concern that Y should be that far up the C-scale, even though neither will match the level of concern that Z should be brought up from a position much further down below them. But in the former case, the egalitarian element may disappear altogether once everyone has reached the threshold C, and the entitlement theorist may be, as Miller suggests, indifferent between all states of affairs in which everyone has reached C but some are ranged variously above it and the state of affairs in which each person just achieves C.[20]

Similar points can be made in relation to the distribution of the goods that are necessary for improving one's position on the C-scale. As Miller observes, entitlement arguments seem to generate a requirement of equality of resources 'only in the very special case where there are just enough resources to satisfy everyone's entitlement'.[21] Above and below that point, the requirement of equality seems problematic. Suppose that there are more than enough resources: then the considerations outlined in the previous paragraph together with an account of the relation between resource-increments and C-increments will determine the nature of our concern about the distribution of the surplus. In the case of the arguments we have been considering in this chapter, it seems likely to be true *both* that C (positive liberty) is an achievement or threshold condition *and* that increments in the amount of resources owned above the level necessary to secure C do not correlate proportionately with increments on the C-scale. Or, to put it more simply: even if positive liberty requires the ownership of private property, still once positive liberty has been achieved, it is not the case that the more property you own the freer you are.

I have said nothing so far about how much private property a person may need in order to be free. If the concern is simply that everyone should have *some* property, it might seem as though it were enough to offer everyone a piece of furniture or a book which he could call his own. It might seem as though the GR-based arguments required nothing more than that sort of minimum. Resources surplus to this requirement might then be distributed unequally or arbitrarily, or even held under different types of property rule. For example, we might give everyone private property in some trivial resource but ensure that all economically

---

[20] Miller, 'Arguments for Equality', p.75.
[21] Ibid.

important resources remained under collective control. Whether such an arrangement would be sufficient depends entirely on the details of the particular GR-based argument, and on what exactly in that argument the contribution of property to liberty is supposed to be. For example, in an argument such as Hegel's, where ownership is supposed to contribute to the development of a settled sense of responsibility, it may turn out that this contribution requires an individual to have property rights in resources that he takes seriously as necessary for his well-being; unless that is true, he may not care enough what happens to them while they are in his hands. But if it is like the Aristotelian argument (discussed in Chapter 1), where the importance of private property is related to an opportunity to practise the moral virtue of generosity, it may be that nothing more than the ownership of a few treasured baubles and trinkets is required.

5. SCARCITY

What if material resources are scarce relative to the demands which a GR-based theory of property places upon them? What if there are simply not enough resources to give everyone the amount of property which our favourite argument deems necessary for the development of his freedom? We need to distinguish two cases here: one is the situation of sheer material scarcity (where the shortage is much more acute than that normally assumed as one of the background circumstances of justice);[22] the other is the familiar situation in which even if there are in principle enough resources to go round, the dynamics of a private property system continually generate situations in which many are left propertyless. I will postpone consideration of the second case until Chapter 12.

Here is one view to consider. I cannot claim that I have the right, as a human being, to some good or opportunity if, as things stand, it is a necessary condition of my having that good or opportunity that it be denied to other human beings who have, so far as my argument is concerned, an equally valid claim to it. Universalizability dictates a rejection of my moral claim in these circumstances or, at least, its reformulation in other (perhaps goal-based or SR-based) terms. Similarly in the case of property. An individual

[22] Cf. Ch. 2, n. 11, above.

cannot claim that his having property is a necessary condition for his development or fulfilment *qua* free man if it is the case that his having private property in scarce resources would necessarily involve its denial to other individuals on behalf of whom an identical case for having property could be made out. On this view, the scarcity of material resources threatens to undermine GR-based arguments in favour of private property.

Another view which might also undermine such arguments is based on the dictum '*Ought* implies *Can*'. I cannot say that an interest of mine is sufficiently important to justify holding others to be under a duty to serve it, if it is in fact the case that there is nothing those others can do which would promote or protect that interest. Thus I cannot say that I have a *right* to private property if nobody is in a position to conjure up the resources that would be needed to satisfy that right. But this view rests on a mistake. Provided only that there are *some* resources in the world rather than none at all, it is true that in the case of each person we *can* see to it that *he* has private property in a significant holding of material resources, even if somebody (or everybody) else has to be dispossessed. So scarcity cannot be used as a basis for denying, in his case, that he has a right to private property which generates duties on us. What is true is that we cannot satisfy *all* these rights jointly; but, of course, since rights claims are made severally, rather than jointly, and since the duties they impose are generated one by one out of the moral importance accorded to individual interests, this is not a logical obstacle.

A right to private property is not the only right which places demands on scarce resources. Others include a right to basic medical care, to a decent minimum standard of living, to an elementary education, and so on. In the case of all these rights, it is not possible to solve the problem of scarcity by distributing resources equally, for an equal distribution might mean that *no one* was brought anywhere near the threshold specified as important in the right. The choice may be between satisfying some rights but not all, and satisfying none. But if that is the choice, how are we to determine rationally whose rights should be satisfied? Some philosophers have used this sort of a dilemma as a basis for arguing that the so-called 'socio-economic' rights do not really exist, and that rights talk should be confined to cases where individual interests impose merely *negative* duties, understood as side-constraints, and where no problem of scarcity can conceivably arise.[23] I do not think, though, that the problem is insuperable. Most of us believe—whether we use the language of rights or not—that all individuals have interests in acquiring an education, in having a basic subsistence, and in receiving the basic medical care that they need, and that these interests are sufficiently important to justify holding anyone who can serve them to be under some sort of moral requirement to do so. Now, when the resources necessary to serve these interests are scarce, we tend to think along the following lines. First, we will say that each person has a claim on the stock of available resources and that, even when there are not enough resources to go round, this claim remains in play constraining the production of other resources (requiring, for example, that we produce more necessities when we have the opportunity rather than more luxuries) and placing demands on the distribution of any further resources of the appropriate sort as and when they come to hand. Secondly, we will look for some principle for determining who should get the benefit of the resources that are currently available. Perhaps we will say that as many rights as possible should be satisfied, or perhaps we will recommend some sort of queuing system ('First come, first served'), or some other principle which respects in a 'second-best' sort of way the equal claim that all have to be served. Thirdly, even when the exigencies of such a situation require trade-offs to be made, we will think that the rights of those who lose out should evoke some degree of compunction, apology, and maybe even compensation in other respects.[24]

A fourth consideration has to do with the connection between rights and self-interest which we considered at the end of Chapter 3; and I am much less certain about it. All of us are inclined at times to prefer serving our own interests to the objectively equally important interests of others, and usually that preference is regarded as antipathetic to morality and moral duty. Talk of rights, however, is a way of drawing attention to the element of self-interest which it is morally respectable for a person to assert and without which he cannot be expected to respond to other more stringent demands of moral duty. Perhaps this has consequences not only for the way rights are asserted but also for the way in which people may respond to the demands imposed by rights when resources are scarce. If an individual is already in fact using scarce resources to promote or protect some interest regarded as the basis

[23] e.g. Nozick, *Anarchy, State, and Utopia*, p. 238.
[24] See Ch.3, sect. 3 (ii), above.

of a right, then perhaps he is entitled to resist any attempt to take those resources away from him, even an attempt made in the name of the equally pressing interests of others. If we accept that his interests have a natural priority *for him* over the identical interests of others, then we can make sense of his saying 'What I have I hold' in circumstances where it is clear that there is not enough for everyone. (It will be worth asking then—though I cannot answer this now—whether the egoistic aspect of rights therefore introduces a minimal agent-relative aspect into the picture, so far as the exercise and vindication of one's rights is concerned.)[25] But I am not sure how far this line can be pushed. Does it, for example, lead us to say that others who have nothing are obliged to respect the holdings of those who take this attitude? Perhaps not: after all, *their* interest in getting hold of the resources will be as compelling in their case as his interest is in hanging on to them. There is, at any rate, no inconsistency in saying that, if two parties have an equal right to some scarce resource in circumstances where there is not enough to satisfy both, it is not impermissible for the one party to try and gain possession of the resource, and it is not impermissible for the party in possession to resist that attempt. Some philosophers have argued that paradoxes of this sort are sufficient to refute ethical egoism; but they do so only on the basis of a hidden premiss that the function of a moral theory is to provide a basis for the resolution of conflict.[26] In the present context—the area of legitimate egoism established by a theory of rights—the assumption of scarcity means that premiss cannot be sustained.

6. APPROPRIATION

If private property is defended on GR-based grounds, what becomes of appropriation?

One answer goes as follows. Since individuals have a right to own private property, it is morally permissible for them to take possession of any natural resources they come across and to use them and exclude others from their use on the basis that the resources are to be regarded as their private property. Since individuals need not only material sustenance but also to be owners

[25] But cf. the discussion of self-interest in Parfit, *Reasons and Persons*, Ch. 6.
[26] See the discussion in Medlin, 'Ultimate Principles and Ethical Egoism', and Kalin, 'In Defence of Egoism'.

(in order to become fully free), no-one can have any objection if someone takes what he needs in this sense. Since each individual has a right to private property, each individual has a right to do what amounts in effect to setting up a private property system as far as his control of material resources is concerned. Even though the right to private property is a universal and equal right, an individual does no wrong in taking what he has a right to unilaterally for himself without considering the needs of others. For either there are enough resources for others to satisfy their need in this respect or there are not: if there are, then they can go ahead and do what he has done, and they have in any case no cause for complaint; if there are not, then it is better, from a right-based point of view, that some get what they have a right to than that none do, and there is no reason why he should not have put himself into the privileged group.

This line of argument is persuasive up to a point. We have already speculated that, under conditions of scarcity, a right-based approach may license an individual's insistence on 'What I have I hold', where what he holds is no more than what he has a right to. But two qualifications need to be noticed. First, appropriation is not the only basis on which a system of private property might be set up, though it has been regarded, largely under the influence of Lockean theories, as the most 'natural'. Other bases for such a system might include Humean conventionalism where in effect an existing distribution of possession established by force is transformed into a system of private property by consent, or a fully consensual arrangement where there is time and opportunity for members of a society to agree upon a private property system and to distribute resources fairly to one another.[27]

Secondly, it does not follow from the argument outlined in the previous paragraph that the full moral weight of the GR-based argument for private property is transferred to the individual holdings acquired by appropriation, so that a man who has taken possession of a piece of land may resist subsequent expropriation in the name of 'the right to property'. Whether he can or not depends largely on the size of his holding. If the appropriated holding is no greater than the minimum that the individual has a right to be the owner of, then the general right to property transfers its moral weight to the defence of that holding, since expropriation to *any*

[27] Hume, *Treatise*, Bk. III, Pt. ii, sect. 2, p. 489. (For a more recent version of the Humean view, see Buchanan, *Limits of Liberty*.)

degree would leave the individual in effect propertyless. But if the holding is larger, expropriation of the surplus cannot be resisted on that ground, particularly if it is undertaken in order to satisfy other people's rights to private property. Thus, the mere fact that an appropriation took place in the name of the right to property does not give it any special moral status and does not create a special entitlement to the holding that is appropriated. Appropriation is simply a *means* whereby individuals come to be the owners of things; it has no special moral significance in its own right, on this sort of approach.

Some right-based theories, however, may give appropriation a more than merely instrumental significance. Perhaps it is the act of taking possession of something which is important from the point of view of liberty: this may be so, for example, in some of the theories of liberty as self-assertion discussed in Chapter 8, and we shall discuss this possibility again in more detail in Chapter 11. But, on the whole, the arguments we have been considering draw attention to the importance of ownership itself, and the exercise of the rights and powers of an owner, rather than to the importance of the *acquisition* of those rights. In terms of the arguments on which we have concentrated, the fact that in capitalist society no one is forbidden to make an appropriation of unowned resources is not good enough. As T. H. Green put it:

[T]he actual development of rights of property in Europe . . . has so far been a state of things in which all indeed *may* have property, but great numbers in fact cannot have it in that sense in which alone it is of value, viz. as a permanent apparatus for carrying out a plan of life, for expressing ideas of what is beautiful, or giving effect to benevolent wishes. In the eye of the law they have rights of appropriation, but in fact they have not the chance of providing means for a free moral life, of developing and giving reality or expression to a good will, an interest in social well-being.[28]

For these arguments, then, the logic of the Proudhon strategy is irresistible:

Well, is it not true . . . that if the liberty of man is sacred, it is equally sacred in all individuals; that, if it needs property for its objective action, that is, for its life, the appropriation of material is equally necessary for all; that if I wish to be respected in my right of appropriation, I must respect others in theirs; and consequently, that though, in the sphere of the infinite, a

[28] Green, *Lectures on Political Obligation*, Lect. N, p. 219.

person's power of appropriation is limited only by himself, in the sphere of the finite this same power of appropriation is limited by the mathematical relation between the number of persons and the space which they occupy? Does it not follow that if one individual cannot prevent another—his fellow-man—from appropriating an amount of material equal to his own, no more can he prevent individuals yet to come; because, while individuality passes away, universality persists, and eternal laws cannot be determined by a partial view of their manifestations? Must we not conclude, therefore, that whenever a person is born, the others must crowd closer together . . . ?[29]

So appropriation must never be considered or justified as an isolated individual action: 'I maintain that the element of time must be considered also; for if the first occupants have occupied everything, what are the new comers to do? What will become of them, having an instrument with which to work, but no material to work upon?'[30] The answer is that the propertyless or their representatives are entitled to intervene collectively to limit or redistribute the appropriated resources so that as many individual rights as possible are satisfied out of the available stock:

One hundred thousand men settle in a large country like France with no inhabitants: each man has a right to 1/100,000 of the land. If the number of possessors increases, each one's portion diminishes in consequence; so that if the number of inhabitants rises to thirty-four millions, each one will have a right only to 1/34,000,000. Now, so regulate the police system and the government, labour, exchange, inheritance, &c., that the means of labour shall be shared by all equally, and that each individual shall be free; and then society will be perfect.[31]

Such social intervention cannot then be resisted in the name of the sacredness of appropriation, for the intervention is undertaken for the sake of the very rights on the basis of which original appropriation was supposed to be justified.

We end up, then, with something like a strong Lockean proviso on the basis of which redistributive intervention may be justified. Everyone when he appropriates must, if he takes more than the minimum, leave enough for others to acquire the resources that they need to own in order to be free. If he appropriates more than that and if the amount he appropriates is more than he needs to

[29] Proudhon, *What is Property?*, pp. 66–7.
[30] Ibid. 65–6.
[31] Ibid. 67.

own in order to be free, then his claim to the surplus is very weak and it is liable to be redistributed. This limit, we see now, can be justified in a GR-based based defence of private property even though, as we saw in Chapter 6, it could not be justified in the Lockean tradition with which it has usually been associated. It derives its force directly from the claim that everyone has a right to be the owner of enough property to make him a free man—a claim that is not made or argued for in Locke's or Nozick's theories of property.

Of course, the whole position may have to be qualified by the proviso which we did insist would have to be inserted into SR-based theories as well: the proviso that ownership rights cannot prevail in the face of abject material need. In the present context, this is a matter of a straight conflict of different rights: the right of all individuals to be the owners of enough property to make them free versus the right of all individuals to the material wherewithal for survival. If we take the contractarian approach to problems of this sort set out in Chapter 7, then we may have to say that the latter right prevails in conflicts of this sort, since the unsatisfied need for material subsistence is likely to be more compelling for individuals than the unsatisfied need to be an owner and to be free. But that is just a hunch; I do not have an argument to show that this must be so.

10

Hegel's Discussion of Property

1. THE NATURE OF HEGEL'S ARGUMENT

Hegel's account of property in the *Philosophy of Right*[1] provides us with the best example we have of a sustained argument in favour of private ownership which is GR-based, in the sense I have given that term. In this chapter, I am going to examine that account in some detail. The interpretation I shall offer highlights Hegel's theory of the importance of property for the development of individual freedom. I shall show that his argument, if taken seriously, requires not just that there should *be* an institution of private property in any society or that existing property entitlements should be respected, but—more radically—that property is something which it is important for every individual to have, so that there is a basis for overriding ethical concern if some people are left poor and property*less*.

The description of Hegel's account of property as a GR-based argument is likely to be controversial. In the first place, it may be disputed whether Hegel is even offering an *argument* for private property. Secondly, even if he is, it may seem odd to describe his argument as *right-based*. Hegel's account of the importance of property has none of the 'absolutist' spirit usually associated with rights-talk: he explicitly cautions us that individual rights of property, such as they are, cannot be expected to prevail over or to 'trump' any of the demands that might be made for the realization or maintenance of a genuine ethical community or state.

Thirdly, even if we are convinced that Hegel's account can be regarded as a right-based argument, we may still doubt whether it is a theory of general, as opposed to special, rights. It is true that Hegel gives an account of the importance of property to individuals

---

[1] Parenthetical references in the text are to section numbers in the Knox translation of the *Philosophy of Right*. The addition R indicates one of the explanatory notes that Hegel appended to many of the sections, and A the less authoritative glosses collected at the end of the book.

and that he takes its importance for each individual as the basis for articulating a demand of justice 'that everyone must have property' (49A). But he also sets out a theory of First Occupancy to account for the genesis and justification of particular property entitlements; and it appears, on the face of it, that this part of the theory simply uses the argument about the general ethical importance of property-owning to underpin an SR-based account of individual entitlements in the style of Locke or Nozick.

This third worry is obviously of crucial importance to my interpretation. But I do not want to discuss it in any more detail at this stage. I have introduced it now only to make explicit the overall problem of this chapter. We are to look at Hegel's account of property to discern how far he compromised the GR-based character of his argument by introducing a First Occupancy element, and how far he ought to have compromised it or needed to compromise it in this respect. The question will be taken up explicitly in the final section of the chapter once we have examined the argument in detail and considered the difficulties it faces.

But the other two worries—(i) does Hegel's discussion yield an argument for private property? And (ii) if so, is it a *right-based* argument?—are difficulties that do have to be dealt with as preliminary points.

(i) Does Hegel Have an Argument for Private Property?

In his preface, Hegel castigates those philosophers who engage in purely speculative thinking in ethics. He contrasts them with natural philosophers in this respect. Philosophers of nature or natural scientists acknowledge 'that it is nature as it is which philosophy has to bring within its ken' and that their task is to discern the rational order and harmony which lie behind the appearances. But in ethics, everyone is convinced that his mere birthright entitles him to put forward ethical schemes, to criticize the status quo for its failure to conform to some speculative Utopia, and to support existing institutions only to the extent that they match the details of some purely intellectual construction. Hegel's invective against this way of doing ethics and his concern about its consequences for philosophy and indeed for the conduct of social and political life is bitter and sustained in the preface. In interpreting his discussion of property in the *Philosophy of Right*, therefore, we must avoid attributing to Hegel the style that he criticized so severely in his contemporaries.[2]

Hegel takes himself to be offering primarily an *understanding* of the institutions of social life: 'to comprehend what is, this is the task of philosophy, because what is, is reason' (preface). Private property was an existent institution that Hegel saw in the world around him. He argued that its existence was a rational necessity, not a merely accidental feature of human history; in other words, he took it upon himself to display the rationality inherent in the actuality of private ownership. This is what he is doing in the discussion of property.

So the account of property in the *Philosophy of Right* is not straightforwardly prescriptive. It would be equally mistaken, however, to characterize it merely as descriptive sociology.[3] The understanding which Hegel is seeking to evince is necessarily an *evaluative* understanding since, on his theory, to comprehend the rational necessity of an institution provides the only standpoint from which evaluation makes sense. We must also bear in mind that Hegel's theory is not an account of social statics: he takes himself to be characterizing society not just as it is but as it is coming to be.[4] If we are led to agree with Hegel that private property is a rational necessity, then we will be inclined to give a positive evaluation of some features of society (those that represent a progressive tendency towards private ownership) and a negative evaluation or an evaluation of tired indifference of others (those features of society and social thought which the institution of private ownership is destined to supersede).

That Hegel's discussion has this critical edge is apparent from one or two peripheral comments that he makes about ancient and contemporary ideas and institutions.

He writes, for example, of 'a clash' in the agrarian laws of ancient Rome 'between public and private ownership of land' and suggests that rationality, as expressed in the argument for property, would favour the latter over the former even at the expense of other vested rights (46R). Certainly the communist Utopias of ancient

---

[2] See Taylor, *Hegel*, pp. 403 ff. and 421.

[3] For the idea of interpreting Hegel's work as 'sociology', see the comment by Ryan, *Property and Political Theory*, p. 119.

[4] There is a lucid account of Hegel's early thought on the historical development of economic and political life in Plant, *Hegel*; see also Chamley, *Économie Politique et Philosophie*.

philosophy are rejected. Hegel attacks Plato's account of the guardians' way of life in the *Republic* (46R and 185R) and the communist ethics of Epicurus (46R). The failure of the ancients to grasp what he calls 'the principle of the freedom of property' (62R) led them to develop accounts of legal personality that were, on his account, quite irrational (40R). For example, the Roman provision which takes children to be the property of their parents is described as 'unjustifiable and unethical' (40R). Moreover, the existence in Greece and Rome of the institution of slavery made it impossible for ancient lawyers to develop simultaneously adequate conceptions of property and man (2R).[5]

If we turn to contemporary institutions, we find Hegel using his account of property to attack the lingering remnants of feudal land law. The distinction between the complete use of an object and the ownership of it—a distinction which lies at the bottom of the system of feudal tenure—is described as 'an "insanity of personality"' (62R) since it implies, on Hegel's understanding of property, the exclusive presence in an object of the will of one person (the sole user) and the simultaneous exclusive presence in that object of the will of someone else (the owner). There is a similar absurdity, he suggests, in certain types of family testamentary trusts (see 46R and 63A). These methods of tying up property, so that it is beyond the ultimate control of the particular people using it, should be done away with if Hegel's principle of the freedom of property were to be accepted.

On the positive side, Hegel argues that a number of apparently objectionable practices may actually be seen to be justified, once his account of property is accepted. The dissolution of the monasteries is one example; it had the excellent result of transferring resources from collective ownership into private hands (46A).[6] Similarly the account justifies various rules of prescription. If, for instance, a public memorial loses its character as a symbol of national remembrance or whatever through the passing of time, then it should cease to count as public property and be open to legitimate appropriation at the hands of the first comer (46R).

Thus, while Hegel rebukes 'the impatience of opinion' that would call for the instant establishment in society of the institutions

---

[5] Note also Hegel's suggestion: 'It is in the nature of the case that a slave has an absolute right to free himself . . . ' (*Philosophy of Right*, sect. 66A).

[6] See also Hegel, 'English Reform Bill', p. 305.

he has shown to be rationally necessary (62R), he is prepared to use his account of that necessity as a basis for some practical criticism and evaluation. We must remember that this evaluation is not intended to have a speculative or Utopian character. But, for all that, it is open to us to interpret the discussion as an evaluatively significant account of the importance of private property and to enquire into the sort of argument that is used to establish that importance.

(ii) Is Hegel's Argument Right-based?

I have defined a right-based argument as an argument based primarily on a concern for the promotion of some individual interest. If an individual's interest in some state of affairs, S, is regarded, taken by itself, as a ground for imposing a duty on others to bring S about or to maintain or protect S, then S is being argued for in a right-based way. Right-based arguments have been distinguished from utilitarian arguments because the latter argue for social arrangements on the basis of their net effect on all individual interests rather than on the basis of individual interests one by one.

Now Hegel did not believe that there was ultimately any distinction between the collective interest of a community and the individual interests of the members of that community. That the goals of the community to which he belongs should be pursued and realized— *that* is the ultimate interest of each individual. Does it make sense, then, to say that Hegel's argument for property is a right-based rather than, say, a utilitarian argument? Certainly, the relation between individual interests and collective goals is more complex in Hegel's philosophy than in most other political theories, including utilitarianism.[7] Nevertheless, there are (at least) two reasons why the distinction still makes sense so far as the argument about property is concerned.

First, Hegel's theory is a developmental theory. He denies that individuals are born *ready* for the ethical community in which rights and collective goals come together. This is something that they must grow up into. Part of that growth—as we shall see, a crucial part—is the establishment of a clear sense of oneself as a person, that is, as an individual right-bearer. It is at this stage that

---

[7] For an excellent discussion, see Taylor, *Hegel*, pp. 378 ff.

property is taken to be important. The fact that individuals may attain a higher stage of development, according to Hegel's theory, at which the distinction between individual interests and social goals appears specious does not mean that the distinction is unimportant at the earlier stages. Certainly, we would misunderstand the nature of the argument for property completely if we were to identify it, in any sense, merely as a collective goal of the Hegelian state.

Secondly, the ethical community or state which represents the final end of the process which Hegel is describing is not regarded as an intrinsically rights-abrogating or rights-transcending collective. On the contrary, Hegel argues that individual rights receive their highest recognition *as such* in a community of this kind:

The essence of the modern state is that the universal be bound up with the complete freedom of its particular members and with private well-being. . . . Thus the universal must be furthered, but subjectivity on the other hand must attain its full and living development. It is only when both these moments subsist in their strength that the state can be regarded as articulated and genuinely organised. (260A)

In such a community, individual rights and social goals no longer appear antagonistic to one another, but it may still make sense to distinguish between them.[8]

This helps us deal with another difficulty involved in calling Hegel's argument for private property right-based. The argument, as we have seen, is a developmental one. Property is shown to be necessary, not in absolute or final terms, but as a stage in a process of individual and social development.[9] Individuals have real interests which justify the demand for private property; but those interests are seen by Hegel only as necessary moments in a wider development of individuality which may, in its later stages, make the case for property or our concern about it appear trite and

---

[8] I believe John Charvet exaggerates the collectivism of Hegel's theory of the state when he writes: 'The individual, as this person, has no value as an end, but only as a means. In this sense, individuality is absorbed into and destroyed by the life of the universal.' (Charvet, *Critique of Freedom and Equality*, pp. 134–5). A better view is found in Taylor, *Hegel*, p. 388, and Ryan, *Property and Political Theory*, p. 133. For changes in Hegel's account of the relation between the individual and society, see Ilting, 'Hegel's Concept of the State', pp. 100 ff.

[9] Ryan puts it this way: 'Property is only one way in which modern man finds himself at home in the modern world' (*Property and Political Theory*, p. 131). But this is misleading if it is meant to suggest Hegel believed that there were other equally good *substitutes* for private property in this regard.

immature. In presenting the case for property, Hegel is at pains to stress that the subject for whom property is demanded is a *natural, immediate,* and *abstract* being rather than a full individual participating in ethical life. The subject for whom property is demanded stands at the beginning of the long and arduous process of education and discipline which Hegal claims is required before final liberation and individuality is achieved (187R). At the stage where property is in question, his individuality is described as 'trivial' (35A) even 'false' (41A and 57R) individuality, and the rights based on it are regarded as 'elementary', purely 'formal' (30R), and, from the sublime perspective of the ethical individual, even 'contemptible' in character (35A).

This has important practical consequences. In the higher phases of individuals' development, they will acquire interests justifying structures and institutions which may, to some extent, be incompatible with the demands of a right to property. In this case, there is no question of the right to property prevailing against or 'trumping' these higher demands.[10] Even as he expounds his principle of property, and draws from it the practical conclusions that we have already discussed, Hegel takes care to warn us that 'the specific characteristics pertaining to "private" property may have to be subordinated to a higher sphere of right (e.g. to a society or a state) . . . ' (46R). For example, the patriotic interest of the state may demand the widespread abrogation of property rights and even the sacrifice of life itself (324). So if the right of property clashes with the demands of ethical life, then, in so far as the latter can be formulated as categorical demands, the former must be subordinated to them. 'It is only the right of the world-mind which is absolute without qualification' (30R). For an individual to insist, say, against the state that his property or his right to property should remain inviolate would, on Hegel's view, be an absurdity: it would be to parade the claims of his lesser self against the demands of his higher self in its final realization.[11]

But a putative right that yields in the face of every collective goal is not a right at all: it does no work of its own in the political theory that postulates it.[12] Perhaps there is a danger that a right to property as submissive as this may turn out in the end to be empty.

[10] For the idea of rights as 'trumps' over social goals, see Dworkin, *Taking Rights Seriously*, p. xi *et passim*. See also Dworkin, 'Rights as Trumps'.
[11] See Stillman, 'Property, Freedom and Individuality', pp. 145–6.
[12] Dworkin, *Taking Rights Seriously*, p. 92

We must be careful not to overstate this danger. First, we should note that Hegel's position is certainly not the position sometimes attributed to Marx: that, at a certain point in history, an economy organized around private ownership is necessary as an indispensable stage on the road to socialism, but that at a later stage in history, when human nature reaches its culminating development, private property will become entirely redundant. Untangling the ontogenetic from the phylogenetic strands in Hegel's developmental theory is not an easy business,[13] but this at least is clear: the case for private property given in the *Philosophy of Right* is a case which may be made by or for any individual at any juncture in history, once the idea of freedom and with it the idea of property have entered the world. Even if a Hegelian state exists and the institutions are there to make the fullest ethical life possible, *still* it is the case, according to Hegel, that 'everyone must have property' (49A). For his thesis is that without property, no man can develop to the stage where he is capable of responding to the sort of demands to which the principle of property might properly be subordinated. So the fact that a society has reached the stage, in terms of its history and institutions, where ethical life is possible does not mean that individuals can take a 'shortcut' to the ethical life without going through the sordid business of property-ownership.[14] The institution of property takes the individual a few steps up the ladder to ethical fulfilment. There are many other steps to be taken before self-realization is achieved. But, even so far as the stage of private property is concerned, it is, on Hegel's theory, only the *individual* who is ever in a position to 'throw away the ladder after he has climbed up it'.[15] Neither the community nor history can do it for him. And for the community to kick away the ladder from someone who had not even got on to it, in the name of some higher stage of his potential development, would be absurd.

It follows that the case for private property has some weight even in societies where an ethical community or Hegelian state is in existence. Even these advanced societies must not embrace communism or tolerate the institutions of feudal tenure, for that would be to deny emergent individuals the opportunity to develop to the point where they can participate fully in the life of that community.

[13] See e.g. the bewildering attack on Condillac in Hegel, *Philosophy of Mind*, sect. 442, pp. 183 ff.

[14] This point is emphasized in Ritter, 'Personne et Propriété selon Hegel', p. 188.

[15] Cf. Wittgenstein, *Tractatus*, prop. 6. 54.

Secondly, although the right to property is not absolute, still it is not just any demand that can override its requirements: 'the exceptions to private property cannot be grounded in chance, in private caprice, or private advantage, but only in the rational organism of the state' (46R). The right of property is to be subordinated only to those rights to which it is, in its basis, functionally subordinate anyway. It has, on the other hand, weight as against purely utilitarian considerations. As we shall see throughout this chapter, Hegel adamantly refuses to make out his case for private property on the grounds that it is an efficient means of satisfying physical wants or needs. It is to be given a rational justification which will be sufficient to trump any argument suggesting that needs would be satisfied more efficiently in a socialist economy. This does not mean that Hegel did not take needs seriously or regard their fulfilment as a worthy aim; on the contrary, he regarded 'the securing of every single person's livelihood and welfare' as an aim of considerable importance in civil society (230). But it is an aim which is subordinate to the ethical case for private property.

Thus it is not altogether out of order to describe Hegel's argument for private property as a right-based argument.

2. PERSONALITY AND THE WORLD

Hegel's claim is that property is something everyone needs in order to develop his freedom and individuality. What are his reasons for this?

(i) Needs, Personality, and Freedom

One might try to state a case as follows. People cannot be free unless their basic physical needs are satisfied. Those needs can be satisfied only by the sort of objects which we usually think of as the objects of property—food, clothing, housing, land, tools, and medicine. Such an argument is no doubt interesting, as far as it goes, but it would be an insecure basis for an argument for *private* property. After all, physical needs could be satisfied under some non-private system of property, under a system of collective property, for instance. Private property is not the only system under which physical needs can be satisfied, and it may not even be true that needs are satisfied more efficiently under private property than under any other system. (Whether this is so is a matter for the utilitarian defenders and critics of the institution.)[16]

In any case, when he discusses property Hegel puts the question of the satisfaction of physical needs to one side. Certainly it is, he says, 'the particular interest satisfied by possession' (45) in the sense that the satisfaction of needs and wants has to be invoked to explain why particular things are taken into possession by particular people. Those who own property are concrete individuals who feed, clothe, house, and enjoy themselves with what they own. But Hegel wants to argue that proprietors will also find a deeper ethical significance in their ownership of property—one that has to do, not with their biological nature, but with their status as potentially free wills.

Hegel's account of the relation between freedom and needs is a complex one. As a natural being, man feels needs, desires, and impulses of every sort. His first experience of freedom is his ability to abstract himself in thought from every particular need or inclination—to say of such needs 'They are not necessarily mine,' and to preoccupy his mind with the pure thought of himself. Now on its own, this is a depraved condition: it is 'the Hindu fanaticism of pure contemplation' or, in practical life, the nihilistic 'fanaticism of destruction' (5R). Its ethical importance lies in the individual's ability to relate the pure abstracted thought of himself straight back to particular needs and desires and to associate them with it, so that they take on the character of chosen rather than merely given aims or ends—aims and ends which are in a strong sense *his* rather than merely happening where he is.[17]

The main thesis in the *Philosophy of Right* (which we will not subject to critical examination here) is that this ability is implicitly universal—not just in the sense that all men have it, but also in the sense that, in each man, the ability is a local manifestation of a single universal ability, which is the Idea or the Concept of

---

[16] See the discussion, above, in Ch.1, sect. 2, Ch.6, sect. 6, and Chapter Nine. For Hegel's attitude towards utilitarianism, see *Philosophy of Right* sect. 187. More generally, see: Walton, 'Economy, Utility and Community', p. 247; Ryan, 'Hegel on Work, Ownership and Citizenship', p. 183; and Cooper, 'Hegel's Theory of Punishment'.

[17] There are affinities here with the notion of autonomy outlined in Ch.8, and in Frankfurt, 'Freedom of the Will'.

freedom.[18] Hegel's undertaking in the *Philosophy of Right* is to show how this universal ability, initially present in every individual, is developed, brought forth, and made explicit as something worthwhile in itself in concrete forms of social life.

That is the agenda. At the stage where property enters the picture, we are dealing with discrete individuals becoming aware of this freedom in themselves. They take themselves to be capable of abstracting their will from given impulses and inclinations, and so the needs and wants on which their will settles take on the character of resolutions or chosen ends rather than mere natural afflictions (13). To conceive of oneself in this way is to regard oneself as a *person*. 'A person', Hegel writes, 'is a unit of freedom aware of its sheer independence' (35A). To be a person is just to be a subject preoccupied self-consciously with the freedom of one's will.

It is with regard to their *personality,* rather than their status as natural beings driven by needs, that private property is important to individuals. As we shall see, Hegel argues that individuals need private property in order to sustain and develop the abilities and self-conceptions definitive of their status as persons. To anticipate: they need to be able to 'embody' the freedom of their personalities in external objects so that their conceptions of themselves as persons cease to be purely subjective and become concrete and recognizable to themselves and others in a public and external world. (These are arcane propositions and they will be examined and discussed in detail in the following sections.)

(ii) Personality and Rights

Before going on it is worth noting the connection that Hegel establishes between the concepts of *personality* and *rights*. Something is a right if it is a condition necessary to sustain or develop personality—if it is, in other words, a *demand* of personality as such. (Hegel's argument is that private property is a right in this sense.) So, when we take up the perspective of rights, we are again abstracting from the particular details of individuals' lives and from the particular contents of their wills, to consider what is necessary

---

[18] I do not want to take sides in the disagreement between those who, like Taylor, see *Geist* as the genuine *subject* of the *Philosophy of Right* (e.g. Taylor, *Hegel*, pp. 71–5) and those who, like Ilting, see the concept merely as a way of expressing the changing perspective of philosophical understanding (Ilting, 'Dialectic of Civil Society').

to sustain and develop this common abstractive power of the will in them. 'Everything which depends on particularity is here a matter of indifference' (37A).[19]

The standpoint of personality and rights is apt to seem somewhat cold and austere (in comparison, say, with the concreteness of a theory of property dominated by the idea of the satisfaction of material needs). As a conclusion or resting place for moral philosophy, a morality of rights would be singularly unattractive.

To have no interest except in one's formal right may be pure obstinacy, often a fitting accompaniment of a cold heart and restricted sympathies. It is uncultured people who insist most on their rights, while noble minds look on other aspects of the thing. Thus abstract right is nothing but a bare possibility and, at least in contrast with the whole range of the situation, something formal. (37A)[20]

But Hegel does not take rights as the final end of his ethics. We are not to imagine the ethical life of the Hegelian state as a community of ghostly beings having no more interesting feature than a common ability to abstract from any content given to their wills. There will be an ultimate reintegration of the individual with his own concrete individuality. So the final development of free will, even as it becomes the development of universal forms of life, is not the utter rejection of the natural and the particular, but a different and more adequate understanding of their significance in human life.

Nevertheless, in the early stages of this development, Hegel indicates that it is necessary to stress some aspects rather than others. As intitially given, man is 'an immediate being, sunk in his particular needs and drives, with only the haziest, most primitive sense of the universal'.[21] For such a being to set off on the road to universal development, it may be necessary for a while to lay great stress on his freedom considered in the abstract, to bring that freedom to his attention in its bare universality, before we begin the process of reintegrating the abstract and the particular at a higher stage. This is what is going on at the stage of the discussion where rights, personality, and property are the central concern.

---

[19] See also Ritter, 'Personne et Propriété selon Hegel', p. 179

[20] See also the comments on the aridity of the concept of the individual in Hegel, *Phenomenology of Spirit*, sects. 479 ff. (Miller trans., pp. 291 ff.).

[21] Taylor, *Hegel*, p. 366.

(iii) Externalization

Hegel begins his discussion of property by asserting: 'A person must translate his freedom into an external sphere in order to exist as Idea' (41). Now, *existence as Idea* represents the end-point of the *overall* process of development which Hegel is describing in the *Philosophy of Right*; so this passage does not specify, as it were, the local or specific end of private ownership. It does not say what unique contribution private property makes to the overall process.

But the notion that ethical development in general involves some sort of 'transition' from the inner subjective world to the external objective world is important if we are to understand the contribution of property. So it is worth pausing briefly to examine the general thesis of externalization.

Fundamental to Hegel's philosophy is the principle that mind or freedom is necessarily embodied—that it does not make sense to conceive of its existence in any 'pure' or transcendent form.[22] That principle applies to free will at every stage of its development. Initially, freedom is embodied in finite human subjects, and thus in a scattered and limited form. As it matures and develops, this sort of embodiment has to be transcended, but embodiment as such can never be transcended. It follows that there must be some other embodiment for free will in the higher stages of its development beyond the particular subjects in which it is initially given. So, at least from the point of view of those subjects, the development of free will, as it moves from its initial towards its higher embodiment, has the aspect of an externalization. Free will must proceed out of its initial embodiment in them into the external world where a genuinely universal embodiment can be established.[23]

Of course, in real terms, the idea of externality here is inappropriate. As free will develops, the standpoint from which its development appears to be an excursion into an alien and external world— the standpoint of its initial embodiment—is a standpoint which is left behind. The free will grows as it is externalized; in a sense, then, the subject does not remain behind, helpless and passive, to see the process as an externalization.

For the person, the first step in this process of externalization is

[22] There is a clear exposition of Hegel's 'principle of embodiment' in Taylor, *Hegel and Modern Society*, pp. 14–31.
[23] See Knox's helpful note in his translation of Hegel, *Philosophy of Right*, pp. 302–3 (note to the Preface).

the establishment of the bare principle of his personality in the public world of material objects. Hegel's thesis is that by appropriating, owning, and controlling objects, a person can establish his will as an objective feature of the world and transcend the stage in which it is simply an aspect of his inner and subjective life. Before going on in section 3 to discuss the details of this process, we must look briefly at Hegel's view of the material world which is to be the locus of this initial excursion of free will.

(iv) The World of Material Objects

The first step in Hegel's argument is to establish that the familiar world of material objects is the appropriate realm for this initial excursion of free will to take place. Two arguments need to be made out here. First, that the world of objects is not, as it were, 'off-limits' to the free will, i.e. that it is an arena in which the externalization of freedom is permissible. And secondly, that the world of material objects is worthy of this exercise—that it is not too lowly or sordid an arena for the first strivings of free will toward objectivity.

The former argument is the easier. External objects could present ethical objections to the externalization of free will only if they were ends-in-themselves. But, on Hegel's view, 'the thing, as externality, has no end in itself; it is not infinite self-relation but something external to itself' (44A). In choosing the realm of external objects as the arena for its first objectification, the will manifests the dominance of entities which are ends-in-themselves over entities which are not. As Hegel puts it, to appropriate is 'to prove that the thing is not absolute, is not a thing in itself' (44A). One 'proves' this by endowing the object with a purpose which is not its own; when this is done, we recognize that the object is such that the *only* purpose it could have is a purpose given to it by a human being.

In appropriating the objects of the natural world, then, man displays his intrinsic superiority over nature.[24] This was one of the themes that most fascinated Hegel in the topic of property. Part of human development as he describes it is the process whereby nature ceases to be 'something alien and yonder' and becomes an

---

[24] This aspect of Hegel's theory is highlighted by Stillman, 'Property, Freedom and Individuality', pp. 137 ff. See also Ritter, op. cit. 190.

environment in which human beings can feel 'at home' (4A). Partly this is a matter of understanding and science—the realization, so important in Western philosophy since Newton and Kant, that the world is intrinsically amenable to human intellect. But understanding and appropriation are deeply related for Hegel. It is largely through the domestication of nature that man attains the insight that nature has discernible laws and structures behind the appearances and that it is not distinct in kind from the mind that confronts it. So it is no accident that Hegel uses the language of appropriation to describe knowledge: 'In thinking an object, I make it into thought and deprive it of its sensuous aspect; I make it into something which is directly and essentially mine' (4A). And it is no accident that he uses the image of the infusion of mind into nature as the organizing metaphor of his theory of property.[25]

The claim that nature is essentially amenable to human appropriation becomes a little clearer when we contrast the institutions of property and slavery. For Hegel, what is wrong with slavery is that the will (of the master) sets out to externalize itself in a realm where such externalization is *not* permissible. All justifications of slavery, Hegel writes, 'depend on regarding man as a natural entity pure and simple' (57R), as a 'being that by nature belongs not to himself but to another . . . a tool or instrument having a separate existence and useful for the purposes of living'.[26] Enslavement is thus distinguished from other crimes by involving a thoroughgoing insult to the free will of the man who is enslaved: the insult of denying the existence or the ethical significance of the slave's free will (96). The slave is treated by his master as if he were an object to be imbued with the master's will. What strikes us as wrong about slavery is that, when we see a slave in whom the master's will is 'objectified', we recognize that this is not the only way such a being could be imbued with purpose. We recognize this, not just because the slave's ability to determine himself eventually breaks through in defiance of the master's will, but also just because of the way the master treats the slave—the sort of tasks he sets him, and so on. The key to the problem of slavery is the tension arising out of the fact that the reason slaves are so useful to their masters—their potential rationality, their ability to take on complex projects

---

[25] See Hegel, *Phenomenology of Spirit*, sects. 244 ff. (Miller trans., pp. 147 ff.). See also Hegel, *Philosophy of Mind*, sect. 381 (pp. 8 ff.) and sect. 388 (p. 29).

[26] Cf. Aristotle, *Politics*, Bk. I, Ch. 5, 1254^a ff. (Sinclair trans. pp. 32–4).

involving intelligence, skill, and judgement, and to care about whether they are completed etc.—is precisely the reason slavery is wrong. Slaves are useful because, not in spite, of their rationality and potential for autonomy.

If there is nothing in nature which gives rise to any ethical objection against man's externalizing his will there, still it remains to be shown that the natural world of objects is a worthy realm for this exercise.

Certainly, Hegel insists that the natural world is not the place for the final realization of free will in its universal form. He describes the externalization of will in objects as a 'false' (41A) and 'inadequate' (33A) realization. But we are proceeding stage-wise and Hegel's argument is that, at the initial stages of human development, the world of naturally given things is an appropriate place for the free will to begin its journey out of subjectivity. At this stage, the crude and primitive world of material objects is exactly matched by the primitive level of development of the free wills seeking their realization therein. 'Abstract personality in its immediacy can have no other embodiment save one characterised by immediacy' (41A).

The contrast between *immediacy* and *mediation* is important. We have already looked at Hegel's thesis that the free will must be embodied at all the stages of its development. Free will is initially presented in the form of separate individual minds; but potentially it is a single rational entity. The realization of this potential must therefore consist in the embodiment of free will in forms which transcend the particularity of the organisms in which it is initially given. From the point of view of these organisms, the growth of free will must be 'mediated' by the establishment of institutions which transcend their particularity, such as the familiar institutions of property, contract, family, economy, and state.

Immediacy is partly the notion of a certain potential in its naturally given form. Knox gives the example of a seed which is 'the whole life of the tree in its "immediacy"'.[27] But this is a poor example. The notion of immediacy has a sense which distinguishes it from the genus terms 'potential' or 'implicit': it is the sense that the growth or development envisaged is one that will be mediated in forms that transcend the particularity of the form in which it is naturally given. When Hegel refers to the individual's will as an

---

[27] Knox, 'Translator's Foreword' to Hegel, *Philosophy of Right*, p. ix.

'immediate' will, he does not mean merely that it is capable of growth; he is also picking out a particular form of growth, a form which denies the ultimate reality of discrete and separate individual development. This is a form of growth which is not that of an acorn growing into an oak tree.

We have an idea of what it is for individual will to be thought of as immediate. But what is it for nature or naturally given objects to be immediate? How can they have an immediacy which matches or is equal to the immediacy of the individual will?

To answer these questions, we have to turn to Hegel's philosophical idealism. The external world does not have any reality apart from its reality *for* individual minds. What the external world *is*, is given by what mind and will are. In its immediacy, the human mind sees the world as a realm distinct from, even alien to, itself. This, then, is the immediacy of the naturally given world. But it too has a higher destiny: to be a world *for* free will once the latter is mediated in the institutions of communal life. Such a world will be a world imbued with human purpose, understood and reclaimed by reason as its own.

Now, I think, we have sorted out what one might call the ontology of property on Hegel's account. On the one hand we have individual human beings; they are immediate beings inasmuch as they embody in an implicit form the concept of free will which is destined to develop through mediation. We are considering the first stage of that development, which is the detachment of abstract personality from the inner life of each of these beings and its embodiment in the external world. On the other hand we have the external world—equally immediate, just because it is the world as seen by mind in its immediate condition. The first stage in *its* development is its conversion from the status of a merely given other to the status of an assemblage of discrete things or objects— entities which are essentially places for the embodiment of personality. Just as the subject of property (the person) is conceived of in a purely abstract way, without considering particular characteristics, so the objects of property are considered, at this stage, merely as *things*. Their detailed characteristics are not in question, nor are we interested at this stage in the particular determinations which they acquire after free will has appropriated them (43). The natural world, then, is as transformed by the process of appropriation as the free will: it is changed from a given nature into a realm of objects. We cannot, on Hegel's account, understand what it is to be an object, except in so far as we take the world to be divided into discrete parcels amenable to the purposes of discrete individuals.

Thus in the process of appropriation, man constitutes himself as a bearer of rights and he constitutes nature as a realm of objects capable of embodying and sustaining his status as right-bearer.[28]

3. EMBODIMENT

What exactly is it for personality or free will to be embodied in an object? On the face of it, the idea is an extremely obscure one. There are obvious connections with Locke's famous idea that the labour of a producer is, in some sense, 'annexed to' or 'mixed with' the substance of the object on which he has been working. In both theories, there seems to be the notion that something essentially pertaining to agency—will, freedom, personality, action, or labour—becomes part of something which, at least initially, is distinct in kind from agency and thus constitutes the latter as the private property of the agent. But, as we saw in the case of Locke, there are grave logical difficulties with views of this kind; we were unable to see how Locke's 'labour-mixing' theory could be stated in any coherent form and still do the work that he wanted it to do.[29] Does Hegel's account run into similar difficulties? We cannot tell until we have produced a clear account of the sort of thought that Hegel was having when he used this language of 'embodiment'; until then we will not know how literally he needs to take the idea of a 'mixture' of will/action and object.

Besides 'embodiment', there are a number of other terms that Hegel uses, apparently to pick out the same relation. He talks of 'the direct presence of my awareness and will' in an object (56; see also 48, 62R, and 64), of an object's being 'penetrated through and through by my will' (62; see also 52R), of an identity being established between myself and an object (59A; see also 66), and of my will's being 'reflected in the object' (90; see also 53). By themselves, none of these is particularly illuminating. All of them (except perhaps the last) seem to involve the troublesome notion

---

[28] 'Sans se trouver sur le même plan, l'objet et le sujet qui se l'approprie sont donc complementaires'—Chamley, *Économie Politique et Philosophie*, p. 20.

[29] Locke, *Two Treatises*, II, sect. 27. See the discussion, above, Ch. 6, secs. 7–9. See also the references at n. 35, below.

that there can be some sort of containment relation between an object and an element of agency usually taken to belong to a different logical category from objects.

In attempting to elucidate the idea of embodiment in Hegel's discussion of property, there are four main sources of clues. First, there is his account of the relation between will or personality and the human body. Hegel argues that the first task of will is to appropriate the body, to take possession of it and to give itself an 'embodiment' therein. For obvious reasons, the sense of the term 'embodiment' is likely to be clearer here than in the case of the relation between will and external objects. So a discussion of what Hegel means by taking possession of one's body may cast some light on the embodying of one's will in external objects. Secondly, once we move out into the external realm, there is Hegel's account, in the later part of his discussion of property, of the exact nature of possession. His thesis is that one's will is embodied in the objects one possesses. So his views about what counts as taking possession and why may give us some assistance in determining what it means to embody one's will in an object. Thirdly, and connected with this, there is Hegel's account of use—that is, of the way in which using something reveals a concrete relation between object and will. And finally, we have his account of the alienation of property -of how it is possible for a person to withdraw his will from an object. Possibly, this account may cast some light on what the embodiment of the will—the condition ended by alienation—is supposed to be.

(i) Taking Possession of One's Body

There is an obvious sense in which a human individual, even in his natural or immediate state, is already embodied. Inasmuch as 'I am alive in this bodily organism, which is my external existence' (47), I am already in possession of my body. But the sense of 'possession' here is the sense in which an animal might be said to possess its body (47A); it is not a sense of 'possession' which has anything to do with personality or free will. The first step in human development, according to Hegel, is for the mind to take possession of its body in some stronger sense and to embue it with its will.[30]

---

[30] Stillman contrasts Hegel's theory of property with Locke's in this respect: that Hegel sees self-ownership as a task to be accomplished whereas Locke 'begins with the assertion that individuals own their. . . bodies' (Stillman, 'Property, Freedom and Individuality', p. 140). This is a mistake. As we saw in Ch. 6, sect. 8, Locke asserts that individuals own their *persons* and their *actions*, not their bodies. (See also Tully, *A Discourse on Property*, pp. 104 ff.)

Notice, though, that my natural possession of my body is not ethically insignificant. It is sufficient to establish that I am not to be treated as 'a beast of burden' (48R). From the point of view of other people, I am to be treated at all times as though I were in possession of my body in the stronger sense. Hegel's argument for this is a little obscure. He says that 'my body is the embodiment of my freedom'; but in the absence of possession in the stronger sense, this can only mean that my body is at all times the necessary medium for the development of my freedom. I will be unable to take possession of myself or of anything else if others have control over my body. Bodily integrity, then, is required at all times as a necessary condition of freedom—even at the most primitive stages of ethical growth—since it is the *sine qua non* of further development. Secondly Hegel also mentions the fact that 'it is with my body that I feel' (48R). This may mean that, at this stage of development, all the material input for the operation of my mind comes in via the body, so that an attack on the body is necessarily an attack on the operation of the mind. He develops the point by criticizing the old Stoic notion that 'the soul . . . is not touched or attacked if the body is maltreated' (48R). Certainly, *I* may be able to distance myself from the agonies of bodily assault or violation and carry on meditating or whatever regardless. But from the point of view of anyone else, no attack is ever justified or mitigated by the assumption that I have managed to do this: 'so far as others are concerned, I am in my body' (48R). For others, the important point is that in attacking my body they are attacking almost the only capacity that I have to act, to develop, to perceive, and to feel.[31]

To explain the stronger sense in which one may possess one's body, Hegel refers to 'the training of my body in dexterity' (52R) and to 'the development of [one's] own body and mind' (57). The notion of dexterity is reasonably clear: it is the idea of an increasingly deeper and more subtle control over one's body so that one becomes capable of performing more complex and delicate actions. Then, there is the notion of self-control—the idea of the body's being increasingly subjected to the will so that its apparent independence of the mind, revealed in clumsiness or awkwardness, is progressively reduced. Connected with self-control is the notion

---

[31] Marcuse, *Reason and Revolution*, p. 199 suggests that Hegel's target here is Luther. For the critique of stoicism, see Hegel, *Phenomenology of Spirit*, sects. 199 ff. (Miller trans. p. 121 ff.)

of training. Training involves the idea that the development of one's bodily capacities is a process taking place in time. One performs certain actions now—exercises and practice—in order to make other actions and further development possible in the future. In training one builds day by day on the various changes that one has wrought in one's body already. Since taking possession of one's body is a developmental process, it necessarily involves the idea of the persistence of the self through time and of one's responsibility in the present for future states of one's physique etc. In developing this sense, obviously the sheer durability of the body and the stability of the changes wrought in it, are factors of considerable importance. These ideas, particularly that of training as a process in time in which actions are performed now to make certain other actions possible in the future, will be very important in our account of embodiment in external objects.

So far, none of this requires the notion that one's will or personality is actually present in one's limbs or sinews, in any literal sense. It is difficult to imagine what such a notion would mean, but anyway the concept of self-possession does not require it. All it requires is that the body be gradually modified and turned to the will's purposes so that it becomes increasingly difficult for the agent or anyone else to view his body, especially in action, without taking into account its essentially will-governed character. To look at a highly trained athlete is to look at a body almost totally subject to wilful control; it is a markedly different experience from watching the movements of an awkward or clumsy man.

(ii) Taking Possession of Objects

Property, according to Hegel, involves the embodiment of my will in an object. But he denies that merely directing one's will on an object is sufficient to embody it therein (51). There has to be some physical relation between the body inhabited by the will in question and the external object in which that will is to be embodied. Sometimes Hegel speaks as though this requirement were purely a matter of letting others *know* that one's will has become embodied in an object: 'The inner act of will which consists in saying that something is mine must also become recognisable by others' (51A). But it is more than that. It is of the essence of appropriation that the will operate in a realm that transcends the subjectivity of inner mental life. Physical possession—the interaction of will and object in a material way—is therefore crucial to an understanding of property.[32]

Hegel's remarks about what it is to take and to be in possession of an external object offer us some clues about the application of the notion of embodiment outside one's own bodily space.

He distinguishes three ways of taking possession of an object (54). First, there is direct physical grasping of an object. To take hold of an object purposely is to subordinate it directly to one's will. Hegel suggests that when I grasp an object 'I am directly present in this possession (*in diesem Besitzen*) and therefore my will is recognisable in it.' (55)[33] No one can understand what it is for an object to be grasped by me without understanding that, at least for the time being, the object is entirely subject to my will. However, in these cases, the relation between my will and the object lasts only as long as the act of grasping itself. So this mode of possession is, as Hegel puts it, 'temporary, and seriously restricted in scope' (55).

Much more important is the case in which I work to bring about some physical change in the object.[34] In this case the will-governed character of the object 'acquires an independent externality' (56). For now there is something about the object itself, quite apart from its contiguity with me, which may be explained only in terms of the working of my will. If the object is inanimate (say, a piece of marble formed into a statue) then the aspect of the object which may be understood only by reference to my will is one of its physical properties—its shape, for example. If the object is organic, then maybe it is not merely some property which is understood in this way but also some ongoing process in the object: 'What I do to the organic does not remain external to it but is assimilated by it' (56R). When I plough and plant a field, I adapt or set in motion natural processes and activities whose occurrence here may then be understood only in terms which make reference to my will.

Notice again that we are not required to believe here that my actions or my will literally enter into or become part of the object on which I work. In Hegel's account, the important thing is that the gap between the subjectivity of will and the perceived externality of

[32] See Ch. 7, sect. 3, above.

[33] This sounds odd if *Besitzen* is taken to refer to the *object* (in the way the English term 'possession' is sometimes used). But if it is taken to refer to the act of possessing, the meaning of the passage is quite clear.

[34] There is a useful discussion of Hegel's early account of the development of the division of labour in Plant, *Hegel*, p. 93.

the objects of the world has been bridged. When the subject labours in the world, his willing is such that it cannot be understood or explained except by making reference to the external objects of his labour; and those objects once they have been worked on become such that certain aspects of them cannot be understood or explained except by making reference to the workings of his will. We do not have to insist (as Locke has to) that the willed actions are actually present *in* the product, only that the condition (and, of course, the value) of the product is such as to be intelligible only by reference to the will which shaped them. As Ryan puts it, 'our aims *permeate* the results'.[35]

The third way of taking possession is the marking of something as one's own. Hegel does not dwell on this mode. But he notes that it shares with the other modes the characteristic that an external object is affected in some way that can only be explained by reference to the workings of an active will (58).

(iii) Possession and Use

So far we have examined Hegel's account of *taking* possession. The *use* of an object reveals a more direct relationship with the will. If I eat a piece of food, one can explain what is happening to the food only by referring to the need or want which is being satisfied in the process. In the course of such explanation, the thing is taken to have a purely subordinate status: it is taken to be the complement of some human need. No longer is it independent object O; now it is the satisfier of need N.

Hegel develops this further, in an obscure way, by arguing that, in use, the object acquires a 'negative' character in relation to the externalization of my will:

[M]y need, as the particular aspect of a single will, is the positive element which finds satisfaction, and the thing, as something negative in itself, exists only for my need and is at its service.—*The use of the thing is my need being externally realised* through the change, destruction and consumption of the thing. (59; my emphasis)

The sentence I have emphasized is important. Hegel, I think, is suggesting that my will can be externalized by the creation of a *gap*

[35] Ryan, *Property and Political Theory*, p. 126. Plant sees here echoes of Locke's theory and conjectures that Hegel was in fact influenced by Locke: Plant, 'Economic and Social Integration', p. 62.

or an *absence* in nature, relative to what was there before. Previously there were thirty apples on a tree but now there are only twenty-nine; the non-existence of one of the apples is a fact about the world which can be explained only by reference to my hunger and my wilful satisfaction of it. In this sense the apple I eat stands in a 'negative' relation to the externalization of my will.

Of course, animals also consume things (and each other); if a monkey eats the misssing apple, then equally its absence can be explained only by reference to the monkey's hunger (44A).[36] The difference in the human case is the relation of the need in question to an emergent will. It is the fact that the need is 'the particular aspect of a single will' (59) which makes its satisfaction ethically significant in the human case.

Hegel places great stress on the use of property objects (not just 'use' in the sense of consumption, but also 'use' in the sense that a tool or a piece of land may be used). Although, at this stage of his theory, he wanted to abstract from the particular wants and needs that drive men to use things, he nevertheless saw that the point of property for humans had to do with the use of the objects in their posession. Merely having something is not enough to constitute a real property relation. 'The relation of use to property is the same as that of substance to accident' (61A). Use—the wilful satisfaction of material need—is the substantial aspect of ownership; from an ethical point of view, it is the most important thing about an individual's ownership of some object.[37] Property is important as a means whereby individuals may perceive the effects of their willing in a concrete form; and one does not understand what it is for a will to affect the material world unless one understands that the will is driven by need. It follows that Hegel must reject the jurisprudence which suggests that an individual can be the owner of an object even while he is not involved at all with the use of it. From an ethical point of view, such 'ownership' is an empty abstraction (61A).

[36] 'Labour lifts man above the animals because man *uses* his environment to satisfy his desires, whereas the animal is a merely passive consumer, annihilating it in appropriating it.' (Plant, *Hegel*, p. 108).

[37] When we talk about use, we have it in mind that for a finite material being, the driving force of will is physical need. This does not mean that will is subordinate to need; on the contrary, the story of the development of will is very much a story of the growth of its autonomous control over needs, wants, and impulses. But even the autonomous will is the will of a human being. Hegel shares sufficient humanistic materialism with Marx to see that it is in terms of men and women struggling for their subsistence in a natural world that the story of freedom must be told.

(iv) Alienation of Property

Hegel evidently believed that ownership involved the power to alienate resources or to transmit them to another by gift or exchange. However, it is far from clear what connection this has with his doctrine of the ethical importance of ownership. We know he was prepared to say that some of the goods I own may be *in*alienable—for example, 'those goods, or rather substantive characteristics which constitute my own private personality and the universal essence of my self-consciousness . . . my personality as such, my universal freedom of will, my ethical life, my religion' (66). This, for example, is why I may not sell myself into slavery. It cannot be the case, therefore, that alienability is crucial for something to be *mine*. If we are going to associate private property with alienability, what we will need is some account of what distinguishes external objects from these inalienable goods, so that we can show that the ethical importance of owning the former requires alienability in a way that the ethical importance of owning the latter does not.

Alan Ryan attempts to provide an argument: 'As a free agent, I rightly bring any and every external object under control as 'mine'. Were men able to *take* but not *relinquish*, this freedom would be a bad joke— we would be much like the monkey who seized the sweets in the sweet jar, but could not extract his clenched fist when he had done so.'[38] But this will not do, for several reasons. First (and pedantically), the monkey's trouble is that he cannot consume the sweets that he has 'acquired' not that he cannot relinquish them; a better example (if we are looking for examples) would be the Ancient Mariner who, having shot the albatross, cannot get rid of it and is condemned to carry it around his neck. Secondly, Hegel himself does not deploy any argument of this kind to link alienability with freedom. He does suggest that 'it is only a thing completely mine which I can so spurn'[39]; but, at best, that has the point the wrong way round. It does not establish that for a thing to *be* completely mine it must be something I can abandon. Thirdly,

---

[38] Ryan, *Property and Political Theory*, pp. 129–30.
[39] See footnote to Hegel, *Philosophy of Right*, sect. 65A (Knox trans., p. 241 n). The only other passage I can think that Ryan is alluding to is sect. 91, where Hegel talks about free will being coerced 'in so far as it fails to withdraw itself out of the external object in which it is held fast, or rather out of its idea of that object.' But this is an account of the wrongness of theft or seizure of another's goods, not of the necessity of alienation.

the Ryan argument fails to distinguish between alienable and inalienable goods. If his point has any force at all, it applies surely with equal force to my embodiment in my limbs and my experience of freedom in ethical life as well. Indeed, Ryan concedes in a later essay, that Hegel's point that life, liberty, ethical involvement, and so on are all *in*alienable goods tends to undercut the argument for alienable property: 'The upshot of this may well be to conclude that lives and liberties simply are not property in any useful sense of the term, but if we draw this conclusion, there is some difficulty in hanging on to Hegel's claim that it is as property-owners that people first exist.'[40]

My own impression is that the relationship of alienability to property is a relation which Hegel accepted as, in the first instance, *historically* given, rather than as a relation for which he wanted to attempt a conceptual deduction. (In this regard, the relation is rather like that between the family and civil society, on K. H. Ilting's account.)[41] In the society Hegel confronted, and which he undertook to explain, private property happened to be alienable and freedom of contract existed. Since his premiss was that the real is rational, and since freedom of contract was actual, it had to be the case that, as Hegel puts it, 'reason makes it just as necessary for men to enter into contractual relationships—gift, exchange, trade, &c.—as to possess property' (71R). However, it is one thing to explain the contribution that contract makes to the development of rational freedom in social life; it is quite another to try and draw freedom of contract dialectically out of the concept of property. In my view, Hegel does not seriously attempt the latter task.

The result is that the account of the importance of alienability and contract in the *Philosophy of Right* is not right-based in the same way as the account of the importance of property is. Rather the importance of contract is located in the beginning of the transcendence of individual personality, and in the realization that free will may have a representation or embodiment apart from particular individuals. The *consensus ad idem* which contract involves is the first instantiation of will outside the mind and

[40] Ryan, 'Hegel on Work, Ownership and Citizenship', p. 187. Doubts about the persuasiveness of the view attributed to Hegel in Ryan's original interpretation (see n. 38, above) are expressed in ibid. 191.

[41] See Ilting, 'Dialectic of Civil Society', pp. 215–160. I find this paper quite the best thing available in English on Hegel's method in his social and political philosophy.

activity of single individuals. Though Hegel's right-based argument for private property is often taken to be an argument for alienable property, the right-based part of the case does not establish this. He does not show that *alienable* property is needed in order for humans to be free persons. Alienability is rationalized in a part of the argument which moves on beyond the stage at which it can be described as right-based or oriented towards individual personality.[42]

So far we have stressed the following interpretation: an individual's will is 'embodied' in an object to the extent that there is something about that object that can be understood only by making reference to the operation of his will. But the introduction of alienation complicates this somewhat. To alienate an object—to sell it or give it away—is to withdraw one's will from it. But an object from which one's will has been withdrawn may still be an object such that some characteristic of it can only be understood by reference to one's will. The shape of the chair I have built is still to be understood by reference to my will, even after I have sold the chair. We need then a richer and more complex understanding of embodiment if we are to avoid the conclusion that my will remains 'embodied' in the objects from which it has been 'withdrawn'.

Consider a chair that I have built. What changes when I sell the chair or give it away? Well, one relation does not change: it remains the case that the shape of these pieces of wood is explicable only in terms that make reference to my will. But on the other hand I cannot *use* the chair; in that respect the relation of the chair to my will has been altered. So, if we want to say that the embodiment of my will in the chair is ended by its alienation, then it must be the case that the embodiment involves something like the *conjunction* of *two* relations between my will and the chair. There is (1) the relation constituted by my having built the chair and (2) the relation constituted by my being in a position to use or further modify the chair. Embodiment then is a two-way process. The chair has been affected by my will and, as a result of that effect, it makes certain uses possible for me that were not possible before. My will

---

[42] I have not discussed Hegel's views on inheritance and bequest: see *Philosophy of Right*, sects. 178–80. Ryan suggests Hegel may have wanted to drive a wedge between *post-mortem* disposition and other forms of alienation: 'Hegel on Work, Ownership and Citizenship', pp. 189–90. This is supported by remarks like: 'The essence of inheritance is the transfer to private ownership of property which is in principle common' (*Philosophy of Right*, sect. 178). Certainly, Hegel was highly critical of the capriciousness of testamentary arrangements, particularly in England (ibid., sect. 180A).

affects the chair and the chair in its affected state affects my willing. To say, then, that my will is embodied in the chair is to regard the chair as the nexus of this dual relation between will and object, object and will. Now to alienate an object is to terminate one relation of this pair, and thus to withdraw from the object this status as a nexus of relations. Interestingly, then, we find ourselves in a position to make central use, in our interpretation, of a term we noted earlier (at the start of this section) as just one among several of Hegel's synonyms for embodiment: the term 'reflection'. My will is reflected in the object inasmuch as there is this dual line of effect from my will to the object and back to my will. This, I submit, is what embodiment is for Hegel.

(The term 'reflection' does not occur often in Hegel's discussion. We do find it, however, in his later discussion of crimes against property: 'In owning property I place my will in an external thing, and this implies that my will, just by being thus reflected in the object, may be seized in it and brought under some compulsion' (90). Of course, 'reflection' remains a metaphor.[43] But the advantage of using it to elucidate Hegel's more frequently used terms 'embodiment' and 'penetration' is that it preserves all the ethical and philosophical significance of this account of property-owning, without committing us to the troublesome Lockean idea that objects need be, in any literal sense, the containers of will and action.)

4. THE ETHICAL IMPORTANCE OF EMBODIMENT

We have noted Hegel's belief that it is important for free will to be embodied at every stage of its development. In the previous section, I sketched an account of what this embodiment was supposed to involve, so far as individual ownership of property is concerned. A person's will is embodied in an object to the extent that (1) his will has made a difference to the object and (2) the object, affected in this way by his will, itself makes a difference in turn to his willing. In this section, I want to examine how the individual will is supposed to be matured and educated by being embodied in this way. In what ways will an individual feel that property-owning is setting him on the path (albeit a long path) to genuine self-

---

[43] See also Plant's use of the term in *Hegel*, p. 108.

realization? And why is it ethically important for individuals to attain this sort of fulfilment?

(i) 'Making Consciousness Concrete'

At the beginning of his discussion of property, Hegel contrasts the nascent objectivity of the embodied will with its previous subjectivity: 'the rationale of property lies in the supersession of the pure subjectivity of personality' (41A). What is subjectivity and why is it important that it be superseded?

There is no sustained or explicit answer to this question in the discussion of property in the philosophy of right. But we can draw some clues from elsewhere. In the famous discussion of lordship and bondage in the phenomenology of spirit, Hegel discusses the effect of actual work and labour on the mind of a slave. Although it is the master who derives all the enjoyment and satisfaction from the objects on which the slave labours, still it is the slave rather than the master who benefits ethically from the process:

Desire has reserved to itself the pure negating of the object and thereby the unalloyed feeling of self. This satisfaction, however, just for that reason is itself only a state of evanescence, for it lacks objectivity or subsistence. *Labour, on the other hand, is desire restrained and checked, evanescence delayed and postponed*; in other words, labour shapes and fashions the thing. The negative relation to the object passes into the form of the object, into something that is permanent and remains; because it is just for the labourer that the object has independence. This negative mediating agency, this activity giving shape and form, is at the same time the individual existence, the pure self-existence of that consciousness, which now in the work it does is externalised and passes into the condition of permanence. The consciousness that toils and serves accordingly comes by this means to view that independent being as its self.[44] (my emphasis)

This is a difficult passage (like every other passage in the *Phenomenology!*). But I believe we can draw the following out of it.[45]

In working on an object and forming it according to his will (even though it is a heteronomous will), the slave experiences a certain mental discipline. Labouring on something is a complex business and takes time. One proceeds step by step, performing

[44] Hegel, *Phenomenology of Spirit,*, sect. 195. (I have preferred Baillie's translation, p. 186.)
[45] Cf. Ch. 8, sect. 4, above.

certain actions now in order to make other steps, other actions, possible in the future. So one must have a plan and, by and large, keep to it. Once the first steps have been taken, for example forming pieces of wood into a chair, constraints are placed on what intentions can be fulfilled with respect to that wood at a later stage. One may not be able to change one's mind and build a table instead, since by then the timber has been cut into lengths too small for a table. In this way, labouring on materials imposes some sort of permanence and stability on the projects of the will. One cannot be always changing one's mind, if one is to work on objects, because the objects themselves will register in a more or less inerasable form the effects of one's earlier willing. Thus the 'evanescence' of speculative idling, the fleetingness and whimsicality of pure thought, is replaced by the objectivity and durability of the concretely efficacious will. 'Labour,' as Hegel put it in an earlier work, 'is the activity of making consciousness concrete.'[46]

In this respect, the master is the poorer for having all the work related to the satisfaction of his needs performed by someone else. For the slave gets the benefit of seeing his will 'embodied' in the material on which he works. Even though his will is not autonomous, even though he is acting under orders and fulfilling desires that are not his own, he at least gets an idea of what it is like to transcend the evanescence of subjective desire and to exert his will in a stable and purposeful manner.

This account of the importance of transcending subjectivity fits well with the account we have given of embodiment. Our notion of embodiment is the notion of a will not just affecting a material object but in turn being itself affected by the possibilities opened to it by its effect. As long as our resolutions, plans, and projects remain purely 'inside our heads', they tend to swirl about in a cloud of indeterminacy and indecision: plans just come and go. But when our wills are reflected in the external world, we have to impose a stronger discipline on our willing. That discipline will be felt as a liberating force in as much as the agent becomes capable of planning, effort, and tangible and permanent achievement in a way that was not possible before.

These points can be related to others made more generally in Hegel's discussion of moral action. In one place, he points out: 'what the subject is, is the series of his actions. If these are a series of

---

[46] Hegel's *Jensener Realphilosophie*, quoted in Plant, *Hegel*, p. 108.

worthless productions, then the subjectivity of his willing is just as worthless. But if the series of his deeds is of a substantial nature, then the same is true also of the individual's inner will' (124).[47] In context, this is the assertion that consequences matter, and a repudiation of all ethics of pure intentions (126R). But Hegel's remark that 'the laurels of mere willing are dry leaves that never were green' (124A) can also be applied to the evanescence of a will that has never been pinned down in the discipline of working on a *material* of its own. Modifying something in the external world changes the character of the subject too. Since he takes responsibility for his production, identifying it as the product of his will, he has to shape his will and his intentions so that they become apt for this sort of stable and constraining realization.

That is the argument. Why does it require *private* property, rather than some other regime of economic life? Hegel's initial moves here are unconvincing. He points out that we are dealing at this stage with individual wills: 'since my will, as the will of a person, and so as a single will, becomes objective to me in property, property acquires the character of private property' (46). But individuality does not in itself imply private property. A system of common (or collective) property may involve assigning rights over objects to individual wills—*this* person has the right to use the tractor today, *that* person has the right to use the tractor tomorrow, and so on. As Hugh Reyburn has noted, Hegel moved too quickly. The argument cannot be based on the individuality of wills as such for 'he does not hold that the privacy of individual wills is ultimately hostile to their community and interpenetration, and accordingly . . . he should not have assumed that common ownership impedes private possession'.[48]

The real work in the argument for *private* property is done by Hegel's account of the importance of property in terms of the relationship over time between an individual person and an object. The importance of property to individual wills is this: the actions that an individual performs on or with this object now may constrain or determine the actions that he can perform on or with it later. This is how an object can embody a will—by registering the effects of willing at one point of time and forcing an individual's willing to become consistent and stable over a period. But this effect

[47] The first sentence of this passage has a remarkable affinity to Locke's doctrine of personal identity: cf. Ch. 6, sect. 8, above.
[48] Reyburn, *Hegel's Ethical Theory*, p. 129.

can be lost if others are also working on the object for purposes of
their own in the meantime. That is why we need *private* property: a
system which assigns enduring objects to the exclusive control of
individuals. Otherwise embodiment and its beneficial effects on
willing would not be possible. This account, then, provides more
substantial backing for Hegel's vehement opposition to communism (46R).[49]

There is one final point to be made before we move on from this
aspect of Hegel's argument. It is important to note how limited the
conception of private property is on Hegel's account. An argument
depending this strongly on the persistence of an individual's control
of the objects he works on is clearly vulnerable to the charge that it
ignores the effects of modern production relations and, in particular, the division of labour, on an individual's relationship to the
objects he is working on. In modern society, the predominant
relation between producer and product is that of a worker in a
large-scale factory rather than that of an individual carpenter
producing a piece of furniture for his own use. To what extent can
property continue to have the beneficial effects that Hegel
identified, in an economy characterized by a thoroughgoing
division of labour, by assembly-line style production, and by
commerce oriented around commodity exchange? I cannot do
anything more here than allude to this problem, except to say that
Hegel was aware of it (e.g. 198), and that his account of property
seems therefore obviously more applicable to a petit-bourgeois
economy of small owner-occupiers than to an advanced capitalist
economy. Hegel's account of civil society fits ill, in many respects,
with his account of the importance of private property; and it is
clear that in a theory less committed than his to the rationality of
the actual the latter account could be used as a basis for criticizing
the former.[50]

[49] Cf. Stace's interpretation: '[Hegel's] teaching is not really inconsistent with
modern socialistic ideas. The true essence of socialism, if it understands itself, is not
an absolute objection to private property as such, but to the inequitable distribution
of private property. No scheme of communism can ever really get rid of the necessity
of private property. For even if wealth become nominally the property of the state, it
must at least be divided among individuals, appropriated and consumed by them.
. . . The necessity of private property in this sense of the appropriation of things by
individual persons is all that really follows from Hegel's deduction, though he may
have imagined that he deduced more than this.' (Stace, *Philosophy of Hegel*,
pp. 383–4.) In my view, Stace underestimates both the communism of socialists and
the extent and nature of Hegel's commitment to private property.

[50] For a discussion of this theme in Hegel's earlier writings, and his echoing the
concerns of Steuart and Ferguson about the effects of the division of labour, see

(ii) Recognition

There is a second aspect of the supersession of subjectivity which needs to be discussed. In a couple of passages, Hegel stresses that it is only in so far as my will is embodied in objects that it becomes capable of being recognized by others.

Some commentators regard this as the most important aspect in the Hegelian justification of property.[51] But it is obvious that the need for mutual recognition of persons cannot do any independent work in justifying *private* property. The need for recognition could be satisfied by *any* system of property, provided it assigned rights in respect of objects by individuals, no matter how temporary or limited those rights were. The assignment of any rights to individuals in a society, no matter what their content, will constitute a system of mutual recognition. As we have seen, *private* property involves a distinctive way of packaging rights over objects. The need for mutual recognition does not require that rights be allocated in this distinctive way. It may be thought that, in order to define myself in distinction from others, I need to be able to distinguish 'mine' from 'thine' and to be assured that this distinction is recognized (46a). But there will be senses for 'mine' and 'thine' (*my* rights of temporary use versus *thy* rights of temporary use) even in a commune, since *any* economy will require some rules to govern individual use of objects. The difference is that in a commune 'mine' and 'thine' will be understood in respect of limited uses of objects for limited periods, whereas *private* property employs 'mine' and 'thine' to denote enduring, exclusive, and relatively unlimited rights of use and decision that persons have in relation to enduring objects.

The need for mutual recognition, then, can hardly be the basis of Hegel's case for private property, since it leaves unanswered the question of the sort of rights we are to recognize one another to have. But once that question has been answered, then the recognition element does become important.

It is no accident that the world of enduring objects on which we work is also the world of public objects and that what is visible and significant to us as the work of our wills on the external world is

Plant, *Hegel*, pp. 21–5 and 110–14. See also: Plant, 'Hegel on Identity and Legitimation', p. 230; Avineri, *Hegel's Theory of the Modern State*, pp. 99–108; and Knowles, 'Hegel on Property', pp. 60 ff. See also Hegel's discussion in 'The Old German Freedom', pp. 147–8.

[51] e.g. Plamenatz, 'History as Realization of Freedom', pp. 40–1.

also perceptible as such by others. By objectifying his will in this sort of world, Hegel's person not only brings that will into a stronger and more mature relation to itself, but also brings it into a relation with the similarly matured wills of other persons.[52]

The need to supersede subjectivity in this second sense is crucial in Hegel's philosophy. It is a commonplace (at least among dialectical idealists) that a being may be defined and understood only by contrasting it with something else. This applies to the self-definition of a human being: a human can only define himself by distinguishing himself from something he is not. Part of the doctrine of dialectic is bound up with this: if X cannot be understood without reference to non-X, then there is a sense in which non-X, far from having nothing to do with X, is actually essential to X. For instance, to define oneself as a natural entity is, first, to distinguish oneself from other natural entities, but then to realize, as a result of the necessity of that distinction, that the idea of a world of other natural entities is bound up in one's own self-definition. Similarly for persons. To define oneself as a person is, first, to mark off the bearer of rights and duties which one takes oneself to be from other bearers of rights and duties, but then to realize that one's place in a network of other persons is itself constitutive of one's personality, and that one could not be a person except in a world of persons.[53]

The subjective individual attempts this process of dialectical self-definition without making any reference to anything outside himself. The subjective ego 'posits itself as its own negative' (7), postulating its particular finite nature as the 'other' by reference to which the identity of its abstract will may be understood. But this purely negative self-definition is inadequate. Ultimately, of course, the individual will be understood only in terms of his own real nature (as part of universal freedom etc.). But at this stage of his development, a purely self-referential understanding is pitifully limited. One must supersede the subjectivity of this point of view by understanding oneself in relation to others.

The exclusionary character of private property plays an important role in the development of this self-understanding. In a world

[52] For the phenomenological importance of recognition, see Hegel, *Phenomenology of Spirit*, sects. 178–86 (Miller trans., pp. 111–13). See also Taylor, *Hegel*, Ch. 5.
[53] I believe Gillian Rose makes unnecessarily heavy weather of this point in *Hegel contra Sociology*, pp. 73 ff.

where resources are moderately scarce, one individual is likely to experience another's ownership of a given object as something of a frustration and to be tempted to violate it. His own needs, he may think, have as much claim to satisfaction as the needs of the man whose will is embodied therein. Now the norms protecting private property in the face of this temptation are, in the first instance, a basis for the distinction of one such need-laden will from another. We are not merely the locations of needs and wants. We are also individual wills in a process of growth. That growth, at the point where property is important, is growth at an individual level. So property protects the development of will by erecting normative fences around the objects in which wills have become embodied.

But, secondly, there is the understanding that such fences make sense only in a common world of property-holders. It is only in terms of such a world that the distinction between self and other that fences presuppose could be sustained. This leads, then, thirdly, to the recognition of an underlying identity as between self and other. We are distinguished from one another as property-holders, but therefore we share property-holding as a common characteristic.

This aspect of mutual recognition reaches its highest form in contract and exchange. As an object passes from one owner to another, it becomes apparent that what is embodied in it is not ultimately the will of this person or that, but rather will and personality as such. As Hegel puts it: 'contractual relationship is the means whereby one identical will can persist within the absolute difference between the property owners' (74). So contract represents the end of the beginning of the process of development which Hegel is sketching in the *Philosophy of Right*. Personality has now come out of its subjective condition into a public world. But not only that; it now begins to be intelligible as something that may be embodied in that world in its own right apart from its relation to particular human beings.

5. POVERTY AND EQUALITY

We have completed our account of Hegel's justification of private property. It is worth pausing to review our conclusions. Property-owning is said to be important to the human individual since it is only through owning and controlling property that he can embody his will in external objects and begin to transcend the subjectivity of his immediate existence. In working on an object, using it, and having control over it, an individual confers on his will a stability and a maturity that would not otherwise be possible, and enables himself to establish his place as one in a community of such wills. Of course, he must not remain forever preoccupied with his status as proprietor; there are other tasks to be undertaken before ethical development is complete. But Hegel is adamant that property is necessary: unless he can establish himself as an owner, an individual's development in other areas of ethical life will be seriously at risk.

It ought to follow immediately from this that *poverty*—the plight of the property*less*—is a matter of the gravest concern. First and foremost, it is of concern because people may starve and perish. But that is only part of it. There is also the fact that, from an ethical point of view, propertyless individuals are left stranded in their natural subjective immediacy. As Hegel points out (but in another context):

[T]o be confined to mere physical needs as such and their direct satisfaction would simply be the condition in which the mental is plunged in the natural and so would be one of savagery and unfreedom, while freedom itself is to be found only in the reflection of mind into itself, in mind's distinction from nature, and in the reflect of mind in nature. (194R)

Private property, as we saw, is important to individuals not just because it satisfies their physical needs—for all that the argument shows, needs might be satisfied as well in a communist system—but because of its liberating contribution to the life of the will. The plight of the propertyless, then, is all the more lamentable in that their condition denies them this liberation. All this ought to follow directly from Hegel's account of the importance of ownership.

(i) Hegel's Concern About Poverty

There is no doubt that Hegel was concerned about poverty. 'The important question of how poverty is to be abolished,' he wrote, 'is one of the most disturbing problems which agitate modern society' (244A).[54] Moroever, he seemed to have a realistic view of the tendency of a capitalist economy to generate poverty. He regarded

[54] For a discussion of this concern, see Plant, *Hegel* p. 232 and Cullen, *Hegel's Social and Political Thought*, pp. 85 ff.

the prosperity of civil society and the formation of what now would be described as a proletariat as, more or less, two sides of the same coin (195 and 243), and he wrote pessimistically of the 'decline of the masses into poverty' (245) as though this had the inevitability of natural law. His use of the term 'inner dialectic' (246) to characterize the process whereby a society is driven to seek markets abroad to solve the problem of poverty at home suggests an anticipation of Marx's central theses of the essential contradictions and crises of capitalist production and of the connection of this with imperialism.

But Hegel's *expressed* concern about poverty turns out to be quite limited in its basis. That concern relates, in the first instance, to the physical predicament of the poor. He articulates this concern as a right to subsistence, demanding 'that the securing of every single person's livelihood and welfare be treated and actualised as a right, i.e. that particular welfare as such be so treated' (230).[55] Hegel went on to assert: 'It is not simply starvation which is at issue: the further end in view is to prevent the formation of a pauperised rabble' (240A). Such a rabble tends to arise, he suggests, when there is joined with poverty a hatred of the rich, of society, and of government (244A). Poverty involves not only unsatisfied need but also certain ethical consequences: 'laziness of disposition, malignity' (241), 'a consequent loss of the sense of right and wrong, of honesty, and of the self-respect which makes a man insist on maintaining himself by his own work and effort . . .' (244).[56]

Reflecting this sort of concern, there is considerable discussion of the ways in which civil society can deal with poverty. Hegel rejects casual alms-giving as a solution since it relies on subjective and contingent contributions to deal with an objective social problem (242). The prime responsibility for individuals' subsistence should lie with their families. But Hegel recognizes that one of the functions of civil society is to tear the individual from his family ties and constitute him as a self-subsistent person (238). So the familial responsibility for subsistence falls now on civil society *in loco parentis*. From the fact that society has a duty in this regard, Hegel infers that it also has certain rights—in particular the right to require the poor to provide by work as far as possible for their own livelihood (240A). He considers the adverse effects on the economy

[55] See also Hegel, *Philosophy of Right*, sects. 240, 240A, and 244.
[56] There is an interesting discussion of propertylessness in Ireland in Hegel, 'The English Reform Bill', pp. 307–9.

which a programme of relief employment may have (245), and concludes the discussion with vague suggestions about the need to found colonies and find markets abroad (247 ff.).

But from our point of view, the significant point is this. There is, in the discussion of poverty in the *Philosophy of Right*, precious little attempt to link the plight of the poor with the ethical arguments in favour of private property. Objectively, the link is there, as we saw at the start of this section; and Hegel is aware that poverty had adverse effects on the ethical condition of the poor. But he never links the ethical effects of poverty with the fact that the poor man is not and cannot be an *owner*. He is worried, it seems, only by the social consequences of individuals' propertylessness. The nearest Hegel comes to an identification of poverty with lack of personhood and the conditions of freedom is in a gloss on his remarks about welfare:

Life as the sum of ends has a right against abstract right. If for example it is only by stealing bread that the wolf can be kept from the door, the action is of course an encroachment on someone's property, but it would be wrong to treat this action as an ordinary theft. To refuse to allow a man in jeopardy of his life to take such steps for self-preservation would be to stigmatize him as without rights, and since he would be deprived of his life, his freedom would be anulled altogether. ... [T]he only thing that is necessary is to live *now*, the future is not absolute but ever exposed to accident. Hence it is only the necessity of the immediate present which can justify a wrong action, because not to do the action would in turn be to commit an offence, indeed the most wrong of all offences, namely the complete destruction of all freedom. (127A)

There are hints here that the clash is not just one of needs versus rights, but rather one of rights versus rights, property against property, as Proudhon put it.[57] But they are no more than hints, and it seems clear that Hegel's main concern is with life as the precondition of all rights, rather than with the propertyless man's right to property as such. The exception here that he allows is strikingly similar to that which I argued for in Chapter 7 and which Locke, as we saw in Chapter 6, imposed as an overarching proviso: that the claims of desperate need prevail against all property rights. But does not amount to any recognition that the needy man has a right to his own property.

What Hegel seems to miss, then, is the point stressed in Chapter 9: that any account of why property-owning is important to individuals is equally and necessarily an account of why property-lessness, in the case of any individual is a matter of concern. Or, to put it the other way round: if our only concern about poverty is concern about unsatisfied physical need and its social effects, how can the *property-owner* have an argument against communism or any other system which might satisfy needs as efficiently as private property? How can there be a concern which is articulated in his case which is not equally articulated in the case of the propertyless? In attempting to insulate the discussion of private property from the question of the evil of poverty, Hegel risks the accusation that he does not really take seriously the argument that private property, as such, is something that all individuals need.[58] If Hegel wants to maintain his position that private property is necessary for the development of free will, then he must answer the question which as we saw was posed by Proudhon: 'Well, is it not true . . . that if the liberty of man is sacred, it is equally in all individuals; that if it needs property for its objective action, that is, for its life, the appropriation of material is equally necessary for all . . . ?'[59]

The point of all this is that, lurking in the background, there is a grave threat to the viability of Hegel's argument for property. If poverty is, as Hegel sometimes suggests, a necessary feature of the operation of an advanced private property economy—if (as Marx argued in *The Communist Manifesto*[60]) there cannot be private property for anyone at all unless nine-tenths of the population is propertyless—then the possibility of a GR-based argument for private property, along the lines of the one we have attributed to Hegel, is in danger. Any thesis about the inevitability of widespread propertylessness threatens the collapse of the sort of argument that Hegel wants to put forward in favour of private property. (We will consider how this danger can be responded to in Chapter 12.)

There are, I think, several possible explanations of Hegel's failure to see these points; they will be discussed in the rest of this section and in the next. But none of them excuses his failure to confront this crucial issue.

[58] See above, Ch. 9.
[59] Proudhon, *What is Property?*, p. 66.
[60] See Marx and Engels, *Communist Manifesto*, pp. 96–8, and the discussion in Ch. 12, below. But cf. Ryan, *Property and Political Theory*, p. 137.

(ii) A Right to a Mere Opportunity?

Hegel may have thought that his argument for private property showed the importance only of the *opportunity* or *liberty* to acquire property, not the importance of property-owning itself. If that were the case, then the concern which lies behind the right-based argument for property would not necessarily carry over into a concern about propertylessness. It would do so only if he believed that one of the reasons for poverty was that some people were effectively banned from private ownership or prevented from attempting to acquire it. This is a position whose merits we shall examine in the next chapter. But for the time being it is worth saying one or two things about it as an interpretation of Hegel.

Certainly, this is how Hegel has been interpreted by some of his commentators. K.-H. Ilting claims that on Hegel's account, 'only the *possibility* of private property is granted to all',[61] seeming to indicate that the Hegelian right to property is nothing more substantial than the right to be *eligible* to be a property-owner.[62] Similarly, Richard Teichgraeber offers this interpretation of Hegel's statement that 'everyone must have property' (49A): 'This statement . . . is not a practical directive; it makes sense only when one keeps in mind that it is *the attempt to have* that really concerns Hegel here.'[63] I think this interpretation of Hegel is mistaken. In regard to the fundamental justification of property, Hegel does not say that a person must *try* to translate his freedom into an external sphere or that his will becomes objective to him in the *attempt* to embody it in an object. His thesis is not that one must *try* to supersede the subjectivity of immediate life or that one does in fact supersede that subjectivity by *trying* to embody one's will in an object. And his claim is certainly not that one embodies one's will in an object by *trying* to become the possessor of it. On the contrary, Hegel claims all the time that what matters is *actual* ownership, *actual* embodiment of one's will, *actual* supersession of immediate subjectivity.

Think back to our discussion of the ethical importance of embodiment in section 4. The will is matured and stabilized by its actual exercise on objects, by the reflection of itself into itself involved in labour and subsequent use. If one never actually gains

---

[61] Ilting, 'Structure of Hegel's *Philosophy of Right*', p. 93.
[62] See Ch. 1, sect. 4.
[63] Teichgraeber, 'Hegel on Property and Poverty', pp. 54–5.

control of any object then one never gets the benefits of the exercise of one's will on objects; one's will, then, never develops in the way that Hegel thinks it is important for it to develop. The liberating discipline which ownership involves never takes place. Similarly with regard to mutual recognition. The recognition which Hegel takes to be important to self-definition at this stage is the mutual recognition of *property-owners*; it is certainly not the sidelong glances that competitors for control of scarce resources are likely to throw at one another.

I am not suggesting that no GR-based argument could be made out for the proposition that Ilting and Teichgraeber take Hegel to be asserting. One might want to argue, for instance, that it is a matter of concern that every individual develop the sense of responsibility, competititiveness, and self-reliance that can be fostered only by participation in a deadly struggle for scarce resources.[64] But that is not Hegel's argument in the *Philosophy of Right*.

(iii) Equality and Inequality

In a number of places Hegel denies that his argument for property dictates any principle of the *equal* distribution of goods. As we saw in section 2, Hegel wants to distinguish at this stage between an individual's bare personality and the details of his particular existence. The argument about property focuses exclusively on the former: it is concerned with individuals *qua* persons—that is, individuals considered merely as free wills and as bearers of rights. Of course, it is our particular needs and desires that attract us to particular goods; but then (as I have stressed throughout) our needs and wants could be satisfied equally well under communism. When we are arguing for *private* property, we are interested only in the relation between person and object in the abstract. In this connection, Hegel believes that the quantity and quality of the particular goods in one person's possession, and their proportion to the goods in somebody else's possession, are irrelevant. The qualitative and the quantitative proportions may matter to them, but they do not matter so far as the abstract argument for private property is concerned.

---

[64] See the discussion of this approach in Ch. 8, sect. 4, above, and Chapter 11, below.

So the demand for material equality is misconceived, if it is supposed to arise out of the argument for property: 'At this point, equality could only be the equality of abstract persons as such, and therefore the whole field of possession, this terrain of inequality, falls outside it' (49R). Elsewhere in the *Philosophy of Right*, Hegel stresses the factual inequality of men in skills, endowments, and other mental and bodily characteristics and he argues (perhaps implausibly) that individuals have a right that this inequality should be permitted to prevail in economic life (200 and 200R). But that is a separate argument. Any demand for equality which arose out of the right to property would outweigh the alleged 'right of particularity'; and certainly the demand that 'everyone must have property' (49A) is bound to do so.[65]

Whatever their basis, Hegel's remarks about equality do nothing to dampen the concern that his theory ought to require for the plight of the propertyless. If we compare two individuals—one a wealthy landowner, the other a pauper—it is clear that the proportion between their respective possessions is not just an accidental feature of the particularities of their lives. The proportion in question is that of *plenty to zero*, and that is a radical difference of kind, not a mere difference of degree or detail. It is a difference that does affect personality as such in its possibilities for development. In fact, Hegel's position on this is stated quite plainly in a passage worth quoting at length:

> Of course men are equal, but only *qua* persons, that is, with respect only to the source from which possession springs; the inference from this is that *everyone must have property*. But this equality is something apart from the fixing of particular amounts, from the question of how much I own. From this point of view, it is false to maintain that justice requires everyone's property to be equal, since *it requires only that everyone shall own property*. The truth is that particularity is just the sphere where there is room for inequality and where equality would be wrong. (49A; my emphasis)[66]

There is room then for genuine concern, from the point of view of *justice* and the right of personality, about the sheer propertylessness of the impoverished man.

[65] Stillman, 'Property, Freedom and Individuality', p. 144, claims that Hegel actually uses the fact that private property produces inequality as an argument for the former. I am inclined to doubt this.

[66] I discuss the relation between equality and a general right to property in sect. 2 of Ch. 12, below.

But now it may be objected that we are hardly ever likely to come across a case of *absolute* propertylessness. Surely even the most destitute beggar owns the rags that he wears and the bowl that he holds out for alms. Is this not enought to satisfy the demand of justice that he, like everyone else, must have property? In other words, how are we to avoid trivializing the demand for property, once we abandon any concern about the amount of property people own? Surely it will be sufficient now to satisfy Hegel's argument that everyone be allocated a little piece of wood on which he can work, while inequality (or perhaps even communism) is permitted to prevail with respect to all other resources.

There is, I believe, an answer to this implicit in Hegel's account. The will that is to be embodied in property is not an idle will or a will whose content is simply a desire for play: it is the will of a natural being driven by needs that relate to its subsistence. We have seen that Hegel does not want to *base* his justification of private property on the satisfaction of physical needs. But that does not mean they drop out of his account altogether. Rather we must understand the relation between needs and property in a slightly different way. Private property is justified because of the way in which a *need-laden will* must be related to objects in order to foster the ethical development of the individual. Clearly, none of the ethical benefits of property-owning—the maturing and stabilizing of the will, and the mutual recognition of persons—is likely to be achieved, unless the will that is reflected in objects is driven by motives that the agent takes seriously.[67]

One might imagine a system of the following sort. Fundamental human needs (food, shelter, etc.) are taken care of by a centralized distribution system based on goods held in common; but some right of private property is recognized and this is indulged by allowing individuals to own relatively unimportant goods.[68] Hegel could have no truck with such a proposal. The case for property requires that the will attain a maturity and an external embodiment with respect to its *more important* projects and resolutions. A person will not take his willing seriously if the only occasions on which he supersedes the subjective evanescence of desire, and the only

---

[67] See also no. 37, above. An analogy can perhaps be developed between the need for serious material motivation behind the will that is embodied in property and the need for serious sexual motivation behind the wills that are involved in marriage: see Hegel, *Philosophy of Right*, sect. 163R.

[68] Cf. Held, 'Property Rights and Interests', pp. 577–9.

projects that he stabilizes in the way we have described, are occasions and projects that are not important to him or to his subsistence.

It follows that propertylessness is a somewhat less clear-cut condition than it seemed. It is not the bare absence of *any* relation of possession and control between a person and an object. Rather, it is the condition of a person whose will, driven as it is by natural needs for subsistence, is unable to find an embodiment in external objects. This is certainly the condition of the beggar, even though he 'owns' his rags and begging bowl. For as far as his more important needs are concerned— food, shelter, even a place to stand—his will finds no embodiment in the external world. His condition, then, is just the sort of condition which Hegel ought to regard as a matter for grave concern, if he takes his argument for private property seriously.

6. FIRST OCCUPANCY

Hegel believed that his account of private property generated a justification for a theory of First Occupancy. His introduction of First Occupancy was abrupt and confident: 'The principle that a thing belongs to the person who happens to be the first in time to take it into his possession is immediately self-explanatory and superfluous, because a second person cannot take into his possession what is already the property of another' (50). And the point was hammered home in an Addition:

The points made so far have been mainly concerned with the proposition that personality must be embodied in property. Now the fact that the first person to take possession of a thing should also be its owner is an inference from what has been said. The first is the rightful owner, however, not because he is the first but because he is a free will, for it is only by another's succeeding him that he becomes the first. (50A)

Alan Ryan appears to accept this line: 'The first taker does not have to justify his taking; the question we ask is negative, not positive, namely whether the thing is already occupied by a will which demands respect.'[69] Since Hegel's view is that objects have no natural ends of their own (44A), the answer to the question is 'No'.

[69] Ryan, *Property and Political Theory*, p. 122.

If First Occupancy follows from the argument for property, then it is, Hegel claims, easy to explain the growth of inequality: 'Occupancy, as an external activity whereby we actualise our universal right of appropriating natural objects, comes to be conditioned by physical strength, cunning, dexterity, the means of one kind or another whereby we take physical possession of things' (52R). As a result, how much a person occupies will depend on accidental and particular factors. Some will end up with more than others, and if resources are even moderately scarce some may end up with nothing at all to occupy. Hegel imposes nothing like the so-called 'Lockean proviso'[70] on initial acquisition. He just assumes that any argument which justifies property will justify an individual's acquisition of any unoccupied object, without any thought for the acquisitive opportunities of anybody else.

It is easy to see why Hegel believed this. The general principle is that personality must be embodied in property; to the individual agent that principle yields a right, perhaps even something like a duty, to advance his own ethical development in this regard if he can. So when an individual who is to embody his will in the external world confronts an object which would satisfy his needs and which (being at this stage ownerless) offers no ethical resistance to his will, what could be more obvious than that he is entitled to go ahead and occupy it as his property? For suppose he refrained from occupying it: then he would have forgone an opportunity to supersede the subjectivity of his immediate existence and set himself on the road to the genuine ethical life. If he were required to satisfy himself at every point that there is 'enough and as good left for others' to embody their wills, the opportunity to get his own will embodied might pass. In a situation where no fairer or more reliable means of allocating objects to individuals for the embodiment of their wills is available—that is, in a Lockean 'state of nature'—the argument seems to go through.

But it is a mistake to think that First Occupancy, understood and justified in this way, is capable of yielding entitlements which can operate as moral constraints on the redistributive efforts of a subsequently instituted government. Certainly, as we saw earlier, Hegel does not believe that property rights are absolute anyway against the demands that might arise out of higher stages of ethical development (see section 1 above). But that is a different point.

[70] See above, Ch. 6, sect. 15, and also Ch. 7, sect. 5.

Even if conflicting 'higher' demands are not involved, still Hegelian
First Occupancy will not yield entitlements resistant to redistribution. For, on Hegel's account, it is a matter of concern (indeed, a
demand of justice and respect for personality) that everyone should
have property. In a 'state of nature', individuals are entitled to
appropriate unilaterally only because they cannot be expected to
shoulder that universal concern. The mechanisms for doing so—for
seeing that there is enough left for others —are not available. But
when these mechanisms do become available, when a government
is set up which shows itself willing and able to redistribute goods in
a way that will satisfy the demands of justice, *then* entitlements
founded upon the assumption of the absence of such mechanisms
cannot prevail. It follows that the natural inequality that one would
expect to arise out of unilateral appropriation by individuals in a
'state of nature' cannot by itself justify or explain away the
persistence of propertylessness in society.[71]

There are passages where Hegel approaches some sort of
recognition of these points. He argues in one place: 'Original, i.e.
direct, titles and means of acquisition (see paragraphs 54 ff.) are
simply discarded in civil society and appear only as isolated
accidents or as subordinated factors of property transactions'
(217R). This is slightly ambiguous. It may be simply a restatement
of Hegel's main theme in paragraph 217, that once civil society is
under way acquisition of property must take place in a legally
prescribed form, and any title acquired in the state of nature must
now be legitimized in the new legal forms.[72] Or it may be a more
radical point: not only are the *modes* of acquisition which prevailed
in the state of nature now invalid, but also the entitlements that
arose under those modes. On this interpretation, all originally
acquired property is liable to be called in and distributed anew once
civil society is under way.[73] It is not clear which claim Hegel
wanted to commit himself to.

In another (rather bewildering) passage Hegel suggests that the
change from the state of nature to civil society may actually be to
the *detriment* of the poor: 'The poor still have the needs common to
civil society, and yet since society has withdrawn from them the
natural means of acquisition (see paragraph 217) . . . their poverty

[71] See above, Ch. 7, sect. 5, and also Ch. 9.
[72] This would be a position close to Kant's, *Metaphysical Elements of Justice*,
sects. 9 and 41–2 (Ladd trans., pp. 65–72).
[73] Cf. Tully's interpretation of Locke: *A Discourse on Property*, Pt. III.

leaves them more or less deprived of all the advantages of society
. . . ' (241). The suggestion here seems to be that the poor are worse
off as a result of the legal ban on unilateral acquisition. Perhaps
Hegel means that they may not now squat on land or poach game.
But those restrictions might be involved in a State of Nature, if
someone had appropriated the land or the game in question. But if,
there is, in civil society, genuinely ownerless land and game, then it
is difficult to see why the *poor*—as opposed to anybody else—
should suffer from a law forbidding the unilateral acquisition of
such goods.

So the First Occupancy theory which Hegel tacked on to his
argument for private property does little to alleviate the concern
which that argument ought to require for the plight of the
propertyless. It certainly does not provide the civil authorities with
any excuse for failing to undertake redistribution to ensure that
everyone has some property since the First Occupancy part of the
theory only works on the assumption that no such redistribution is
possible.

It remains to be seen whether Hegel *could* have repaired the gaps
that we have seen in his theory. That is, it remains to be shown that
the ideals of maintaining a system of *private* property and seeing to
it that everyone has some significant property of his own are
compatible. Marx's challenge in this respect has not been answered
(though the basis for an answer is sketched in Chapter 12.) But
Hegel never even confronted the question. Though his account of
the justification of property is deep, plausible, and attractive, his
central mistake was his failure to see that private property can be
justified as a right of personality only if it can be made available to
every person on whose behalf that argument can be made out.

11

Self-Ownership and the Opportunity
to Appropriate

I. A COMMON VIEW

In discussions I have had, it is common to hear people say that there
is indeed a human right to private property, but that it is a right
which is adequately respected so long as everyone has the
opportunity to acquire private property. It is not, they say, a right
which requires that everyone should actually *own* something: a
propertyless person has his right to property respected as long as he
has the chance of becoming the owner of something substantial.

At the same time, however, this right is held to be one that
prohibits taking things away from their owners (or doing so
'arbitrarily' or without compensation or whatever). Even though
one can *satisfy* the right by seeing to it merely that everyone has a
chance to become an owner, it is sufficient for a *violation* of the
right that one take actual property even if the victim of the
expropriation is left with the chance to acquire some more. Though
guaranteeing the opportunity to acquire is sufficient for respecting
the right in the case of a poor man, taking away that opportunity is
not necessary for something to count as a violation of the right in
the case of a rich man. The right to property, then, according to this
common view, is strangely asymmetrical in its character. But that
oddness pales into insignificance when compared with its rhetorical
advantages. A right like this has the immense advantage that it
enables us to congratulate a capitalist society for protecting and
upholding property as a universal human right, even though many
or most of the members of that society are in fact the owners of
little or nothing. Of course, those who hold this view do not
necessarily deny that poverty and radical inequality are matters of
considerable concern. It is a pity perhaps that so much of the wealth
of the society is concentrated in so few hands, and that so many go
hungry or have no chance to make a decent life for themselves. But
it is not a concern connected with the right to property.

We have encountered this view several times already. In Chapter 1, we took it as the third of four possible interpretations of the claim—made in the 1789 Declaration of the Rights of Man and the Citizen, and elsewhere—that property was one of the fundamental rights of man. The other three were (1) that existing property rights should be associated with an immunity against expropriation, (2) that property rights could be regarded as natural rights, and (4) that everyone had the right to actually be an owner of property. Interpretation (3) was that everyone has the right not to be excluded from the class of potential property-owners, in the way, for example, that slaves and women have been excluded in the past; but, as I have already mentioned, the common version of this view associates it with something like (1) as well. In recent political philosophy, this interpretation of the right to property, has been championed by John Rawls as one of the basic liberties included under the first of his principles of justice. Rawls, however, did not attempt to make any argument for this position; and he indicated that it was to apply only to personal goods and that it left quite open the issue of property in the means of production in an economy.[1] We saw in Chapter 9 that this interpretation of the right to property might also be a way of avoiding the 'Proudhon strategy'— that is, the strategy that infers the imperative of 'Property for all' from the claim that private ownership is necessary for genuine freedom. Finally in Chapter 10, we saw it put forward as an interpretation of Hegel's position on property by K.-H. Ilting and J. Teichgraeber: they both maintained (I think quite mistakenly) that Hegel's argument about the relation between property and the development of personality required only that 'the *possibility* of private property is granted to all'.[2]

In this chapter I want to examine in more detail the view that people have a general right only to an *opportunity* to acquire property. I want to ask what this view amounts to, and how it might possibly be justified.

To ask what it amounts to is to concentrate primarily on the concept of an *opportunity*. What is it to have an opportunity to acquire property but not actually to own any property? Is opportunity merely a legal characteristic of personality—a

[1] Rawls, *Theory of Jusitce*, pp. 61 and 265 ff.

[2] Ilting, 'Structure of Hegel's *Philosophy of Right*', p. 93; Teichgraeber, 'Hegel on Property and Poverty', pp. 54–5. See also Ch. 10, above, particularly the text to nn. 60–4.

Hohfeldian power to acquire and perhaps also a liability to be the recipient of someone's gift, transfer, or bequest? Or is it a concept that tells us something more, for example, something about the material situation that a person is in—that there are (or have been or will be) resources available which he is physically as well as legally capable of acquiring, or that (in some other way) there is, was, or will be some substantial likelihood of his becoming a proprietor should he choose to make the effort to do so? That is one set of questions we should consider.

The other set of questions concerns justification. From one point of view, it is easy to justify a right to an opportunity; that will be done if any of the general lines of justification for property considered in Chapters 8 and 10 go through. To say that people have a general right actually to be owners, but to deny that they have a right to an opportunity to become owners, is almost to contradict oneself. The real difficulty, however, lies not in justifying the opportunity claim, but in justifying that *and no more*. Let me put the point in abstract terms. To justify the sort of distinctive position we are considering in this chapter, one has to show that the opportunity to become X is sufficiently important in political morality to form the basis of a human right while simultaneously denying that *actually being* X has that degree of importance. The question that must be faced is this: if an individual's interest in having the opportunity to become X is important enough to warrant holding others to be under a duty to provide him with that opportunity, why is his interest in being X not also important enough to warrant holding others to be under a duty to make him X? I am not saying there cannot be an argument which leads to the former sort of conclusion but not to the latter; but if there is, it has to be shown. The background point is that we must keep faith with the justificatory values we invoke to defend our modest claims, and we must be prepared to follow through on them even if they lead beyond the position we want to defend in the direction of politically uncongenial conclusions.

2. SPECIAL RIGHTS AND UNIVERSALIZATION

The weakest interpretation of the opportunity claim is that it is simply the universalization of an SR-based theory of property, of the sort held by Locke and Nozick.

We say that if a person is the first to labour on a resource (or occupy it, or whatever), then he gets to be its owner, or that if a person receives something in a just transfer from someone else who is its owner, then he gets to be its owner. We assert that; then we universalize it (quantifying universally over the *x* who may acquire or the *x* who is a potential transferee); and then we present it as a general right to an opportunity which everybody has. Everyone has the right, by his actions, to acquire resources if he can; and everyone has the right to own what others give him, in an exchange, or by way of gift or bequest.

Taken in this sense, the 'opportunity' which the claim involves is nothing but the existence—literally, *in principle*—of a Hohfeldian power (to make oneself an owner) and/or a liability (to be made an owner by somebody else). It is nothing but the expression of a principled connection between the occurrence of a certain contingency and a change in normative relations. Any argument for the 'opportunity', then, will simply be an argument for establishing that connection—between labouring and becoming an owner, or between being chosen by a testator and becoming an owner, or whatever it is. If those connections can be defended, there is nothing more to do in the way of establishing that people should have these 'opportunities'. For people to have an 'opportunity', in this sense, is simply for it to be the case that an SR-based defence of property, like Locke's or Nozick's, is implemented. In Chapters 6 and 7, we considered whether such theories might be justified. Our conclusions there were largely negative: the most famous theory of this sort—that of John Locke—failed to make a convincing case for acquisition by labour; and the failure of Robert Nozick's argument seemed to indicate that no such theory could be made defensible, at least in an unqualified form. But if they *were* justified, the claim that people had a right to an opportunity to own property, but not an actual right to property, would be justified too. Only it would be very modest and formalistic talk. Talk about a right to an 'opportunity' to acquire, or talk of a right to receive what others give you, would be nothing more or less than a way of talking about the operation of a principle of justice in acquisition or of a principle of justice in transfer.

To put it another way, this sort of talk does not really take us beyond special rights to general or human rights. It is just a way of talking about the general application to persons of the principles under which special rights come into existence. As we saw in

Chapter 4, any principle governing special rights, may be reformu-
lated (with perhaps some slight difficulty) as a principle attributing
a right which is general, albeit conditional, to everyone. But that
reformulation contributes nothing of substance. It remains the case
that the 'opportunity' to acquire property is nothing but the
possession of the right that, *if* one should labour (or whatever) on
an unowned resource, *then* one will become its owner.

Now, as it is usually understood, the opportunity claim is always
at least slightly stronger than this. It is taken to involve also the
assertion that there should not be any disqualifications of status in
relation to the basis of property-holding. 'Anyone who is the first to
labour on something gets to be its owner' is a universal principle;
but so is 'Any *male* who is the first to labour on a resource gets to be
its owner'. One of the intentions behind the opportunity claim is, I
think, to rule out principles of the second kind. The acquisitive
opportunity (even if it is nothing more than the existence in
principle of an Hohfeldian power or liability) must be available,
without discrimination, to *everyone*, not just males (or free-born
citizens or whites or whatever). So the idea of a universal right to an
opportunity, on this interpretation, might be used as a a basis for
criticizing things like the old legal doctrine that women could not
own real estate in their own right or the Group Areas Act in South
Africa.

But even this universal doctrine remains well within the overall
SR-based approach. The argument against discrimination might
simply be, for example, that the gender of the labourer is irrelevant
to the argument from labour to acquisition, and so there is as much
reason for respecting the interest that a woman creates in an object
by labouring on it as there is for respecting the interest of a man
under similar circumstances. If our theory is Lockean, we will argue
that a woman stands to lose as much if an object embodying her
labour is taken away from her as a man does. If it is a theory of First
Occupancy, we will say that all the right-based reasons for making
an owner out of the first man to occupy a piece of land apply
unproblematically to the first woman too. If it is based on desert,
we will argue that a woman's work, other things being equal, is as
morally deserving as a man's. And so on. Put bluntly, the claim
would be that nothing except whether a person has performed the
appropriate acquisitive action (or been the recipient in a just
transfer) should be allowed to determine whether that person is to
be a property-owner or not. Allowing other considerations like

gender, birth, or race to enter the picture would be to submit to reasons which were morally irrelevant.

Suppose, however, it were shown that the acquisitive action (A) required by our theory of property was an action that in fact men were better or more adept at performing than women. Men might be better than women at mixing their labour with things; they might, through nature or nurture, be more aggressive and competitive, and thus more likely to do better in a land rush where people were let loose on a territory and where the first to stake out a claim to a piece of land got it as his property. There might be an 'old boy network' in existence, so that men were many times more likely to be beneficiaries of transfers than women were. Nothing in the idea of a right to property, as we are presently interpreting it, would indicate the slightest reason for concern about these inequalities of real opportunity. The theories we are considering hold only that, *if* one mixes labour on a resource or receives it in a transfer, *then* one acquires an interest in it which is a matter of right-based concern. But the concern is entirely contingent: no acquisition, no concern. The fact that—for whatever reason—one class of people is less likely than another to fall under this contingency is as irrelevant to the principle of property (on this account) as the fact that lepers are unlikely to have promises made to them is to the principle that promises, when made, must be kept. The promising principle is concerned with the new expectations of those who have had promises made to them, not with the vague wishes of those who, for one reason or another, have not. And equally, an SR-based theory of property is concerned with the fortunes of people who happen to have forged the moral links with a resource that the theory deems to be important. From this point of view, the fact that one class is less likely to forge those links than another is neither here nor there. Of course, it is true that there are senses of 'opportunity' and 'discrimination' in terms of which these situations would undoubtedly amount to discriminatory denials of equal opportunity. But we cannot simply invoke these other senses. The sense of the concepts we deploy is given by the arguments with which we defend them; and the sort of arguments used by an SR-based theorist will not justify the use of these more demanding conceptions of opportunity.

There is another way in which the position we are considering might be strengthened. Locke recognized that the idea of private property as a matter of special right, acquired through acquisition and transfer, was quite compatible with the existence of widespread common or collective property.[3] A society might decide that certain pieces of land should remain common in perpetuity and be declared 'off-limits' to private acquisition, while at the same time recognizing the legitimacy of unilateral acquisition in relation to resources not restricted in this way. Even a communist society might give private acquisition a role to play: it might provide, for example, that anyone who catches a fish in a public river or shoots a deer in a public forest may keep his catch as his own private property, and it might justify that on SR-based grounds, while at the same time insisting that neither industrial plant nor agricultural land could be appropriated by those means. Forbidding people to make an appropriation is no more a violation of a principle of justice in acquisition than forbidding people to make promises is a violation of the principle that promises must be kept. If people are given notice that it is unlawful to labour on one's own initiative on certain types of resource, then it may be perfectly reasonable to hold that doing so does not generate any rights, even though similar labour on a different sort of resource would generate such rights. (The analogy is that we forbid certain promises—such as promises to commit murder for a fee—and do not regard them as generating enforceable rights, should anyone purport to enter into them.) Now to avoid or diminish the possibility of this sort of restriction, someone might want to insist, not only that everyone should have the legal power to acquire property, but also that *all resources* or *as many resources as possible* should be available for acquisition in this way. One gets the impression that those who support the SR-based approach to the justification of property also support this position: they would be unhappy with a situation in which substantial new resources, when discovered, were not left available for private acquisition in the normal way, or in which *res nullius*, as they came to hand through intestacy, for example, were simply taken over by the state.[4]

But while the first way of strengthening the principle (non-discrimination) is easy to defend, this second way is much more difficult. Why exactly is it thought important that resources should be made available for private acquisition rather than dealt with by a

---

[3] Locke, *Two Treatises*, II, sect. 35.
[4] CF. Locke's suggestion, ibid. I, sect. 90, that goods which are ownerless 'come into the Hands of the Public Magistrate'.

society in some other way (when there is a choice)? A utilitarian argument may be made against establishing too many commons (but then one wonders why utilitarian considerations are not also used to determine who becomes the owner of what).[5] Certainly it will be difficult for the defender of this position to find right-based reasons for strengthening it in this way. The SR-based approach provides no support. As we have seen, it establishes only a conditional position; it provides no reason for seeing that the condition is fulfilled. A GR-based argument, on the other hand, opens up a whole new can of worms for the defender of this sort of position. If they say that people need to appropriate things, or that this is something they have a right to—and that this is why as many resources as possible must be legitimate targets for acquisition—then consistency requires that they be ready to articulate that concern on behalf of those who do not, or who are unable to, make any appropriation even under the most favourable conditions. And if they say people are entitled to an opportunity to appropriate, which is unjustly denied them when some resources are made unavailable for appropriation, then they may (as I shall argue in section 4) have a hard job holding the line against those who believe that the very same considerations require an assurance of property for everyone. For the 'opportunity' that they will be invoking now will be much more substantial than that which was simply derived from the SR-based theory. That was just an opportunity to be an owner, and it amounted to nothing more than an Hohfeldian power. But now what is called for is the provision of an opportunity to do what is necessary to become an owner, and that is a much more demanding and may lead to a much more radical position.

It is worth noting, by the way, how similar this strengthened position is to the so-called 'Lockean proviso'—that every appropriator leave 'enough and as good in common for others' to appropriate.[6] Both positions require it to be the case not only that appropriation, when it happens, generates property rights, but also that people have a right to make an appropriation. I argued in Chapter 6 that Locke did not actually adhere to this 'Lockean' proviso. But if anyone else does, they are likely to find themselves in

---

[5] See Hardin, 'Tragedy of the Commons', in Ackerman (ed.), *Economic Foundation of Property Law*.

[6] Locke, *Two Treatises*, II, sects. 27 and 33; see Ch. 6, sect. 15, above.

a difficulty similar to the one we are indicating here: the argument for the proviso, if there is one, may generate rather more radical conclusions than its defenders would be willing to adopt.

3. THE IDEA OF SELF-OWNERSHIP

One reason, perhaps, for thinking that people have a right to make an appropriation is that nothing less than this is consistent with the doctrine of self-ownership.

The idea of self-ownership has been made popular in modern discussions of property by Robert Nozick. But it can be traced back to Locke's claim in the *Second Treatise* that 'every Man has a Property in his own Person. Thus no Body has any Right to but himself.'[7] In Locke's theory, the claim was used as a premiss for the argument about mixing one's labour: since I own my person, I own my actions, and therefore I can come to own whatever my actions are irretrievably mixed with. I argued in Chapter 6 that both this argument and the underlying idea of owning one's actions were problematic: since actions are dated events, it is quite incoherent to talk of ownership rights in them after they have been performed; and it is even more incoherent to think that the ownership of one's past actions (whatever that means) is somehow imperilled by certain ways of dealing with external objects.

Nozick, however, does not put the idea of self-ownership to this use. Instead, he uses it initially as a way of expressing a point about liberty. To say that I own myself is to say that nobody but me has the right to dispose of me or to direct my actions. *I* have rights to do these things (though I must not harm others in doing so; that is, I must not exercise my self-ownership in a way which violates theirs), and those rights are exclusive of anyone else's privilege in this regard, for they are correlative to others' duties to refrain from interfering with what, in this sense, I own. G. A. Cohen elucidates Nozick's idea in terms of an analogy with slave-owning:

[The] thought is that each person is the morally rightful owner of himself. He possesses over himself, as a matter of moral right, all those rights that a slaveholder has over a complete chattel slave as a matter of legal right, and he is entitled, morally speaking, to dispose over himself in the way such a

---

[7] Locke, *Two Treatises*, II, sect. 27; also Nozick, *Anarchy, State, and Utopia*, pp. 171 ff.

slaveholder is entitled, legally speaking, to dispose over his slave. Such a slaveholder may not direct his slave to harm other people, but he is not legally obliged to place him at their disposal to the slightest degree: he owes none of his slave's services to anyone else. So, analogously, if I am the moral owner of myself, and therefore of this right arm, then, while others are entitled to prevent it from hitting people, no one is entitled without my consent, to press it into their own or anybody else's service . . . [8]

Nozick even suggests that, just as a slave-holder may sell his slave to another, so I, if I am the owner of myself, may sell myself into slavery.[9] But we do not need to go that far in order to make sense of the ownership idea in this context. As we saw in Chapter 2, though many conceptions of ownership entail a power of complete alienation, not all do. I can be the owner of something in the sense that it is for me rather than for anyone else to make decisions about its use (and in the sense that society will back up my decisions with force if need be), without it being the case that I can, by my say-so, transfer exactly that power of decision over the resource to somebody else.

The Nozickian idea of self-ownership gets its attraction not only from ideas about liberty, but also from the fears, 'intuitions', and hunches we have about the use and cannibalizing of one another's bodies and one another's body parts. In John Harris's article 'The Survival Lottery' and elsewhere consequentialists have argued that, as organ transplant techniques improve, it may be impossible to resist the demand that the organs of some healthy people should be cannibalized in order to save the lives of a larger number of sick people. A's heart may save the life of B, his lungs may save the life of C, his kidneys the life of D, his blood the life of E, and his corneas could be thrown into the bargain. Of course, this would result in A's death; but *failing* to do it would result in the death of B, C, D, and E; and so the cannibalizing seems to be a necessary evil from a consequentialist point of view.[10] Nozick and others are alarmed at this prospect, and they are alarmed that modern theories of justice and rights provide no principled basis for opposing such a course of action. A commitment to maximizing utility or even a Rawlsian commitment to maximizing the prospects of the worst-off group in society may require us to redistribute body parts, unless

---

[8] Cohen, 'Self-Ownership, World-Ownership and Equality, p. 109.
[9] Nozick, *Anarchy, State, and Utopia*, p. 331.
[10] Ibid. 206–7; Harris, 'The Survival Lottery', pp. 81–7.

we are prepared to recognize a basic entitlement to self-ownership. Utilitarians and Rawlsians alike believe that such entitlements will emerge naturally in the working out of their principles: it is doubtful, they say, that utility or the welfare of the worst off will ever *really* be promoted by such ghastly interventions, but they add that we must beware of simply committing ourselves to our 'intuitions' on these matters without exploring their basis in utility or justice. In other words, as Nozick points out, they assume that there are no *fundamental* entitlements; they assume that 'there is some level [of moral thought] so deep that no entitlements operate that far down'.

May all entitlements be relegated to relatively superficial levels? For example, people's entitlements to the parts of their own bodies? An application of the principle of maximizing the position of those worst off might well involve forceable redistribution of bodily parts ('You've been sighted for all these years; now one—or even both—of your eyes is to be transplanted to others'), or killing some people early to use their bodies in order to provide material necessary to save the lives of those who otherwise would die young. To bring up such cases is to sound slightly hysterical. But we are driven to such extreme examples in examining Rawls' prohibition on micro counterexamples. That not all entitlements in microcases are plausibly construed as superficial, and hence as illegitimate material by which to test our suggested principles, is made especially clear if we focus on those entitlements and rights that most clearly are not socially or institutionally based. On what grounds are such cases, whose detailed specification I leave to the ghoulish reader, ruled inadmissible?[11]

The implication is that only a right of self-ownership—as Nozick puts it, 'a line (or hyper-plane) [which] circumscribes an area in moral space around an individual'[12]—can provide protection for individual integrity against these proposals, and that such a right has simply to be accepted as a axiom, rather than established as an theorem, of our thinking about these matters.

But even if a right of self-ownership is necessary, how can it connect up with property in external resources? Locke tried to use it as a premiss for his SR-based account; but that, as we saw, did not work. More recent theorists have argued, however, that self-ownership gives us a right to deploy, exploit, and keep the fruits of our own abilities, and that this is what requires society to ensure that the opportunity to appropriate is not taken away.

[11] Nozick, *Anarchy, State, and Utopia*, pp. 206–7.
[12] Ibid. 57.

The argument, as far as I understand it, goes like this. The 'self' or 'person' which I own is not merely a passive lump of flesh; it is an active self with talents and abilities. Those talents and abilities must also be said to be owned by me, for otherwise somebody else might be thought to have a power—rather like a slave-holder's—to direct their exercise. Some of these talents and abilities are not just capacities to act, they are capacities to make something of the resources of the world. An 'industrious and rational' Lockean farmer has the ability to turn a wilderness into a cultivated field; a talented prospector has the ability to find precious metals in a hitherto undiscovered location; and so on. They would not exercise these capacities apart from the prospect that they might better their material condition in this way. If that prospect is not open to them, their capacities will lie idle; and if, once they have exercised their capacities, the fruits of their labour are taken away from them, the exercise will have been, from their point of view, worthless. Either way, a regime which does not give people the opportunity to appropriate and improve resources for themselves renders worthless their ownership of the talents they might use in doing so. It is not essential to the exercise of a capacity like this that one actually succeed in the aim of the exercise. Though the capacities are exercised with an aim in view, what is essential for their exercise is that one *strive* towards the aim, with some realistic prospect of success, rather than that one necessarily achieve one's goal. Respect for self-ownership, then, does not require that everyone should succeed in acquiring property. But it does require that everyone should have the opportunity to appropriate property, and be able to pit his acquisitive talents against nature. This generates in turn a requirement that the resources of the world, or of the territory controlled by a state, must not be put off-limits to this sort of appropriative activity.

I have reconstructed this argument from various hints in the work of Nozick and others.[13] I do not think it holds water. Sometimes it is put forward in the form of a critique of a claim made by John Rawls; and if we see why the criticism does not work against Rawls, we can begin to see what is wrong with the overall position.

In *A Theory of Justice*, Rawls argued that the natural distribution

[13] Apart from Nozick, *Anarchy, State, and Utopia*, see Cohen, 'Self-Ownership, World-Ownership and Equality', and Sandel, *Liberalism and the Limits of Justice*, pp. 54–9.

of talents and abilities (together with the contingencies of their nurture and development in society) must be regarded as 'arbitrary from a moral perspective':

> It seems to be one of the fixed points of our considered judgements that no one deserves his place in the distribution of natural endowments, any more than one deserves one's initial starting place in society. The assertion that a man deserves the superior character that enables him to make the effort to cultivate his abilities is equally problematic; for his character depends in large part upon fortunate family and social circumstances for which he can claim no credit.[14]

The appropriate response to this arbitrariness, Rawls believes, is the Difference Principle, which requires any inequalities that result from natural capacities or social privilege to be sustained only to the extent that they contribute to the prospects of the least well-off group.

> We see then that the difference principle represents, in effect, an agreement to regard the distribution of natural talents as a common asset and to share in the benefits of this distribution whatever it turns out to be. Those who have been favored by nature, whoever they are, may gain from their good fortune only on terms that improve the situation of those who have lost out. The naturally advantaged are not to gain merely because they are more gifted, but only to cover the costs of training and education and for using their endowments in ways that help the less fortunate as well.[15]

This passage has been interpreted by Robert Nozick, Michael Sandel, and G. A. Cohen as a denial of self-ownership, so far as talents and natural endowments are concerned. Rawls regards 'natural talents as a common asset . . . as a collective resource', writes Nozick, whereas on his own view, people should be regarded as *entitled* to their talents, whether their distribution is morally arbitrary or not.[16] Cohen writes that Rawls (and also other egalitarians like Ronald Dworkin) 'treat people's personal powers as subject . . . to the same egalitarian principles of distribution that they apply, less controversially, to external wherewithal'.[17] And Sandel insists that Rawls's 'notion of society as the owner of natural assets for which individuals are the guardians' makes sense only on the basis of a

[14] Rawls, *Theory of Justice*, pp. 74 and 104.
[15] Ibid. 101–2.
[16] Nozick, *Anarchy, State, and Utopia*, pp. 225–6 and 228–9.
[17] Cohen, 'Self-Ownership, World-Ownership and Equality', p. 113; cf. Dworkin, 'What is Equality?: II. Equality of Resources'.

repudiation of the individualism that characterizes other aspects of the theory.[18] All of them imply that the doctrine leaves Rawls with an unacceptably thin notion of self-ownership. Though Rawls wants to insist that men may not be used as mere means to others' welfare, that position can be sustained, Nozick argues,

> only if one presses *very* hard on the distinction between men and their talents, assets, abilities, and special traits. Whether any coherent conception of a person remains when the distinction is so pressed is an open question. Why we, thick with particular traits, should be cheered that (only) the thus purified men within us are not regarded as means is also unclear.[19]

The consensus seems to be that if only a more full-blooded sense of self-ownership were accepted, Rawls's position would collapse.

It is not, I think, merely pedantic to point out that Rawls never says that personal talents are to be regarded as collective property. What he says is that *their distribution* is to be treated as a common asset—in other words, the fact that talents have been distributed thus and so is to be exploited for the benefit of all. Since this involves *acceptance* of the fact that X's talents are X's and Y's talents are Y's, and asks simply what we should do about that fact, it is hard to see how it can possibly be interpreted as the claim that the talents in question are not X's or Y's at all.

More tellingly, perhaps, the Rawlsian position rests on the insight that though the distribution of talents over individuals is natural, the design of the institutions within which these talents are exercised is not. 'The natural distribution is neither just nor unjust; nor is it unjust that men are born into society at some particular position. These are simply natural facts. What is just or unjust is the way that institutions deal with these facts.'[20] In any conceivable society, which might be the subject of speculations about justice, talents will be nurtured and exercised in an institutional framework. That framework will make a difference to what happens, socially and economically, when somebody exercises his talents. A man sings in the street; perhaps he is arrested for obstructing the sidewalk, or perhaps there is a custom that people throw money into his hat. A woman trains as a doctor and is willing to practise

[18] Sandel, *Liberalism and the Limits of Justice*, p. 102, and see generally Ch. 2 of that work.

[19] Nozick, *Anarchy, State, and Utopia*, p. 228.

[20] Rawls, *Theory of Justice*, p. 102.

her skills; perhaps she can charge her patients what she pleases, and recover the money from them in a court of law if they will not pay up; but perhaps she also has to pay taxes on her fees. A man has a talent for mineral prospecting; but he finds there are complicated arrangements for issuing mining licences to cover wilderness areas. And so on. There is no sense to the idea that talents can simply be *exercised* by those who own them apart from any social framework whatsoever. And there is no sense to the idea that there is a natural phenomenon called 'reaping the benefits of one's talents' which is understood apart from the social arrangements and institutions that define one's relationships to other people. Maybe people naturally get a good feeling from singing or digging in the earth; and in that sense benefiting from one's own talents may be 'naturally' bound up with exercising them. But I doubt whether even that is true; and it is certainly false that 'reaping the benefits' is a natural incident of self-ownership, if the benefits are supposed to flow from, or be gained at the expense of, other people. So, firstly, the mere fact that there *exists* a framework within which talents are exercised and within which the talented and their clients relate to one another cannot on its own amount to a derogation from self-ownership. Otherwise self-ownership would be impossibly (or incoherently) demanding. Secondly, it cannot be a derogation from self-ownership for us to consider as a society what we want this framework to be. After all, it is going to be *our* framework— we will have to live with it, and relate to one another under its auspices. Moreover, though utopian redesign of our society may be out of the question, there are certain choices that we face in relation to the remodelling or improvement of the framework, and it cannot be the case that it is wrong to address those questions. Further, since the framework affects not only the conditions under which people benefit from the exercise of their talents, but also the conditions under which their clients and others can be forced to pay for those benefits, and, more generally, the conditions under which everyone makes a life for himself, it cannot be a derogation of self-ownership from the point of view of the talented if we face those questions with the interests of all in mind.

This is not to say that no answers we come up with could ever amount to such a derogation. Forcing people to exercise their talents when they would rather not (conscription) is one way of doing that.[21] Handicapping them (breaking a pianists' fingers,

---

[21] Cf. Nozick, *Anarchy, State, and Utopia*, p. 229 and n.

giving an entrepreneur a frontal lobotomy to remove his competitive streak) is another. But neither of these is suggested by Rawls. What he suggests is the setting up of fiscal, redistributive, property, and welfare institutions which ensure that the framework in which fees are charged, salaries earned, profits made, debts collected, property sold, and so on, and without which none of that could possibly take place, is also a framework which ensures that the bottom of the ladder of well-being in society is as high as it can be, to the extent that the society faces practicable choices in the area. The suggestion may be inadequate as a theory of distributive justice for various reasons (and we cannot canvass its wider merits here). But it simply cannot be said that designing a system with this end in view is a way of encroaching on the self-ownership of the talented.

In *Anarchy, State, and Utopia*, Nozick argues that a proportional tax on earnings is the moral equivalent of forced labour, and so there is no distinction between, for example, forcing a pianist to play (which would be a violation of his self-ownership) and taxing his fees (which, on the account I am giving here, would not).[22] But his argument to this effect works—if it works at all—only on account of an analogy between limiting someone's alternatives and coercing, that is, threatening them. We say that a person is coerced to do X, on Nozick's account, if someone else says (credibly) that they will attach consequences to his not doing X which it would not have 'in the normal and (morally) expected course of events'. However, we have already established that there is no 'normal and (morally) expected course of events' so far as profiting from one's talents is concerned, apart from the specification of a social structure in which talents are exercised, fees charged, and so on. As Nozick himself points out, in another place, if it is unclear what the normal and expected course of events is, it is unclear whether there is coercion.[23] To take a position one way or the other, one would have to have *independent* reasons for thinking that taxing pianists' earnings was morally objectionable. (And I conjecture that the mere fact that the pianist is not benefiting from his talent as much as he might is unlikely to be accepted as the basis of such an independent moral objection.)

In all of this, I have been insisting that owning a talent is one thing, and benefiting from it in a scheme of social co-operation is quite another. What, then, does a person own when he owns a

---

[22] Ibid. 169–70.
[23] Nozick, 'Coercion', pp. 114 ff.

talent? If talk of ownership makes any sense in this area at all (which I doubt), I guess what he owns is a capacity that he can, as it were, 'plug in' or relate to any of an array of possible social structures to produce various levels of benefit, for himself and others. To own a great gymnastic talent, for example, is to be in a position to benefit in a certain way in the United States, to be in a position to benefit in a slightly different way in the Soviet Union, to not be in any particularly special position of benefit at all in a subsistence economy, and so on. I suspect, by the way, that serious work on this subject (which is almost never done by those who talk glibly about self-ownership) would reveal either that it is impossible to identify talents cross-culturally or that in doing so one packages up so much other social baggage in its description that it becomes impossible to use ownership of talents as a critical standard to evaluate the society in which the talent is understood. But even if that is not the case, a talent has to be understood as a sort of a function that takes social structures as its argument. To have one's ownership of a talent respected is for it to be the case that the function itself is not meddled with; but it can hardly be regarded as a demand that its domain should be restricted to only one or to a narrow range of arguments.

With all this in mind, let us return to the issue of appropriation. People have talents (as entrepreneurs, prospectors, farmers, etc.) which in a favourable situation they might use to derive particular benefits for themselves from the resources that they grab. Do we have a duty to provide that situation for them? Maybe we do; but if so, it is not on account of respect for their ownership of the talents that they have.

To see this, let us focus on the case of a prospector. A prospector's talent for self-motivation, crossing rough country, and divining or recognizing the signs of the presence of minerals is a capacity which when exercised will yield different benefits in different social structures. In a society where all the land (and everything in it, discovered or undiscovered) is already privately owned, and where there are never any breaks in that ownership, he will benefit from his talents only by hiring his services out to landowners and working to their instructions. In a 'new frontier' society, on the other hand, he will be able to benefit from the exercise of his canny abilities in appropriation, eschewing the easy farmland on the plains, and wandering into the hills where the real mineral wealth is to be found. In a socialist society, he may find himself having to work as a salaried employee of the state if he wants to exercise his talents; and though he may still receive considerable benefit from his abilities, they may not be as high as those he could earn in a different society as an entrepreneur acting on his own account. Now it seems to me that in all these situations, the prospector remains the owner of himself and his talents and is respected by others and by the state as such. No doubt there are other reasons for choosing between these types of society, but it does not seem as if this business of the ownership of talents is one of them.

What about a situation in which there is no opportunity at all for him to benefit from the exercise of his prospecting skills? Suppose there is a socialist state pledged to environmentalist principles which owns all the land, and will not allow anyone, under either private or public auspices, to develop mineral wealth. Is this a society which attacks the self-ownership of talented would-be prospectors? I do not think that this is among the (many) objections we could legitimately raise against such a regime (though it is obliquely connected with one or two of them). For even in such a set-up, the prospector retains his ability to recognize good spots for mineral development; he can go hiking and say to himself (and anyone else who will listen), 'There's probably some uranium over there. And some gold in them thar hills.' And everyone can acknowledge that these are his skills, and use them in party games etc. What he cannot do is make a living—either as an employee or as an entrepreneur—out of his skills. But lots of people have skills (tying knots, playing hopscotch) that they cannot make a living out of, and that is no derogation from their self-ownership.

There are doubtless talents which can only be exploited in a socialist bureaucracy—the talent of making one's way in a massive array of faceless offices, working the system, or whatever. When state enterprises are privatized, these opportunities may disappear, and there will no longer be any call for the skilled capacities of the talented *apparatchik*. If there is anything to the self-ownership argument I am criticizing, these reforms would amount to an attack on the self-ownership of the official, as much so as if we had cut his fingers off. But clearly that is absurd. By reforming the system, we are not taking his talents away from him; we are simply changing the social circumstances under which he may exercise them. It may be objected that the difference between the frustrated prospector in a socialist society and the frustrated *apparatchik* in a capitalist one, is that the talents of the latter are socially undesirable (like the talents of a good hit-man or the talents of a burglar). But that is exactly the point: self-ownership confers no right whatsoever to be able to exercise one's talents for one's own benefit. Everything depends on what the talent is, and whether the independent moral reasons for having a society of this sort rather than that provide a framework for their legitimate exploitation.

4. THE OPPORTUNITIES OF THE PROPERTYLESS

We have seen that an SR-based theory can define a bare, formal sense of opportunity in terms of which everyone has the opportunity to acquire property. But we have seen too that neither those theories themselves, nor the associated idea of self-ownership, provide any reason for holding that resources must be left available for private appropriation. I want to turn now to arguments for the opportunity claim derived from GR-based theories of property.

In Chapters 8 to 10 we examined various GR-based arguments for private ownership. All of them purport to show that owning property is morally important for individuals—important for their independence, for their sense of themselves, for their ethical development, for the growth of a sense of prudence and responsibility, for their ability to make good citizens, and so on. It is a feature of most of these arguments that the alleged benefits of private property accrue to the individual only from his actual ownership of some significant resources—that is, from the actual exercise of property rights and from the thinking and planning that is associated with that exercise. In Hegel's discussion, for example, we saw that the ethical importance of property was associated, firstly, with the discipline which owning something and working on it imposes on the will, and secondly, with the recognition that is accorded to a property-owner when others take the ethical importance of property-owning to him to be a reason for constraining their own actions so far as his resources are concerned. A person who has no property gets none of these benefits. There is nothing external on which he can work which will register in concrete and inerasable form the effects of his having a particular intention, and so that particular basis for stabilizing his intentionality is not open to him. And none of the benefits of recognition accrue to him either; others in their use of resources do not take themselves to be constrained in any way by respect for the relation between resources and his will, for he has no rights over any resources. He is nothing to them as far as their use of resources is concerned.

(It is no good saying, by the way, that there may be other means by which a propertyless person can stabilize his will, or other modes of recognition available to him. To the extent to which this is true, the Hegelian arguments no longer provide conclusive reasons for property at all. Certainly they will no longer provide conclusive arguments against the expropriation of those who do have property. For these other means to ethical development will be available to them as well.)

Is any of this altered if the propertyless man has the *opportunity* to acquire some property? Is any of it altered if he is actively pursuing that opportunity? By itself, the existence of the opportunity does little to promote the things that the Hegelian argument takes to be important. Admittedly, the *denial* of the opportunity would be an especially insulting affront. If by 'opportunity', we simply mean the power to acquire property or the liability to receive it, then explicitly denying somebody *that* would be a way of incorporating formally into law contempt and indifference to that person's ethical development. The denial would be a kind of negative recognition—an explicit determination to treat someone as 'invisible' so far as legal personality was concerned. There is no doubt then that these arguments can be used to criticize restrictions on the class of people who may own property, and in this sense they are arguments for an opportunity. But they are arguments that *also* show that, while the opportunity to acquire property is necessary, it is not in itself sufficient for the promotion of ethical development.

To see this, imagine a person without any significant property, but who is eligible to be an owner and for whom it is not, as a practical matter, out of the question that some day he might come to own a significant holding. What contribution does the mere existence of that opportunity make to the development of his personality and freedom? One thing it might do is encourage him in industry and frugality so that he can build up his wealth. Another thing it might do is encourage him to keep a sharp eye out for various ways in which he might become rich. But our experience of those who try to improve their position in this way is that, while some of them succeed, it is as often through luck as through single-mindedly planning, and that the majority who fail over a lifetime to acquire significant wealth, fail pathetically despite the constancy with which they have kept their acquisitive aim in view. Worse still, the effort to acquire property—particularly in circumstances where it is continually unsuccessful—often takes on exactly the inconstancy and effervescence of scheming and intention that Hegel thought the actual possession of property would mitigate. Every day there is a new 'Get rich quick' scheme; every day a new investment opportunity, pursued half-heartedly and doomed from the outset. My point here is not that the effort to acquire wealth is inevitably corrupting or that the opportunity to do so is worthless; it is that the mere pursuit of the opportunity, in and of itself, serves none of the values which, on the Hegelian account, are served by the actual possession of property and may actually disserve some of them. So it simply cannot be argued that the opportunity to acquire is all that the Hegelian argument calls for. The opportunity may be welcomed, but only as an indispensable means to the outcome— actually owning something—and it is the interest in that outcome that the Hegelian argument shows to be important.

The same can be said of a number of the other arguments we have been considering. In Chapter 8, we suggested various links between property and the idea of freedom. Private property might be thought to serve a general interest that people have in negative liberty; or it might be thought to serve certain specially important basic liberties; or it might be thought indispensable for the development of freedom in some positive sense. In all three areas, it can be shown that if there is any plausible argument available at all, it is an argument not only for an acquisitive opportunity but also for the importance of people actually owning property.

If private property serves negative liberty, it does so because owning something just *is* a matter of being free to use it and of its being the case that one is not to be opposed in that use by the interference of others. But then the distribution of property has a direct impact on the distribution of negative liberty. A person who owns nothing in a society (where everything is privately owned) is not at liberty, in a negative sense, to make use of anything—indeed for everything that he *might* use, someone else has a right that he should refrain from using it, and it is a right which they are entitled to enforce. If it is true that all (or most) human actions require a material component over and above the use of one's own body—a location, for example, or an implement—then the unfreedom in a negative sense of the propertyless man is more or less comprehen-

sive. There is literally nothing or next to nothing that he is free to
do. This point is mitigated by the existence of some common
property even in the most comprehensively capitalist societies:
tramps have the streets to walk in and the bridges to sleep under.
But that is all they have and all they can do, without falling foul of
the prohibitions enforced by the property system of the society in
which they have to make a life for themselves.

The point is also sometimes obscured by the way we talk about
negative liberty. When we are asking how free a society is, we tend
to ask what *types* of action are permitted and prohibited: are
people free to demonstrate, to speak their minds, to start small
businesses, to walk the streets after dark, to travel, and so on. But if
we really want to know how free the people are, we have to ask, not
about action-types, but about action-tokens, that is, particular acts
performed with particular objects or resources. An action such as
riding a bicycle may not be subject to any general prohibition; but
the laws of property will still prohibit anyone from riding a
particular bicycle that does not belong to him. The action of *fishing*
may not be prohibited in a society, but if one or two people own all
the river-banks, then concentration on the act-type will obscure the
fact that the overwhelming majority of the people are not free to
engage in any particular act of river-fishing. In other words,
concentration on *types* of action will produce an easy impression of
general and indeed equal negative liberty which is belied by the fact
that unequal property leaves people unequally free to perform
particular actions.[24]

If we concentrate our attention, then, on the propertyless man,
we may say that he is free in general but not free in particular, and
his general freedom just is his opportunity to acquire the property
that would make him free to perform the particular actions that fall
under general descriptions. But an opportunity to become free is
not freedom (though of course it is better, for instrumental reasons,
than the lack of such an opportunity). So any argument for private
property on the basis of the interest we all have in negative liberty,
is an argument for actual ownership, not merely for an opportunity
to become an owner. So long as the opportunity remains
unconsummated, the person who possesses it and who is even
actively pursuing it, remains in a negative sense unfree.

A similar point is made by G. A. Cohen, though he phrases it

[24] See Cohen, 'Capitalism,. Freedom and the Proletariat'; see also my book,
Property and Libery, forthcoming, Ch. 4.

rather misleadingly in self-ownership terms. One of the objections to 'joint' or collective ownership, he says, is that people cannot exercise their self-ownership except with the permission of others: 'For people can do (virtually?) nothing without using parts of the external world. If, then, they require the leave of the community to use it, then, effectively, they do not own themselves, since they can do nothing without communal authorization.'[25] As it stands, this is a bit like saying I cannot be said to own a car unless I own a garage and a road to drive it on. But if we drop the stuff about self-ownership, and talk directly about freedom, the point is clear. Freedom requires private property, and freedom for all requires private property for all. Nothing less will do.

If we move from liberty generally to important basic liberties, the same point may be thought to apply: nobody gets the benefit of a basic liberty unless he actually has it, and so if certain of these basic liberties are constitutive of ownership, then the argument from liberty requires ownership, and not just the opportunity to own, for everybody. In fact, the point does not quite apply across the board. Some of the basic liberties which are believed to be promoted by the existence of private property may be promoted for everyone even though not everyone is a property-owner. For example, Milton Friedman argues that political liberty is in danger if the means of intellectual and political production (printing presses, photocopiers, meeting places, etc.) are not in private hands.[26] But if they are in private hands (particularly if they are distributed across a plurality of owners), then freedom for all is enhanced, because a dissident has the option of dealing with any of a number of people besides officials of the state he is opposing if he wants to get his message across. It is clear, though, that this argument does not require everyone to have even the opportunity to own things. Even if radicals of a certain hue are banned from owning property, their chances of access to political resources are enhanced if they can borrow or hire things from private owners.

Other basic liberties thought to be promoted by private property include privacy and free trade. For these liberties, it *is* the case that ownership and not just the opportunity to own is required. Consider privacy first. If I do not own a home to hide in, a place where I can withdraw from others' gaze and from their constant

²⁵ Cohen, 'Self-Ownership, World-Ownership and Equality', pp. 113–14.
²⁶ Freidman, *Capitalism and Freedom*, Ch. 1.

demands that I should acount for myself, then merely having the *opportunity* to acquire such a hiding place will not afford me much relief. So long as it remains unconsummated, my active pursuit of the opportunity to own something must be conducted in the public realm, for I do not yet have access to the resources that would enable me to close myself off from it.

Freedom of trade has a similar character. The argument in Chapter 8 was that free trade was important in that it enabled people to reach accommodations with one another and pursue mutually beneficial arrangements in the material realm on their own terms without the mediation of any other party, and that this was an important aspect of respect for the sociability of every human individual. But I can enter into these accommodations only if I can bring something to them, that is, only if I have something to deal with which would make it as much in the interest of another to treat with me as it was in my interest to treat with him. If I have a firm expectation of coming into wealth in the future, then perhaps I can deal with that (if others have even a proportion of the confidence that I have). But if all I have is the opportunity of acquiring wealth, and no wealth and no firm expectation of receiving any, then I am to all intents and purposes excluded from the net of sociability which we call the marketplace. Deals will be struck, bargains made, mutually advantageous arrangements arrived at, but the man who has nothing but an opportunity will not be party to any of that.

There are other aspects to human sociability which do not depend on property in this way, and even aspects of economic interaction (like begging or offering oneself for work) that a propertyless man may engage in. But if being able to engage in these is sufficient for the arguments I am considering, then it is important to note, first, that those arguments are not, as they are usually paraded, arguments in favour of an opportunity to own private property— for these interactions do not even require that—and, secondly, they are not arguments that can be used to oppose the expropriation of those who are owners—for on this account, there are adequate substitutes for free trade available even to the expropriated man.

The category of arguments we explored at greatest length in Chapter 8 were arguments about the connection between private ownership and liberty in one of its 'positive' senses. One of those arguments was the Hegelian one; and we have already seen that it cannot be construed as an argument for a mere opportunity. Others concerned independence, recognition, and the capacity to act as a citizen. It would be tedious to go through and make the same point again and again; I will concentrate on the argument from independence, and let the reader work out for himself how the point applies to the other arguments.

The argument from independence took as its basic conception of liberty an ideal of 'self-mastery': 'I wish my life and decisions to depend on myself. . . . I wish to be the instrument of my own, not of other men's acts of will.'[27] Independence in this sense goes beyond being negatively free from force or coercion exercised by others. It is also concerned with the way in which one makes one's decisions even in circumstances of negative freedom. No person can be wholly free of his socialization or of the ideas and values embedded in his culture. But a person can reflect on the values and conceptions that he adopts, and deploy them critically, and not slavishly in response to fashion, public opinion, or the views of somebody he simply imitates. The link with property lies in the fact that a person without property is likely to become economically dependent—for his income and livelihood—on someone who has property, and so he is that much more likely to be sensitive to his patron's or employer's views and wary of crossing them. A person with a reasonable amount of property, on the other hand, has not only the leisure but the independence to trust his own judgement and develop patterns of reflection and deliberation which embody values that appeal to him, not just values he has adopted because they appeal to someone else.

If this is a good argument, it is an argument for seeing to it that everyone has property (or, more broadly, for ensuring that no one is ever in a situation in which economic dependence is likely to undermine his independence of thought, action, and evaluation). The civic humanist tradition has always emphasized the importance of independence in the actions and deliberations of the citizen, and the same point can be made here: if we have good reasons for making everyone a citizen—for having universal suffrage and a democratic republic—then they are also good reasons for seeing to it that everyone has the amount of property and economic security which, in the past, principled defenders of the property franchise have always thought citizens should have.[28]

[27] Berlin, 'Two concepts of Liberty', p. 131.
[28] See King and Waldron, 'Social Citizenship'.

Does giving everyone the opportunity to acquire property answer this concern? Once again, the reply must be 'No'. Though a denial of eligibility to hold property would be an insult in these terms, the mere existence of that eligibility goes no way towards guaranteeing independence except to the extent that it is connected with a substantial probability that the opportunity will be consummated. The more probable that is, the closer we are to the goal of freedom-as-independence. But that is simply another way of saying that it is the consummation of the opportunity that is called for by this argument, and not the opportunity as such.

5. OPPORTUNITY AND OUTCOME

Egalitarians are often accused by their opponents of confusing equality of opportunity with equality of outcome. Anthony Flew's indictment is typical:

So many people today—including, indeed most particularly including, professing social scientists—collapse the distinction between equality of opportunity and equality of outcome. They mis-take it that evidence of unequal outcomes, or of big differences between the probabilities of success among several competitors and non-competitors, is sufficient to show that these never had equal opportunities to compete. Very possibly, of course, they did not. But as a conclusion this has to be established, if at all, in some other way.[29]

Flew points out quite rightly that if the opportunity in question is an opportunity to compete for scarce goods or positions (for example, an opportunity in a competitive race or other contest), then necessarily there will be an unequal outcome, and it would be ridiculous to infer from that to any inequality of opportunity. But the 'mis-take' he is criticizing happens most often in regard to goods that are not (or at least not obviously) scarce, competitive, or positional in this way. In these cases, though it is true that unequal outcomes do not *imply* unequal opportunities, still if they are sustained and striking they may provide a good reason for looking again at the opportunities, particularly when there are independent background reasons for suspecting that the group doing less well in its outcomes has in the past had fewer opportunities as well. Nothing Flew or other critics say about the conceptual difference

---

[29] Flew, *The Politics of Procrustes*, pp. 47–8.

between opportunity and outcome can detract from this pragmatic point.

The point I want to make about the distinction, however, is slightly different. Often what is going on when a social scientist or anybody else 'collapses' the distinction between opportunity and outcome is that they have become convinced, quite rightly, that the two are not in fact independent ideals. Politicians commit them-selves to 'equality of opportunity' in some field such as educational achievement, suspecting that this is probably an easier ideal to live up to than any sort of equality of outcome. They defend that commitment with values like the importance of education to the growing youngster, to his future possibilities, and his development as a citizen. But they fail to see that, if those values establish anything, they establish that we should be concerned not only with the opportunity each person has to become educated, but with the level of education that each person actually attains. In terms of values and justifications, the commitment to an equal opportunity is unstable; for the very concerns that underpin it drive us beyond opportunity to attainment and outcome as well.

This, I think, is exactly what is going on in the arguments I have been examining. People say that the right to property is important in our society, and they defend it with reference to freedom, autonomy, and the development of independence and responsibility in the individual. They then claim that the right is merely a right to an opportunity to acquire things, thinking (quite correctly) that this is easier to attain than the ideal of property for all. But they fail to notice that the values with which they defend it, if they are followed through, take us far beyond a mere opportunity. They are values which are simply not satisfied, in anyone's case, until that person is in possession of significant property of his own. Opportunity as an ideal is unstable in this sense; and it is no wonder that those who take seriously the values with which it is defended are tempted to collapse it into a concern for outcomes.

There is a more general point here which informs everything I have been arguing for in Chapters 9 and 11. It is time for those who make arguments in political philosophy to start keeping faith with the values and concerns they invoke. It is no good calling on 'liberty' or 'autonomy' as a way of defending one's favourite position, if one is not prepared to follow through on that commitment and accept whatever other, perhaps less congenial, positions those values would also imply. We cannot play fast and loose with our values in that way. If a value is invoked to support a political position, then the logic of justification implies that the person who invokes it thinks it important enough that whatever flows from that value should be accepted. Otherwise why should anyone who is not already convinced of the position he is defending pay any attention at all to what he says? To make an evaluative case for something against an opponent is to say to him: 'Look, I know you dislike position P. But if you take value V—which I know you agree with—and follow through on its implications for this sort of case, you will find that P is its necessary consequence. So P should be accepted, on grounds of V, despite your initial distrust.' No one can say this sincerely unless he himself would be prepared to accept a similar argument from V for another position Q, of which *he* was initially distrustful.

Of course, other values may cut across the argument in other cases, and their proponent may be pulled both ways. Though V is a justification for Q, Q might disserve another value W, to which our proponent is also committed. That is fair enough. Then the complicated version of my point is that he must be prepared to keep faith with the whole array of values he is prepared to invoke and with the priorities he is willing to establish between them in any particular case.

This is something which utilitarians have always been better at than their opponents. Having committed themselves to the proposition that the maximization of utility is the most important thing, they are prepared to follow that commitment where it leads, rather than simply abandon it in the embarrassing cases. But theorists of rights should be equally committed to this sort of consistency. If we are not to have a simple 'intuitionistic' array of rights[30]—each taken on its own merits as a first principle—then we shall want to articulate some of the deep concerns that underlie our principles of right and give them their coherence as a theory. One of the reasons for that articulation—indeed part of what it means to be coherent—is to enable us to tease out of the deep values that our commitments reveal other positions that we might not have thought about.

If we are sophisticated, we can do this in a sort of 'reflective equilibrium' way, and nothing in this section is supposed to imply that, once a value is invoked, we are stuck with it and its implications forever. We may often want to revise our deep values

[30] See Rawls, *Theory of Justice*, pp. 34 ff.

once we see what their implications are.[31] But if we do that, we must do it across the board. We cannot simply stick with the pre-reflective value in those cases where its implications are congenial, and abandon or revise it for the cases where they are not.

This is the approach I have tried to take in evaluating GR-based arguments for property. We discover an argument that says, for example, that private property is defensible because it promotes responsibility in the individual, and that argument seems attractive and plausible. But we do not leave the matter there. We ask what else this value of promoting responsibility in the individual implies for private property, apart from a defence of the institution. On examination, it seems to imply that we should see to it that everyone has some property. Now that is a radical conclusion, and it may be a difficult one to live up to. But we cannot simply abandon the argument so far as this implication is concerned, and yet hang on to it as a general defence. If both arms of the argument are plausible, then both have got to be accepted. If we want to reject one of them, then we have to reject the other, unless we can find some principled distinction between them (which we are also prepared to follow through on). Making an evaluative argument for property is a serious business, for it involves an attempt to convince those who are suspicious of or hostile towards this institution that it serves some values they believe in. If this is anything more than a cynical manipulation using slogans that simply resonate in the culture, then we must keep faith with the arguments we invoke, and be prepared ourselves to draw conclusions from them that are as uncongenial to us as our conclusions are to those whom we are trying to convince.

6. IS OPPORTUNITY EVER IMPORTANT?

I have argued *ad nauseam* that most of the GR-based defences of private property establish that property is something everyone should have, and not merely that everyone must have the opportunity to acquire some property. Arguments for opportunity quickly become arguments for attending to outcomes, once the values underlying them are explored. However, it would be unfair to conclude this chapter without some consideration of the

---

[31] Rawls, *Theory of Justice*, pp. 34 ff.; see also Hare, *Freedom and Reason*, Ch. 6.

arguments that might be made for taking the opportunity to acquire seriously in its own right.

These arguments fall into two categories. On the one hand, someone might claim that the competitive struggle for resources is itself the *locus* of the interests that are served by the existence of private property. It is the invigorating effort to acquire that people have a right to, not the actual acquisition itself. On the other hand, someone might argue that though it is the possession of property that matters, its impact on individuality, responsibility, or whatever is spoiled if it is not acquired in a certain sort of way. I shall examine the second of these arguments first.

I have said that the tenor of most of the GR-based arguments that we have been examining is that, in Hegel's words, 'everyone must have property'.[32] The interest which each person has in being an owner of some significant holding of resources is so important that it warrants our saying that other people, particularly governments, are under duties to him in this respect. What sort of duties are these? In the case of those who are propertied, the main duty that falls on governments is the negative one of not expropriating their holdings. But for people who are at present propertyless, the right to property seems to call for some sort of hand-out: these people must be *given* wealth so that they can enjoy the ethical benefits of ownership. Now we will explore the tension between these two sorts of duties in Chapter 12—the concern that it may be impossible to carry out our duty to the poor without violating our duty to the rich. But leaving that aside, is it likely that a person will derive ethical benefit from a property holding that he has just been *given* as a hand-out? Is that likely to enhance his sense of responsibility, or stabilize his will, or any of the other things we have been talking about, if wealth simply falls into his lap? Surely this sort of hand-out would be as corrupting as his original propertylessness; it would encourage rather than dispel general fecklessness and irresponsibility. Maybe property can only do the work that, in our GR-based arguments, we want it to do, if the holder acquires it for himself, by his own actions and efforts. For then the responsibility and so on that his holding of it is supposed to engender will be prefigured in the means by which it has arrived in his possession.

On this account, then, though the arguments in question give us a

---

[32] Hegel, *Philosophy of Right*, sect. 49 (addition).

reason to *hope* that everyone acquires property, they also give us a reason not to dole property out to them, but to stand clear and see if they can acquire it for themselves. Though it is the outcome that is valued, it is only the opportunity that we should be manipulating politically. It is important that people themselves consummate their opportunities, through their own action and initiatives, rather than have those opportunities consummated for them. Just as a concern that everyone needs a life partner is not a reason to set up a system of arranged marriages, so a concern that everyone should have property is not necessarily a reason for the state to involve itself in distribution.

There are several things to say in response. The first is that this line works better for some of our arguments than for others. It looks plausible for those arguments that stress the development of a sense of responsibility for one's own fate etc. But it does not get much of a grip on arguments which defend property on the basis of the contribution it makes to independence. Whether my wealth is due to my own efforts or to a one-off hand-out from the state, once I have it, I can afford to trust my own opinions and cock a snook at those on whom I would otherwise be economically dependent. And similarly for arguments about privacy etc.: a home is a refuge from the public realm and from public accountability whether it has been given to me by the state or acquired through my own efforts.

Secondly, if the argument works at all, it is equally an argument against those who acquire their property through the lottery of inheritance or succession. So far as they are concerned, wealth has arrived in their laps as a hand-out, with no action or effort on their part. If hand-outs undermine the ethical importance of property, then the arguments against confiscating deceased estates are weakened accordingly.

Thirdly, even if we accept the concerns articulated in the argument, there are other ways of addressing them. Perhaps a system of hand-outs is undesirable. But there are many other ways in which we could alter and manipulate the framework of property to increase the real likelihood that everyone will end up with something. We could insist on breaking up large holdings, set a maximimum level for any individual bequest, target the privatiz-ation of previously state-owned resources to particular social groups, increase the value of the lowest incomes to encourage savings, provide incentives for home-or share-ownership, and so on. While stopping short of any direct manipulation of outcomes, we could set up the opportunities in a way that made it much easier for each individual to consummate them. Though that would not guarantee that each person ended up with property, it would make it much more likely that there was something each person could plausibly do to put himself in that position. It would therefore be oriented towards the goal of property for all even if it did not achieve that directly.

The other sort of argument we had to consider was a more radical reversal of priorities. Instead of saying that people have a right to property, someone might say that people have only a right to participate in the invigorating struggle for property, and that it is this which enhances true liberty, develops the character, compels recognition, and promotes self assertion.

The view might be developed with various clichés drawn from the sports-field. It does not matter whether you win or lose; from a right-based point of view, it is playing the game that counts. On this view, the only reason property-holdings should be protected is that otherwise winning the game would be meaningless. The game has got to be a struggle that matters, with high stakes; otherwise it is not worth playing. But there is no question of setting things up so that everyone wins. The competition can promote self-assertion and what-not only in the bracing atmosphere of a struggle in which some are likely to lose and lose badly. But even if they lose, they can still retain their self-respect, for that will have been forged in the course of the desperate struggle in which they are continually engaged.

The position has resonances of Social Darwinism, though the latter is better understood as a goal-based view extolling the natural means by which the human species becomes adapted to its environment.[33] Competition for scarce resources, for the Darwinists, was essentially a process by which humanity built up its capital and nature rid itself of the weak, and so it was judged instrumentally in terms of the overall fitness of the species. But many Social Darwinists also held rather more individualistic views. Some saw the struggle for resources as a process whereby virtue was rewarded; and others moved close to the position of extolling the right to compete, and the individual interest in competition, that I have been alluding to here.[34]

There is not space to go into any detailed discussion of Social

---

[33] See Bannister, *Social Darwinism: Science and Myth*.
[34] See e.g. Sumner, *Social Darwinism: Selected Essays*, Ch. 5.

Darwinist theories of property, nor to examine the merits of this sort of position. But it is important to say that the direction of this line of argument cannot be faulted on logical grounds: it is an argument for the importance of an opportunity to appropriate and not for the importance of everyone's consummating that opportunity. It does therefore do the sort of work conservative defenders of private property have often wanted their arguments to do. And I would go further and suggest that *this* sort of argument, such as it is, with whatever conviction it carries, is the only sort of right-based argument people are going to be able to invoke if they want to be serious and consistent in their claim that there is a general right to an opportunity to acquire private property, but no general right to private property itself.

12

Property for All

1. THE CHALLENGE: NOZICK AND MARX

Could private property be the subject of a general right? Is it something we could plausibly provide *for everyone* in the way we try to provide political rights, civil liberty, health, education and welfare? Or—to put it another way—is the ideal of a 'property-owning democracy' anything more than a *petit-bourgeois* utopian pipe-dream?[1]

In this final chapter, I want to consider two negative answers to these questions which amount to quite radical challenges to the idea that private property could be one of the general rights of man. The challenges come from utterly different political perspectives.

(i) Nozick

The first comes from the Right and is most lucidly expressed in an argument adapted from Nozick's work.

A principle of justice requiring private property for everyone would, if implemented, soon be frustrated by the exercise of the very property rights that were distributed. Suppose access to and control of resources were distributed so that everyone was the owner of at least the share deemed necessary for liberty or ethical development by whatever GR-based argument we favoured. What would happen subsequently when someone lost his shirt in a poker game or invested his share imprudently in an enterprise that went bust? The required pattern of distribution of private property would be disrupted by these events and the GR-based case for a distribution of private property would no longer be satisfied on a universal scale. But yet that would have happened as a result of the

---

[1] The idea of a property-owning democracy is found in Rawls, *Theory of Justice*, p. 274. See also Meade, *Efficiency, Equality and Ownership*, Ch. 5, and Forsyth, *Property and Property Distribution*. The idea was earlier associated with thinkers like Chesterton: see e.g. Canovan, *G. K. Chesterton*, pp. 81 ff.

free exercise of the rights which it was the whole point of the argument to make available. As Nozick puts it:

Any favored pattern would be transformed into one unfavored by the principle, by people choosing to act in various ways; for example, by people exchanging goods and services with other people, or giving things to other people, things the transferrers are entitled to under the favored distributional pattern. To maintain a pattern one must either continually interfere to stop people from transferring resources as they wish to, or continually (or periodically) interfere to take from some persons resources that others for some reason chose to transfer to them. (But if some time limit is to be set on how long people may keep resources others voluntarily transfer to them, why let them keep resources for *any* period of time? Why not have immediate confiscation?)[2]

(The answer to the last question, I suppose, will refer to difficulties of administration.) The point of Nozick's challenge in the present context is that the only way to ensure that everyone has a specified amount of private property seems to involve prohibiting or frustrating the exercise of the very rights which constitute the private property that we want everybody to have.

In my view this is the only interesting interpretation of what has become known as 'the Wilt Chamberlain argument' in *Anarchy, State, and Utopia*. There is no doubt that Nozick intends it to establish a lot more: he intends it to establish that any theory of justice with an end-state or patterned component built into it would be oppressive or self-defeating or both. He purports to show that since voluntary actions by individuals with the holdings assigned to them will tend to upset patterns of distribution favoured on grounds of social justice, attempts effectively to implement a theory of social justice over time are bound to be oppressive. But this is not shown. It is *not* always oppressive to prohibit people from trading in holdings or in goods assigned to them: everything depends on the basis on which the goods were distributed and received in the first place. Jobs, office furniture in a university, council-house tenancies, and so on are all goods received on the explicit understanding that they are to be used exclusively by the people to whom they are assigned but not to be transferred or traded by them. *Pace* Nozick, the fact that a given distribution D of these goods has been established does *not* show that '[t]here is no question about whether each of the people was entitled to control over the

----

[2] Nozick, *Anarchy, State, and Utopia*, p. 163.

resources they held in D$_1$,'[3] if 'control' is supposed to include giving it to others (such as Wilt Chamberlain) in exchange for their holdings or services. As C. C. Ryan points out:

[F]or any set of holdings, sustaining a pattern implies coercive restrictions (restrictions on personal liberty) only if the 'holdings' are private property—holders have full rights of ownership in them. . . . *Without* the assumption that private property rights extend to all present and potential economic holdings, Nozick's general contention that sustaining patterns of distribution implies the restriction of liberty simply will not hold: if each individual's holdings are not assumed to be his private property, then there is no reason to conclude that restrictions on the 'free exchange' of holdings constitutes coercion.[4]

It *is* oppressive, as Bentham pointed out, for legislators to frustrate expectations which they themselves have engendered.[5] But it is not necessarily oppressive for them to discourage certain expectations from the start in the interests of justice. The Wilt Chamberlain argument does not, therefore, have the general force that Nozick thought it had.

However, if there are *independent* reasons for distributing holdings as private property, then the argument is important. For those independent reasons—for example, GR-based arguments for private property—may show that it is oppressive to say to citizens even at the outset that no economic holding assigned to them may be dealt with as private property. If private property is what we think people need, we must not give it to them on terms which derogate, as it were, from its privacy. But if private property is what we want to distribute on the basis of a certain pattern, then the very nature of the rights we are distributing will make it difficult for that pattern to be sustained.

(ii) Marx

The second attack comes from the opposite direction. It is the challenge laid down by Karl Marx in a furious response to bourgeois critics of the socialist programme outlined in *The Communist Manifesto*:

[3] Ibid. 161.
[4] Ryan, 'Yours, Mine, and Ours', pp. 330–1. See also Cohen, 'Robert Nozick and Wilt Chamberlain'.
[5] Bentham, 'Principles of the Civil Code', p. 113.

You are horrified at our intending to do away with private property. But in your existing society, private property is already done away with for nine tenths of the population; its existence for the few is solely due to its non-existence in the hands of these nine-tenths. You reproach us, therefore, with intending to do away with a form of property the necessary condition for whose existence is the nonexistence of any property for the immense majority of society. In one word, you reproach us for intending to do away with your property. Precisely so; that is just what we intend.[6]

Throughout his work, Marx is adamant that the indictment against capitalism is not merely the fact that private property happens to be distributed unequally or in a way that leaves millions without any guaranteed access to the means of production; the problem is that private ownership is a form of property that has this characteristic *necessarily*. No matter how noble your egalitarian intentions, the existence of any distribution of private property rights in the means of production will lead quickly to their concentration in the hands of a few. Thus egalitarian intentions, so far as private property is concerned are hopelessly utopian, for they underestimate the dynamic tendencies of the system they are interested in: 'for us the issue cannot be the alteration of private property but its annihilation'.[7] GR-based arguments for private property therefore would stand condemned on this approach just to the extent that they have egalitarian or quasi-egalitarian implications.

This is not Marx's only criticism of private property. The main critique throughout his work is the one we mentioned in Chapter 8: private property as a form for productive relations divides man from man, disguises the underlying co-operative nature of production and economic endeavour, and thus prevents the development of conscious and rational freedom in the economic sphere—the only sphere where man can find his true self-realization.[8] If there is a moral basis to Marx's indictment of capitalism, it is not a theory of equality but, as George Brenkert and others have argued, a theory of freedom.[9]

Nevertheless, according to Marx, it is no accident that *petit-*

[6] Marx and Engels, *Communist Manifesto*, p. 98.

[7] See e.g. Marx, 'Address to the Communist League', p. 280, and *Critique of Gotha Programme*, pp. 14 ff.

[8] For Marx's attack on private property see e.g. 'On the Jewish Question', p. 146; 'On James Mill', pp. 194 ff.; *Capital*, Vol. I, Ch. 32, pp. 927 ff.; and 'Results of the Immediate Process of Production', pp. 1083–4.

[9] Brenkert, *Marx's Ethics of Freedom*. See esp. Marx and Engels, *German Ideology*, pp. 117–18.

bourgeois theories of distributive justice are hopelessly impractical. They fly in the face of the logic of the institutions they purport to be dealing with:

> The justice of transactions between agents of production rests on the fact that these arise as natural consequences out of the production relationships. . . . [The content of a transaction] is just whenever it corresponds, is appropriate, to the mode of production. It is unjust whenever it contradicts that mode. Slavery on the basis of capitalist production is unjust; likewise fraud in the quality of commodities.[10]

But accumulation and the concentration of capital in a few hands, leading to mass propertylessness, is not only 'appropriate to' a capitalist mode of production; it is its inevitable result.

There is a controversy as to whether Marx offers a moral indictment of injustice of capitalism at all.[11] Certainly, in *Capital*, Marx argues that capitalist exploitation depends on proletarian propertylessness—that is, on the worker being, as Marx put it ironically, 'free in the double sense that . . . he can dispose of his labour power . . . and that, on the other hand, . . . he is *free of* all objects needed for the realization of his labour power'—and that it got under-way initially on the basis of forcible and bloody expropriation.[12] The justice of this process was dubious even relative to the relations of production prevailing at the time. But those relations were pre-capitalist relations and expropriation was in those circumstances a revolutionary act by the bourgeoisie against social and political forces stifling their progressive aspirations. Relative to the capitalist relations that it ushered in, that revolutionary beginning is (retrospectively) legitimate. Certainly, on the Marxian account, there is no suggestion either of the possibility or the desirability of rectificatory redress or reversal for any putative injustice that accompanied the birth of capitalism. That would be a wholly reactionary step.

Often the most Marx appears to be saying is that private property is doomed historically, that it is obsolescent, that it will eventually, under pressure, give way to social control. If there is an evaluative dimension, it may be nothing more substantial than a

[10] Marx, *Capital*, Vol. III, pp. 339–40. See also Marx, *Critique of Gotha Programme*, pp. 14 and 17.

[11] The debate is aired in Cohen *et al.*(eds.), *Marx, Justice and History*. See also Wood, *Karl Marx*, Ch. 9, and Buchanan, *Marx and Justice*.

[12] Marx, *Capital*, Vol. I, p. 273. For capitalist accumulation, see ibid. Chs. 27–8.

commitment to the value of historical progress: 'From the standpoint of a higher economic form of society, private ownership of the globe by single individuals will appear quite as absurd [*abgeschmacht*] as private ownership of one man by another.'[13] From this point of view, it is wrong to see Marx condemning the inevitability of propertylessness under capitalism. Nevertheless, even on this account, Marx is always prepared to get involved in moral polemics in a characteristic 'counter-punching' sort of way. If someone offers to *defend* private property on the sort of moral grounds that we have been considering, then Marx (as much as Proudhon) is ready to expose the contradictions and inconsistencies in that defence. That, I think, is the context of the challenge we are considering. (I should add that, on Marx's view of ideology, it is to be expected that the historically transient and contradictory character of a form of society like capitalism should be reflected in similar inconsistencies in the superstructural ideas involved in its defence.)[14]

(iii) Nozick and Marx on the Possibility of Equality

It is tempting to say that these challenges are identical, despite the fact that they come from opposite ends of the political spectrum. In a way this is true: both point to a source of resistance, inherent in the very idea of private property, to the imposition of the sort of distributive requirements that a GR-based argument is likely to engender. Of course, they evaluate that resistance in different ways. For Marx, it is part of the case against a private property economy that it cannot be made subject to the sort of conscious control that would be necessary for a society 'in which the free development of each is the condition for the free development of all'.[15] For Nozick, it is, if anything, a virtue of capitalism that distributional patterns emerge unplanned and therefore uncontrolled in the free interplay of individual choices.[16]

But there are also important differences in the account each

[13] Marx, *Capital*, Vol. III, p. 776.

[14] See Marx, 'Preface to *Critique of Political Economy*', p. 390. See also Avineri, *Social and Political Thought of Karl Marx*, p. 65 ff. and Seliger, *Marxist Conception of Ideology*.

[15] Marx and Engels, *Communist Manifesto*, p. 105.

[16] Nozick, *Anarchy, State, and Utopia*, Pt. III (though see the doubts expressed on pp. 157–9).

thinker would give of the unmanageability of a private property distribution.

Nozick appears to concede that in theory it is just possible that individuals might exercise their property rights voluntarily in a way which preserved an overall pattern of fair distribution.[17] But he has doubts about the practicality of this suggestion. First, it underestimates the diversity of motivations involved in economic transactions: people play poker, invest their life savings, and buy and sell for all sorts of reasons, and it is unlikely that the desire to preserve a given distributional pattern will always be uppermost in their minds as they exercise their property rights. But unless it is, each will engage in transactions that are not calculated to maintain fair shares of private property either in his own case or in the case of others affected by his actions. In places, Nozick appears to take a stronger position: that even in a socialist society, people would (naturally?) want to set up private competitive enterprises for themselves regardless of the implications for others. When he writes that 'small factories would spring up in a socialist society, unless forbidden' and that a 'socialist society would have to forbid capitalist acts between consenting adults',[18] we can read these passages perhaps as ill-thought-out gestures towards the GR-based position that private property answers to some deep and universal human need (though such a view is incompatible with the SR-based character of his historical entitlement theory). But in context it also seems to indicate his subscription to the widespread view that something called 'human nature' militates against egalitarianism[19] and would be the undoing of any distributional scheme based on a general right to private property. Secondly, Nozick points out that even if everyone most wanted to uphold a given distribution, he would be unable to obtain enough information or to co-ordinate his activity sufficiently well with others' to see that he did not upset the pattern in spite of his good intentions.[20] (He does not explain why it might not be a proper function of government to make this information available and provide the basis for co-ordination.)[21]

[17] Ibid. 163–4.
[18] Ibid. 162–3.
[19] Cf. Bentham, 'Principles of the Civil Code', p. 120: 'The levelling apparatus ought to go incessantly backward and forward, cutting off all that rises above the line prescribed.'
[20] Nozick, *Anarchy, State, and Utopia*, p. 163.
[21] I owe this suggestion to Leslie Green.

Nozick's account of the distributional unmanageability of private property is based, then, on considerations of individual motivation and rational choice.

Marx's account is somewhat more complicated. It appeals beyond individual rationality to the historical changes which underlie and condition it. In the modern age, the existence of private property systems is associated with the acquisitive mentality of capitalism,[22] and it is worthless to try and abstract the idea of private property from that historical context and ask what would happen if that mentality were to mysteriously evaporate. Of course, that mentality is not a permanent feature of human psychology. But the possibilities of change are limited and for Marx any change is likely to be associated with the abolition of private property and the institution of collective economic relations rather than with the distribution of private property on an equal or universal basis.

There is also a Marxian argument based on historical materialism against the feasibility of anything like the sort of property-owning democracy that a GR-based argument would require. For Marx the concentration of control of the means of production in fewer and fewer hands is not an accidental feature of modern society, nor even a feature associated exclusively with capitalism. It is, in a contradictory way, an indication that advanced economic production necessarily involves very large-scale control and large-scale decision-making.[23] In this regard, as we noted in Chapter 2, the growth of corporate capitalism is seen as an adumbration of the collective control over production that will eventually have to be exercised.[24] It is one of the symptoms of socialism with which capitalism is pregnant. Capitalism is now potentially what socialism will be in practice. As Marx puts it, corporate production

is a necessary transitional phase towards the reconversion of capital into the property of producers, although no longer as the private property of the individual producers, but rather as the property of associated producers, as outright social property. On the other hand, the stock company is a transition towards the conversion of all functions in the reproductive process which still remain linked with capitalist property, into mere functions of associated producers, into social function . . . [25]

---

[22] For an account along Marxian lines, see Macpherson, *Democratic Theory*, Ch. 1.

[23] See Avineri, *Social and Political Thought of Karl Marx*, pp. 174 ff.

[24] See Marx, 'Preface to *Critique of Political Economy*', p. 390.

[25] Marx, *Capital*, Vol. III, pp. 427–9.

But to imagine that we could move to or sustain anything like equal or universal private property for individuals is to postulate a move in the *other* direction, against the historical current, from modern capitalism back to its historical forebears. This, then, is the reason why ideas like property-owning democracy are dismissed so scathingly by Marxists as a futile *petit-bourgeois* ideal. From their point of view, a requirement that every individual should have private property in the means of production flies directly in the face of historical experience which tells us that the development of production, under the conditions of modern industry, is inexorably, necessarily, and desirably in the direction of large-scale collective control.

If Marx is right about this, we can have no reasonable expectation at all under modern conditions that people will voluntarily refrain from exercising the private property rights assigned to them in ways which are non-pattern-disruptive. (Marx's theory has also more radical consequences for GR-based arguments. Since politics is determined at least in the last analysis by class, we can have no reasonable expectation that a government in capitalist society will even attempt to put a general right to private property into effect, still less that it would intervene to prevent subsequent accumulation and concentration of capital.[26] That sort of determinism of course undermines *any* attempt to grapple with problems of justice in capitalist and late-capitalist societies.)

2. CONCEPTIONS OF PRIVATE PROPERTY

Let us concentrate now on the tighter point posed by the Nozickian and Marxian challenges. Apart from the bare possibility that private property rights could be exercised in a way which fortuitously sustained the pattern required for their distribution, and leaving aside the suggestion that the direction of history is bound to defeat the ideal of a property-owning democracy, is it the case that private property rights *as such* are essentially unamenable to the sort of distributional constraints that would flow, as we saw, from a GR-based argument? If they are, then those arguments are not just utopian but self-contradictory. In calling for something,

[26] See e.g. Miliband, *Marxism and Politics*, Ch. 6.

they are also calling for the conditions that are bound to defeat it.

Proudhon appears to have been convinced on this score. As we have seen, his intention was to show that 'every argument which has been invented in behalf of property, *whatever it may be*, always and of necessity leads to equality; that is, to the negation of property'.[27] Later he elaborated the indictment:

They did not foresee, these old founders of the domain of property, that the perpetual and absolute right to retain one's estate,—a right which seemed to them equitable, because it was common,—involves the right to transfer, sell, give, gain, and lose it; that it tends, consequently, to nothing less than the destruction of that equality which they established it to maintain.[28]

Now if the right to retain control of certain resources did involve these other powers, then the Wilt Chamberlain argument would apply and the objection would be sustained. Not only would we expect equality to be destroyed in a short time, but we would expect also that before long a large number of people would have little or no private property of their own at all and certainly much less than was deemed necessary for each individual by any plausible GR-based argument for that institution.

But as we saw in Chapter 2, private property is a concept of which there are many conceptions. The tight logical connection that Proudhon saw between 'the right to retain one's estate', on the one hand, and 'the right to transfer, sell, give, gain, and lose it', on the other, does not exist. The various rights are separable in thought and in fact, and a conception of private property is imaginable in which individuals would be assigned an exclusive right to determine what use should be made of particular resources without their necessarily having the power to transfer that right, on their own initiative, to anyone else. Such a 'no-transfer' system of private property might then in effect prevent disruption of the pattern of initial distribution, at least disruption of the sort envisaged in the Wilt Chamberlain argument.

It is, however, not enough simply to say that 'no-transfer' conceptions of private property are conceivable, and that we can avail ourselves of them in order to avoid the present difficulties. Although private property is a concept of which there are many conceptions, we may not simply pluck the conception that we want to use out of the air. Just because a conception would help us to

---

[27] Proudhon, *What is Property?*, pp. 39–40.
[28] Ibid. 78.

avoid a certain difficulty does not mean that we are entitled to use it. Everything depends, as always, on what the upshot is of the particular *argument* for private property that we want to deploy. If the argument focuses, for example, on the importance to individuals of being able to trade freely or to exercise virtues like generosity and discrimination in gift-giving, then it is clearly an argument for private property; but it is also an argument which requires exchange and which precludes any deployment of a 'no-transfer' conception of the concept. If, on the other hand, it focuses purely on the importance to individuals of making responsible decisions about how to draw subsistence over a period of time from a given stock of resources, it may not require exchange and it need not rule out a 'no-transfer' conception. To repeat: the conception of private property we adopt is not a matter of independent choice; it is the upshot of the arguments we are convinced by. (The same seems true of other contestable concepts in political philosophy. For example, we cannot simply opt for one conception of harm or another in the context of Mill's famous 'Harm Principle'. Everything depends on the arguments used to defend the 'Harm Principle': for example, one set of arguments may have as its upshot a conception of harm that necessarily includes moral offence; another set of arguments may have as its upshot a conception that excludes this.[29] Since our arguments are our connection with the considerations that ultimately *matter* to us, we should take their upshot more seriously than we take the results of any independent 'conceptual analysis'. For if we are really worried about the 'proper' analysis of the concepts we are using, we can always express our conclusions in terms of fresh concepts, even ones we have newly invented.)

The objection we are considering, then, is an embarrassment primarily to those GR-based arguments for private property that lay great importance on individuals' being able to exercise powers of transfer. These arguments cannot avoid deploying a conception of ownership that includes powers whose exercise would generate the embarrassment that Nozick's and Proudhon's arguments predict. Fortunately, as a matter of fact, few of the arguments we are considering have this feature. Hegel thought it important that individuals should be able to withdraw their will from the objects in which they had 'embodied' it; but in our interpretation of his

[29] See Waldron, 'Mill and Value of Moral Distress', Pt. I.

account of the ethical importance of private property, that did not play a significant role.[30] One argument we considered, however, did attribute importance to freedom of trade and contract: it was based on an idea of respect for the individual capacity to enter into arrangements and reach accommodations in the economic sphere with other individuals without the need for overarching direction, and on the view that this required respect for the arrangements and accommodations that were actually entered into. (The underlying notion here is respect for a capacity that is as distinctively human as the capacity to plan on a communal scale.)[31] This argument, then, is prima facie vulnerable to the objection we are considering. It makes it a matter of importance that all individuals should have the wherewithal to enter into arrangments with others on matters of economic significance, but the result of the exercise of that capacity will almost certainly be that some individuals come in time to be deprived of the wherewithal to exercise it.

Moreover, even though Proudhon is wrong in discerning a *logical* connection between private property and powers of transfer, and even though our favourite argument for private property may permit as its upshot a 'no-transfer' conception of ownership, still there may be other non-logical but none the less contingently important connections between being a private owner and having the power to transfer one's holding to another. As we saw in Chapter 2, most societies that face the problem of allocation will also face the problem of *re*allocation from time to time as individuals' circumstances change. It will tend to be overwhelmingly inconvenient to call in all resources and redistribute them on every occasion when such changes are deemed appropriate, for those occasions are likely to be very numerous indeed. If there is any possibility at all that transfers arranged by individuals between individuals could solve the problem of reallocation, then that will appear the more attractive solution. This then is an independent reason (arising out of the allocation problem) for including a power of transfer in any practicable conception of ownership. (It is not, by the way, a reason for instituting such a conception of ownership as opposed to a system of collective property, since in a collective regime the problem of reallocation can be solved much more easily; but it is a reason for adopting such a conception *if* we are already well-disposed towards private property.)

---

[30] See above, Ch. 10, sect. 4.
[31] See above, Ch. 8, sect. 3(ii).

These points suggest that it may not be open to us to adopt a pure 'no-transfer' conception of private property. But they suggest also that there may be room for compromise in other directions. Whether or not a conception of private property includes powers of transfer is not an all-or-nothing affair. To begin with, there are several powers to be considered: gift, sale and purchase, abandonment, bequest, inheritance, and so on. It is possible that the points just made could be met by a conception which included some of these powers but not others. Many people have argued that powers of transfer *post mortem*, such as bequest and inheritance, are much more inimical to equality than powers of transfer *inter vivos* such as sale and purchase: the disruption to a favoured distribution of property caused by the latter may be trivial, whereas the former may upset distributional patterns in a more significant way.[32] It is possible that the powers whose exercise threatens the pattern are not those that our argument for property requires. For example, the principle of respecting the arrangements people have entered into may be thought to apply more to arangements *inter vivos* than to *post mortem* arrangements.[33] Similarly, if the problem of reallocation is the source of our concern that powers of transfer should be included in a conception of ownership, it may be that this concern is much less in the case of the reallocation of deceased estates than it is in the case of goods that somebody is currently holding. As Bentham argued, a general principle of escheat (and redistribution by the state) does not threaten to disrupt expectations in the way that expropriation of living proprietors would.[34]

Further, we should remember that there are a number of different ways in which any given power of transfer may be limited or curtailed. An extreme case is one in which the purported exercise of the power is given no effect in law at all: a man purports to leave his estate to his friend, but because the system does not recognize a power of bequest that exercise is null and void. A much less extreme case is one in which transactions are taxed, either as far as the transferor is concerned (e.g. death and gift duties, payroll taxes, VAT, etc.), or as far as the transferee is concerned (e.g. income tax, capital gains tax, etc.). In this case, the transfer is recognized but made subject to certain conditions: for example, no one in New

[32] For arguments to this effect, see: Crosland, *Future of Socialism*, Ch. 12 and Atkinson, *Unequal Shares*, Ch. 3–4 *et passim*; and Van Doren, 'Redistributing Wealth'.

[33] See my discussion in Waldron, 'Locke's Account of Inheritance'.

[34] Bentham, 'Supply Without Burthern', esp. pp. 290–4.

Zealand may make a gift of more than $10,000 without paying a
proportion of that sum to the government in gift duty; and no one
in Britain may receive income of any sort from another person
without paying a (rather large) proportion of that to the state in
income tax. When Nozick discusses taxes of this sort, he suggests
that their intention is to defeat or partially to defeat the transaction
or the point of the transaction.[35] This may be the case but it need
not be. Suppose the *point* of my transferring a large sum of money
to my son is to disrupt the pattern of the equal distribution of
private property. Then it is true that the point of the gift duty we
are considering would be to defeat that intention. But that is
because the intention, in its content, is explicitly at odds with the
ideas of rights, liberty, and justice as we conceive them; it does not
seem oppressive in a society committed to those ideals to set out to
defeat intentions which are calculated to undermine them. But most
transfers will not be motivated in this way. For those that have
ordinary commercial or philanthropic motivation, our fiscal
experience suggests that taxation is *not* perceived as defeating
or undermining the point of a transfer. People adjust their expectations of what they can do in transferring and receiving goods to
the exigencies of the fiscal regime, and seem able to carry on
transferring goods freely within the constraints it imposes. Once
again, whether a power of transfer constrained by taxation is
sufficient for the conception of ownership yielded by a particular
GR-based argument will depend on the details of the argument. But
it is difficult to imagine an argument placing such great value on
absolutely untrammelled transfer that it required a conception of
ownership that was stronger than this.

   So far the argument has concerned the powers of transfer that
might be connected with particular conceptions of private ownership. Our response to the objection has been that although many of
the conceptions we are dealing with will involve powers of transfer,
they will seldom involve any requirement that there should be
unlimited powers of transfer. If the powers of transfer that we
recognize are qualified by a system of taxation, understood to be
imposed for the express purpose of maintaining a wide distribution
of the property rights in question, then that system can be used to
redress any disruption of the distributional patterns favoured by the
arguments which have generated the conceptions of private
ownership that are giving us this difficulty.

[35] Nozick, *Anarchy, State, and Utopia*, pp. 163 and 167–8.

We should note, however, that Proudhon does not rest his argument against private property purely on this putative incompatibility between equality and powers of transfer. At times he seems prepared to make an even stronger claim—that the very element of exclusive and indefinite control that private property involves is incompatible with the demand for equality that the arguments he is considering give rise to. Considering questions of First Occupancy, for example, he writes:

For, since every man, from the fact of his existence, has the right of occupation, and, in order to live, must have material for cultivation on which he may labor; and since, on the other hand, the number of occupants varies continually with the births and deaths,—it follows that the quantity of material which each laborer may claim varies with the number of occupants; consequently, that occupation is always subordinate to population. Finally, that, inasmuch as possession, in right, can never remain fixed, it is impossible, in fact, that it can ever become property. . . . *All have an equal right of occupancy. The amount occupied being measured, not by the will, but by the variable conditions of space and number, property cannot exist.*[36]

The suggestion is that private property involves the idea of the allocation of a resource to the control of a single individual for an indefinite period (or for a period determined only by his own say-so). But since the population varies, the number of people whose right to property must be satisfied varies with it, and the rightful demands placed on the stock of available resources will change accordingly. An increase in population will mean that the satisfaction of a universal right to property demands a reduction in the amount of resources allocated to individuals before the increase. Since such an increase is always likely, putative proprietors must always hold themselves ready to give up some of their resources in favour of newcomers. But holding resources in this spirit, Proudhon contends, is incompatible with the idea of property as that is usually understood.

Once again, no doubt there are conceptions of private property which make this a plausible objection. On some conceptions, a man cannot be said to be the owner of a resource if his holding is subject continually or even periodically to a redistributive wealth tax. The private property rights of each individual, on these conceptions, are absolutely resistant to redistributive considerations. But it seems

[36] Proudhon, *What is Property?*, pp. 82–3.

unlikely that any of these conceptions will be the upshot of the GR-based arguments we have been considering; that is, it seems unlikely that any of those arguments will establish that private property must be either absolute in this sense or not worth having.

Whether the ethical importance of owning property is under-mined significantly by periodic taxation will depend in part on how frequent, how drastic, and how unpredictable such taxation would have to be. If the population varies greatly at irregular intervals, and if the stock of resources available for private holdings remains constant or is liable to diminution, then there is a danger that the redistribution required to ensure that everyone has private property will make it almost impossible for individuals to make medium-or long-term plans about the use of the resources assigned to them. For example, if the population of a small society is periodically increased by the influx of large numbers of refugees, then land redistribution may be so drastic that farmers are unable to follow through on their own plans for development, crop rotation, and so on. In this case, Proudhon's objection is sustained: those to whom land is initially assigned hold it not as owners but, at best, as 'usufructuaries', owing a duty to society at large to keep it in a condition where it can be easily transferred to the use of others.[37] In societies not subject to such vicissitudes, however, the effect will be much less drastic. For example, in a society where the birth-rate is not overwhelmingly greater than the death rate, and where the increase in population is matched by economic growth, the need for redistribution in favour of newcomers can possibly be accommo-dated by a system of taxation on deceased estates, and the owners of property can be confident that their holdings will not normally be subject in their lifetime to compulsory and debilitating transfers.

In all of this, we should bear in mind the possibility of approaching the problem also from the other direction. The GR-based arguments we are considering have important distributive implications, as we have noticed. But, as we saw in Chapters 8 to 10, they are not implications of strict egalitarianism or anything like it; they are requirements that everyone must have private property in some significant holding, not that everyone must have at most a certain or an equal amount. There is the further point that, though a given argument may require that everyone have property, it may not necessarily require that everyone should

[37] Proudhon, *What is Property*, p. 82.

continue to be the owner of a significant holding at all times. Indeed, in relation to some arguments, a guarantee of this sort might be counter-productive: for example, it might diminish the contribution that owning property makes to the development of prudence, thrift, and responsibility. This means that the GR-based case for private property may allow for a certain amount of flexibility in distributive patterns. Those concerned for it need not be upset by every fluctuation in the relative wealth and fortunes of individuals. What they will be on the lookout for will be tendencies towards the accumulation of enormous holdings, particularly of capital resources, on the one hand, and the accompanying development of long-term propertylessness, on the other. The danger with these trends is that they give rise to the possibility of what Marxists have called 'exploitative' economic relations—relations which are unwelcome in the present context, not because of their injustice or putative coerciveness, but because of the way in which they tend to preclude the autonomous development or occurrence of the sort of transactions and relationships which could shift the distributive balance back in a more egalitarian direction. When these trends become apparent, intervention will be necessary. It does not seem to be unduly optimistic or utopian to suggest that they can be kept in check, at least in a relatively prosperous society, by action which falls considerably short of threatening the very basis of individual ownership.

3. GENERAL AND SPECIAL RIGHTS AND THE CLAIMS OF NEED

In Chapter 7 I argued that no SR-based system of private property would be acceptable if it were not qualified by a principle of provision for basic human needs. No one can be expected voluntarily to refrain from using what is putatively the property of another if that is the only way he can see to satisfy his most pressing bodily needs. Since this is so, no-one can agree in advance in good faith to abide by a system of property which has, as one of its rules, that an owner's decision to withold resources from the relief of desperate need must be respected. Accordingly, no system which included such a rule could possibly have been the subject of an original contract or agreement for the establishment of a just society.

This argument, however, does not merely concern the case for special rights. It is quite general in its application, and applies equally to the implementation of a GR-based case for private property. So the private property rights which are justified by a GR-based argument will be subject, not only to the distributive requirements which that argument itself is likely to generate, but also to this independently-grounded principle of need. In Chapter 9 we discussed briefly the possibility that these requirements might conflict under conditions of great scarcity: *if* basic needs could be provided for more efficiently under a system of collective control of resources, then we would have to decide which of these considerations—the considerations invoked in the GR-based argument for private property or the considerations involved in the principle of need—should prevail. Fortunately, however, if the situation is not one of great scarcity or if the argument about the greater efficiency of collective provision does not go through, then the two principles will not conflict, and indeed are likely to converge, in terms of their practical implications. The argument for their convergence goes as follows. As we saw in our discussion of Hegel, a GR-based argument for private property is not satisfied by the assignment of one or two trivial or useless resources to each individual; it requires the assignment to individuals of resources that they take seriously as the basis of their individual economic well-being.[38] Thus the universal distribution of private property required by a GR-based argument is likely, as a matter of fact, to satisfy the demands of the principle of need, for in seeing to it that everyone has private property, the proponents of that argument will also in effect be seeing to it that everyone has the wherewithal to satisfy his basic needs.

There is also perhaps a more subtle point involved here. The principle of need provides an independent basis for qualifying and restricting otherwise unlimited rights of private property. So even if it is true that a given GR-based argument for private property, considered on its own, requires something like absolute rights of ownership, not limited by any possibility of a wealth tax or by restrictions on traditional powers of transfer, still, when that argument is considered in conjunction with other independent moral considerations, such as the principle of need, the upshot is likely to be a system of limited property rights. In our discussion in

[38] See above Ch. 10, sect. 5(iii).

the previous section, we did not think it likely that very many GR-based arguments would have such extreme implications. But if any did, there would have been contradictions of the sort to which Proudhon drew our attention: these would be arguments at the same time *for* private property on a certain conception and also, in so far as they had distributive implications, *against* private property on that conception. So long as such arguments are considered in isolation, that is a problem: they appear contradictory and self-defeating. But once their force is adjusted to take account of other moral considerations, the danger that they will be self-defeating in practice will disappear. The distributive implications generated by GR-based argument will converge in fact with the implications of principles which the argument would have had to be subject to in any case.

In a SR-based system of private property, there is no such convergence. SR-based arguments do not, as we have seen, have in themselves any universal distributive implications. Those who have got hold of resources (by the specified procedures) are entitled to retain exclusive control of them; those who have not have no right to have property at all. Though SR-based theories sometimes talk of private property as one of the rights of man, it is clear that they do not mean anything like a general right to be the owner of private property. They mean at most a conditional right to-be-an-owner-*if*-certain-events-or-transactions-have-taken-place. There is no basis for any suggestion that one person can demand respect from another for his property only on condition that he respect the other's property as well. The suggestion at most would be: 'You should respect my property for I would respect yours if you had any.' The principle of need, then, cuts right across the SR-based case for private property in a way that it does not cut across the GR-based case.

It may be objected that we have been, till now, far more generous to GR-based arguments for private property than to SR-based ones. For the former, we have been willing to argue that there are all sorts of different conceptions of private property, and to insist that the fact that an argument does not generate anything like a case for absolute property does not deprive it of all interest for us. The argument in Chapter 7 might indicate that we are likely to be much more dismissive of an SR-based argument if it does not establish the absolutist conclusions that its proponents want it to establish. The point is perhaps a fair one. Partly it is a matter of tactics. Often proponents of an SR-based approach (such as Nozick) are endeavouring explicitly to use that approach as a basis for attacking redistribution, welfare provision, and any limitation on owners' control or powers of transfer over the resources they hold.[39] It is worth pointing out in the strongest possible terms that SR-based arguments fall woefully short of adequately establishing that sort of conclusion.

Having said that, we must beware of dismissing SR-based arguments altogether simply because they do not establish the extreme positions that their proponents want to occupy. The point of stressing throughout this work that private property is a concept of which there are several conceptions is to draw attention to the contribution that an argument may make to the debate about private property even when it fails woefully to vindicate absolute *laissez-faire* capitalism. The debate about the merits of different types of property system is not a simple one. Often, in the real world, we face questions like: 'How and in what direction should the property institutions of a mixed economy be modified or reformed?' A modest argument in favour of private property, under some very mild conception, may make an important contribution to answering this question even if we are sceptical about its ability to generate a justification for a pure private property system. Of course, if an argument is simply incoherent, then it makes no contribution at all: this, I have urged, is how we should treat the literal interpretation of Locke's argument about the 'mixing' of labour. But arguments can be weak in other ways, and their weakness does not always mean they should be ignored altogether. For example, in Chapter 6 I argued that a desert-based argument cannot be regarded as a plausible interpretation of the Lockean case for property since, among other things, it falls far short of generating the sort of conception of private property that Locke wanted to defend. But considerations of desert may still be relevant to the case for private property, and the argument based on desert—even if it cannot sustain the burden of justifying a system of private property— should not be dismissed until we are sure that it draws to our attention nothing that we ought to consider. Or, to take another example, we found that the idea of a person's *identifying* himself with an object (regarded by Olivecrona as

[39] Nozick, *Anarchy, State, and Utopia*, Ch. 8.

crucial to Locke's theory of entitlement)[40] could not lie at the basis of a theory of entitlement, or in its 'infrastructure' as Nozick puts it,[41] because the psychology of identification would already presuppose the stability of a set of property rules of a certain sort. Nevertheless, when we are considering, not which property system to *institute*, but rather where to go from here—how to reform already existing property institutions—the idea of identification will have an important role to play. For once a property system gets under way, it will be wrong simply to push aside people's expectations in the interests of distributive justice, even if those expectations have been generated by unjust institutions. The idea of identification, as a broadly SR-based consideration, helps explain why.

4. CONCLUDING REMARKS

This has been an exercise in the exploration of the space for argument in favour of private property. I wanted to consider what arguments were possible on a right-based approach and, in broad terms, what the conditions of their plausibility would be. The aim was not to *argue* in favour of private property, nor was it to extol the virtues of one form of argument against another. It was rather to sketch a map of the terrain of argument in this area—a map whose necessity was indicated by the disarray and disrepute into which the suggestion that private property was one of the rights of man had fallen.

As I indicated in Chapter 1, I began with the suspicion that quite radically different claims were being put forward under the rubric of '*The Right to Property*' and that no real progress could be made in assessing these claims until those differences were brought to the surface. I hope I have shown how deep-set the differences are between SR-based and GR-based modes of right-based argument. The former, associated with Lockean political theory, sees private property as a right that someone may have rather in the way that he has certain promissory or contractual rights; he has it because of what he has done or what has happened to him. The latter, associated in the last hundred years with Hegelian political theory,

---

[40] Olivecrona, 'Locke's Theory of Appropriation'.
[41] Nozick, *Anarchy, State, and Utopia*, p. 238.

sees private property as a right that all men have rather in the way they are supposed to have the right to free speech or to an elementary education; not because they have contingently acquired it, but because its recognition is part and parcel of respect for them as free moral agents. These are basic differences in the *structure* of the respective moral positions: they are not merely differences in content. As we saw in Chapter 4, the structural difference may be elucidated in different ways: perhaps it is the difference between conditional and unconditional rights, though I preferred to view it as the difference between special or contingent rights and general rights which the holders were conceived to have *ab initio*.

However they are characterized, the differences have important practical implications. A GR-based argument is *radical* in its distributive implications: even if it is not obsessively egalitarian, it generates a requirement that private property, under some conception, is something all men must have. SR-based theories *may* have radical implications: if the procedures by which wealth has been accumulated in a society are not the procedures specified by the theory, then the theory may generate quite radical requirements as a matter of rectification. But the distributional implications inherent in the arguments are not radical: there is no case for distributing private property in resources more widely than those who have legitimately appropriated them choose to do.

These differences of structure and implication are not merely of academic interest. Politicians and theorists alike often try to bring the two strands of argument together in a single case, saying for example, that those who have acquired private property ought to be able to keep it since property is an indispensable condition for the development of a sense of individual responsibility. That juxtaposition needs to be exposed as fraudulent eclecticism, aligning as it does considerations that pull in different directions from utterly different and in fact mutually incompatible theoretical perspectives. Once this has been acknowledged, it may still be the case, as I suggested at the end of the previous section, that the two strands of argument both have contributions to make to the discussion of the moral importance of private property. But that discussion is not merely a matter of *assembling*, on one list, considerations in favour of private property and, on another list, considerations against. It must be informed by an understanding of how different considerations, with different provenances can be related to one another, and by an awareness of the difficulties as well as the possibilities of fitting them together into a single case. It is to that understanding that I have tried to make a contribution in the present work.

BIBLIOGRAPHY

In this bibliography all cross-references to edited collections of articles, etc. are by author or editor and short title. Each such collection is listed in its own right under the editor's or author's name, with full bibliographical details.

ACKERMAN, BRUCE A., *Private Property and the Constitution* (New Haven, Yale University Press, 1977).

—— *Social Justice in the Liberal State* (New Haven, Yale University Press, 1980).

ACKERMAN, BRUCE (ed.), *Economic Foundations of Property Law* (Boston, Little, Brown and Company, 1975).

AMERICAN LAW INSTITUTE, *Restatement of the Law of Property*, Volume I (New York, American Law Institute, 1936).

ANDERSON, PERRY, *On the Tracks of Historical Materialism* (London, Verso Books, 1983).

ANSCOMBE, G. E. M., 'Modern Moral Philosophy', in her *Ethics, Religion and Politics: Collected Philosophical Papers, Volume III* (Oxford, Basil Blackwell, 1981).

ARBLASTER, ANTHONY, *The Rise and Decline of Western Liberalism* (Oxford, Basil Blackwell, 1984).

ARENDT, HANNAH, *The Human Condition* (Chicago, University of Chicago Press, 1958).

—— 'What is Freedom?', in her *Between Past and Future* (London, Faber and Faber, 1961).

—— *On Revolution* (Harmondsworth, Penguin Books, 1973).

ARISTOTLE, *The Nicomachean Ethics*, translated by Sir David Ross (London, Oxford University Press: The World's Classics, 1954).

—— *The Politics*, translated by Sir Ernest Barker (Oxford, Clarendon Press, 1946).

—— *The Politics*, translated by T.A. Sinclair (Harmondsworth, Penguin Books, 1962).

ARTHUR, C. J. and SHAW, W. (eds.), *Justice and Economic Distribution* (Englewood Cliffs, N. J., Prentice-Hall, 1978).

ASHCRAFT, RICHARD, 'Locke's State of Nature: Historical Fact or Moral Fiction?' *American Political Science Review*, 62 (1968).

ATIYAH, PATRICK, *The Rise and Fall of Freedom of Contract* (Oxford, Clarendon Press, 1979).

ATKINSON, A. B., *Unequal Shares: Wealth in Britain* (Harmondsworth, Penguin Books, 1974).

AUSTIN, JOHN, *Lectures on Jurisprudence (or The Philosophy of Positive Law)* 5th edition, edited by Robert Campbell (London, John Murray, 1885).

AVINERI, SHLOMO, *The Social and Political Thought of Karl Marx* (Cambridge, Cambridge University Press, 1970).

—— *Hegel's Theory of the Modern State* (Cambridge, Cambridge University Press, 1972).

BANNISTER, ROBERT, *Social Darwinism: Science and Myth in Anglo-American Social Thought* (Philadelphia, Temple University Press, 1979).

BARRY, BRIAN, *Political Argument* (London, Routledge and Kegan Paul, 1965).

BECKER, LAWRENCE C., *Property Rights: Philosophic Foundations* (London, Routledge and Kegan Paul, 1977).

BENN, S. I. and GAUSS, G. F. (eds.), *Public and Private in Social Life* (London, Croom Helm, 1983).

BENN, S. I. and PETERS, R. S., *Social Principles and the Democratic State* (London, George Allen and Unwin, 1959).

BENN, S. I. and WEINSTEIN W. L., 'Being Free to Act and Being a Free Man', *Mind*, 80 (1971).

BENNETT, JONATHAN, *Locke, Berkeley, Hume: Central Themes* (Oxford, Clarendon Press, 1971).

BENTHAM, JEREMY, 'Principles of the Civil Code', in Ogden (ed.), *Theory of Legislation*.

—— 'Supply Without Burthern or Escheat *vice* Taxation', in Stark (ed.), *Bentham's Economic Writings*.

—— 'Anarchical Fallacies' in Waldron (ed.), *Nonsense Upon Stilts*.

—— *An Introduction to the Principles of Morals and Legislation*, edited by J. H. Burns and H. L. A. Hart (London, Athlone Press, 1982).

BERKI, R. N., 'Political Freedom and Hegelian Metaphysics', *Political Studies*, 16 (1968).

BERLE, ADOLF A. and MEANS, GARDINER C., *The Modern Corporation and Private Property*, Revised Edition (New York, Harcourt, Brace and World, 1967).

BERLIN, ISAIAH, *Four Essays on Liberty* (Oxford, Oxford University Press, 1969).

BLACKBURN, SIMON, *Spreading the Word* (Oxford, Oxford University Press, 1984).

BLUMENFELD, SAMUEL L., *Property in a Humane Economy* (La Salle, Ill., Open Court, 1974).

BOTTOMORE, TOM (ed.), *Karl Marx: Early Writings* (London, C. A. Watts, 1963).

BOUCHER, DAVID, 'New Histories of Political Thought for Old?', *Political Studies*, 31 (1983).

BRAMSTEAD, E. K. and MELHUISH, K. J. (eds.), *Western Liberalism: a History in Documents from Locke to Croce* (London, Longmans, 1978).

BRENKERT, GEORGE C., *Marx's Ethics of Freedom* (London, Routledge and Kegan Paul, 1983).

BRIDGE, J. W. *et al.* (eds.), *Fundamental Rights* (London, Sweet and Maxwell, 1973).

BUCHANAN, ALLEN, *Marx and Justice: The Radical Critique of Liberalism* (London, Methuen, 1982).

BUCHANAN, JAMES, *The Limits of Liberty: Between Anarchy and Leviathan* (Chicago, University of Chicago Press, 1975).

CALABRESI, G. and MELAMED, A. D., 'Property Rules, Liability Rules and Inalienability: One View of the Cathedral', *Harvard Law Review*, 85 (1972).

CALDWELL, L. K., 'Rights of Ownership or Rights of Use?: The Need for a New Conceptual Basis for Land Use Theory', *William and Mary Law Review*, 15 (1974).

CANOVAN, MARGARET, *G. K. Chesterton: Radical Populist* (New York, Harcourt Brace Jovanovich, 1977).

CHAMLEY, PAUL, *Économie politique et philosophie chez Steuart et Hegel* (Paris, XII Annales de la faculté de droit et des sciences politiques et économiques de Strasbourg, 1963).

—— 'Les Origines de la pensée économique de Hegel', *Hegel-Studien*, 3 (1965).

CHARVET, JOHN, *A Critique of Freedom and Equality* (Cambridge, Cambridge University Press, 1981).

CHAUDHURI, J., 'Toward a Democratic Theory of Property and the Modern Corporation', *Ethics*, 81 (1977).

CHESHIRE, G. C., *Cheshire's Modern Law of Real Property*, 12th edition, edited by E. H. Burn (London, Butterworth, 1976).

CLARK, BARRY, 'Eccentrically Contested Concepts', *British Journal of Political Science*, 9 (1979).

—— 'Beyond the "Banality of Evil"' *British Journal of Political Science*, 10 (1980).

CLARK, BARRY and GINTIS, HERBERT, 'Rawlsian Justice and Economic Systems', *Philosophy and Public Affairs*, 7 (1978).

CLARKE, L. M. G., 'Who Owns the Apples in the Garden of Eden', *Canadian Journal of Philosophy*, 7 (1977).

COHEN, G. A., 'Capitalism, Freedom and the Proletariat', in Ryan (ed.), *The Idea of Freedom*.

—— 'Freedom, Justice and Capitalism', *New Left Review*, 126 (1981).

—— 'Robert Nozick and Wilt Chamberlain', in Arthur and Shaw (eds.), *Justice and Economic Distribution*.

—— 'Self-Ownership, World-Ownership and Equality', in Lucash (ed.), *Justice and Equality*.

COHEN, MARSHALL (ed.), *Ronald Dworkin and Contemporary Jurisprudence* (Totowa, N. J., Rowman and Allenheld, 1984).

—— et al. (eds.), *Marx, Justice and History: A Philosophy and Public Affairs Reader* (Princeton, Princeton University Press, 1980).

COHEN, M. R. and COHEN, F. S. (eds.), *Readings in Jurisprudence and Legal Philosophy* (New York, Prentice Hall, 1951).

CONNOLLY, W. E., *The Terms of Political Discourse* (Lexington, Mass., Heath, 1974).

—— *The Terms of Political Discourse*, revised 2nd edition (Oxford, Martin Robertson, 1983).

COOPER, DAVID E., 'Hegel's Theory of Punishment', in Pelczynski (ed.) *Hegel's Political Philosophy*.

CRANSTON, MAURICE, *John Locke: a Biography* (London, Longmans Green and Co., 1957).

—— 'Human Rights: Real and Supposed', in Raphael (ed.), *Political Theory and the Rights of Man*.

CROSLAND, C. A. R., *The Future of Socialism* (London, Jonathan Cape, 1967).

CULLEN, BERNARD, *Hegel's Social and Political Thought: An Introduction* (Dublin, Gill and MacMillan, 1979).

DAVIDSON, DONALD, 'The Logical Form of Action Sentences', in his *Essays on Actions and Events* (Oxford, Clarendon Press, 1980).

—— *Inquiries into Truth and Interpretation* (Oxford, Clarendon Press, 1984).

DAVIS, LAWRENCE, 'Nozick's Entitlement Theory', in Paul (ed.), *Reading Nozick*.

DAY, J. P., 'Locke on Property', *Philosophical Quarterly*, 16 (1966).

DEMSETZ, HAROLD, 'Toward a Theory of Property Rights', *American Economic Review: Proceedings and Papers*, 57 (1967).

D'ENTRÈVES, A. PASSERIN, *Natural Law: An Introduction to Legal Philosophy* (London, Hutchinson's University Library, 1951).

DENYER, NICHOLAS, 'Chess and Life: The Structure of a Moral Code', *Proceedings of the Aristotelian Society*, 82 (1981–2).

DIAS, R. W. M., *Jurisprudence* 4th edition (London, Butterworth, 1976).

DUNN, JOHN, *The Political Thought of John Locke: An Historical Account of the Argument of 'Two Treatises of Government'* (Cambridge, Cambridge University Press, 1982).

—— *Locke*, Past Masters Series (Oxford, Oxford University Press, 1984).

—— *The Politics of Socialism* (Cambridge, Cambridge University Press, 1984).

DURRANT, R. G. (ed.), *Essays in Honour of Gwen Taylor* (Dunedin, Otago Philosophy Department, 1982).

DWORKIN, RONALD, *Taking Rights Seriously*, Revised Edition (London, Duckworth, 1979).

—— 'Liberalism', in Hampshire (ed.), *Public and Private Morality*.

—— 'Is There a Right to Pornography?', *Oxford Journal of Legal Studies*, 1 (1981).

—— 'What is Equality?: II. Equality of Resources', *Philosophy and Public Affairs*, 10 (1981).

—— 'Rights as Trumps', in Waldron (ed.), *Theories of Rights*.

—— 'A Reply by Ronald Dworkin', in Cohen (ed.), *Dworkin and Contemporary Jurisprudence*.

—— *Law's Empire* (London, Fontana Books, 1986).

EXSHAW, E. Y., 'The Right of Private Ownership', in Bridge *et al* (eds.), *Fundamental Rights*.

FICHTE, J. G., *The Science of Right,* translated by A. E. Kroeger (Oxford, Clarendon Press, 1970).

FILMER, ROBERT, *Patriarcha and Other Political Works*, edited by Peter Laslett (Oxford, Basil Blackwell, 1949).

FINER, S. E. (ed.), *Five Constitutions* (Harmondsworth, Penguin Books, 1979).

FLEW, ANTONY, *The Politics of Procrustes: Contradictions of Enforced Equality* (London, Temple Smith, 1981).

FOOT, PHILIPPA (ed.), *Theories of Ethics* (Oxford, Oxford University Press, 1967).

—— *Virtues and Vices* (Oxford, Basil Blackwell, 1978).

FORSYTH, MURRAY, *Property and Property Distribution Policy* (London, Policy Studies Institute, 1977).

FOUCAULT, MICHEL, *Power/Knowledge: Selected Interviews and Other Writings* (New York, Pantheon Books, 1980).

FRANKFURT, HARRY G., 'Freedom of the Will and the Concept of a Person', *Journal of Philosophy*, 68 (1971).

—— 'Coercion and Moral Responsibility', in Honderich (ed.), *Freedom of Action*.

FREY, R. G. (ed.), *Utility and Rights* (Minneapolis, University of Minnesota Press, 1984).

FRIEDMAN, DAVID, *The Machinery of Freedom: Guide to a Radical Capitalism* (New York, Harper and Row, 1973).

FRIEDMAN, MILTON, *Capitalism and Freedom* (Chicago, University of Chicago Press, 1962).

FRIEDMANN, W., *Law in a Changing Society*, 2nd edition (London, Stevens and Sons, 1972).

GALLIE, W. B., 'Essentially Contested Concepts', *Proceedings of the Aristotelian Society*, 56 (1955–6).

GAUTHIER, D. P. (ed.), *Morality and Rational Self-Interest* (Englewood Cliffs, N. J., Prentice Hall, 1970).

—— 'The Role of Inheritance in Locke's Political Theory', *Canadian Journal of Economics and Political Science*, 32 (1966).

—— *Morals By Agreement* (Oxford, Clarendon Press, 1986).

GEWIRTH, ALAN, *Reason and Morality* (Chicago, University of Chicago Press, 1978).

—— *Human Rights: Essays in Justification and Application* (Chicago, University of Chicago Press, 1982).

—— 'Are There Any Absolute Rights?', in Waldron (ed.), *Theories of Rights*.

GIBBARD, ALAN, 'Natural Property Rights', *Nous*, 10 (1976).

GLAZER, NATHAN, 'Individual Rights Against Group Rights', in Kamenka and Tay (eds.), *Human Rights*.

GLOVER, JONATHAN, *Causing Death and Saving Lives* (Harmondsworth, Penguin Books, 1977).

GOLDIE, MARK, 'John Locke and Anglican Royalism' *Political Studies*, 31 (1983).

GOLDING, M. P., 'The Primacy of Welfare Rights', *Social Philosophy and Policy*, 1 (1984).

GOUGH, J. W., *John Locke's Political Philosophy* (Oxford, Clarendon Press, 1950).

GRAY, JOHN N., 'On the Contestability of Social and Political Concepts', *Political Theory*, 5 (1977).

—— 'On Liberty, Liberalism and Essential Contestability', *British Journal of Political Science*, 8 (1978).

—— 'Political Power, Social Theory, and Essential Contestability', in Miller and Siedentop (eds.), *The Nature of Political Theory*.

GREEN, LESLIE, 'Rights for Rights' Sake' (unpublished typescript; York University, Toronto).

GREEN, THOMAS HILL, *Prolegomena to Ethics*, 5th edition (Oxford, Clarendon Press, 1906).

—— *Lectures on the Principles of Political Obligation* (London, Longmans Green and Co., 1941).

—— 'Liberal Legislation and Freedom of Contract' in Bramstead and Melhuish (eds.), *Western Liberalism*.

GREGOR, MARY, *Laws of Freedom: A Study of Kant's Method of Applying the Categorical Imperative in the 'Metaphysik der Sitten'* (Oxford, Basil Blackwell, 1963).

GREY, T.C., 'The Disintegration of Property', in Pennock and Chapman (eds.) *NOMOS XXII: Property*.

GRIFFIN, JAMES, 'Towards a Substantive Theory of Rights', in Frey (ed.) *Utility and Rights*.

GRIFFITHS, A. PHILIPS (ed.), *Of Liberty*, Royal Institute of Philosophy Lecturers, Series 15 (Cambridge, Cambridge University Press, 1983).

GROTIUS, HUGO, *The Rights of War and Peace*, translated by A. C. Campbell (New York, M. Walter-Dunne, 1901).

GUEST, A. G., 'Family Provision and *Legitima Portio*', *Law Quarterly Review*, 73 (1957).

GUEST, A. G. (ed.), *Oxford Essays in Jurisprudence* (Oxford, Oxford University Press, 1961).

HACKER, P. M. S. and RAZ, JOSEPH (eds.), *Law, Morality, and Society: Essays in Honour of H.L.A. Hart* (Oxford, Clarendon Press, 1982).

HAMPSHIRE, STUART, *Thought and Action* (London, Chatto and Windus, 1959).

—— (ed.), *Public and Private Morality* (Cambridge, Cambridge University Press, 1979).

HARDIN, GARRETT, 'The Tragedy of the Commons', in Ackerman (ed.), *Economic Foundations of Property Law*.

HARE, R. M., *Freedom and Reason* (Oxford, Oxford University Press, 1963).

—— *Moral Thinking: Its Levels, Method and Point* (Oxford, Clarendon Press, 1981).

HARGREAVES, A. D., 'Terminology and Title in Ejectment', *Law Quarterly Review*, 56 (1940).

—— 'Modern Real Property', *Modern Law Review*, 19 (1956).

HARRIS, JOHN, 'The Survival Lottery', *Philosophy*, 50 (1975).

HART, H. L. A. 'Definition and Theory in Jurisprudence', *Law Quarterly Review* 70 (1954).

—— *The Concept of Law* (Oxford, Clarendon Press, 1961).

—— *Punishment and Responsibility: Essays in the Philosophy of Law* (Oxford, Clarendon Press, 1968).

—— 'Bentham on Legal Rights', in Simpson (ed.), *Oxford Essays in Jurisprudence*.

—— *Essays on Bentham: Jurisprudence and Political Theory* (Oxford, Clarendon Press, 1982).

—— *Essays in Jurisprudence and Philosophy* (Oxford, Clarendon Press, 1983).

—— 'Rawls on Liberty and its Priority', in his *Essays in Jurisprudence*.

—— 'Between Utility and Rights', in his *Essays in Jurisprudence*.

—— 'Are There Any Natural Rights?', in Waldron (ed.), *Theories of Rights*.

HASTIE, W., *Kant's Philosophy of Law* (Hastie's translation of Kant's *Metaphysical Elements of Justice*) (Edinburgh, W. Clarke, 1887).

HAYEK, FRIEDRICH A., *The Mirage of Social Justice*, Volume II of *Law, Legislation and Liberty* (London, Routledge and Kegan Paul, 1976).

HEGEL, G. W. F., *The Phenomenology of Mind*, translated by J. B. Baillie (London, George Allen and Unwin, 1949).

—— 'The English Reform Bill', in Pelczynski and Knox (eds.), *Hegel's Political Writings*.

—— 'The Old German Freedom', in Pelczynski and Knox (eds.), *Hegel's Political Writings*.

—— *The Philosophy of Right*, translated with notes by T. M. Knox (Oxford, Oxford University Press, 1967).

—— *The Philosophy of Mind*, Part III of *Encyclopaedia of the Philosophical Sciences* (1830), translated by W. Wallace (Oxford, Clarendon Press, 1971).

—— *Jensenser Realphilosophie*, excerpts in Plant, *Hegel*.

—— *Phenomenology of Spirit*, translated by A. V. Miller (Oxford, Oxford University Press, 1977).

HELD, VIRGINIA, 'John Locke on Robert Nozick', *Social Research*, 43 (1976).

—— 'Property Rights and Interests', *Social Research*, 46 (1979).

HILPINEN, RISTO (ed.), *Deontic Logic: Introductory and Systematic Readings* (Dordrecht, D. Reidel, 1981).

HINTIKKA, JAAKO, 'Some Main Problems of Deontic Logic', in Hilpinen (ed.), *Deontic Logic*.

HOBBES, THOMAS, *Leviathan: Or The Matter, Forme and Power of a Commonwealth, Ecclesiastical and Civil*, edited by C. B. Macpherson (Harmondsworth, Penguin Books, 1968).

—— *De Cive, The English Version*, edited by Howard Warrender (Oxford, Oxford University Press, 1983).

HOBHOUSE, L. T., *Liberalism* (London, Williams and Norgate, n.d.).

HOHFELD, WESLEY N., *Fundamental Legal Conceptions, as Applied in Judicial Reasoning, and Other Legal Essays*, edited by W. W. Cook (New Haven, Yale University Press, 1919).

HOLDSWORTH, W., 'Terminology and Title in Ejectment: A Reply', *Law Quarterly Review*, 56 (1940).

HONDERICH, TED (ed.), *Essays on Freedom of Action* (London, Routledge and Kegan Paul, 1973).

—— *Violence for Equality: Inquiries in Political Philosophy* (Harmondsworth, Penguin Books, 1980).

HONORÉ, A. M., 'Ownership', in Guest (ed.), *Oxford Essays in Jurisprudence*.

—— 'Social Justice', *McGill Law Journal*, 8 (1962).

—— 'Property, Title, and Redistribution', *Archiv für Rechts-und Sozialphilosophie*, 10 (1977).

HUME, DAVID *A Treatise of Human Nature*, edited by L. A. Selby-Bigge (Oxford, Clarendon Press, 1888).

—— 'An Enquiry Concerning the Principles of Morals', in *Hume's Enquiries*, edited by L. A. Selby-Bigge (Oxford, Clarendon Press, 1902).

IGNATIEFF, MICHAEL, *The Needs of Strangers* (London, Chatto and Windus, 1984).

ILTING, K.-H., 'The Structure of Hegel's *Philosophy of Right*', in Pelczynski (ed.), *Hegel's Political Philosophy*.

ILTING, K.-H., 'The Dialectic of Civil Society', in Pelczynski (ed.), *State and Civil Society*.

—— 'Hegel's Concept of the State and Marx's Early Critique', in Pelczynski (ed.), *State and Civil Society*.

KAHN FREUND, OTTO, 'Introduction' to his edition of Renner, *Institutions of Private Law*.

KALIN, JESSE, 'In Defence of Egoism', in Gauthier (ed.), *Morality and Rational Self-Interest*.

KAMENKA, EUGENE and TAY, ALICE ERH-SOON (eds.), *Human Rights* (London, Edward Arnold, 1978).

KANT, IMMANUEL, *The Moral Law* (*The Groundwork of the Metaphysics of Morals*), translated and edited by H. J. Paton (London, Hutchinson's University Library, 1956).

—— *Critique of Practical Reason*, translated by Lewis White Beck (Indianapolis, Bobbs Merrill, 1956).

—— *The Metaphysical Elements of Justice*, translated by John Ladd (Indianapolis, Bobbs Merrill, 1965).

—— 'On the Common Saying: "This may be true in theory, but it does not apply in practice"' ('Theory and Practice'), in Reiss (ed.), *Kant's Political Writings*.

KEITH, K. J. (ed.), *Essays on Human Rights* (Wellington, Sweet and Maxwell, 1968).

KENDALL, WILLMOORE, *John Locke and the Doctrine of Majority Rule* (Urbana, University of Illinois Press, 1965).

KING, DESMOND and WALDRON, JEREMY, 'Citizenship, Social Citizenship, and the Defence of Welfare Rights', *British Journal of Political Science* (forthcoming 1988).

KIRALFY, A., 'The Problem of the Law of Property in Goods', *Modern Law Review*, 12 (1949).

KIRZNER, ISRAEL, 'Entrepreneurship, Entitlement and Economic Justice', in Paul (ed.), *Reading Nozick*.

KNOWLES, DUDLEY, 'Hegel on Property and Personality', *Philosophical Quarterly*, 33 (1983).

KNOX, T. M., 'Translator's Introduction', to his translation of Hegel, *Philosophy of Right*.

KOCOUREK, A., *Jural Relations*, 2nd edition (New York, Bobbs Merrill, 1928).

KOHR, LEOPOLD, 'Property and Freedom', in Blumenfeld (ed.), *Property in a Humane Economy*.

KOLAKOWSKI, LESZEK and HAMPSHIRE, STUART, *The Socialist Idea: A Reappraisal* (London, Quartet Books, 1977).

KONTOS, A. (ed.), *Powers, Possessions and Freedom: Essays in Honour of C. B. Macpherson* (Toronto, University of Toronto Press, 1979).

LASLETT, PETER, 'Introduction' to his edition of Locke, *Two Treatises*.

LASLETT, PETER, RUNCIMAN, W. G., and SKINNER, QUENTIN (eds.), *Philosophy, Politics and Society*, 4th series (Oxford, Basil Blackwell, 1972).

LAWSON, F. H., *The Law of Property* (Oxford, Clarendon Press, 1958).

LESSNOFF, MICHAEL, 'Capitalism, Socialism and Democracy', *Political Studies*, 27 (1979).

—— 'Not Talking About Jerusalem: A Reply to Miller', *Political Studies*, 28 (1980).

LINDSAY, A. D., 'The Principle of Private Property', quoted in Cohen and Cohen (eds.), *Readings in Jurisprudence*.

LLOYD-THOMAS, D. A., 'Liberty, Equality and Property', *Proceedings of the Aristotelian Society*, 81 (1981).

LOCKE, JOHN, *Some Considerations of the Lowering of Interest and Raising the Value of Money*, in *The Works of John Locke*, Volume III (London, W. Strahan *et al.*, 1777).

—— *Two Treatises of Government*, Critical edition, edited by Peter Laslett (Cambridge, Cambridge University Press, 1960).

—— *An Essay Concerning the Human Understanding*, two volumes (London, J. M. Dent, 1961).

—— *Essays on the Law of Nature*, edited by W. von Leyden (Oxford, Clarendon Press, 1970).

—— *A Letter Concerning Toleration*, in Locke, *The Second Treatise*.

—— *The Second Treatise of Government* and *A Letter Concerning Toleration*, edited by J. W. Gough (Oxford, Basil Blackwell, 1976).

LOPATA, BENJAMIN B., 'Property Theory in Hobbes', *Political Theory*, 1 (1973).

LOWIE, R. H., 'Incorporeal Property in Primitive Society', *Yale Law Journal*, 37 (1928).

LUCASH, FRANK (ed.), *Justice and Equality: Here and Now* (Ithaca, Cornell University Press, 1986).

LUKES, STEVEN, *Individualism* (Oxford, Basil Blackwell, 1973).

—— *Power: A Radical View* (London, Macmillan, 1974).

—— 'Reply to Macdonald', *British Journal of Political Science*, 6 (1976).

LYONS, DAVID, *Forms and Limits of Utilitarianism* (Oxford, Clarendon Press, 1965).

—— 'Rights, Claimants and Beneficiaries', *American Philosophical Quarterly*, 6 (1969).

—— 'The Correlativity of Rights and Duties', *Nous*, 4 (1970).

—— 'Utility and Rights', in Waldron (ed.), *Theories of Rights*.

MacCormick, Neil, 'Rights in Legislation', in Hacker and Raz (eds.), *Law, Morality, and Society*.

—— *Legal Right and Social Democracy: Essays in Legal and Political Philosophy* (Oxford, Clarendon Press, 1982).

—— 'Children's Rights: A Test-Case for Theories of Rights', in his *Legal Right and Social Democracy*.

MacDonald, K., 'Is "Power" Essentially Contested?', *British Journal of Political Science*, 6 (1976).

Mackie, J. L., *Ethics: Inventing Right and Wrong* (Harmondsworth, Penguin Books, 1977).

—— 'Can There Be a Right-Based Moral Theory?', in Waldron (ed.), *Theories of Rights*.

Macpherson, C. B., *The Political Theory of Possessive Individualism: Hobbes to Locke* (Oxford, Oxford University Press, 1962).

—— *Democratic Theory: Essays in Retrieval* (Oxford, Clarendon Press, 1973).

—— (ed.), *Property: Mainstream and Critical Positions* (Oxford, Basil Blackwell, 1978).

—— 'The Meaning of Property', in his *Property: Mainstream and Critical Positions*.

Marcuse, H., *Reason and Revolution: Hegel and the Rise of Social Theory* (London, Routledge and Kegan Paul, 1967).

Marx, Karl, *Critique of the Gotha Programme* (Moscow, Progress Publishers, 1960).

—— 'On the Jewish Question', in Waldron (ed.), *Nonsense Upon Stilts*.

—— 'On James Mill', in Bottomore (ed.), *Karl Marx: Early Writings*.

—— *Capital: A Critique of Political Economy*, Volume III, edited by F. Engels (Moscow, Progress Publishers, 1971).

—— *Capital: A Critique of Political Economy*, Volume I, translated by Ben Fowkes (Harmondsworth, Penguin Books, 1976).

—— 'Results of the Immediate Process of Production', Appendix to Marx, *Capital*, Volume I.

—— 'The Law on Thefts of Wood', in McLellan (ed.), *Karl Marx: Selected Writings*.

—— *Grundrisse*, excerpted in McLellan (ed.), *Karl Marx: Selected Writings*.

—— 'Preface to *A Critique of Political Economy*', in McLellan (ed.), *Karl Marx: Selected Writings*.

—— 'Address to the Communist League', in McLellan (ed.), *Karl Marx: Selected Writings*.

—— and Engels, F., *The German Ideology*, Part I; Students' Edition, edited by C. J. Arthur (London, Lawrence and Wishart, 1977).

—— —— *The Communist Manifesto* (Harmondsworth, Penguin Books, 1967).

MAURICE, S. G., *Family Provision Practice*, 4th edition (London, Oyez Publishing, 1979).

McCLOSKEY, H. J., 'A Note on Utilitarian Punishment', *Mind*, 72 (1963).

—— 'Rights', *Philosophical Quarterly*, 15 (1965).

—— 'Rights: Some Conceptual Issues', *Australasian Journal of Philosophy*, 54 (1976).

McLELLAN, DAVID (ed.), *Karl Marx: Selected Writings* (Oxford, Oxford University Press, 1977).

McMURRIN, S. (ed.), *The Tanner Lectures on Human Values* (Salt Lake City, University of Utah Press, 1980).

MEADE, J. E., *Efficiency, Equality and the Ownership of Property* (London, George Allen and Unwin, 1964).

MEDLIN, BRIAN, 'Ultimate Principles and Ethical Egoism', in Gauthier (ed.), *Morality and Rational Self-Interest*.

MEGARRY, P. E. and WADE, H. W. R., *The Law of Real Property*, 4th edition (London, Stevens and Sons, 1975).

MELDEN, A. I. (ed.), *Human Rights* (Belmont, Calif., Wadsworth, 1970).

—— *Rights and Persons* (Oxford, Basil Blackwell, 1977).

MILIBAND, RALPH, *Marxism and Politics* (Oxford, Oxford University Press, 1977).

MILL, JOHN STUART, *Principles of Political Economy*, edited by W. J. Ashley (London, Longmans Green and Co., 1909).

—— *On Liberty* (Indianapolis, Bobbs Merrill, 1956).

—— *Utilitarianism*, edited by Mary Warnock (London, Fontana Library of Philosophy, 1962).

MILLER, DAVID, 'Justice and Property', *Ratio*, 22 (1980).

—— 'Jerusalem not yet Built: a Reply to Lessnoff on Capitalism, Socialism and Democracy', *Political Studies*, 28 (1980).

—— 'The Macpherson Version', *Political Studies*, 30 (1982).

—— 'Arguments for Equality', *Midwest Studies in Philosophy*, 7 (1982).

—— 'Linguistic Philosophy and Political Theory', in Miller and Siedentop (eds.), *The Nature of Political Theory* .

MILLER, DAVID and SIEDENTOP, LARRY (eds.), *The Nature of Political Theory* (Oxford, Clarendon Press, 1983).

MILLER, W. G., *Lectures on the Philosophy of Law* (London, Charles Griffen, 1884).

MOSS, LAURENCE S. (ed.), *The Economics of Ludwig von Mises: Towards a Critical Reappraisal* (Kansas City, Sheed and Ward, 1974).

NAGEL, THOMAS, 'Libertarianism Without Foundations', in Paul (ed.), *Reading Nozick*.

—— 'The Limits of Objectivity', in McMurrin (ed.), *Tanner Lectures*.

NELSON, WILLIAM N., 'Special Rights, General Rights, and Social Justice', *Philosophy and Public Affairs*, 3 (1974).

NOVE, ALEC, *The Economics of Feasible Socialism* (London, George Allen and Unwin, 1983).

NOVE, ALEC and NUTI, D.M. (eds.), *Socialist Economics: Selected Readings* (Harmondsworth, Penguin Books, 1972).

NOYES, C. REINHOLD, *The Institution of Property* (London, Humphrey Milford, 1936).

NOZICK, ROBERT, 'Coercion', in Laslett et al. (eds.), *Philosophy, Politics and Society*.

—— *Anarchy, State, and Utopia* (Oxford, Basil Blackwell, 1974).

—— *Philosophical Explanations* (Cambridge, Mass., Harvard University Press, 1981).

—— 'On the Randian argument', in Paul (ed.), *Reading Nozick*.

OGDEN, C. K. (ed.), *Jeremy Bentham: The Theory of Legislation* (London, Routledge and Kegan Paul, 1931).

OLIVECRONA, KARL, 'Locke's Theory of Appropriation', *Philosophical Quarterly*, 24 (1974).

O'NEILL, ONORA, 'Nozick's Entitlements', in Paul (ed.), *Reading Nozick*.

OPPENHEIM, FELIX, *Political Concepts: A Reconstruction* (Oxford, Basil Blackwell, 1981).

PANICHAS, GEORGE E., 'Prolegomenon to a Political Theory of Ownership', *Archiv fur Rechts- und Sozialphilosophie*, 64 (1978).

PARFIT, DEREK, *Reasons and Persons* (Oxford, Clarendon Press, 1984).

PASHUKANIS, EVGENY B., *Law and Marxism: A General Theory (Towards a Critique of the Fundamental Juridical Concepts)*, translated by B. Einhorn (London, Ink Links, 1978).

PATON, GEORGE WHITECROSS, *A Textbook of Jurisprudence*, 3rd edition, edited by David P. Derham (Oxford, Clarendon Press, 1964).

PAUL, JEFFREY (ed.), *Reading Nozick: Essays on 'Anarchy, State, and Utopia'* (Oxford, Basil Blackwell, 1982).

PEASLEE, AMOS J., *Constitutions of Nations*, revised 3rd edition, 4 volumes (The Hague, Martinus Nijhoff, 1965–70).

PELCZYNSKI, Z. A. (ed.), *Hegel's Political Philosophy: Problems and Perspectives* (Cambridge, Cambridge University Press, 1978).

—— (ed.), *The State and Civil Society: Studies in Hegel's Political Philosophy* (Cambridge, Cambridge University Press, 1984).

—— and KNOX, T. M. (eds.), *Hegel's Political Writings*, translated by T. M. Knox (Oxford, Clarendon Press, 1964).

PENNOCK, J. R., 'Thoughts on the Right to Private Property', in Pennock and Chapman (eds.), *NOMOS XXII: Property*.

PENNOCK, J. R. and CHAPMAN, J. W. (eds.), *NOMOS XXII: Property* (New York, New York University Press, 1980).

PHILBRICK, F. S., 'Changing Conceptions of Property in Law', *University of Pennsylvania Law Review*, 86 (1936).

PLAMENATZ, JOHN, *Man and Society*, Volume I (London, Longmans, 1963).

—— 'History as the Realization of Freedom', in Pelczynski (ed.), *Hegel's Political Philosophy.*

PLANT, RAYMOND, *Hegel* (Political Thinkers series) (London, George Allen and Unwin, 1973).

—— 'Economic and Social Integration in Hegel's Philosophy', in Verene (ed.), *Hegel's Social and Political Thought.*

—— *Equality, Markets and the State*, Fabian Pamphlet 494 (London, The Fabian Society, 1984).

—— 'Hegel on Identity and Legitimation', in Pelczynski (ed.), *State and Civil Society.*

PLATO, *The Republic*, translated by Desmond Lee (Harmondsworth, Penguin Books, 1974).

POLLOCK, F., *Jurisprudence and Legal Essays* (London, Macmillan, 1961).

PROUDHON, PIERRE-JOSEPH, *What is Property?*, translated by Benjamin R. Tucker (New York, Dover Publications, 1970).

PUFENDORF, SAMUEL, *Of the Law of Nature and Nations* (Oxford, J. Churchill *et al.,* 1703).

QUINE, W. V. O., *Word and Object* (Cambridge, Mass., MIT Press, 1960).

RAPHAEL, D. D. (ed.), *Political Theory and the Rights of Man* (London, Macmillan, 1967).

—— 'Human Rights: Old and New', in Raphael (ed.), *Political Theory and the Rights of Man* .

RAWLS, JOHN, 'Two Concepts of Rules', in Foot (ed.), *Theories of Ethics.*

—— *A Theory of Justice* (Oxford, Oxford University Press, 1971).

—— 'Kantian Constructivism in Moral Theory: The John Dewey Lectures', *Journal of Philosophy*, 77 (1980).

RAZ, JOSEPH, 'Promises and Obligations', in Hacker and Raz (eds.), *Law, Morality, and Society.*

—— 'Liberalism, Autonomy and the Politics of Neutral Concern', *Midwest Studies in Philosophy*, 7 (1982).

—— 'Legal Rights', *Oxford Journal of Legal Studies*, 4 (1984).

—— 'On the Nature of Rights', *Mind*, 93 (1984).

—— 'Right-Based Moralities', in Waldron (ed.), *Theories of Rights.*

—— *The Morality of Freedom* (Oxford, Clarendon Press, 1986).

REEVE, ANDREW, 'Political Obligation and the Strict Settlement', *Locke Newsletter*, 13 (1982).

—— *Property* (London, Macmillan, 1985).

—— and WARE, ALAN, 'Interests in Political Theory', *British Journal of Political Science*, 13 (1983).

REICH, CHARLES A., 'The New Property', *Yale Law Journal*, 73 (1964).

REISS, HANS (ed.), *Kant's Political Writings*, translated by H. B. Nisbet (Cambridge, Cambridge University Press, 1970).

RENNER, KARL, *The Institutions of Private Law and their Social Functions*, translated by Agnes Schwarzschild (London, Routledge and Kegan Paul, 1976).

REYBURN, HUGH A., *The Ethical Theory of Hegel: A Study of 'The Philosophy of Right'* (Oxford, Clarendon Press, 1921).

RITCHIE, D. G., *Natural Rights* (London, George Allen and Unwin, 1924).

RITTER, JOACHIM, 'Personne et propriété selon Hegel', *Archives de Philosophie*, 31 (1968).

ROSE, GILLIAN, *Hegel contra Sociology* (London, Athlone Press, 1981).

ROSS, W. D., *The Right and the Good* (Oxford, Clarendon Press, 1930).

ROTHBARD, MURRAY, 'Von Mises and Economic Calculation', in Moss (ed.), *Economics of von Mises*.

ROUSSEAU, JEAN-JACQUES, *The Social Contract and Discourses*, translated by G. D. H. Cole (London, J. M. Dent, 1973).

—— *A Discourse on the Origin of Inequality*, in Rousseau, *Social Contract and Discourses*.

—— *A Discourse on Political Economy*, in Rousseau, *Social Contract and Discourses*.

—— *The Social Contract*, in Rousseau, *Social Contract and Discourses*.

RYAN, ALAN, 'Locke and the Dictatorship of the Bourgeoisie', *Political Studies*, 13 (1965).

—— (ed.), *The Idea of Freedom: Essays in Honour of Isaiah Berlin* (Oxford, Oxford University Press, 1979).

—— 'Property, Liberty and *On Liberty*', in Griffiths (ed.), *Of Liberty*.

—— 'Public and Private Property', in Benn and Gauss (eds.), *Public and Private*.

—— 'Hegel on Work, Ownership and Citizenship', in Pelczynski (ed.), *State and Civil Society*.

—— *Property and Political Theory* (Oxford, Basil Blackwell, 1984).

RYAN, CHEYNEY C., 'Yours, Mine, and Ours: Property and Liberty', in Paul (ed.), *Reading Nozick*.

SALMOND, J., *Salmond on Jurisprudence*, 12th edition, edited by P. J. Fitzgerald (London, Sweet and Maxwell, 1966).

SANDEL, MICHAEL, *Liberalism and the Limits of Justice* (Cambridge, Cambridge University Press, 1982).

—— (ed.), *Liberalism and its Critics* (Oxford, Basil Blackwell, 1984).

SCANLON, THOMAS A., 'Nozick on Rights, Liberty and Property', in Paul (ed.), *Reading Nozick*.

SCHUMPETER, JOSEPH A., *Capitalism, Socialism and Democracy*, 5th edition (London, George Allen and Unwin, 1976).

SCHWEICART, DAVID, 'Should Rawls be a Socialist?', *Social Theory and Practice*, 5 (1978).

SCRUTON, ROGER, *The Meaning of Conservatism* (Harmondsworth, Penguin Books, 1980).

SELIGER, MARTIN, *The Marxist Conception of Ideology: A Critical Essay* (Cambridge, Cambridge University Press, 1977).

SEN, AMARTYA and WILLIAMS, BERNARD (eds.), *Utilitarianism and Beyond* (Cambridge and Paris, Cambridge University Press and Maison des Sciences de l'Homme, 1982).

SIDGEWICK, HENRY, *The Methods of Ethics*, 5th edition (London, Macmillan, 1893).

SIMPSON, A. W. B. (ed.), *Oxford Essays in Jurisprudence*, Second Series (Oxford, Clarendon Press, 1973).

SKINNER, QUENTIN, 'Meaning and Understanding in the History of Ideas', *History and Theory*, 8 (1969).

SMART, J. J. C. and WILLIAMS, BERNARD, *Utilitarianism: For and Against* (Cambridge, Cambridge University Press, 1973).

SMITH, ADAM, *An Inquiry into the Nature and Causes of the Wealth of Nations* (Chicago, University of Chicago Press, 1976).

SMITH, J. C., *The Law of Theft*, 4th edition (London, Butterworth, 1979).

SNARE, FRANK, 'The Concept of Property', *American Philosophical Quarterly*, 9 (1972).

STACE, W., *The Philosophy of Hegel: A Systematic Exposition* (New York, Dover Publications, 1955).

STARK, W. (ed.), *Jeremy Bentham's Economic Writings*, Critical Edition, Volume I (London, George Allen and Unwin, 1952).

STEINBECK, JOHN, *The Grapes of Wrath* (London, Pan Books, 1975).

STEINER, HILLEL, 'The Structure of a Set of Compossible Rights', *Journal of Philosophy*, 74 (1977).

—— 'How Free?: Computing Personal Liberty', in Griffiths (ed.), *Of Liberty*.

STEVENSON, CHARLES, 'Persuasive Definitions', *Mind*, 47 (1938).

STILLMAN, PETER G., 'Person, Property and Civil Society in the *Philosophy of Right*,' in Verene (ed.), *Hegel's Social and Political Thought*.

—— 'Property, Freedom and Individuality in Hegel's and Marx's Political Thought', in Pennock and Chapman (eds.), *NOMOS XXII: Property*.

STRAUSS, LEO, *What is Political Philosophy?* (New York, Free Press, 1959).

STRAWSON, P. F., 'On Referring', in his *Logico-Linguistic Papers* (London, Methuen, 1971).

SUMNER, W. G., *Social Darwinism: Selected Essays* (Englewood Cliffs, N. J., Prentice Hall, 1963).

SWANTON, CHRISTINE, 'The Concept of Interests', *Political Theory*, 8 (1980).

TAWNEY, R. S., 'Property and Creative Work', in Macpherson (ed.), *Property: Mainstream and Critical Positions* .

—— *The Sickness of an Acquisitive Society* (London, George Allen and Unwin, 1920).

TAYLOR, CHARLES, *Hegel* (Cambridge, Cambridge University Press, 1975).

—— *Hegel and Modern Society* (Cambridge, Cambridge University Press, 1979).

—— 'What's Wrong With Negative Liberty?', in Ryan (ed.), *Idea of Freedom*.

—— 'Atomism', in Kontos (ed.), *Powers, Possessions and Freedom*.

TAYLOR, MICHAEL, *Community, Anarchy, and Liberty* (Cambridge, Cambridge University Press, 1982).

TEICHGRAEBER, J., 'Hegel on Property and Poverty', *Journal of the History of Ideas*, 38 (1977).

TEITELMAN, M., 'The Limits of Individualism', *Journal of Philosophy*, 69 (1972).

TUCK, RICHARD, *Natural Rights Theories: Their Origin and Development* (Cambridge, Cambridge University Press, 1979).

TULLY, JAMES, *A Discourse on Property: John Locke and his Adversaries* (Cambridge, Cambridge University Press, 1980).

—— 'A Reply to Waldron and Baldwin', *Locke Newsletter*, 13 (1982).

TURNER, J. W. C., 'Some Reflections on Ownership in English Law', *Canadian Bar Review*, 19 (1941).

TYLER, E. L. G., *Family Provision* (London, Butterworths, 1971).

VAN DOREN, J. W., 'Redistributing Wealth by Curtailing Inheritance', *Florida State University Law Review*, 3 (1975).

VERENE, D. P. (ed.), *Hegel's Social and Political Thought: The Philosophy of Objective Spirit* (Sussex, Harvester Press, 1980).

VON MISES, LUDWIG, *Socialism: An Economic and Sociological Analysis*, New Edition (London, Jonathan Cape, 1951).

—— 'Economic Calculation in the Socialist Commonwealth', in Nove and Nuti (eds.), *Socialist Economics*.

WALDRON, JEREMY, 'Enough and as Good Left for Others', *Philosophical Quarterly*, 29 (1979).

—— 'Locke's Account of Inheritance and Bequest', *Journal of the History of Philosophy*, 19 (1981).

—— 'A Right to Do Wrong', *Ethics*, 92 (1981).

—— 'The Turfs My Servant Has Cut', *Locke Newsletter*, 13 (1982).

—— 'Producers' Entitlements', in Durrant (ed.), *Essays in Honour of Gwen Taylor* .

—— 'Reply to Galston on Rights', *Ethics*, 93 (1983).

—— 'Two Worries About Mixing One's Labour', *Philosophical Quarterly*, 33 (1983).

—— 'Locke, Tully, and the Regulation of Property', *Political Studies*, 32 (1984).

—— (ed.), *Theories of Rights* (Oxford, Oxford University Press, 1984).

—— 'What is Private Property?', *Oxford Journal of Legal Studies*, 5 (1985).

—— 'Critical Notice of Hart, *Essays in Jurisprudence*', *Mind*, 94 (1985).

—— 'Welfare and the Images of Charity', *Philosophical Quarterly*, 36 (1986).

—— 'Mill and the Value of Moral Distress', *Political Studies*, 35 (1987).

—— (ed.), *Nonsense Upon Stilts: Bentham, Burke and Marx, on the Rights of Man* (London, Methuen, 1987).

—— 'When Justice Replaces Affection: the Need for Rights', *Harvard Journal of Law and Social Policy*, 11 (1988).

—— 'Can Communal Goods be Human Rights?', *Archives européennes de sociologie*, 27 (1987).

—— *Poverty and Freedom*, forthcoming (Routledge, 1991).

—— 'John Locke: Social Contract versus Political Anthropology', *Review of Politics*, 51 (1989).

WALTON, A. S., 'Economy, Utility and Community in Hegel's Theory of Civil Society', in Pelczynski (ed.), *State and Civil Society*.

WALZER, MICHAEL, *Obligations: Essays on Disobedience, War and Citizenship* (Cambridge, Mass., Harvard University Press, 1970).

—— *Spheres of Justice: A Defence of Pluralism and Equality* (Oxford, Martin Robertson, 1983).

WEBER, MAX, *Economy and Society*, edited by G. Roth and C. Wittich (Berkeley, University of California Press, 1968).

—— *The Protestant Ethic and the Spirit of Capitalism*, 2nd edition (London, George Allen and Unwin, 1976).

WIGGINS, JAMES W., 'The Decline of Private Property and the Diminished Person', in Blumenfeld (ed.), *Property in a Humane Economy*.

WILLIAMS, BERNARD, 'A Critique of Utilitarianism', in Smart and Williams, *Utilitarianism: For and Against*.

—— 'The Idea of Equality', in his *Problems of the Self: Philosophical Papers 1956–72* (Cambridge, Cambridge University Press, 1976).

WITTGENSTEIN, LUDWIG, *Tractatus Logico-Philosophicus*, translated by D. F. Pears and B. McGuiness (London, Routledge and Kegan Paul, 1961).

—— *Philosophical Investigations*, translated by G. E. M. Anscombe (Oxford, Basil Blackwell, 1974).

WOLFF, R. P., 'Nozick's Derivation of the Minimal State', in Paul (ed.), *Reading Nozick* .

WOOD, ALLEN, *Karl Marx*, Arguments of the Philosophers Series, (London, Routledge and Kegan Paul, 1981).

INDEX